CAREER COUNSELING INTERVENTIONS

Wendy K. Killam, PhD, LPC, CRC, NCC, is a professor in the Department of Human Services at Stephen F. Austin State University. Her research interests include students adjusting to college, wellness throughout the life span, issues faced by older adults, and issues faced by veterans and military families. She enjoys working with college students and, in addition to working as a counselor educator, has worked in student affairs.

Suzanne Degges-White, PhD, LPC, LMHC, NCC, is a licensed counselor and professor and chair of the Department of Counseling, Adult and Higher Education at Northern Illinois University. She is the coauthor of three books that all touch on the ways in which relationships play out across the life span. These include her most recent book, *Toxic Friendships: Knowing the Rules and Dealing With the Friends Who Break Them* (Rowman & Littlefield, 2015); *Mothers and Daughters: Living, Loving and Learning Over a Lifetime* (Rowman & Littlefield, 2014); and *Friends Forever: How Girls and Women Forge Lasting Relationships* (Rowman & Littlefield, 2011). Suzanne has also coedited four books addressing clinical counseling practice and innovative counseling interventions.

Rebecca E. Michel, PhD, LCPC, is an assistant professor and doctoral coordinator within the Division of Psychology and Counseling at Governors State University. Her research interests include career development, international counseling, and strengths-based education. She is passionate about helping people to discover and capitalize on their unique personal strengths to enhance educational and career success across the life span.

CAREER COUNSELING INTERVENTIONS

Practice With Diverse Clients

Wendy K. Killam, PhD, LPC, CRC, NCC
Suzanne Degges-White, PhD, LPC, LMHC, NCC
Rebecca E. Michel, PhD, LCPC
Editors

SPRINGER PUBLISHING COMPANY
NEW YORK

Springer Publishing Company, LLC
11 West 42nd Street
New York, NY 10036
www.springerpub.com

Acquisitions Editor: Nancy Hale
Composition: Newgen KnowledgeWorks

ISBN: 978-0-8261-3216-1
e-book ISBN: 978-0-8261-3217-8

Instructor's Manual: Qualified instructors may request supplements by e-mailing textbook@springerpub.com

16 17 18 19/ 5 4 3 2 1

Library of Congress Cataloging-in-Publication Data
Names: Killam, Wendy K., editor. | Degges-White, Suzanne, editor. | Michel, Rebecca E., editor.
Title: Career counseling interventions : practice with diverse clients / Wendy K. Killam, PhD, LPC, CRC, NCC; Suzanne Degges-White, PhD, LPC, LMHC, NCC; and Rebecca E. Michel, PhD, LCPC, Editors.
Description: New York, NY : Springer Publishing Company, LLC, 2016. | Includes bibliographical references.
Identifiers: LCCN 2015039329 | ISBN 9780826132161 | ISBN 9780826132178 (e-book)
Subjects: LCSH: Vocational guidance—Psychological aspects. | Career development—Psychological aspects. | Personality and occupation. | Counseling psychology.
Classification: LCC HF5381 .C265234 2016 | DDC 650.14—dc23
LC record available at http://lccn.loc.gov/2015039329

Printed in the United States of America by McNaughton & Gunn.

We dedicate this book to all of the counselors who are called upon to provide assistance and support to the clients who bring career concerns into their sessions. Our hope is that the knowledge and interventions shared within this book will provide readers with creative and innovative techniques and perspectives that will help clients follow, and achieve, their career aspirations and dreams.

CONTENTS

CONTRIBUTORS

Beheshteh Abdi Master's Student, Department of Counseling, Adult and Higher Education, Northern Illinois University, DeKalb, Illinois

Samantha Barbieri, BA Master's Candidate, Clinical Mental Health Counseling, The College of New Jersey, Ewing, New Jersey

Susan R. Barclay, PhD, NCC, LPC, ACS, GCDF_I Assistant Professor, Department of Leadership Studies, College of Education, University of Central Arkansas, Conway, Arkansas

Shalom Bond Master's Candidate, Clinical Mental Health Counseling, The University of New Mexico, Albuquerque, New Mexico

Imelda N. Bratton, PhD, LPCC, RPT-S, NCC School Counseling Program and Clinical Coordinator, Codirector of Talley Family Counseling Center, Western Kentucky University, Bowling Green, Kentucky

Laura Bruneau, PhD Associate Professor, Department of Counselor Education, Adams State University, Alamosa, Colorado

Michelle Cap, BA Master's Candidate, Clinical Mental Health Counseling Program, The College of New Jersey, Ewing, New Jersey

Montserrat Casado-Kehoe, PhD, LMFT, RPT Associate Professor, Department of Counseling Psychology, Palm Beach Atlantic University, Ocoee, Florida

Marion Cavallaro, PhD Associate Professor and Coordinator, Clinical Mental Health Counseling Program, Department of Counselor Education, The College of New Jersey, Ewing, New Jersey

Alyce R. Clark, MS Master's Student, University of Louisiana at Lafayette, Lafayette, Louisiana

Katrina Cook, PhD, LPC-S, LMFT-S, CSC Assistant Professor, Department of Leadership and Counseling, Texas A&M University—San Antonio, San Antonio, Texas

Penny Dahlen, EdD, LPC Core Faculty, Clinical Mental Health Program, Walden University, Denver, Colorado

Ryan Day, PhD, LPC, NCC Assistant Professor, Department of Counseling, Foundations, and Leadership, Columbus State University, Columbus, Georgia

Suzanne Degges-White, PhD, LPC, LMHC, NCC Professor and Chair, Department of Counseling, Adult and Higher Education, Northern Illinois University, DeKalb, Illinois

Sabina R. de Vries, PhD, LPC-S, NCC Assistant Professor, Department of Leadership and Counseling, Texas A&M University—San Antonio, San Antonio, Texas

Robert A. Dobmeier, PhD, LMHC, CRC Associate Professor, Counselor Education, The College at Brockport, State University of New York at Brockport, Brockport, New York

Diane M. Dryja, MAT ElEd, MEd, NCC Clinical Specialist, Psycamore, LLC, Hernando, Mississippi

Nakeshi L. Dyer, MS, NCC Doctoral Student, The University of Memphis, Memphis, Tennessee

LaWanda S. Edwards, PhD, ALC, NCC Associate Professor, Counselor Education, Alabama State University, Montgomery, Alabama

Amanda M. Evans, PhD, LPC, NCC Assistant Professor, Coordinator Clinical Mental Health Counseling Program, Special Education, Rehabilitation, and Counseling, Auburn University, Auburn, Alabama

Nancy L. A. Forth, PhD, NCC, LPC Professor, Department of Educational Leadership and Human Development, University of Central Missouri, Warrensburg, Missouri

Erin N. Friedman Master's Candidate, Northern Illinois University, DeKalb, Illinois

Marta M. Garrett, LPC-S, LMFT-S, RPT-S Associate Professor and Director of the Graduate Counseling Program, University of Mary Harden-Baylor, Belton, Texas

Kristopher M. Goodrich, PhD Associate Professor, Counselor Education, Department of Individual, Family, and Community Education, The University of New Mexico, Albuquerque, New Mexico

Cynthia B. Greer, PhD Associate Professor of Counseling, Trinity Washington University, Washington, DC

Karen J. Haas, PhD Assistant Professor of School Counseling, Co-Coordinator of Master's in School Counseling Program, Keene State College, Keene, New Hampshire

Zach J. Hebert, MS Master's Student, University of Louisiana at Lafayette, Lafayette, Louisiana

Carly Heckathorn, MA, EdS School Counselor, Marion County Public Schools, Ocala, Florida

Bridget Tuohy Helms, MSEd Student Support Advisor/School Counselor, Tri-Creek School Corporation, Oak Hill Elementary School, Lowell, Indiana

Katherine M. Hermann, PhD, PLCP, NCC Assistant Professor, University of Louisiana at Lafayette, Lafayette, Louisiana

Vincent D. Hinton, EdS, LPC, NCC Instructor, Alabama State University, Montgomery, Alabama

James R. Huber, PhD, LMFT Associate Professor of Counseling Psychology, Holy Family University, Newtown, Pennsylvania

Edward F. Hudspeth, PhD, NCC, LPC, RPh, RPT-S, ACS Assistant Professor of Counselor Education, Henderson State University, Arkadelphia, Arkansas

Kathryn S. Jaekel, PhD Assistant Professor, Department of Counseling, Adult and Higher Education, Northern Illinois University, DeKalb, Illinois

Andre Joachim Master's Student, Department of Counseling, Adult and Higher Education, Northern Illinois University, DeKalb, Illinois

Michael A. Keim, PhD Assistant Professor, Department of Counseling, Foundations, and Leadership, Columbus State University, Columbus, Georgia

Bethany Kennedy, EdS, NCC Counselor, Oxford Play Therapy Institute, Oxford, Mississippi

Wendy K. Killam, PhD, LPC, CRC, NCC Professor, Department of Human Services, Stephen F. Austin State University, Nacogdoches, Texas

Carrie A. Kortegast, PhD Assistant Professor, Department of Counseling, Adult and Higher Education, Northern Illinois University, DeKalb, Illinois

Elsa Soto Leggett, PhD, LPC-S, RPT-S, CSC Associate Professor in Counselor Education, University of Houston—Victoria, Sugar Land, Texas

Sandra Logan, MA, NCC, NCSC, DCC, CSC Lead Field Supervisor, Counseling and Special Populations, Lamar University, Beaumont, Texas

Chad Luke, PhD Assistant Professor, Counseling and Psychology, Tennessee Technological University, Cookeville, Tennessee

Melissa Luke, PhD Associate Professor, Counseling and Human Services Department, Syracuse University, Syracuse, New York

Laurel Malloy, MEd, LPC, CSC Counselor, John Paul Stevens High School, Northside ISD, San Antonio, Texas

Mary Mayorga, PhD, LPC-S, NCC, CCDS, CART Associate Professor, Educational Leadership and Guidance Counseling Department, Texas A&M University—San Antonio, San Antonio, Texas

Tony Michael, PhD, LPC-S, ACS, RPT, NCC Assistant Professor, Counseling and Psychology, Tennessee Technological University, Cookeville, Tennessee

Rebecca E. Michel, PhD, LCPC Assistant Professor, Department of Psychology and Counseling, Governors State University, University Park, Illinois

Eric J. Michel, MBA Doctoral Candidate, University of Illinois at Chicago, Chicago, Illinois

Anne G. Morring, MS Doctoral Student, Department of Counseling, Adult and Higher Education, Northern Illinois University, DeKalb, Illinois

Suzanne Mudge, LPC-S, NCC, NCSC Professor, Program Coordinator School Counseling, Interim Department Chair, Counseling, Health, and Kinesiology, Texas A&M University—San Antonio, San Antonio, Texas

Patrick D. Murphy, MS, LPC-MHSP, NCC Doctoral Student, Counselor Education and Supervision, Graduate Teaching Assistant, Auburn University, Auburn, Alabama

Charles E. Myers Associate Professor, Department of Counseling, Adult and Higher Education, Northern Illinois University, DeKalb, Illinois

Lori Notestine, PhD, LPC, NCC Instructor, University of Colorado–Colorado Springs, Colorado Springs, Colorado

Jonie Oliver Doctoral Student, The University of Memphis, Memphis, Tennessee

Lucy Parker, MA, NCC Doctoral Student, Department of Counseling, Adult and Higher Education, Northern Illinois University, DeKalb, Illinois

Ricardo Phipps, PhD Executive Director, Catholic Charities of Jackson, Jackson, Mississippi

Diandra J. Prescod, PhD, NCC, ACS Assistant Professor, The Pennsylvania State University, State College, Pennsylvania

Jane Rheineck, PhD Associate Professor, Department of Counseling, Adult and Higher Education, Northern Illinois University, DeKalb, Illinois

Gail K. Roaten, PhD, LPC-S, CSC Associate Professor, Department of Counseling, Tarleton State University, Waco, Texas

Hewitt B. Rogers, EdS, NCC Doctoral Student, Department of Counseling Psychology, University of Georgia, Athens, Georgia

Varunee Faii Sangganjanavanich, PhD, LPCC-S, NCC, RPT-S School of Counseling, College of Health Professions, The University of Akron, Akron, Ohio

Corie N. Schoeneberg, EdS, LPC, RPT-S, NCC Adjunct Faculty, Counselor Education Program, University of Central Missouri, Warrensburg, Missouri

Atsuko Seto, LPC, NCC, ACS Associate Professor, The College of New Jersey, Ewing, New Jersey

Kevin B. Stoltz, PhD, NCC, ACS Associate Professor, Counseling, University of Central Arkansas, Conway, Arkansas

Margo D. Sutorius-Milano, LCPC, NCC, CFEL Instructor, School of Family, Consumer and Nutrition Sciences, Northern Illinois University, DeKalb, Illinois

Bill Weber, PhD, LPC, CRC, CVE Professor and Coordinator of Undergraduate Rehabilitation Training, Stephen F. Austin State University, Nacogdoches, Texas

Melissa A. Wheeler, NCC, ACS Distance Clinical Professor, Counseling and Special Populations, Lamar University, Beaumont, Texas

Jakendra D. Williams, MS, Ed, NCC, LPC Master's Candidate, Northern Illinois University, DeKalb, Illinois

Barb C. Wilson, PhD, LPC, NCC Middle School Counselor, West Hall Middle School, Oakwood, Georgia

Suzanna M. Wise, EdS, LPC, NCC Doctoral Student, Department of Counseling, Adult and Higher Education, Northern Illinois University, DeKalb, Illinois

Katherine M. Wix, PhD, LPC, NCC, ACS Assistant Professor, Division of Psychology and Counseling at Governors State University, University Park, Illinois

Steven D. Wright, MED, NCC Counselor Education and Supervision Doctoral Student, Auburn University, Auburn, Alabama

PREFACE

A growing number of adults find themselves struggling with career choices and options at different points within their life span. It is not uncommon for people to decide to change occupations at midlife, reenter the workforce after children are in school, or return to work in later adulthood. Facing an uncertain economy, many workers have found themselves in need of obtaining new job skills in order to advance in careers. Dual-career couples might have to make tough decisions regarding work opportunities; likewise, returning or retired military service personnel might find the civilian workforce expectations much different from those experienced in the military. Finding ways to encourage individuals in different career situations is a task that can be challenging for career counselors.

THE SCOPE OF THE BOOK

This book is designed for both dedicated career counselors and personal counselors who find themselves helping clients make sense of career concerns as they work to make sense of their lives. This book offers chapters with case vignettes in which creative career interventions are applied. Each of these chapters provides a thorough exploration of the career-related challenges and needs of each unique group. In this book, we provide an overview of the unique needs of several populations including caregivers; unwed mothers; formerly incarcerated individuals; lesbian, gay, bisexual, and transgender (LGBT) individuals; veterans; and many other populations. The background information provides counselors with a broadened understanding of the unique frames of reference and worldviews clients may bring to counseling. Although each client is unique, there are some common elements that most members of various groups share. These elements are highlighted in the population chapters along with specific information that can be beneficial to consider when providing counseling services.

Each population chapter opens with a case vignette in which a client's story is presented for readers to consider. These cases highlight the diverse array of career- and lifestyle-related concerns that clients may bring to counseling. The vignettes are revisited at the close of the chapter to illustrate potential ways of helping clients resolve their concerns. The use of specific career counseling interventions provides the reader with a greater understanding of how practical applications can be applied to various clients. The book contains more than 50 innovative career interventions that are located at the end of the book. These interventions can help one to have greater insight into how creativity can be used when working with clients facing career changes and challenges. Although these interventions are organized by specific populations, each one can be modified by the clinician to be effective with a diverse array of clients. We have also included several expressive arts interventions that can be used for career-specific counseling; these are found in Appendix O. The interventions were written by practitioners in the field who have worked with numerous clients on career-related issues.

WHO WILL BENEFIT FROM THE BOOK?

The intended audience for this book includes those professionals who specialize in career counseling, as well as any clinical mental health counselor working with adults. It is often difficult to unravel career counseling and life counseling, as our career concerns can affect all aspects of our lives, from the personal to the professional. It is beneficial for students as well as seasoned professionals who are seeking creative and innovative methods of enhancing their work with clients wrestling with issues related to their careers. The book provides a practical application of creative career interventions that can be useful when working with a wide variety of clients. Furthermore, although the book focuses on the specific needs of adults, one can use some of the interventions with teenagers who are considering college majors and career choices.

OVERALL VALUE OF THE BOOK

Although there are numerous career-counseling books on the market, this book provides a new perspective and an innovative twist on other resources. We wanted to go beyond providing information regarding career counseling and provide a book that is practical and, hopefully, inspirational in nature. The population chapters provide basic information but go beyond what is normally presented in career counseling books by using vignettes and applying creative career interventions. The book provides more than 50 interventions that can be used by career counselors in the field when working with a variety of clients who are facing different career issues and challenges.

ACKNOWLEDGMENTS

The editors would like to thank Nancy Hale for her support and guidance from the earliest stages of this project's development. We also would like to thank the insightful, knowledgeable, and creative contributors who shared their expertise through this book.

Wendy K. Killam, Suzanne Degges-White, and Rebecca E. Michel

To my coeditor Suzanne: Thanks for your guidance and support. You helped us to move forward with this idea and have an amazing amount of energy. To my coeditor Becky: You have a great eye for detail and I appreciate your patience. I am also grateful to my husband Bil and son Michael. You have been encouraging and have taken care of yourselves at times when I have been working on this project. To my mentors (too many to mention, but you know who you are) who have challenged me to continue to keep growing both professionally and personally, thank you! Finally, to my dad: Thanks for your constant encouragement.

Wendy K. Killam

To my amazingly brilliant and thorough coeditors, Becky and Wendy: I express my appreciation for all of the learning that I enjoyed through the development of this book! Collaborating with colleagues who care as much about "doing good" as you two do is a very satisfying experience. Thanks, too, to all of those who have had a hand in helping me grow as a counselor, a counselor educator, and a person. This includes my amazing spouse, Ellen, and our three "emerging adult" children, each of whom is on a different path to career satisfaction and career success.

Suzanne Degges-White

Wendy and Suzanne, it has been an incredible honor to collaborate with you both on this book. Thank you for giving me this opportunity to learn and grow. I would not be here today without the wisdom and guidance of all my teachers, mentors, and colleagues, who have supported me to create a meaningful life and career. Mom and Dad, thank you for teaching me the value of hard work. Eric, you are an exemplar of work–life balance and I appreciate everything you do to support our family. Raney and Hartley, being your mom has brought so much joy into my life—thank you for reminding me each day about what is most important.

Rebecca E. Michel

CHAPTER 1

HIGH SCHOOL GRADUATES

Rebecca E. Michel

CASE VIGNETTE: ALEJANDRO

Alejandro was the youngest of four boys in the hard-working, blue-collar Martinez family. Alejandro's father, Andrew, did not attend college, yet became a well-established journeyman electrician. Upon graduation from high school, Alejandro's three older brothers, Diego, Nathan, and Daniel, all accepted electrician apprenticeships with the International Brotherhood of Electrical Workers (IBEW) local union. Given the family's long history with the IBEW, a career in the electrical trades was understood to be Alejandro's postsecondary vocational education.

However, Alejandro was not sure if he wanted to follow in the footsteps of his father and brothers. For one, electrical work was the least interesting of all the trades he was exposed to while enrolled in the career and technical education (CTE) program at High School. Although he was good with his hands and preferred the mechanical environment as opposed to the classroom, he just was not sure that electrical work was for him. With apprenticeship positions across the trades filling up quickly, Alejandro was pressured to make a career decision soon.

DESCRIPTION OF THE POPULATION

High school graduates include individuals who have earned a high school diploma or its equivalent, such as a general educational development (GED) certificate, and who have not enrolled in postsecondary education. In 2014, approximately one third of high school graduates did not enroll in college, and more than 70% of these individuals were working or seeking employment (Bureau of Labor Statistics [BLS], 2015a). Socioeconomic status is a strong indicator of college attendance. Individuals who graduated from a high-poverty public high school were the least likely to attend college (National Student Clearinghouse, 2014).

People living in poverty may not believe that higher education is worth the financial investment (Packard, Leach, Ruiz, Nelson, & DiCocco, 2012) and may choose jobs based on survival rather than vocational interest (Blustein et al., 2002). Thus, high school graduates often pursue shorter term positions rather than investing time to prepare for a career aligned with their values, skills, and abilities (Laird, Chen, &

Levesque, 2006). Millennial high school graduates (born after 1980) are three times more likely than college graduates to describe work as *just a job to get by* compared to a *career or stepping stone to a career* (Pew Research Center, 2014). The occupational opportunities for high school graduates have changed in the past few decades.

HISTORICAL CAREER PATHS FOR HIGH SCHOOL GRADUATES

Historically, graduates entered the workforce directly following high school and found available entry-level employment in many different sectors. In recent decades, the educational requirements for jobs across the career spectrum have increased, changing the types of available positions for individuals without postsecondary education. In the United States today, approximately 6 out of 10 jobs require some postsecondary education (Carnevale, Smith, & Strohl, 2013). However, despite significant changes in the career landscape, there are still many occupations that do not require a college degree. Currently, 200 to 350 occupations are featured for high school graduates in the *Occupational Outlook Handbook* (BLS, 2015b), O*Net Online (2015), and the BLS (2014) websites. Over the next decade, the projected growth rate for occupations that require only a high school diploma is 9.1%, and these positions are expected to account for more than half of all new jobs (BLS, 2013). High school graduates are expected to be eligible for two thirds of the occupations with the largest projected employment increases (e.g., home health aides, construction workers, and carpenters). Individuals can also receive career training and education in apprenticeship programs while also earning a paycheck. Although the types of jobs available for high school graduates have changed over the past several decades, there are many career opportunities for high school graduates in various sectors of the labor force. However, despite their job options, high school graduates still face unique career challenges.

CAREER OBSTACLES FACING HIGH SCHOOL GRADUATES

One of the most significant obstacles high school graduates face today reflects the current economic landscape. The Great Recession that lasted from 2007 to 2009 (National Bureau of Economic Research, 2012) and the subsequent slow economic recovery have negatively impacted the jobs available for high school graduates. These individuals are more likely to be unemployed (28.8%) than recent high school graduates enrolled in college (BLS, 2015a). Although most high school graduates are seeking jobs, in 2014 the employment rate of high school graduates aged 20 to 24 years was only 63% (National Center for Education Statistics, 2015). Additionally, the value of high school education has dramatically declined over the past several decades. The average wage for high school graduates without further education declined from $31,400 in 1965 to $28,000 in 2013 (Pew Research Center, 2014). As a result of these factors, approximately 22% of high school graduates are living in poverty today (Pew Research Center, 2014). It is vital to understand the unique needs facing high school graduates as they strive to develop skills to be competitive on the job market.

CAREER DEVELOPMENT NEEDS OF HIGH SCHOOL GRADUATES

As high school graduates transition into the working world, they must develop a comprehensive understanding of how to utilize their own skills, abilities, and interests to secure a job. Young adults who understand themselves and the demands of the world of work are better able to make career choices congruent with their values and interests. High school graduates who are adaptable and open minded in their job search will likely retain employment in a workforce that is constantly changing. However, some high school graduates lack work ethic, problem-solving abilities, and timeliness, which make them unprepared to transition into entry-level positions. It is ideal for individuals to have their academic and behavioral needs met during high school so that they can seamlessly transition into a career following graduation.

Comprehensive school counseling programs prepare high school graduates to make informed career and educational choices to navigate different life roles and events (Gysbers, 2013). Following high school, these career-ready students are prepared to enter the workforce, apprenticeship program, technical school, community college, or university. Many high school students also gain real-world job training that provides a realistic preview of various careers.

SUPPORTS FOR HIGH SCHOOL GRADUATES

High school graduates need help to transfer skills learned in school into the world of work. In 1994, the U.S. Congress allocated funding for the School-to-Work Opportunities Act to enhance career preparation in U.S. public schools (Neumark & Rothstein, 2007). This included diverse transitional programs, such as career planning, internships, cooperative education, and job shadowing (Stern, Finkelstein, Stone, Latting, & Dornsife, 1995). These initiatives expose high school students to career-related experiences to connect what they are learning in high school with the world of work (U.S. Department of Education, 2015).

CTE programs were developed to improve academic, technical, and job-specific skills to increase employability of high school graduates by helping them develop skills in critical thinking, communication, problem solving, collaboration, teamwork, and innovation. Students can gain education and experience in 16 different career areas, including science, technology, engineering, and math (STEM); human services; and manufacturing (Association for Career and Technical Education, 2015). More than 90% of high school graduates have earned CTE credits (National Center for Education Statistics, 2011), and participation in CTE has been shown to reduce dropout rates and help students obtain industry-endorsed certificates and technical endorsements (Plank, DeLuca, & Estacion, 2005). These individuals demonstrated more realistic expectations about their job opportunities, more consistent ideas about possible career options, and greater job satisfaction following high school (Blustein, 1997). Young adults aged 16 to 24 years interested in career technical training and education could also enroll in Job Corps (2015), which provides hands-on career training, job assistance, education, and transitional support in more than 100 different career areas (e.g., construction, business, and health care). Programs like these help people living in poverty secure employment following graduation.

There are also many relevant web resources available to support high school graduates (see Additional Resource Suggestions). The BLS features career-planning articles appropriate for high school graduates. For example, Torpey (2015) provided a guide to learning about oneself and possible careers with information about how to gain relevant job experience. There is also information about apprenticeship programs and vocational schools. High school graduates can access these resources on their own or with the support of a career counselor.

CAREER COUNSELING INTERVENTIONS WITH HIGH SCHOOL GRADUATES

Career counselors work with high school graduates using various approaches to meet their needs. Effective career interventions during and following high school expose individuals to role models who can share information about careers and expand their social networks (Brown & Krane, 2000) as well as help them make informed decisions about how to gain relevant work experience to improve their resume and career outlook (Packard et al., 2012). High school graduates who are adaptable and used social networks have more successful school-to-work transitions (Blustein, Phillips, Jobin-Davis, Finkelberg, & Roarke, 1997). It is especially helpful for low-income individuals to adaptively respond to unexpected events and setbacks in their careers (Bright & Pryor, 2005). Career construction theory (CCT; Savickas, 2005) can be used to assist high school graduates improve adaptability during career transitions.

In CCT, counselors use the Career Style Interview (CSI; Savickas, 2005) to encourage the client tell his or her story. Throughout this narrative process, clients gain awareness about life themes (e.g., aspects that give an individual meaning and purpose), vocational identity (e.g., abilities, skills, needs, values, and interests), and career adaptability (e.g., coping skills to overcome career challenges). This approach is helpful with high school graduates striving to construct their identities and discover jobs that may be enjoyable. By gaining self-awareness and enhancing career adaptability, high school graduates are better equipped to make career-related decisions.

It is also important that career counselors assist high school graduates with career decision making in order to facilitate intentional choices regarding occupations based on their interests, skills, projected job growth, and decline. Career counselors could administer various assessments to help clients discover their career skills and interests and new career possibilities (Wood & Hays, 2013). Assessments such as Holland's (1959, 1997) RIASEC Interest Inventory (i.e., Realistic, Investigative, Artistic, Social, Enterprising, and Conventional) provide information to high school graduates about the types of careers they might be interested in based on different work environments. Additionally, the StrengthsFinder (Rath, 2007) helps students discover their natural talents and the types of jobs that would be most rewarding. After taking assessments, high school graduates could search for specific careers using O*Net Online (2015) based on their interests and talents. Such information empowers high school graduates to evaluate potential occupations.

High school graduates might also consider the different *possible selves* (Markus & Nurius, 1986) they could become depending on their choices (Pisarik & Shoffner, 2009). To facilitate this process, career counselors have the option to use Possible Selves Mapping (Shepard & Marshall, 1999) with high school graduates to help them discover more about their identity and improve career decision making (Michel, 2013). This assessment encourages clients to think about who they *could* become, *hope* to become, and *fear* they might become in the future (Shepard & Marshall, 1999).

It is important for high school students to receive realistic information about their skills, interests, and the job market so that they can make effective career decisions about which occupations to pursue or avoid. Recent high school graduates could access the employment projections from the BLS. Career counselors help high school graduates establish realistic expectations and develop strategies to remain flexible as they transition into the working world. See Appendix A for additional suggestions.

REVISITING THE CASE OF ALEJANDRO

Alejandro connected with a counselor from his former high school to help him decide his next steps regarding employment. He admitted to feeling conflicted for wanting to establish a career outside of electrical work because this would break an important family tradition. However, Alejandro wanted to explore different options and choose a career he would enjoy, not just one that he would get because of family connections. The career counselor administered different assessments to Alejandro to help him discover more about his interests, talents, and career identity. After receiving the results, he wrote down words that described himself.

Alejandro took the RIASEC (Holland, 1997) to evaluate his interests. His codes and personalized descriptions included Realistic (like to work with hands and machines; prefer to solve concrete problems), Artistic (creative and unconventional; enjoys designing and creating art with different materials), Enterprising (goal-oriented; leader). Alejandro also took the StrengthsFinder Assessment (Rath, 2007) to obtain information about his natural talents. His top five strengths and personalized descriptions were as follows:

- *Responsibility: follow through with what I say I will do and value honesty and loyalty.*
- *Deliberative: anticipate obstacles and take time to make decisions or choices.*
- *Focus: take and follow through with directions in order to stay on track with progress.*
- *Restorative: good at resolving problems.*
- *Analytical: consider factors that might affect a situation in order to brainstorm reasons and causes (Rath, 2007).*

*Alejandro generally agreed with the results from both assessments and felt empowered to learn more about what types of occupations might be satisfying based on his interests and talents. For homework, he used his assessment results to access online resources (e.g., O*Net) and brainstormed 43 possible occupations of interest. Next, he used a worksheet to evaluate the occupations he wanted to learn more about based on* *several factors (e.g., skills/knowledge/task fit, average income, projected job openings, potential job satisfaction, and overall rating of the occupation). His final list consisted of the following occupations: automotive worker, construction carpenter, heating and air conditioning mechanic, pipe fitter, welder, sheet metal worker, boilermaker, steel worker, and layout worker.*

Next, the counselor led Alejandro through the Possible Selves Mapping Exercise (PSME; Shepard & Marshall, 1999) to explore more about his career identity. Using the list of occupations he brainstormed and researched, Alejandro shared the following list of hoped-for selves and feared selves:

What I Hope to Become: I hope to be employed in a position as a construction carpenter, heating and air conditioning mechanic, welder, or sheet metal worker. I want to become trained in a career that will be fulfilling and where there is a lot of job growth expected. One day, I even hope to become a manager. I want to create my own career path. I think it is likely that I can obtain employment as long as I determine the steps required to enter these occupations.

What I Fear, Dread, or Don't Want for Myself: I don't want to be unemployed or train in an occupation that will become obsolete in the near future. I also don't want to follow in the footsteps of my family and become an electrician.

Ultimately, Alejandro decided to apply to a 4-year sheet metal worker apprenticeship program. He accepted a full-time job that also included 250 hours of classroom training a year. He received paid on-the-job training to learn about building code requirements, how to read blueprints, and mathematical concepts. Eventually, he would become a journeyman, and with additional years of training, experience, and skills, he could have the opportunity to move up within the industry to project manager, foreman, general foreman, superintendent, or owner of a sheet metal company. At this point, though, Alejandro was simply relieved that he took the initiative to make his own career decision that was not dictated by his family. Ultimately, although his family was surprised, they were also very supportive of his decision to become a sheet metal worker. Regardless of where his career path would take him, Alejandro was now equipped with the tools to investigate and evaluate occupations and make a self-authorized career choice.

ADDITIONAL RESOURCE SUGGESTIONS

CareerOneStop (www.careeronestop.org) includes career resources appropriate for many types of job seekers. The website includes information about how to plan a job search, including information about the labor market, employment trends, and training opportunities. High school graduates specifically would benefit from the resources provided to entry-level workers, including how to choose a job goal and gain hands-on experience and information on networking, using social media, developing resumes and cover letters, preparing for interviews, and negotiating job offers.

My Next Move (www.mynextmove.org) is a tool that high school graduates can use to explore different career options, regardless of their stage of career decision making. Job seekers with some self-awareness about what they would like to do can describe their dream career or search for more than 900 different careers by industry (such as construction, mining, oil and gas, retail, or service). Other high school graduates who are undecided about their career can take an assessment (O*Net Interest Profiler) to obtain a list of possible occupations based on their interests and current level of education. Individuals can also download the *What's My Next Move Career Guide* (www.careeronestop.org/whats-my-next-move.aspx) that provides a seven-step career planning process with ideas for self-assessment, career exploration, goal setting, and starting a career.

Occupational Outlook Handbook (www.bls.gov/ooh) includes information for job seekers. High school graduates could search for occupations by their current educational level, level of on-the-job training required, number of projected jobs, and the median pay. There is an overview about what people in this career do, the work environment, important qualities to possess, similar occupations, and how to obtain a position in this occupation.

O*Net Online (www.onetonline.org) features occupations based on the level of education, experience, and training required. High school graduates could search for occupations in job zones one and two. Each occupation featured includes a brief overview of the position, job titles, work activities, tasks, knowledge, skills, abilities, interests (based on Holland codes), work styles, and work values important to possess in this occupation. Related occupations are also listed as well as a search engine to explore available job openings.

REFERENCES

Association for Career and Technical Education. (2015). *CTE information: What is CTE?* Retrieved from http://www.acteonline.org/cte/#.VZ7fWEWPlbE

Blustein, D. L. (1997). A context-rich perspective of career exploration across the life roles. *The Career Development Quarterly, 45*, 260–274.

Blustein, D. L., Chaves, A. P., Diemer, M. A., Gallagher, L. A., Marshall, K. G., Sirin, S., & Bhati, K. S. (2002). Voices of the forgotten half: The role of social class in the school-to-work transition. *Journal of Counseling Psychology, 49*, 311–323.

Blustein, D. L., Phillips, S. D., Jobin-Davis, K., Finkelberg, S. L., & Roarke, A. E. (1997). A theory-building investigation of the school-to-work transition. *The Counseling Psychologist, 25*, 364–402.

Bright, J. E. H., & Pryor, R. G. L. (2005). The chaos theory of careers: A user's guide. *The Career Development Quarterly, 53*, 291–304.

Brown, S. D., & Krane, N. E. R. (2000). Four (or five) sessions and a cloud of dust: Old assumptions and new observations about career counseling. In S. D. Brown & R. W. Lent (Eds.), *Handbook of counseling psychology* (3rd ed., pp. 740–766). New York, NY: Wiley.

Bureau of Labor Statistics. (2013). *Employment projections: 2012–2022 summary.* Retrieved from http://www.bls.gov/news.release/ecopro.nr0.htm

Bureau of Labor Statistics. (2014). *Employment projections.* Retrieved from http://www.bls.gov/emp/ep_data_occupational_data.htm

Bureau of Labor Statistics. (2015a). *College enrollment and work activity of 2014 high school graduates*. Retrieved from http://www.bls.gov/news.release/hsgec.nr0.htm

Bureau of Labor Statistics. (2015b). *Occupational outlook handbook, 2014–2015 edition*. Retrieved from http://www.bls.gov/ooh/home.htm

Carnevale, A. P., Smith, N., & Strohl, J. (2013). *Recovery: Job growth and education requirements through 2020.* Washington, DC: Georgetown University Center on Education and the Workforce. Retrieved from https://cew.georgetown.edu/report/recovery-job-growth-and-education-requirements-through-2020/

Gysbers, N. C. (2013). Career-ready students: A goal of comprehensive school counseling programs. *The Career Development Quarterly, 61*, 283–288.

Holland, J. L. (1959). A theory of occupational choice. *Journal of Counseling Psychology, 6*, 35–45.

Holland, J. L. (1997). *Making vocational choices: A theory of vocational personalities and work environments* (3rd ed.). Odessa, FL: Psychological Assessment Resources, Inc.

Job Corps. (2015). *Job corps: Success lasts a lifetime!* Retrieved from http://www.jobcorps.gov

Laird, J., Chen, X., & Levesque, K. (2006). *The postsecondary educational experiences of high school career and technical education concentrators.* Washington, DC: National Center for Educational Statistics. Retrieved from http://goo.gl/c93gkX

Markus, H., & Nurius, P. (1986). Possible selves. *American Psychologist, 41*(9), 954–969. doi: 0.1037/0003–066X.41.9.954

Michel, R. E. (2013). Possible selves mapping. In C. Wood & D. Hays (Eds.), *A counselor's guide to career assessment instruments* (6th ed., pp. 503–507). Broken Arrow, OK: National Career Development Association.

National Bureau of Economic Research. (2012). *U.S. business cycle expansions and contractions.* Retrieved from http://www.nber.org/cycles.html

National Center for Education Statistics. (2011). *Postsecondary and labor force transitions among public high school career and technical education participants.* Retrieved from nces.ed.gov/pubs2011/2011234.pdf

National Center for Education Statistics. (2015). *Employment rates and unemployment rates by educational attainment.* Retrieved from http://nces.ed.gov/programs/coe/indicator_cbc.asp

National Student Clearinghouse. (2014). *High school benchmarks: National college progression rates.* Retrieved from http://nscresearchcenter.org/hsbenchmarks2014

Neumark, D., & Rothstein, D. (2007). Do school-to-work programs help the "forgotten half"? In D. Neumark (Ed.), *Improving school-to-work transitions* (pp. 87–133). New York, NY: Russell Sage Foundation.

O*Net Online. (2015). *Job zone two: Some preparation needed.* Retrieved from https://www.onetonline.org/find/zone?z=2&g=Go

Packard, B. W., Leach, M., Ruiz, Y., Nelson, C., & DiCocco, H. (2012). School-to-work transition of career and technical education graduates. *The Career Development Quarterly, 60,* 134–144.

Pew Research Center. (2014). *The rising cost of not going to college.* Retrieved from http://tinyurl.com/nrc7u6o

Pisarik, C. T., & Shoffner, M. F. (2009). The relationship among work possible selves, socioeconomic position, and the psychological well-being of individuals in early adulthood. *Journal of Career Development, 35,* 306–325.

Plank, S., DeLuca, S., & Estacion, A. (2005). *Dropping out of high school and the place of career and technical education: A survival analysis of surviving high school.* St. Paul, MN: National Research Center for Career and Technical Education.

Rath, T. (2007). *StrengthsFinder 2.0.* New York, NY: Gallup Press.

Savickas, M. L. (2005). The theory and practice of career construction. In S. D. Brown & R. W. Lent (Eds.), *Career development and counseling: Putting theory and research to work* (pp. 42–70). Hoboken, NJ: Wiley.

Shepard, B., & Marshall, A. (1999). Possible selves mapping: Life-career exploration with young adolescents. *Canadian Journal of Counselling, 33,* 37–54.

Stern, D., Finkelstein, N., Stone, J., Latting, J., & Dornsife, C. (1995). *School to work: Research on programs in the United States.* London, UK: Falmer Press.

Torpey, E. (2015). *Career planning for high schoolers.* Retrieved from http://www.bls.gov/careeroutlook/2015/article/career-planning-for-high-schoolers.htm

U.S. Department of Education. (2015). *High schools and career readiness: Strengthening the pipeline to the middle class.* Retrieved from http://www.ed.gov/highschool

Wood, C., & Hays, D. (2013). *A counselor's guide to career assessment instruments* (6th ed.). Broken Arrow, OK: National Career Development Association.

CHAPTER 2

COMMUNITY COLLEGE STUDENTS

Kathryn S. Jaekel and Carrie A. Kortegast

CASE VIGNETTE: NICOLE

Nicole, a 30-year-old single mother with a 4-year-old daughter, has been contemplating returning to school. With only a high school diploma, Nicole has struggled to make enough money to support herself and her daughter. She wants a better life for her daughter, but needs a job that pays more but also allows for flexible hours. In her search for a higher paying position, she has realized that she needs some postsecondary education. Although it is becoming clear that the only way to make more money is to get a degree, Nicole is unsure what courses she needs to take and what vocational opportunities are available to her. Nicole decides to enroll part time in the closest community college to her, which is 10 miles away from her home. She begins taking classes although she is still unsure of the career path she would like to follow. She knows she wants a career in which she can help people and that offers flexible hours, but she is unsure about the best person with whom to discuss her plans.

THE ROLE OF COMMUNITY COLLEGES

Community colleges serve a critical role within higher education. An open access system can be both affordable and flexible; community colleges prepare students for the increasing need for skilled and educated individuals in the workforce. Roughly 7.4 million students have chosen to enroll in community colleges across the nation. Of those 7.4 million students, 4.5 million were enrolled part time and 5 million as noncredit-seeking students (National Center for Education Statistics [NCES], 2011). These institutions have created more access and opportunity for many individuals who struggle with academic performance, have limited finances, or have limited English-language proficiency (Grubb, 2006).

In particular, community colleges have become avenues by which millions are able to gain skills and experience in the workforce. Also, businesses and industries have developed their trainings around community colleges (Jacobs & Dougherty, 2006). Statistically, individuals with an associate's degree have higher earnings and earning potential than those with only a high school diploma (Marcotte, Bailey, Borkoski, & Kienzl, 2005). Thus, the long-term payoff is often worth making the short-term sacrifices required to pursue a degree. Although community colleges play a crucial role in helping maintain a career or gain entry into the workforce, many offer limited career counseling (Grubb, 2006).

DESCRIPTION OF COMMUNITY COLLEGE STUDENTS

Although community colleges serve many different goals, two primary goals are academic and vocational preparation (Berkner, Horn, & Clune, 2000). Because they offer such a wide variety of programs, there is no "one type" of community college student. Instead, community colleges boast a diverse student body, both in terms of demographic makeup and student motivation for pursuing higher education (American Association of Community Colleges [AACC], 2015). Although there is no single type of community college student, research detailing students' demographics and circumstances offers a cross-sectional look into who community colleges serve.

More than half of students who enroll in community college do so on a part time basis. Only 41% of students reported being full-time students (AACC, 2015). As in other sectors of higher education, more women are enrolled in community college than men; according to the AACC (Juszkiewicz, 2014), 61% of students at community college are women. Additionally, Horn, Nevill, and Griffith (2006) noted that community college students are typically financially independent of parents or guardians and are typically older than 24 years. The average age, however, of the community college student is 28 years, and 49% are between the ages of 22 and 39 years (AACC, 2015). Although the majority of community college students are White (68%), community colleges serve more racially diverse students than 4-year institutions (Horn et al., 2006). In addition, there are many community college students who may have special considerations such as military veteran students, first-generation students, and students with children. Of all community college students, 36% were identified as being first-generation college students (AACC, 2015). One third of community college students had children and one fourth of those students were single parents (AACC, 2015).

Student completion and graduation rates at community colleges are tricky to measure. For instance, the Department of Education only counts fall enrolled, full-time, first-time degree undergraduates that graduate from the same institution. Using these metrics, many community college students go uncounted. However, the most recent report from the National Student Clearinghouse (Shapiro, Dundar, Ziskin, Yuan, & Harrell, 2013) revealed that 6-year student outcomes indicated that 26.5% of students who began their education at a 2-year public institution completed their degree at the same institution and 18.9% were still enrolled. Although some students completed degrees at other 2- and 4-year institutions, most students (41.2%) were no longer enrolled and did not receive degrees (Shapiro et al., 2013).

Given this information, it is clear that community colleges serve a wide variety of students. Many students are already on their career paths and are honing their existing skills, while other students attend community college to change careers. Some are hoping to gain entry into the workforce for the first time. Given the richness of the community college population, it is important that these institutions utilize a system that will serve students' diverse career needs effectively.

HISTORICAL CAREER PATHS OF COMMUNITY COLLEGE STUDENTS

Historically, Americans have relied heavily on community colleges for workplace preparedness (Jacobs & Dougherty, 2006). Dating back to the beginning of the 20th century, the American community college arose out of a need for a skilled workforce and new pathways toward social equity and mobility (Cohen & Brawer, 2008). Schooling in the United States, at all levels, was seen as a way to solve both personal and social problems. For instance, one means to "solve problems of unemployment" was to provide public funds to support vocational education in the schools (Cohen & Brawer, 2008, p. 2). The rise of community colleges aligned with the increase in the number of high school graduates in the 20th century and movement toward credentialing. Previously, apprenticeships were the most common pathway into the workforce; however, this shifted toward formal credentials with the belief that education needed to be externally sanctioned by an institution (Cohen & Brawer, 2008).

During the Progressive Era and the passing of the Smith Hughes Act in 1917, vocational education was formalized by providing lower income students with training of trade skills (Morest, 2013). Although these trade skills were first a part of high school curricula, they were later expanded into community college curriculum. The Vocational Educational Act of 1963 and later amendments expanded the role of community college in providing vocational and technical education through increased funding. These funds served to bolster vocational, technical, and career education at community colleges as well as increase access for historically marginalized students such as women, part-time, disabled, older, low-income, and minority students (Cohen & Brawer, 2008).

The career paths for community college students are generally closely aligned with the curricular offerings and pathways. There are four common pathways: academic transfer, vocational–technical, continuing education, and developmental education. The academic transfer pathway prepares students to transfer to a 4-year-degree-granting institution. With the higher education boom in the late 1960s and 1970s, this pathway served to relieve some of the pressure public universities were facing to increase the number of freshman they admitted and, thus, maintaining their selective admission requirements (Cohen & Brawer, 2008). Preparing students to transfer, predominantly through the completion of general education course work and articulation agreements with 4-year institutions, remains an important function of community colleges.

The vocational–technical pathway was developed to prepare individuals for entry-level positions in business and industry. This training was designed to enhance and expand the vocational training provided at the high school level. Currently, the majority (64%) of community college students are enrolled in occupational associate's degrees programs (NCES, 2011) with the largest numbers of degrees granted in the health and business fields. Additionally, many students pursue short-term certificate training in particular fields such as health, business, mechanics, and culinary arts (Morest, 2013).

Continuing education fosters lifelong learning opportunities. These opportunities span hobbies, such as photography or gardening, to development of professional skills, such as computer programming and manufacturing. Importantly, there is no direct pathway, that is, continuing education is not bound by a particular curricular pattern or grade level. Instead, it is dedicated to personal development, and professional development is often a noncredit-bearing endeavor.

The need for community colleges to provide developmental education or remedial education pathways arose out of a need to address deficiencies in individuals' educational preparation. As a result of the breakdown of basic education, coupled with an increased need for postsecondary education, developmental education was needed to address this gap (Cohen & Brawer, 2008). For some students this might mean taking courses to pass the graduate education diploma (GED) examination (Ryder & Hagedorn, 2012), and for others it might mean obtaining the math and language skills needed to pursue college-level courses. Developmental and remedial courses are often noncredit bearing and thus do not count toward an associate's degree.

HISTORY OF CAREER OBSTACLES

Although many choose to attend community colleges due to the community college's open access, affordable, and flexible education, career development and placement continue to be a struggle for community college students, staff, and administrators. One primary reason for this struggle is a lack of guidance. Although some community colleges have stand-alone career centers, many combine the role of academic advising and career counseling into one position. According to Grubb (2006), students may have little career counseling while enrolled in community college. The community college system seems to wrongly assume that this population of students already knows their desired career path (O'Banion, 1994). Due to high caseloads, advisers do not have time to reach out to all their students, instead relying on students to seek out advice and answers to questions and problems. Institutional personnel, then, may be unaware of issues or problems until it is too late (Scott-Clayton, 2011).

Moreover, advisers often have caseloads that span 800 to 1,200 students (Grubb, 2006; Scott-Clayton, 2011), making individualized career counseling difficult, if not impossible. Due to such high caseloads, advisers often have time to attend to only class registration instead of discussion around larger career roles and paths (Scott-Clayton, 2011). Because of poor institutional data collection, advisers often struggle keeping track of students due to the part-time status of students and due to the frequent practice of community college students skipping some semesters instead of remaining continuously enrolled (Scott-Clayton, 2011).

Finally, because many students who attend community colleges are frequently first generation, low income, and/or underprepared, they lack access to different family and peer networks for help in navigating academic and career advice (Bailey, Jenkins, & Leinback, 2005). Access to networks of people who have experience navigating college and the transition into a career is often denied to those in community colleges.

EXPECTED CAREER DEVELOPMENT NEEDS OF COMMUNITY COLLEGE STUDENTS

For most students, "pursuing a postsecondary degree is fundamentally an economic decision" (Morest, 2013, p. 51). However, the academic preparation needed for particular careers is not always apparent or easily understood by students as the relationship between "school and work remains vague" (Morest, 2013, p. 51). Further complicating the expected career development needs of community college students is the diversity of community college students and their academic and professional aspirations.

Community college students pursuing vocational, occupation, or technical training are motivated by obtaining "employable skills" (Morest, 2013, p. 57). They turn to community colleges in order to provide them with the knowledge, skills, and competencies to secure a job that will provide financial security for themselves and often their family. Career counselors must communicate to students the importance of pursuing course work that will prepare them for the jobs and careers they desire. Additionally, clients may need assistance in identifying majors and courses that align with their career interests. Clients may not know precisely which occupational and career fields they are interested in pursuing or which fields they would be well suited to pursue. Without accurate insights and a good major fit, students may flounder, drop out, or pursue generic majors such as "general studies" or "liberal arts" (Morest, 2013), which do not have clear career pathways. Career counselors need to work with clients in identifying individual skills, talents, and occupational interests in order to advise appropriately.

NEEDED SUPPORTS AND RELEVANT CAREER COUNSELING INTERVENTIONS

Although there are several career and educational pathways available to community college students and graduates, the clearest and most strongly supported are the transfer and vocational–technical pathways. Typically, academic advisers support community college students who are preparing to transfer by advising in courses that will transfer as well as assisting with the application processes. However, academic advisers also provide important information and guidance regarding course work that aligns with particular career preparation.

Career centers and career counselors at community colleges offer all students a range of services. These services include providing career assessment and counseling, offering job and internship search assistance, reviewing resumes and cover letters, and sponsoring mock interviews. Additionally, many career centers partner with business and industry to provide career fairs, maintain a clearinghouse of local job postings, and present career development workshops. However, there is no consistency of offerings across the country. In addition, many community colleges are underresourced, particularly in the area of career services. Thus, flexible and innovative approaches to career counseling might better support the needs of students and graduates. For instance, offering appointments beyond the standard 9 to 5 workday is essential, providing counseling via Skype or other virtual means is advised, and answering questions via a chat function or Twitter might reach more students. There are issues regarding confidentiality, but general questions and advice might reach more clients via social media. Social media outreach efforts might encourage more clients to schedule individual appointments for guidance.

Although it is assumed that community college students and graduates know what career options and opportunities are available to them, often this is not the case. Students often are not cognizant of their needs for assistance nor do they know exactly what resources are available. Thus, campus-based career counselors should consider intrusive advising techniques by reaching out to students directly. Finally, because of the diversity of community college students and graduates, a "one-size fits all" approach will not work. Counselors need to be culturally responsive and understand clients' histories regarding work, education, and family. Being thoughtful of clients' backgrounds, social identities, and life constraints will allow counselors to provide more relevant guidance. In particular, career counselors need to bear in mind the economic realities of their clients. As Morest (2013) stated, "By failing to embrace the economic lives of students and leverage their desire to get jobs, community colleges are missing a major opportunity to engage and motivate them to degree completion" (p. 58). Regardless of the community pathway a client participates within, ultimately, the focus remains providing support to individuals pursuing their personal and professional aspirations.

REVISITING THE CASE OF NICOLE

After a successful first semester, Nicole's career counselor sets up a Skype meeting with her during Nicole's lunch break. After Nicole described her interests in helping people as well as her interests in science and math, the career counselor suggested nursing as a career. The counselor explained there is a demand for nurses in Nicole's community and that nursing would allow her flexible hours. The counselor then advised her on course work and internships that would help her to be competitive in the job market. Nicole's career counselor continues to check in with her every semester to make sure Nicole is still on track and to answer any questions that may come up over the course of her education. The counselor also provided information on job applications, interview skills, and ways to broaden her marketability. After 3 years, Nicole is able to graduate with an associate's degree in nursing and secures a position at her local hospital.

ADDITIONAL RESOURCE SUGGESTIONS

American Association of Community Colleges (AACC): www.aacc.nche.edu
Community College Research Center (CCRC): ccrc.tc.columbia.edu

REFERENCES

American Association of Community Colleges (AACC). (2015). *The 2015 community college fact sheet*. Retrieved from http://www.aacc.nche.edu/AboutCC/Pages/fastfactsfactsheet.aspx

Bailey, T., Jenkins, D., & Leinbach, T. (2005). *What we know about community college low-income and minority student outcomes: Descriptive statistics from national surveys.* Community College Research Center. New York: Columbia University.

Berkner, L., Horn, L., & Clune, M. (2000). Postsecondary students. *National Center for Education Statistics, 2*(2), 79.

Cohen, A. M., & Brawer, F. B. (2008). *The American Community College* (5th ed.). San Francisco, CA: Wiley.

Grubb, W. N. (2006). "Like, what do I do now?": The dilemmas of guidance counseling. In T. Bailey & V. Morest (Eds.), *Defending the community college equity agenda* (pp. 195–222). Baltimore, MD: Johns Hopkins University Press.

Horn, L., Nevill, S., & Griffith, J. (2006). *Profile of undergraduates in US postsecondary education institutions, 2003–04: With a special analysis of community college students. Statistical analysis report. NCES 2006–184.* Washington, DC: U.S. Department of Education, National Center for Education Statistics.

Jacobs, J., & Dougherty, K. J. (2006). The uncertain future of the community college workforce development mission. *New Directions for Community Colleges, 2006*(136), 53–62.

Juszkiewicz, J. (2014). *Recent national community college enrollment and award completion data.* Washington, DC: American Association of Community Colleges.

Marcotte, D. E., Bailey, T., Borkoski, C., & Kienzl, G. S. (2005). The returns of a community college education: Evidence from the National Education Longitudinal Survey. *Educational Evaluation and Policy Analysis, 27*(2), 157–175.

Morest, V. S. (2013). *Community college student success: From boardrooms to classrooms.* Lanham, MD: Rowman & Littlefield.

NCES. (2011). *Condition of education.* Washington, DC: National Center for Educational Statistics.

O'Banion, T. (1994). An academic advising model. *NACADA Journal, 14*(2), 10–16.

Ryder, A. J., & Hagedorn, L. S. (2012). GED and other noncredit courses: The other side of the community college. *Data use in the community college: New directions for institutional research, number 2012*(153), 21–31.

Scott-Clayton, J. (2011). *The shapeless river: Does a lack of structure inhibit students' progress at community colleges?* (CCRC Working Paper No. 25, Assessment of Evidence Series). New York, NY: Columbia University, Teachers College, Community College Research Center.

Shapiro, D., Dundar, A., Ziskin, M., Yuan, X., & Harrell, A. (2013, December). *Completing college: A national view of student attainment rates–Fall 2007 cohort* (Signature Report No. 6). Herndon, VA: National Student Clearinghouse Research Center.

CHAPTER 3

TRADITIONAL-AGED COLLEGE GRADUATES

Rebecca E. Michel

CASE VIGNETTE: NANCY

Sitting in bumper-to-bumper traffic, Nancy was trying to figure out how her life led her to this point. Here she was, a 22-year-old African American female college graduate, now driving a produce truck for Christine Organic Farms. This was not how she envisioned her first "real" job out of college. Nancy began thinking about how her college years unfolded and how her career search had gone awry.

Nancy had majored in psychology at Western State. Although Nancy performed adequately in the classroom, she really devoted her attention to activities outside of class. In fact, some might argue that Nancy's true passion was participating in extracurricular activities at Western State. She was pledge chair of her social sorority, captain of her intermural volleyball team, and covered the student body senate for the school newspaper. As senior year rolled around, Nancy was feeling anxious about leaving Western State and found it easier "not to think about" her impending graduation and career preparations. Accordingly, she did not attend the job fair on campus and only visited a campus career counselor once during her senior year after constant badgering by her mother.

Upon graduation, Nancy moved back in with her parents and began to look for work. Her job search thus far has been a frustrating and humbling experience. Despite holding a college degree, the only job she could land was as a produce truck driver at a company owned by her mother's friend, Christine. Dejected, she was now trying to figure out her next steps.

DESCRIPTION OF THE POPULATION

"Traditional" college students, like Nancy, enrolled in college full time following high school and, when successful, graduated college in their early 20s. During college, these individuals progressed from adolescence into emerging adulthood (Arnett, 2000). This distinct life stage between the ages of 18 to 25 years is characterized by identity exploration, instability, self-focus, feeling *in between*, and discovering possibilities (Arnett & Tanner, 2006). During this critical time, individuals face a significant turning point as they transition from college to career.

Whether due to their career development, personal attributes, or the current economy, many recent U.S. graduates have delayed transitioning into the traditional world of work. Instead, during and immediately after college, they invested time exploring their identities and life possibilities. Some emerging adults view this time following college as exhilarating and full of opportunities while others, like Nancy, are paralyzed by the burden of attempting to discover a meaningful career (Kenny & Sirin, 2006; Mortimer, Zimmer-Gembeck, Holmes, & Shanahan, 2002). The decisions made during this transition often determine whether emerging adults launch or languish in their careers during the years that follow.

HISTORICAL PERSPECTIVE

Historically, education has been seen as the great equalizer—that regardless of cultural background, if an individual worked hard and earned a college degree he or she could irrevocably change his or her career and life trajectory. A college diploma set individuals apart from their peers in the job market and allowed them to earn higher income and pursue various career paths. With college graduates reporting higher quality of life than high school graduates, it is not surprising that over the past 150 years higher education in the United States has experienced tremendous growth. For example, in 1870, 1% of the 18- to 24-year-old population was enrolled in college and 9,371 college degrees were conferred (Snyder, 1993; U.S. Department of Commerce, 2013). By 2012, 41% of the 18- to 24-year-old population enrolled in colleges and more than 1,791,000 individuals graduated with their bachelor's degrees (U.S. Department of Commerce, 2013, 2014).

Over the past several decades, colleges and universities have made intentional efforts to recruit and retain diverse students; thus, the "typical" college student of today looks very different from the one in the past. Nontraditional students (those who have delayed college enrollment, are older than 25 years, attend school part time, work full time, are financially independent, and/or are responsible for dependents) are enrolling in college at unprecedented rates. Many scholars argue that nontraditional students have become the new traditional college student (Jenkins, 2012; see Chapter 4 of this book for a comprehensive discussion about the career development of nontraditional college students).

These diverse students expect that their educational investment will pay off over their career. On average, recent college graduates working full time earn approximately $17,500 per year more than high school graduates (Pew Research Center, 2014); a college graduate can anticipate earning $1 million more than a high school graduate during one's lifetime (Carnevale, Rose, & Cheah, 2011). Additionally, the expected growth rate for occupations that require a college degree is 14% per year (Bureau of Labor Statistics [BLS], 2013b). These occupations are typically clustered into career areas including business, education, computer science, arts, engineering, health care, and social science (BLS 2013a). However, changes in the labor market have led to a reduced number of high-skilled jobs available to college graduates, which has caused significant barriers to the career choices available to college graduates today.

CHALLENGES FOR COLLEGE GRADUATES

As college graduates transition from school to the world of work, they can experience many career challenges that are largely reflective of the economic landscape. The Great Recession of 2007 through 2009 disproportionately impacted young adults and college graduates. Greenleaf (2014) posited, with the exception of individuals seeking employment during the Great Depression, "no generation of college graduates in American history has faced more daunting obstacles to their career development than the current one" (p. 159). College graduates are often unable to distinguish themselves from other college graduates unless they have advanced degrees or significant career experience. This fierce competition in the labor market has left many recent college graduates without sustainable or meaningful work.

The slow recovery after the Great Recession resulted in fewer available jobs for college graduates. Many have found themselves unemployed or underemployed (Greenleaf, 2014). Underemployed individuals possess more skills than a job requires, work in a job unrelated to their field of study, are employed part time, or earn significantly less than recent graduates entering the labor market (McKee-Ryan & Harvey, 2011). Mal-employment is one type of underemployment that has steadily increased over the past decade.

Between 2000 and 2010, the mal-employment rate increased from 29.8% to 39.1% for young college graduates aged 20 to 24 years (Fogg & Harrington, 2011). Almost 4 out of 10 employed young college graduates are underemployed; thus, they earn less income, report less job satisfaction, and experience less well-being than their working peers (Kahn, 2010; McKee-Ryan & Harvey, 2011). The long-term psychological and financial effects of starting a career unemployed or underemployed can be overwhelming. In order to support college graduates through these challenges, career counselors can explore the career development needs of emerging adults during this critical life stage.

THE NEEDS OF EMERGING ADULTS

The career needs of emerging adults relate to the major developmental tasks of this phase of life, including identity exploration, self-focus, feeling *in between*, instability, and discovering possibilities (Arnett & Tanner, 2006). The primary need during this stage is to develop autonomy, a key factor in the transition to adulthood (Erikson, 1963). Emerging adults are more likely to experience a successful adjustment from college to their career when they learn to become autonomous and establish financial independence, work salience, self-efficacy, and fulfilled career expectations (Murphy, Blustein, Bohlig, & Platt, 2010).

Many emerging adults utilize the time following college to solidify their work values and career identity (Murphy et al., 2010). Successful transitions from college to career require graduates to have the space to develop autonomy, while also being socially supported (Galambos, Barker, & Krahn, 2006; Murphy et al., 2010). Helicopter parents accustomed to being intimately involved in their children's lives may find it difficult not to intervene at this critical juncture (Hunt, 2008; Schiffrin et al., 2014). However, autonomy is enhanced when parents maintain supportive involvement, establish adult relationships, and foster responsibility (Cullaty, 2011). It is imperative that college graduates learn to function autonomously and establish their own unique career identity.

Recent college graduates who have not yet obtained meaningful full-time employment find themselves in a space *in between* adolescence and adulthood (Arnett & Tanner, 2006). Although they have surpassed the societal milestones leading to adulthood (e.g., obtaining a driver's license, earning the right to vote, graduating with a college degree), they do not feel prepared to take the final leap to vocational and financial independence. Emerging adults experience instability during this time of life (Arnett & Tanner, 2006), as the career landscape has made it challenging for many college graduates to obtain meaningful employment immediately following college. Graduates without work may move home with their parents, contributing to instability and conflicting with the goal of becoming autonomous. These individuals would benefit from increasing their level of adaptability. Murphy et al. (2010) found that college graduates who exemplified adaptability in the face of unexpected career challenges and transition still reported high levels of life satisfaction. For, as many college graduates have learned, instability can also bring about the opportunity for new possibilities.

College graduates are likely to have numerous jobs throughout their career, especially as young adults. A longitudinal study of baby boomers born from 1957 through 1964 suggested that individuals held an average of 5.5 jobs between the ages of 18 and 24 years (BLS, 2013a). Emerging adults tend to be engaged in a prolonged career decision-making process, leaving them open to discover interesting careers in the years following college graduation (Arnett, 2014). Emerging adults working in part-time jobs or positions outside their disciplines are often optimistic and believe that their current position will serve as a stepping stone to a more meaningful career (Murphy et al., 2010). Because the job search is typically self-directed and autonomous, college graduates need to learn the most effective career behaviors to engage in while seeking employment. Specifically, they must develop proactive career behaviors to increase their chances of moving into an occupation aligned with the skills and knowledge they attained during college. These individuals have a wide range of career supports in place to help them manage their transition into the world of work.

SUPPORTS FOR COLLEGE GRADUATES

College graduates have access to numerous career supports. Once they graduate, alumni can continue to utilize career services at their college and universities. These robust lifelong career development services may include career coaching or counseling, job search seminars and webinars, networking events, career fairs, and other online tools (such as career assessments, strategies to write resumes and cover letters, and information about interviewing and negotiating job offers), as well as university-specific resources (Fouad et al., 2006). There are also often directories and job databases to specifically connect and support alumni on the job market. Several websites have also been designed for college graduates (see Additional Resource Suggestions). College graduates can independently utilize these career supports or work with a career counselor to target which supports would be most beneficial to their specific needs.

CAREER COUNSELING WITH COLLEGE GRADUATES

Career counseling can be helpful for college graduates transitioning from school to work. Career counselors working with college graduates must be prepared to address how they can navigate the career landscape when a college diploma is no longer enough to land them their first job. The significant reduction of available positions in the aftermath of the Great Recession has made it difficult for emerging adults to find meaningful work aligned with their educational level and skills. Thus, emerging adults have delayed, either intentionally or as a result of bleak job prospects, launching into the workforce as their college graduate predecessors have done for decades. Career counselors must take these economic and developmental factors into consideration when working with individuals within this population.

Krumboltz's (2009) happenstance learning theory (HLT) can be a helpful framework for working with college graduates to meet their developmental needs during this transitional time (Greenleaf, 2014). Career counselors utilizing HLT (Krumboltz, 2009) understand that career transitions are both expected and desirable. Rather than becoming paralyzed during a transition, college students can take action and obtain assistance from career counselors in order to learn new career-related knowledge and skills and open up new possibilities (Krumboltz, 2009). Career counselors can follow a three-step process to encourage clients to take action and respond to chance events:

1. Before the unplanned event, take actions that position you to experience it.
2. During the event, remain alert and sensitive to recognize potential opportunities.
3. After the event, initiate actions that enable you to benefit from it (p. 144).

In addition to preparing for unplanned events, in order to increase the likelihood of obtaining employment it is important for college graduates to engage in several types of proactive career behaviors, which are intentional actions individuals take to support their career goals, such as networking (Sturges, Guest, Conway, & Davey, 2002) and connecting with people who have information about career opportunities (Claes & Ruiz-Quintanilla, 1998). For college graduates, proactive career behaviors might include joining civic organizations, interviewing, accessing university career centers, and intentionally connecting with alumni.

When college graduates engage in proactive career behaviors they create favorable circumstances that increase the likelihood of new career opportunities, and they are ready to take timely action when such opportunities arise. Emerging adults who proactively search for a job prior to graduation experience greater career and salary satisfaction than their peers (De Vos, De Clippeleer, & Dewilde, 2009). Additionally, recent college graduates who networked in their community experienced greater career success (Sturges et al., 2002). Career counselors can help college graduates identify strategies to increase these proactive career behaviors.

In the current economy, it is expected that individuals will change jobs, and even occupations, several times throughout their careers (Greenleaf, 2014). College graduates willing to explore and engage in various career choices outside of the occupations they anticipated for themselves are at an advantage over individuals who remain stuck on their original career plans (Krumboltz, 2009). College graduates must be willing to take on part-time positions or internships and be open to unforeseen opportunities and chance events that might lead to a more fulfilling career (Bright, Pryor, Chan, & Rijanto, 2009).

Adaptable college graduates will be able to see possibilities and open doors when their career plans are flexible. Career counselors can work with traditional college graduates to increase their ability to adapt to predictable and unpredictable events along their career path. Career counselors support clients to increase their adaptability by encouraging clients to engage in proactive career behaviors and take risks when unforeseen opportunities arise (Krumboltz, 2009). See Appendix C for additional suggestions.

REVISITING THE CASE OF NANCY

Nancy had done everything she thought she was supposed to do, so she did not understand why she was living in her parents' house and driving a produce truck. She did not have a fulfilling career and was uncertain about her next steps. Her parents were very involved in her previous educational decisions, and now she looked to them to help her determine what to do after college. Like many helicopter parents, their over-involvement and hovering caused Nancy to feel insecure about her own decision-making abilities. She felt paralyzed and unable to make progress because she did not know where to begin.

Using Krumboltz's (2009) HLT, the career counselor helped Nancy develop autonomy to take actions and capitalize on employment opportunities should they arise. The counselor heard and normalized her feelings, experiences, and concerns. They both agreed that many college graduates find themselves underemployed because the Great Recession had changed the career landscape for college graduates. The counselor helped Nancy develop realistic expectations about career possibilities in the current economy. Nancy came to understand that driving a produce truck was just the first of many jobs she was likely to have in her life. This realization helped her recognize she had been sulking about her job but not doing anything about it. She decided to stop feeling sorry for herself and start taking action to change the situation.

The career counselor then turned to address Nancy's specific career concerns. Because Nancy was not satisfied in her current employment as a produce truck driver, she and the counselor explored what would bring her satisfaction in a career. The counselor asked Nancy, "What does career success look like to you?" The counselor emphasized that Nancy needed to discover these answers for herself (rather than from her parents) so that she developed more autonomy over her identity and ultimate life decisions.

Nancy took time to investigate many different elements of a career, including work, hobbies, community involvement, family, entertainment, affiliations, and nourishment (Krumboltz, 2009). Because she enjoyed photography, she took several pictures of objects and people that represented each important aspect she imagined in a successful career. She used the images to create a picture vision board of what career success looked like to her. She realized that, since leaving college, she was missing several important aspects of her life, including hobbies, community involvement, entertainment, and affiliations. Nancy determined that there were many steps she could take to increase her satisfaction and took the initiative to join a volleyball league, write stories for the local newspaper, and spend time with her sorority sisters.

As time passed, Nancy was feeling more fulfilled in several important areas of her life. However, she still had not found another job. As homework from her career counselor, Nancy was encouraged to utilize her journalism skills to conduct interviews with people about their career experiences and keep a blog about what she discovered. Nancy enthusiastically got to work. She began by interviewing all the people in her social network and asked everyone she interviewed for a referral. This unexpectedly led to Nancy connecting with the executive director of a regional newspaper who appreciated her initiative and blog. The director offered Nancy a position working full time with the newspaper to write about issues facing young adults. Nancy took the position and moved into her own apartment. To this day, she still keeps a blog to celebrate career stories and adventures.

ADDITIONAL RESOURCE SUGGESTIONS

After College (www.aftercollege.com) allows recent college graduates to post their resume and search among 400,000 entry-level jobs and internships.

Campus Career Center (www.campuscareercenter.com) features a job search database, a job blog, and support from a graduate career coach on topics such as interviewing, branding, and identifying career paths.

College Career Life Planning (www.collegecareerlifeplanning.com) includes more than 50 career and life planning tools with tutorials about networking, interviewing, and negotiation.

One Day One Job (www.onedayonejob.com) aims to help individuals determine what they want to do after college by featuring more than 1,700 employers hiring young adults. The site also includes a free course called "Found your career: Job search prep for college grads."

Quintessential Careers (www.quintcareers.com/grad_jobs.html) features job-search articles, e-books, and a job interview question database. There are also several tutorials, including one on "conquering the real world: a guide for achieving success after college."

The Career Outlook (www.bls.gov/careeroutlook) includes career planning articles, features unique and interesting occupations ("You're a what?"), includes interviews with employees in numerous careers, and highlights data that can be helpful for job seekers.

There are also numerous job search engines specifically designed for college graduates seeking employment, such as CollegeGrad.com, StudentCentral.com, CollegeRecruiter.com, Collegestudentjob.org, ihipo.com, and college.monster.com.

REFERENCES

Arnett, J. J. (2000). Emerging adulthood: A theory of development from the late teens through the twenties. *American Psychologist, 55*, 469–480.

Arnett, J. J. (2014). *Emerging adulthood: The winding road from the late teens through the twenties.* New York, NY: Oxford University Press.

Arnett, J. J., & Tanner, J. L. (2006). *Emerging adults in America: Coming of age in the 21st century.* Washington, DC: APA Books.

Bright, J., Pryor, R., Chan, E., & Rijanto, J. (2009). Chance events in career development: Influence, control and multiplicity. *Journal of Vocational Behavior, 75*, 14–25.

Bureau of Labor Statistics. (2013a). *College to career: Projected job openings in occupations that typically require a bachelor's degree.* Retrieved from http://goo.gl/XaPxKm

Bureau of Labor Statistics. (2013b). *Employment projections: 2012–2022 summary.* Retrieved from http://www.bls.gov/news.release/ecopro.nr0.htm

Carnevale, A. P., Rose, S. J., & Cheah, B. (2011). *The college payoff: Education, occupations, lifetime earnings.* Washington, DC: Georgetown University Center of Education and the Workforce. Retrieved from https://cew.georgetown.edu/report/the-college-payoff

Claes, R., & Ruiz-Quintanilla, S. (1998). Influences of early career experiences, occupational group, and national culture on proactive career behavior. *Journal of Vocational Behavior, 52*, 357–378.

Cullaty, B. (2011). The role of parental involvement in the autonomy development of traditional-age college students. *Journal of College Student Development, 52*, 425–439.

De Vos, A., De Clippeleer, I., & Dewilde, T. (2009). Proactive career behaviours and career success during the early career. *Journal of Occupational and Organizational Psychology, 82*, 761–777.

Erikson, E. H. (1963). *Childhood and society.* New York, NY: Norton.

Fogg, N. P., & Harrington, P. E. (2011). Rising mal-employment and the Great Recession: The growing disconnection between recent college graduates and the college labor market. *Continuing Higher Education Review, 75*, 51–65.

Fouad, N. A., Guillen, A., Harris-Hodge, E., Henry, C., Novakovic, A., Terry, S., & Kantamneni, N. (2006). Need, awareness, and use of services for college students. *Journal of Career Assessment, 14*, 407–420.

Galambos, N. L., Barker, E. T., & Krahn, H. J. (2006). Depression, self-esteem, and anger in emerging adulthood: Seven-year trajectories. *Developmental Psychology, 42*, 350–365.

Greenleaf, A. T. (2014). Making the best of a bad situation: Career counseling young adults in the aftermath of the Great Recession. *Journal of Employment Counseling, 51*, 158–169.

Hunt, J. (2008). Make room for daddy . . . and mommy: Helicopter parents are here. *The Journal of Academic Administration in Higher Education, 4*, 9–11.

Jenkins, R. (2012). The new traditional student. *Chronicle of Higher Education, 59*(8), A31–A32.

Kahn, L. B. (2010). The long-term labor market consequences of graduating from college in a bad economy. *Labour Economics, 17*, 303–316.

Kenny, M. E., & Sirin, S. R. (2006). Parental attachment, self-worth, and depressive symptoms among emerging adults. *Journal of Counseling & Development, 84*, 61–71.

Krumboltz, J. D. (2009). The happenstance learning theory. *Journal of Career Assessment, 17*, 135–154.

McKee-Ryan, F. M., & Harvey, J. (2011). I have a job, but . . . : A review of underemployment. *Journal of Management, 37*(4), 962–996.

Mortimer, J. T., Zimmer-Gembeck, M. J., Holmes, M., & Shanahan, M. J. (2002). The process of occupational decision making: Patterns during the transition to adulthood. *Journal of Vocational Behavior, 61*, 439–465.

Murphy, K. A., Blustein, D. L., Bohlig, A. J., & Platt, M. G. (2010). The college-to-career transition: An exploration of emerging adulthood. *Journal of Counseling & Development, 88*, 174–181.

Pew Research Center. (2014). *The rising cost of not going to college.* Retrieved from http://tinyurl.com/nrc7u6o

Schiffrin, H. H., Liss, M., Miles-McLean, H., Geary, K. A., Erchull, M. J., & Tashner, T. (2014). Helping or hovering? The effects of helicopter parenting on college students' well-being. *Journal of Child and Family studies, 23*, 548–557.

Snyder, T. D. (1993). *120 years of American education: A statistical portrait.* Washington, DC: U.S. Department of Education, Office of Educational Research and Improvement, National Center for Education Statistics. Retrieved from http://goo.gl/B0OScX

Sturges, J., Guest, D., Conway, N., & Davey, K. M. (2002). A longitudinal study of the relationship between career management and organizational commitment among graduates in the first ten years at work. *Journal of Organizational Behavior, 23*, 731–748.

U.S. Department of Commerce. (2013). *Degrees conferred by degree-granting postsecondary institutions, by level of degree and sex of student: Selected years, 1869–70 through 2023–24.* Retrieved from http://nces.ed.gov/programs/digest/d13/tables/dt13_318.10.asp?current=yes

U.S. Department of Commerce. (2014). *Census Bureau, current population survey (CPS), October 1967 through 2013.* Retrieved from http://nces.ed.gov/programs/digest/d14/tables/dt14_302.60.asp

CHAPTER 4

NONTRADITIONAL HIGHER EDUCATION STUDENTS

Susan R. Barclay

CASE VIGNETTE: NESSA

Nessa is a 43-year-old multiethnic woman who entered into a committed relationship directly out of high school. She and her partner began raising a family shortly after the union. Nessa was a full-time parent until her children began school, after which she took a job as a receptionist and office manager at a local construction company. Over the course of several years, Nessa progressed in her career. Currently, Nessa's youngest child is preparing to enter college, and, after 12 years in the construction industry, Nessa is ready for a change. She realizes she is unfulfilled in her work and wants something more meaningful. As a young girl, Nessa dreamed of teaching, but she is unsure if she wants to pursue that dream anymore. She likes helping people yet does not know what career field she desires. She does know that, if she is to exit construction work and pursue a new career, she needs a college education. To accomplish her career goal, Nessa enrolls in courses at a local college known for its Working Adult programs. Nessa believes that core classes will help her acclimate in an environment in which she has no experience (school). Nessa hopes that being in college will help her discover the field in which she might be most interested in pursuing a career.

DESCRIPTION OF THE POPULATION

According to the American Council on Education (ACE, 2014), 40% of the U.S. college population are nontraditional students. Others (Aslanian & Clinefelter, 2012; Soares, 2013) estimated that the percentage might be as high as 80%. The National Center for Education Statistics (NCES, 2011) placed that number at approximately 64.5%. Regardless, nontraditional students continue to attend college, and the primary reason is career related (Aslanian & Clinefelter, 2012), a trend uniquely similar to that in the 1970s and 1980s (Aslanian & Brickell, 1980).

Although one specific definition for *nontraditional student* does not exist, the NCES (n.d.) described the nontraditional student as an individual older than 25 years managing multiple life responsibilities, such as work and family, while attempting to complete educational goals. Most often, nontraditional students work full time (Kenner & Weinerman, 2011); are financially independent (Baptista, 2013; Kenner & Weinerman, 2011); are supporting children or others financially (Pelletier, 2010); and, often, hold a nontraditional high school completion certificate (e.g., General Equivilency Diploma [GED] or certificate of completion).

Nontraditional students at American universities have many faces. They are parents (Butt, 2012), caretakers (Pelletier, 2010), and veterans (Kenner & Weinerman, 2011). Sometimes, life changes, such as empty nest (Butt, 2012; Ibarra, 2003), divorce (Taniguchi & Kaufman, 2007; White, 2001), or retirement (Scott & Lewis, 2012), provide adults with an opportunity to seek a college education. Others return to upgrade career credentials or for personal growth (Cullity, 2006). One of the defining features of nontraditional students is having to cope with the strain of multiple roles that students experience while attempting to complete educational objectives (Luzzo, 1999; Pelletier, 2010; Ross-Gordon, 2011; Veney, O'Geen, & Kowalik, 2012).

The United States is not the only nation to experience the upsurge of the nontraditional student population. Cullity (2006) reported that, in 2002, 38% of undergraduate students in Australian universities were nontraditional; Baptista (2013) noted the increasing numbers of nontraditional students in Portugal entering college for the first time as undergraduates. Orr (2010) cited that, in 2008, 56% of undergraduates in Sweden were older than 25 years, and in Europe, nontraditional students represented "an invisible majority" (p. 26). Jenkins (2012) posited that nontraditional students were the "new traditional student." Small segments of these students enter college for changing careers (29%; Aslanian & Clinefelter, 2012) or are unsure of their goals (8%; Kruger, 2014). This is in contrast to those trying to advance their career (46%), keep up-to-date in their current career (12%), meet credentialing or licensure requirements (5%), or achieve personal growth (4%; Aslanian & Clinefelter, 2012).

HISTORICAL CAREER PATHS/CHOICES AVAILABLE

Before World War II (WWII), the typical household included a man, who supported the family financially, and a woman, who stayed at home caring for the household and children. With the onset of WWII, increasing numbers of women entered the workforce filling jobs left open by men who were at war. These jobs were seen as masculine in nature, and at the close of WWII, women left those jobs. However, women were not content in returning to their homes; they wanted to remain a part of the workforce (Domenico & Jones, 2006).

For most of the 20th century, people entered the workforce pursuing stereotypical jobs, and many entered right after high school. Workers could depend on employers providing a lifetime of employment, medical and retirement benefits, and advancement in their careers. Career development efforts consisted of theories and interventions that aligned with what became known as the "fit" model. This model advocated assessing a person's interests and directing the person to pursue occupations within a specific vocational field. This worked well, from a career guidance perspective; however, many individuals experienced emptiness and meaninglessness in their work. Moreover, career aspirations for both men and women began to overlap (Domenico & Jones, 2006), blurring the boundaries between gender-specific careers.

Savickas (2012) proposed that, "entering today's work world requires more effort, deeper self-knowledge, and greater confidence than ever before" (p. 13). The 21st-century work world differs from that of the 20th century, and employers no longer contract with employees to provide stable employment, retirement packages, or assurance of lifetime employment. In what Savickas calls a "social reorganization of work" (p. 13), employees manage their own careers. This requires self-knowledge. However, other components are also necessary for workers to understand who they are in relation to the world. That world embraces family, identity, and how a person envisions life apart from work. Savickas et al. (e.g., Maree, 2010; Taber et al., 2011) advocated for a different approach in career counseling. This approach includes interventions used during the 20th century but encompasses narrative approaches to create a holistic approach.

HISTORY OF NONTRADITIONAL STUDENT CHALLENGES

The Learning House and the Aslanian Market Research groups (Aslanian & Clinefelter, 2012) provided data on reasons students attend college. Findings indicated that students attend for several reasons. Study results showed that, overall, 90% of students attend for career issues, and 46% indicated that their primary motivation was to advance in their current careers, while 29% indicated that their primary motivation was to change careers. Participants in this study were students of all ages, but nontraditional students (older than 25 years) comprised 80% of the survey participants.

Reasons for the increasing number of nontraditional students vary, although Dacey and Travers (2004) suggested that many adults desire to change careers yet lack a career-related identity. Providing career services and interventions for this group is vital. Traditional career development interventions may not be as effective with nontraditional students because traditional interventions fail to respect the life experiences of nontraditional students.

Kasworm (2010) highlighted the anxiety and self-consciousness nontraditional students experience concerning their place in a traditionally youth-oriented educational environment. They face challenges with the traditional format and structure of course offerings (Pelletier, 2010) because of conflicts with job situations. Higher education institutions are increasing course offerings later in the day, evenings, and weekends; yet, nontraditional students may find these accommodations challenging and resort to online environments. However, with online environments, these students may experience intimidation, depending on their level of technological skill. These students have expressed confusion regarding navigating the higher education system (Pelletier, 2010). They may lack family support and guidance related to application procedures, financial aid processes, registration, and student support services.

EXPECTED CAREER DEVELOPMENT NEEDS

Because the reasons for seeking postsecondary education vary among nontraditional students, their expected career development needs will also vary. Butt (2012) and Kenner and Weinerman (2011) blamed the 2008 economic downturn as a primary motivation for adults to seek postsecondary education. Likewise, Melkun (2012) posited that the decision for many nontraditional students to begin or continue their education was based on financial or occupational motivations. In their study, Larkin, LaPort, and Pines (2007) noted that 61 out of 141 (43%) nontraditional student participants indicated that they were in jobs that were not relevant to their careers and were motivated to seek further education to increase opportunities.

One of the primary career development needs of nontraditional students may be transitional. Nontraditional students must incorporate an additional role strain and transition to being a student. Schlossberg (1984, 2011) highlighted the adjustment individuals experience not only in relationships and behaviors, but also in their beliefs about themselves and the world. These shifts in self-concept may require identity exploration and a rewriting of life needs (Barclay, 2015). Drawing on the work of Markus and Nurius (1986), Rossiter (2009) spoke to the need of nontraditional students to develop a future-focused orientation in developing "possible selves." This task may be difficult during states of transition and requires the support of others (Barclay, 2015; Rossiter, 2009; Schlossberg, 2011). Rossiter argued that the type of support for nontraditional students will be different from the support other students need.

Often, nontraditional students are in the process of midlife renewal (Engels, 1995; Super, 1957) and are reevaluating their lives (Barclay, Stoltz, & Chung, 2011). Power and Rothausen (2003) indicated that adult career changers are no longer interested in the work they have been doing and are looking for a fresh start. In particular, Dacey and Travers (2004) posited that these adults make career changes due to the lack of a career-related identity. The absence of a career-related identity may be applicable to their current profession but could be associated with the absence of a career-related identity with a future career. Often, these students delayed college attendance due to other life constraints. Thus, they may find themselves in careers that developed over their early adult life but only as a means of survival rather than as a career of choice.

Career construction theory (CCT; Savickas, 2013) offers a framework for assisting nontraditional students in shaping and articulating career identity. More so, CCT interventions aid career specialists working with individuals to construct their *self* and their *identity*. Savickas (2011) made a distinction between the two; yet, nontraditional students may be engaged in constructing both. First, an individual constructs self through internal reflections on past interpersonal experiences. Savickas (2011) insisted that individuals "need each other to make sense of [them]selves and the world in which [they] live" (p. 17); however, individuals accomplish construction of *self* by understanding who they are as a person separate from others. Together, construction of self and identity coalesce into the art of life design (Savickas, 2012). Savickas argued that life design counseling could be effective during occupational transitions. Life design encompasses the processes of constructing both self and identity and provides coherence and continuity during career transitions. Building on the concept that identity works as a lifelong process, Savickas (2012) advanced that, often, individuals must renegotiate their identity as they face points of change or transition, especially in the 21st century when constructing a life requires navigating a unique societal organization of work. One such intervention useful in this process is the career construction interview (CCI; Savickas, 2011, 2013).

The CCI is a series of questions career specialists use in helping clients explore and discover themselves. The responses to each question merge to provide meaning to client identity. This meaning aids clients in moving forward in career decision-making tasks and in resolving career challenges (Taber et al., 2011). Savickas (2011, 2013) expressed the importance of this career intervention for assisting clients in moving past the "pauses" in their lives. Likewise, Ibarra (2007) called for interventions to help clients move through and past those in-between periods. Rossiter (2009) advocated for client encouragement and self-efficacy-building interventions that aid clients in making career decisions. The CCI meets these requirements as clients gain greater self-knowledge, and they achieve greater self-efficacy in moving forward with increased purpose (Maree, 2010). Finally, the CCI is an age-appropriate intervention, which Luzzo (1999) insisted was vital in providing career counseling to nontraditional students.

SUPPORTS IN PLACE

In recognition of the increasing number of nontraditional students, programs and services have been developed or existing programs modified. For example, many universities provide working adult programs offering flexible learning options, multiple entry points during the year, and certificate programs to help adults desiring to advance in their careers. Many institutions have on-campus offices providing student services for nontraditional students. Services range from a space where students might lounge to information about scholarship and grant options. Housed, usually, under the auspices of career services, institutions have been slow to create these nontraditional student offices, and these offices may lack an online or easy-access presence.

One professional organization (Association for Nontraditional Students in Higher Education [ANTSHE]) exists that addresses the needs of nontraditional students in particular; however, this organization is geared most specifically toward educational institutions. Information for the general public is minimal. Other, more student-friendly, resource sites include *School Soup* (www.schoolsoup.com), which provides information about available nontraditional student scholarships and financial aid. Registration is free, and students are able to create a matching system for increased opportunities. Likewise, *College Scholarships* (www.collegescholarships.org) offers links to scholarship and grant funding opportunities for nontraditional students. Although not targeted toward nontraditional students only, the National Career Development Association (NCDA; www.ncda.org) offers a plethora of research, information, and resources for both career specialists and consumers. In 2012, the Advisory Committee on Student Financial Assistance (ACSFA, 2012) provided a report to the U.S. Congress and Secretary of Education addressing the need for the integration of life roles and learning for increasing college completion among the nontraditional student population. According to the report, there remains a dearth of service and support for nontraditional students. Within the report is an account of best practice recommendations. Those recommendations include creating flexible and integrated learning environments (e.g., competency-based online programs); bundling support services; and providing federal, state, or institutional grants that support both educational and life (e.g., transportation and child care) components. Other practices cited in the ACSFA report include Florida's common course number and curriculum system that respects the mobility of many nontraditional students and allows credit for learning outcomes based on life experiences. Although helpful, these resources do not provide specific career interventions to assist nontraditional students in exploring "self," working through identity issues, and moving forward in career decision making. In addition to these resources and services, nontraditional students benefit from personalized postmodern career counseling (Cardoso, 2012; Cardoso, Silva, Gonçalves, & Duarte, 2014), which affords exploration of self and meaning making.

CAREER COUNSELING INTERVENTIONS

Given the continual changes in the 21st-century work paradigm, many have called for career interventions that respect a constructivist view. In particular, Rossiter (2009) argued that career counseling with nontraditional students requires an approach distinct from the 20th-century methodology of administering career inventories and assigning students to a particular career trajectory. Although traditional approaches have their place, the 20th-century approach to career development falls short in helping students explore their identity and preparing them for the current work environment. This new environment has ushered in the need for more subjective interventions. Nash and Jang (2013) called for universities to develop meaning-making centers to respond to students' existential questions, echoing Kasworm's (2010) argument that nontraditional students typify identity via decisions reflecting a process of constructing meaning.

CONCLUSION

The link between career counseling and identity development is clear in the literature (Rossiter, 2009; Savickas, 2011, 2013). Nontraditional college students in the midst of making career changes may need assistance in reconnecting with past identities or constructing new identities. The CCI is one postmodern intervention that respects the perspective and authorship of the student's narrative and presents a nontraditional approach as called for in the literature (Ibarra, 2007; Kenner & Weinerman, 2011; Rossiter, 2009). Pelletier (2010) found that nontraditional students prefer hybrid interventions, when possible. To that end, the CCI is available to practitioners in varying formats.

REVISITING THE CASE OF NESSA

As Nessa works through her first semester of courses, she realizes that she is not getting any closer to knowing what career she wants to pursue. She decides to visit the college's career services office to discuss her situation. After completing basic paperwork, Nessa meets with Franklin, a career counselor in the center. After Nessa explains the reason for her visit, Franklin tells Nessa that he would like to use a career construction intervention, and to do so, he will need to ask her questions that—on the surface—may seem unrelated to career. Nessa agrees to the process. Before beginning, Nessa and Franklin agree that the most important way in which Franklin can assist Nessa is by helping her determine and plan a meaningful career trajectory.

In moving through the CCI questions with Nessa, Franklin learns that early role models included Ms. Beadle, the schoolteacher from Little House on the Prairie, *and Dr. Cory, Nessa's dentist when Nessa was a child. She appreciated that these women were gentle and caring yet performed jobs that Nessa believed were necessary to the betterment of all. When Franklin asked Nessa about favored magazines, television shows, and websites, Nessa identified the show* Family Ties, *the story of liberal parents raising their three children in times that were more conservative. Nessa noted, in particular, Elyse (the mother), a self-employed architect who was able to balance her roles as an independent woman and a mother. In addition, Nessa shared with Franklin that she enjoyed the Mayo Clinic website. Her interest in this site stemmed from Nessa's desire to learn what she could about some of the latest medical interventions and techniques—those used with children in particular. When Franklin asked Nessa to tell him about two or three early childhood memories, Nessa offered Franklin the memory of when Nessa was 5 years old and playing outside on the swing set in her backyard. As Nessa swung higher and higher, she decided to jump from the swing seat as she had seen her older brother do. Instead of landing on her feet, Nessa landed on her hands and knees and then fell forward onto her face. As a result, Nessa knocked several teeth loose, breaking one. When asked by Franklin to provide a title for this memory, Nessa responded, "Little Girl Damages Her Mouth." The second early memory Nessa reflected to Franklin was when she was approximately 6 years old. Nessa remembered being on the schoolyard playground during recess and becoming fascinated by an ant colony. As Nessa watched the ants scurrying about the ground and their colony, a few other children came to investigate. Two of the boys began kicking the dirt and collapsing the colony mound. Nessa tried to rebuild the colony mound but realized that her efforts were futile. The title Nessa gave to this memory was, "Little Girl Loses in Her Effort to Help Others."*

In aligning his counseling approach with CCT, Franklin explained to Nessa that all individuals construct a life story based on several factors, including their perceptions of other individuals and characters in their lives. Through these perceptions, humans build a reputation for themselves from which life themes develop. Franklin told Nessa that he wanted to share some of his observations from Nessa's story. One of the first observations affirmed Nessa's lifelong desire to work with children. Franklin noted Tessa's schoolteacher role model and Nessa's identification with Elyse, the mother who cared for her children in Family Ties. *Juxtaposed against this gentle, nurturing reputation was the independence exhibited by Elyse, who functioned in the nonstereotypical roles of self-employment and architect. Franklin asked tentatively, "Could it be that you desired independence but became frightened of the risks? For example, you jumped bravely from the swing seat, which represents a risk; however, the outcome was not what you expected and resulted in what you might consider a failure." Nessa nodded her head, indicating her agreement. A similar incident Franklin noted was Nessa's attempt to help the ants on the playground, but, again, the outcome was very different from Nessa's expectations. "Yeah," Nessa exclaimed. "Every effort I made to rebuild the ant colony failed. I realized trying to help those ants was useless. I couldn't do it." Franklin and Nessa continued to discuss Nessa's responses to the CCI. Franklin highlighted another trend he noticed. "Nessa, one of your role models was Dr. Cory, your childhood dentist, and I cannot help but notice that one of your early memories involves damage to your mouth when you jumped from the swing. I wonder whether there is any connection between those and your interest in the Mayo Clinic website you identified as one of your favorites." Nessa thought a few moments before responding. "You know," she said, "I remember after the swing incident that my mom scooped me up and rushed me to Dr. Cory's office. I know that, at the time, I must have been in terrible pain, but what I remember most is how gentle Dr. Cory was with me. Her fingers felt so soft on my face, and she was very careful in my mouth when she repaired the broken tooth. That's what I remember the most. That, and thinking she must be the most wonderful dentist in the world...and she was a woman!! Women weren't supposed to be dentists; men were!" Franklin observed, "You respected her independence as a woman and how caring and helpful she was. You wanted to emulate her. However, your effort at independence (jumping from the swing) and being helpful (the ant colony) ended poorly. I wonder if, based on those experiences, you decided you could not seek independence through a non-gender–specific career. Teaching is safer; lots of women do that, and being a teacher keeps you around children, which is something you love." Nessa responded, "You could be right" while pondering Franklin's observation.*

Franklin and Nessa continued to discuss the career intervention process and decided to meet again. A week later, Nessa arrived at Franklin's office excited. "You won't believe what I've been doing since we met!" exclaimed Nessa. She shared with Franklin that she had been researching not only the Mayo Clinic website but stumbled across a health school guide website. There, Nessa learned more about pediatric dentistry. "I don't know for sure that I can do this," said Nessa, "but according to what I am reading, I will need to complete my bachelor's in health care before going to a dental institute for an advanced degree. I realize I'm not the typical 20-something-year-old college student, so I may be thinking too big; however, this possibility excites me. At the very least, I can gain enough education to work in a pediatric dentist office as an assistant or hygienist. Either way, I'm excited, and I think I am going to go for it!"

ADDITIONAL RESOURCE SUGGESTIONS

Savickas, M. L. (2011). *Career counseling.* Washington, DC: American Psychological Association.

Vocopher (n.d.). *Career Construction Interview Online intervention.* Retrieved from www.vocopher.com/CSI/CCI.pdf

Vocopher (n.d.). *My career story.* Retrieved from www.vocopher.com/CSI/CCI_workbook.pdf

REFERENCES

Advisory Committee on Student Financial Assistance (ACSFA). (2012). *Pathways to success: Integrating learning with life and work to increase national college completion: A report to the U.S. Congress and Secretary of Education.* Washington, DC. Retrieved from http://www2.ed.gov/about/bdscomm/list/acsfa/ptsreport2.pdf

American Council on Education (ACE). (2014). *Nontraditional students.* Retrieved from http://www.acenet.edu/higher-education/topics/Pages/Nontraditional-Students.aspx

Aslanian, C. B., & Brickell, H. M. (1980). *Americans in transition: Life changes as reasons for adult learners.* New York, NY: College Board.

Aslanian, C. B., & Clinefelter, D. B. (2012). *Online college students 2012: Comprehensive data on demands and preferences.* Louisville, KY: The Learning House, Inc., and Education Dynamics.

Baptista, A. V. (2013). Non-traditional adult students: Who are they and what are the implications for higher education? *Cypriot Journal of Educational Sciences, 8,* 235–246.

Barclay, S. R. (2015). Turning transition into triumph: Applying Schlossberg's Transition Model to career transition. In A. Di Fabio & K. Maree (Eds.), *Exploring new horizons in career counselling: Converting challenges into opportunities.* Rotterdam, The Netherlands: Sense Publications.

Barclay, S. R., Stoltz, K. B., & Chung, Y. B. (2011). Voluntary midlife career change: Integrating the transtheoretical model and the life-span, life-space approach. *The Career Development Quarterly, 59*, 386–399.

Butt, J. E. (2012). Career services and the non-traditional student. *National Career Development Association.* Retrieved from http://associationdatabase.com/aws/NCDA/pt/sd/news_article/58650/_PARENT/layout_details_cc/false

Cardoso, P. (2012). Maladaptive repetition and career construction. *Journal of Vocational Behavior, 81*, 364–369.

Cardoso, P., Silva, J. R., Gonçalves, M. M., & Duarte, M. E. (2014). Narrative innovation in life design counseling: The case of Ryan. *Journal of Vocational Behavior, 85*, 276–286.

Cullity, M. (2006). Challenges in understanding and assisting mature-age students who participate in alternative entry programs. *Australian Journal of Adult Learning, 46*(2), 175–201.

Dacey, J. S., & Travers, F. F. (2004). *Human development across the lifespan.* New York, NY: McGraw Hill.

Domenico, D. M., & Jones, K. H. (2006). Career aspirations of women in the 20th century. *Journal of Career and Technical Education, 22*(2), 1–7.

Engels, D. W. (1995). Common themes in midlife career transitions. *The Career Development Quarterly, 44*, 83–88.

Ibarra, H. (2003). *Working identity: Unconventional strategies for reinventing your career.* Boston, MA: Harvard Business School Press.

Ibarra, H. (2007). *Identity transitions: Possible selves, liminality and the dynamics of career change.* INSEAD, Working Paper Series, Fontainebleu Cedex, France: INSEAD.

Jenkins, R. (2012, October 19). The new traditional student. *Chronicle of Higher Education, 59*(8), A31–A32.

Kasworm, C. E. (2010). Adult learners in a research university: Negotiating undergraduate student identity. *Adult Education Quarterly, 60*(2), 143–160.

Kenner, C., & Weinerman, J. (2011). Adult learning theory: Applications to non-traditional college students. *Journal of College Reading and Learning, 41*(2), 87–96.

Kruger, K. (2014, Fall). The demographic dilemma. *Leadership Exchange, 12*(3), 4.

Larkin, J. E., LaPort, K. A., & Pines, H. A. (2007). Job choice and career relevance for today's college student. *Journal of Employment Counseling, 44*, 86–94.

Luzzo, D. A. (1999). Identifying the career decision-making needs of nontraditional college students. *Journal of Counseling & Development, 77*, 135–140.

Maree, J. G. (2010). Brief overview of the advancement of postmodern approaches to career counseling. *Journal of Psychology in Africa, 20*, 361–368.

Markus, H., & Nurius, P. (1986). Possible selves. *American Psychologist, 41*, 954–969.

Melkun, C. H. (2012). Nontraditional students online: Composition, collaboration, and community. *The Journal of Continuing Higher Education, 60*, 33–39.

Nash, R. J., & Jang, J. J. J. (2013). The time has come to create meaning-making centers on college campuses. *About Campus, 18*(4), 2–9.

NCES. (n.d.). Nontraditional undergraduates: Definitions and data. Retrieved from http://nces.ed.gov/pubs/web/97578e.asp

NCES. (2011). *Digest of Education statistics 2011.* Retrieved from http://nces.ed.gov/programs/digest/d12/tables/dt12_226.asp

Orr, D. (2010). Integrating an aging student population into higher education: Challenges for evidence-based policy in Europe. *Canadian Journal of Higher Education, 40*(3), 25–42.

Pelletier, S. G. (2010, Fall). Success for adult students. *Public purpose.* Retrieved from http://www.aascu.org/uploadedFiles/AASCU/Content/Root/MediaAndPublications/PublicPurposeMagazines/Issue/10fall_adultstudents.pdf

Power, S. J., & Rothausen, T. J. (2003). The work-oriented midcareer development model: An extension of Super's maintenance stage. *The Counseling Psychologist, 31*, 157–197.

Ross-Gordon, J. M. (2011, Winter). Research on adult learners: Supporting the needs of a student population that is no longer nontraditional. *Peer Review*, 26–29.

Rossiter, M. (2009). Possible selves and career transition: Implications for serving nontraditional students. *Journal of Continuing Higher Education, 57*, 61–71.

Savickas, M. L. (2011). *Career counseling.* Washington, DC: American Psychological Association.

Savickas, M. L. (2012). Life design: A paradigm for career intervention in the 21st century. *Journal of Counseling & Development, 90*, 13–19.

Savickas, M. L. (2013). Career construction theory and practice. In R. W. Lent & S. D. Brown (Eds.), *Career development and counseling: Putting theory and research to work* (2nd ed., pp. 147–183). Hoboken, NJ: John Wiley & Sons.

Schlossberg, N. K. (1984). *Counseling adults in transition.* New York, NY: Springer Publishing Company.

Schlossberg, N. K. (2011). The challenge of change: The transition model and its applications. *Journal of Employment Counseling, 48*, 159–162.

Scott, L. M., & Lewis, C. W. (2012). Nontraditional college students: Assumptions, perceptions, and directions for a meaningful academic experience. *The International Journal of Interdisciplinary Social Sciences*, *6*(4), 1–10.

Soares, L. (2013). *Post-traditional learners and the transformation of postsecondary education: A manifesto for college leaders.* Washington, DC: American Council on Education.

Super, D. E. (1957). *The psychology of careers: An introduction to vocational development.* New York, NY: Harper & Row.

Taber, B. J., Hartung, P. J., Briddick, H., Briddick, W. C., & Rehfuss, M. C. (2011). Career style interview: A contextualized approach to career counseling. *The Career Development Quarterly, 59*, 274.

Taniguchi, H., & Kaufman, G. (2007). Belated entry: Gender differences and similarities in the pattern of nontraditional college enrollment. *Social Science Research, 36*, 550–568.

Veney, C., O'Geen, V., & Kowalik, T. F. (2012). Role strain and its impact on nontraditional students' success. *SEM Source—American Association of Collegiate Registrars and Admissions Officers.* Retrieved from http://www4.aacrao.org/semsource/sem/index0790.html?fa=view&id=5292

White, J. (2001). *Adult women in community colleges.* Retrieved from ERIC database (ED451860).

CHAPTER 5

DUAL-CAREER COUPLES

Katherine M. Hermann

CASE VIGNETTE: RACHEL AND ANDREW

It was a Wednesday evening in March, just past 6:30 p.m., and Rachel was rushing home, which meant she had already left her office. She quickly learned the unfortunate repercussion of leaving work during daylight hours: sitting in endless traffic on I-14. She was anxious to get home and had hopes of making a nice dinner. This Wednesday was not an extremely special day, not a birthday or wedding anniversary—there would be the 5-year anniversary in June. But today was the anniversary of the day she and Andrew had met in a corporate finance study group 9 years earlier as juniors in college, and she wanted it to be a little special.

As she sat in traffic, she let her mind wander—"What time would Andrew be home? What did she need from the grocery store? Would she really have to travel to Mobile next week to complete that audit? When was the last time she called her parents? Whose turn was it to pick up the dry cleaning? When were she and Andrew going to have children?" As these thoughts raced through Rachel's mind, she wondered if she was doing the right thing.

When she put her list of questions aside, she reminisced about when she had accepted the job with her accounting firm that last semester of college. She had always been the one with a clear focus, sights set on a business degree. So when a job that provided a master's degree in accounting and a guaranteed position within the company was offered, she and Andrew decided it could provide the security they needed. Those first years, she had done okay in the master's program and had learned how to perform audits. She had great organizational skills. Now, 7 years later, anyone could recognize that she had advanced within the company, earning increased responsibility and commensurate financial benefits.

Andrew had been more of a free spirit. As a freshman in college, he wanted to go to medical school, but after he almost failed chemistry he knew that the medical field was not the ideal career path. He considered law school but was concerned his low GPA would hurt his chances. Eventually, he decided to follow Rachel and enter business school. It was great for their relationship—they had time together studying, but it was clear that they had different gifts. Rachel was good with the mechanics of business, Andrew was great with people.

As their undergraduate programs drew to a close, Andrew struggled to find a job. With graduation looming, he received and accepted his first offer as a sales executive at an oil and gas company. The position offered potential for advancement. Over the years, Andrew had worked his way to the head of a sales team. He was well liked and respected by his colleagues and financially comfortable in a salaried position. The problem with his career path was long hours and too much travel. It seemed like he and Rachel never had quality, focused time together as they both spent "down time" catching up with household or job-related tasks.

As Rachel looked at the rows of taillights and pondered seared scallops versus chicken parmesan, she wondered if this was the life that she and Andrew had planned, or wanted. Should she be working in a profession she felt more passionate about? Could Andrew find a job with less travel and better hours? How were they ever going to add kids to this equation? What would happen if their parents became sick? What could be different?

DUAL-CAREER COUPLES

Dual-career households are composed of couples in which both members are committed to professional occupations. The individuals have an advanced education or specific content knowledge in their field (Bird & Schnurman-Crook, 2005). They generally find their jobs meaningful, work toward a career goal, possess a high degree of commitment, and enjoy the opportunity for both independence and collaboration (Duxbury, Lyons, & Higgins, 2007). In addition, the occupations often require high levels of responsibility and significant time to develop and maintain professional involvement.

In the United States, the number of dual-income households has grown. According to the U.S. Department of Labor: Bureau of Labor Statistics (2014a, 2014b, 2014c), 47.4% of married couples are dual-income households. Also, 59.1% of married couples with children have two working parents (U.S. Department of Labor: Bureau of Labor Statistics, 2014a, 2014b, 2014c). The makeup of these households varies greatly over the course of the family life cycle (Carter & McGoldrick, 2005). Couples in their 20s and 30s may not have children and are referred to as *DINKS* (dual or double income no kids) in nonscholarly literature, while other dual-career couples in their 50s and 60s may have launched children (Becker & Moen, 1999). Regardless of the phase of the life cycle, dual-career couples face unique stressors related to time constraints, work responsibilities, and flexibility. According to the American Time Use Survey (U.S. Department of Labor: Bureau of Labor Statistics, 2014b), the average employed individual works 7.6 hours on workdays. In households without children younger than 18 years, adults spend 4.5 hours a day in leisure activities, roughly an hour more than adults with children younger than 6 years (U.S. Department of Labor: Bureau of Labor Statistics, 2014b).

In addition to time working at an office, a common arrangement affecting couples' decisions and family life is working from home. According to the American Time Use Survey (U.S. Department of Labor: Bureau of Labor Statistics, 2014b), 36% of employed individuals older than 25 years with bachelor's degrees spend time working from home. The data do not differentiate whether this is in addition to, or in place of, time spent at the work place. The two arrangements can have different effects on family life as one provides for increased flexibility and the other could impinge on a healthy work–life balance.

HISTORICAL CAREER PATHS TYPICALLY TAKEN

Historically, unlike many populations, career opportunities for dual-career couples have remained static. The most salient influence on couples' career decisions surround the question, "How can a couple continue to build a relationship and a family given work related stressors and time constraints?" Often, as couples negotiate their answer to this question, they explore various career avenues and opportunities. The decision to add children to the family blurs the cultural and environmental influences as the addition of children results in the arrival of new and significant time demands. According to the U.S. Department of Labor: Bureau of Labor Statistics (2014a, 2014b, 2014c), the average amount of time devoted to childcare in families with children under age 6 is 5.4 hours per day. Also, couples with young children are more stressed than those *without* children or couples with *older* children (Entricht, Hughes, & Tovey, 2007). Because of these and other factors, a woman's odds of leaving her career are 300% higher if she has children than if she had not become pregnant (Shafer, 2011).

HISTORY OF CAREER OBSTACLES

Because of the more recent increase in dual-career households, only a short history of career obstacles can be uncovered with rather stagnant primary complications. A crucial barrier to couples maintaining an ideal career trajectory is the availability of meaningful employment within a confined geographical area. A second influential factor is cultural assumptions surrounding gender roles.

Often, a professional must relocate in order to continue career advancement. The average salaried worker in the United States stays with an employer for only 4.6 years (U.S. Department of Labor: Bureau of Labor Statistics, 2014a, 2014b, 2014c). The need to relocate may arise from the desire to work within a larger market or have international experience to improve marketability. Regardless of the reason, when couples are confronted with the decision to relocate, they have to evaluate whose career will take precedence. Ideally, a company provides spousal job placement assistance, but these services may be unavailable.

A second obstacle to maintaining a dual-career household relates to finding a balance within the household. Researchers have confirmed that if a member of a couple is going to leave the workforce it will most likely be the woman, and the woman is more likely to take on greater responsibility at home while continuing to work (Cha, 2010; Duxbury et al., 2007; Tatman, Hovestadt, Yelsma, Fenell, & Canfield, 2006). In addition, females typically experience higher levels of stress (Higgins, Duxbury, & Lyons, 2010) and more interference between family responsibilities and work schedules than males (Tatman et al., 2006).

The more hours a male partner works, the more likely it is that his partner will leave the workforce (Cha, 2010; Shafer, 2011), but the reverse is not true. In fact, for couples with equally high-achieving and lucrative careers, women are still more likely to defer to their husbands' careers (Stone, 2007). The decision for a woman to leave the workforce is frequently based on her gross, rather than proportional, contribution to family income—if the wife's income is constant, the more her husband makes, the more likely she is to leave the labor force (Shafer, 2011). A final cultural influence on women leaving the workforce is pressure to be a successful homemaker (Cha, 2010).

EXPECTED CAREER DEVELOPMENT NEEDS

Because the dual-career population is generally well educated, clients may appear to have a large number of opportunities. However, career specialization creates limitations. To facilitate the career counseling process, counselors may address alternative careers, advanced education, expansion of support systems, the negotiation of role conflict, and the assessment of career values. A therapist may find it helpful to review the negative effect of work obligations and stressors on both the couple's individual careers and each partner's work performance, as emotional and physical fatigue from weekly routines can cause added strain on families (Crossfield, Kinman, & Jones, 2005; Duxbury et al., 2007; Tatman et al., 2006). The ongoing process of reviewing a couple's needs, stressors, and values is essential. Specific areas of therapeutic exploration may surround career values. For instance, Wils, Wils, and Tremblay (2014) described some of the most significant values to be in the areas of challenge, dedication, security, and competence.

In addition to balancing values, couples may find it helpful to develop a better understanding of future opportunities, the financial effects of changes, the influence of relocation and commuting, and how the household division of labor will affect their career and relationship. Each couple presents unique concerns and it is important that counselors attend to each client couples' specific issues.

SUPPORTS IN PLACE

Despite the many stressors dual-career households experience, a growing number of resources are available. These resources range from household maintenance support to assistance with job placement. Specific assistance may include community-based support, employer-assistance programs, and other regional opportunities.

Household Resources

The division of household responsibilities can be a point of conflict in dual-career families. To better handle the increased need for external assistance, the additional financial flexibility generally available within this family structure may enable couples to outsource to various professional services. Services may be available, thus improving home life by reducing stressors and creating time for leisure. The range of assistance can include services that handle the following types of tasks: food delivery/preparation services, grocery shopping, prescription delivery, gift shopping, picking up and dropping off children, dry cleaning drop off/pickup, baking for school events, tutoring for children, paying bills, garage sale assistance, vacation planning, dog walking, winterizing homes, plant watering, trash-to-curb, pool maintenance, landscaping, household cleaning, diaper delivery, and many others. While some services may seem idealistic, support in each of these areas can provide the necessary support to enable a couple to engage in activities that are not problem oriented.

Childcare

An additional constraint on working families is availability and accessibility to childcare. For many dual-career families, childcare is a factor when deciding if and how many children can be accommodated into their lifestyle. When funding childcare becomes a concern, couples may seek financial assistance through government-funded childcare subsidy programs, such as the Child Care and Development Fund (CCDF). Another government-funded program, the Child and Dependent Care Credit, reduces federal income taxes for individuals who paid for childcare over the course of the year. While programs are based on financial need and may not be available to all dual-career couples, an awareness of the possibility may facilitate career exploration, comfort transitioning into a new position early in a career, or exploration of single-income household opportunities.

Situational Advantages

Aside from resources available in metropolitan communities, intrinsic supports may be in place that can be highlighted in counseling. First, the nature of a dual-income household allows for greater flexibility during times of job transition and termination. This support may come in the form of emotional security during difficult times (Bird & Schnurman-Crook, 2005) or a second income, reducing pressure if one member of a couple explores other employment options. A supportive, committed partnership, where both individuals take pride in the other's accomplishments, will enable selective job exploration and, ideally, more satisfying employment.

Finally, some couples may live in close proximity to extended family. In these cases, couples may have established support systems to assist with childcare, adjustment during transitions to a new position, and possibly career-networking opportunities. Using existing resources can facilitate options exploration and increase comfort during times of change.

RELEVANT CAREER COUNSELING INTERVENTIONS

Many couples are drawn to therapy because of relational dissatisfaction, with more clients identifying marital problems as a presenting complaint than any other concern (Gottman, 1999). Nevertheless, by the time couples seek services, they often already experience conflicting obligations or work–family overload (Bird & Schnurman-Crook, 2005). Through an assessment of work–life balance, a counselor may discern concerns and stressors surrounding current career issues. Interventions with dual-career couples are unique because they have the added opportunity and challenge of developing a couple's relationship. Communication building, the exploration of values, and practicing perspective taking are important long-term skills within a couple's relationship that are especially beneficial during a period of transition.

Clinical Focus

An ideal focus for clinicians working with dual-career couples is on sensitivity, positivity, and intentionality. Clinical sensitivity is important since professionals often construct their identities around careers. Generally, this population derives validation from maintaining a positive reputation, displaying competence in their field, and being capable employees (Bird & Schnurman-Crook, 2005). Positivity in highlighting the couple's overall ability to share beliefs and expectations (Bird & Schnurman-Crook, 2005) can be important for improving individual self-efficacy as well as the couple's relationship, as both work and family obligations can cause role conflict (Higgins et al., 2010; Tatman et al., 2006). In addition, Bird and Schnurman-Crook (2005) described several characteristics of dual-career couples that counselors may find helpful in clinical work. First, dual-career couples generally use individual, dyadic, and communal strategies to solve problems (Bird & Schnurman-Crook, 2005). Therefore, counselors should address these three levels when discussing careers. Helpful questions may include: *How does this decision affect your career? Your partner's opportunities? Your current employer?* Using this multilayered systemic approach can accurately address the concerns of a professional. Furthermore, when working with a couple, interventions should focus on both problems and emotions (Bird & Schnurman-Crook, 2005). A twofold tactic will best match the more complex nature of problem solving surrounding dyadic career counseling by addressing both career concerns and relational development.

Career Exploration Goals

When focusing on career goals, a therapist must consider the multifaceted effects of each decision. Finding a way to undergo career adjustments that balance and improve on the constraints within the household can be challenging. Exploring the clients' values as well as sources of stress such as finances, time limitations, domestic responsibilities, and flexibility can be an intense process. At the same time, maintaining a focus on balancing two individuals' careers concurrently should remain a focus. According to a study by Becker and Moen (1999), three strategies become particularly important in dual-career households: creating boundaries for when and how work affects personal time, understanding differences between a job and a career, and trading off whose career is a priority throughout the relationship. Attention to these areas helps the members of the couple feel heard. As each of these areas is addressed, a therapist must not lose focus on concrete needs able to be explored.

Couples' Therapy Goals

Due to the dyadic nature of counseling couples, additional therapeutic benefits beyond career development are probable. For instance, as a counselor learns about the couple's goals and aspirations, effective communication modeling and instruction can occur, including skills related to reflective listening and I-statements. Counselors can coach clients to develop perspective and awareness of blind spots in understanding value differences. The couple can be challenged to make compromises in decisions. Couples can grow in their repertoire of caring skills and use the career counseling experience to enhance their overall relationship.

Couples may also take the therapeutic process as an opportunity to develop a healthy lifestyle to cope with dual-career obligations. They may find it beneficial to discuss topics such as shared parenting and household responsibilities, work-related concerns, attentiveness to one another's emotions, offering a welcome distraction, and creating the feeling of collaboration during the household and career decision-making processes (Bird & Schnurman-Crook, 2005).

Clinical Recommendations

For many couples who seek couple's counseling, career frustrations often go unaddressed. In order to accurately address the reciprocal nature of work and family stress (Higgins et al., 2010), researchers recommend including intake questions that address both work and family (Tatman et al., 2006). Because of the unique nature of couple's career counseling, openness to career challenges and knowledge of community resources are helpful in serving client needs. See Appendix E for additional suggestions.

REVISITING THE CASE OF RACHEL AND ANDREW

Given this body of information, one may wonder what happens to couples like Rachel and Andrew. Do they move forward in their careers until they eventually drift apart, decide to have children, or experience other shifts in their careers or personal lives? As described, every couple must make decisions and plans based on their own unique circumstances. Ideally, the couple is able to create a mutually satisfying shared lifestyle. When Rachel arrived home that Wednesday evening, exhausted, but happy to have Kroger bags in hand, she was ready to discuss her concerns with Andrew. Initially, she was surprised how nervous and apprehensive she was to suggest that they might need outside help, but Andrew was relieved at the prospect of change. The next morning, he found a couple's therapist and made an appointment.

Two weeks later, the nervous couple entered counseling as a couple. During their first session, they were surprised how the counselor, Lindsey, made them feel comfortable. She was friendly and seemed to care about their concerns. In response, they were open about their concerns with drifting apart; how they seemed to have no time together; and how, when they were together, they were not focused on one another but rather thinking about work.

Lindsey recognized that they were both under a lot of stress at work, which was affecting other aspects of their relationship; she explored their values as individuals and as a couple. She challenged Rachel and Andrew to make eye contact and share their feelings. Since this was the first counseling experience either had attended, they felt a little awkward; however, they grew to appreciate having someone facilitate a discussion, offer feedback, and challenge their thoughts about how their choices affected themselves and one another.

Leaving the first session, they realized how little time they had spent working on their relationship the last few years. They also grasped how little they communicated outside of problem solving, discussing events, or other work-related conversations. Overall, they were comforted to know they had options and things could improve. While Rachel and Andrew may not have developed a solution to solve their concerns, they both recalled how they had communicated early in their relationship and felt confident that, in time, they would learn how to balance their careers and connect so that their relationship would be successful on their own terms.

ADDITIONAL RESOURCE SUGGESTIONS

Resources for Working Parents

Center for American Progress—The importance of preschool and childcare: www.americanprogress.org/issues/education/report/2013/05/08/62519/the-importance-of-preschool-and-child-care-for-working-mothers

Mums@work—Benefits of working parents programs: www.mumsatwork.com.au/employers-creating-working-parents-program.html

World Economic Forum—Working Parents Program (WPP): www.weforum.org/gender-parity/philips-working-parents-program-wpp

Dual-Career Employment Resources

The International Dual Career Network (IDCN) is an association of companies that work together to provide resources for dual-career couples (www.idcn.info).

Tech Valley Connect provides new hire support and spousal support to facilitate the success of dual-career households (www.techvalleyconnect.com).

Resources for Dual-Career Couples in Higher Education

The Clayman Institute for Gender Research provides resources, recommendations, and reports for dual-career academic couples (gender.stanford.edu/dual-career-academic-couples).

Higher Education Recruitment Consortium provides job search tools and resources for dual-career couples (www.hercjobs.org/dual_career_couples).

International Higher Education Dual Career Association offers information, an active listserv, directory, and other tools for dual-career couples (ihedca.com/wp).

REFERENCES

Becker, P. E., & Moen, P. (1999). Scaling back: Dual-earner couples' work-family strategies. *Journal of Marriage and Family, 61*(4), 995.

Bird, G. W., & Schnurman-Crook, A. (2005). Professional identity and coping behaviors in dual-career couples. *Family Relations, 54*(1), 145.

Carter, B., & McGoldrick, M. (2005). *The expanded family life cycle: Individual, family, and social perspectives*. Boston, MA: Allyn & Bacon.

Cha, Y. (2010). Reinforcing separate spheres: The effect of spousal overwork on men's and women's employment in dual-earner households. *American Sociological Review, 75*(2), 303–329.

Crossfield, S., Kinman, G., & Jones, F. (2005). Crossover of occupational stress in dual-career couples. *Community, Work & Family, 8*(2), 211–232.

Duxbury, L., Lyons, S., & Higgins, C. (2007). Dual-income families in the new millennium: Reconceptualizing family type. *Advances in Developing Human Resources, 9*(4), 472–486.

Entricht, T. L., Hughes, J. L., & Tovey, H. R. (2007). Relationships among work and family conflict, stress, and parenthood in dual-income couples. *Psi Chi Journal of Undergraduate Research, 12*(3), 116–121.

Gottman, J. M. (1999). *The marriage clinic: A scientifically-based marital therapy*. New York, NY: W. W. Norton & Company.

Higgins, C. A., Duxbury, L. E., & Lyons, S. T. (2010). Coping with overload and stress: Men and women in dual-earner families. *Journal of Marriage and Family, 72*(4), 847–859.

Shafer, E. F. (2011). Wives' relative wages, husbands' paid work hours, and wives' labor-force exit. *Journal of Marriage and Family, 73*(1), 250–263.

Stone, P. (2007). *Opting out?: Why women really quit careers and head home*. Berkeley, CA: University of California Press.

Tatman, A., Hovestadt, A., Yelsma, P., Fenell, D., & Canfield, B. (2006). Work and family conflict: An often overlooked issue in couple and family therapy. *Contemporary Family Therapy: An International Journal, 28*(1), 39–51.

U.S. Department of Labor: Bureau of Labor Statistics. (2014a, April 25). *Employment characteristics of families summary*. Retrieved from http://www.bls.gov/news.release/famee.nr0.htm

U.S. Department of Labor: Bureau of Labor Statistics. (2014b, June 18). *American time use survey summary.* Retrieved from http://www.bls.gov/news.release/atus.nr0.htm

U.S. Department of Labor: Bureau of Labor Statistics. (2014c, September 18). *Employment tenure summary*. Retrieved from http://www.bls.gov/news.release/tenure.nr0.htm

Wils, T., Wils, L., & Tremblay, M. (2014). Revisiting the career anchor model: A proposition and an empirical investigation of a new model of career value structure. *Industrial Relations, 69*(4), 813–838.

CHAPTER 6

STAY-AT-HOME MOTHERS RETURNING TO WORK

Suzanne Degges-White

CASE VIGNETTE: SANDY

Sandy is a 37-year-old married woman with two daughters, aged 7 and 12 years. Married to Xavier for 15 years, she has not held a full-time job since their wedding day. Now that her younger daughter has been in school for a couple of years, Sandy is eager to find a job and begin earning money for her daughters' extracurricular expenses and college funds. Sandy has an undergraduate degree in English and worked for almost a year as a technical writer for a large engineering firm before her marriage; however, having been out of the workplace for so long, she is concerned that her skill set is obsolete, and she is also wrestling with indecision about putting a job ahead of her family. Although she believes that the "first three years" of a child's life are the most pivotal in terms of development, she fears that not being present for her daughters as they move into adolescence and young adulthood may negatively affect the girls' decision making and behavior.

Sandy is unsure of what direction she should take in her job hunt, and she is unsure of whether or not she has adequate skills or experience to even be offered a job. She notes that she is not afraid of hard work and that the family truly would benefit from the extra income as she realizes that the cost of raising children in her community includes a multitude of associated expenses that she and Xavier had not thought about when they first began their family. A job for Sandy would ease the burden on Xavier and allow their daughters to participate in more activities than they currently are able to afford.

WHO STAYS AT HOME TO RAISE CHILDREN?

According to the U.S. Census Bureau (2014) figures, there were approximately 5 million mothers staying home with their children in 2012; this number has held relatively steady over the past few years. Of these 5 million, 44% of these mothers were younger than 35 years; they were also more likely to be less educated than working mothers and to have a child younger than 5 years. Although Lovejoy and Stone (2012) noted that it is predominantly White women who have the option to *choose* to step out of the professional workforce and opt into a fully domestic role, U.S. Census Bureau (2014) figures reveal that women who are stay-at-home mothers are more likely to have been born outside the United States. These demographic factors all suggest that finding paid employment may pose significant challenges for many of these women when they decide it is time to return to work. Furthermore, even well-educated mothers who are veterans of the workforce face obstacles when they decide to orchestrate a return to their careers (Warner, 2013).

Stay-at-home *fathers* are a relatively new demographic group that has been growing significantly since the past couple of decades of the prior century (Solomon, 2014). This group was roughly 189,000 strong in the most recent census (U.S. Census Bureau, 2013). Although many men make the decision to be primary caregivers due to changes in their own employment (i.e., job loss, relocation request, layoff, etc.), there are also men who intentionally walk away from the role of breadwinner for this new role (Solomon, 2014). Regardless of the reasons behind the shift, fathers who later decide that they are ready to return to the work world may face unique obstacles in their own job hunts. They may endure stigmatization for their choice to become full-time parents, which may result in challenges securing employment after a lengthy period away from full-time employment, as many stay-at-home mothers often face.

OBSTACLES TO FINDING AND KEEPING A JOB

There are many different subgroups of "stay-at-home moms" and "stay-at-home dads," and members of each of the various groups may face unique obstacles to employment. Some stay-at-home parents have always "stayed home," never having established a work history, whereas others may have left well accomplished and respected careers to stay home with their children. Although men's career trajectories are expected to follow a specific path, women's paths often show a great deal of variety (Lovejoy & Stone, 2011). Some of these women may be very well educated, whereas others may not have completed high school.

Partner's Attitude

In some cases, a stay-at-home mother's partner may prefer that she stay in her role as full-time, primary caregiver. This can be due to many individual or traditional traits and expectations. Choosing to leave or reconfigure any role within a family system can lead to upset. If financial pressures are motivating a return to work, the family "breadwinner" may feel threatened or may lose a sense of competence in caring for the family. Each family will need to address the unique concerns individually.

Stigma

There is a large, nonprofit organization devoted to supporting stay-at-home mothers of color called Mocha Moms (www.mochamoms.org). The national president,

Kuae Mattox, revealed that in a study of its members (who span 29 states and fill 100 chapters) more than a third of the respondents affirmed that they were trying to return to the paid workforce, but they were meeting unexpected obstacles; chief among the obstacles, according to more than half of the respondents, was employers' resistance to hiring them due to their current unemployed, stay-at-home mother status (Wallace, 2013). The clash of values between traditional gender roles and economic necessity creates personal difficulties that can be frustrating for women trying to get back into the work world.

Education

For instance, "stay-at-home moms" who also are young, single mothers may face significant challenges in terms of educational status or career readiness. This group is further addressed in a focused chapter in this book on job seekers with less than 4-year degrees.

Language Barriers

For the large number of foreign-born stay-at-home mothers, language skills may present an obstacle to a wide variety of positions. Within her family or her community, there may be few difficulties presented in lack of fluency in a new country's language; however, the ability to learn a second language easily has been found to diminish with age (Johnson & Newport, 1989), so finding employment in the wider community may present a significant challenge.

Work–Life Balance

When mothers are able to secure jobs once their children reach school age, they may still find it difficult to relinquish the caregiver role within the family. Unless clear expectations are set by the couple, mothers may still be the parent expected to pick up sick kids from school, stay home with a sick child, or take off on days when the kids have off from school. Unfortunately, while hiring personnel may deny it, there is a bias against working mothers (Vinkenburg, van Engen, Coffeng, & Dikkers, 2012); this is due to employer expectations that family responsibilities will interfere with employment responsibilities.

Economic Disadvantaging

If a mother is returning to work before her children are old enough to look after themselves, the cost of day care or other caregiving arrangements must be considered. It is a lament of many stay-at-home mothers that they "cannot afford to go back to work." This may be factually accurate, especially when Rose and Hartmann (2004) noted that women may sacrifice 30% of their annual earnings if they are unemployed for 2 or 3 years.

Shifting Career Goals

Career changes are often desired by women who left inflexible "8 to 5" type jobs to raise their families. Rose and Hartmann (2004) found that many women mellow in their career ambitions over time and long for positions that revolve around care and service for others, such as teaching. As women's career aspirations shift, their preparation for the return to work may require additional education, which can delay the return to work and create its own set of challenges for the family system.

Stay-at-home mothers potentially face obstacles both within and outside their families and their households. Whether it is finding childcare for their young children or successfully advocating for their decision to return to work to significant others or extended families, this can be a difficult transition as women add the role of employee to the current 24-hour-a-day job of parent. As Bianchi and Milkie (2010) revealed, running a household and caring for children largely remain the responsibility of mothers rather than fathers.

FACILITATIVE CIRCUMSTANCES AND HELPFUL RESOURCES

Perhaps not unexpectedly, other mothers may be the most useful resource in terms of seeking support and sounding boards as mothers consider the decision to return to work (Degges-White & Borzumato-Gainey, 2011). In fact, the most relevant and rich resources available for this group include websites created by women who have experienced similar challenges in their own career paths. A summary of current and useful sites are included in a following section.

As our work world has shifted over the past few decades, there appears to be a growing trend toward acceptance of the need for all employees—male and female alike—to seek out and practice work–life balance. The new understanding of the value of happiness and career satisfaction also provide support to returning mothers who are seeking a workplace that appreciates their unique skills and does not penalize them for their unique needs.

RELEVANT CAREER COUNSELING PRACTICES

For women who feel a need to return to work to support their own personal well-being, the family's overall well-being, or economic need, basic resume building and job hunting skills may be the best place for career counseling to begin. Although a 5- or 10-year gap in work history due to raising children may be much more easily understood than a similar unexplained gap on another person's resume, it is important to help clients develop a clearly articulated summary of the skills they used during this period and how these skills translate to increased proficiencies in the workplace. With the rapidity of the creation of totally new jobs, it is likely that a few years away from the work world may result in a completely different opportunity landscape on reentry. Encouraging clients to do research on the field in which they are hoping to find jobs is an important "first step." This may include the client taking a "30,000 foot" view of the industry via broad web searches as well as closer examinations of relevant fields via subscriptions to trade journals, attendance at relevant conferences, personal interviews, or job shadowing with those in the relevant field. Career education may be the best place to begin. If clients are developing new resumes, it may be more effective for them to use the functional resume format in lieu of the traditional chronological format. Helping clients determine which experiences and skills would be valuable and transferable to their targeted career is also an important task in the career planning.

In some cases, clients may seek out career counseling to help them determine whether or not to return to work. In these instances, the client may need to engage in personal exploration, weigh a number of interpersonal and intrapersonal circumstances, and assess the potential fit of a new job with his or her current day-to-day obligations and activities. This reflects the aspect of personal counseling that career counseling often incorporates. In the activity section of this book is an intervention named "Sharing Recipes for Success" by Bruneau and Notestine, which provides a framework for helping women find meaning as they reimagine their life paths. See Appendix F for additional suggestions.

REVISITING THE CASE OF SANDY

Sandy's counselor recognized that Sandy's ambivalence about returning to work was worth addressing through the use of a "pros and cons" list. This rational approach to the dilemma made sense to Sandy and she was easily able to list the positives she saw in finding a job. These included such benefits as providing a positive role model to her children; providing an economic advantage to the family that would ease the financial burden of increasingly costly extracurricular activities for her children; providing her with an emotional/social outlet beyond the family, which was something that Sandy expressly desired; and providing additional funds for travel, another benefit for her children, according to Sandy. The list of cons centered around the loss of time in the home to manage its upkeep, having to add more structure to their weeks, and possibly having to arrange for childcare for both girls. Xavier had his own list of benefits and costs related to this role shift, and he felt the costs outweighed his calculation of perceived benefits. However, he was supportive of Sandy's strong desire to return to work and he was willing to find a way to make the shift work for everyone, as Sandy's happiness was the most important outcome for this decision.

Sandy's willingness to accept a job that was different from her former position allowed her to broaden her search. Moreover, because her motivation for job hunting was for the enhancement of her family's overall well-being, not to pursue a specific ambition, she was willing to take jobs that others might have considered "beneath her," as she described it. When she was offered a part-time position in her younger daughter's school cafeteria, she gladly accepted it as she appreciated the mid-day hours and the absence of the need to find childcare for her children. This anecdote underscores the need for counselors working with this population to recognize and support the wide range of motivating factors, perceived costs, and perceived benefits of employment for their clients.

ADDITIONAL RESOURCE SUGGESTIONS

www.workingmother.com: *Working Mothers* magazine includes news and information about the business world as well as ideas for managing a career and a family.

www.working-families.org: This is the website for the Labor Project for Working Families, which is a national advocacy and policy center that provides technical assistance, resources, and education for union members. It also provides information regarding family issues in the workplace.

www.hbwm.com: This is the website for home-based working mothers, a professional association addressing the needs of parents who work from home or who would like to do so. It provides support information and a wide variety of resources to its members.

www.momcorps.com/index: This is the website of Mom Corps, which matches employees to positions. The goal of this organization is to help individuals seeking fractional, interim, and flexible positions find the right job. The website provides a wealth of information, including position listings and resource information.

REFERENCES

Bianchi, S. M., & Milkie, M. A. (2010). Work and family research in the first decade of the 21st century. *Journal of Marriage and Family, 72*, 705–725.

Degges-White, S., & Borzumato-Gainey, C. (2011). *Friends forever: How girls and women forge lasting relationships.* Lanham, MD: Rowman & Littlefield.

Johnson, J. S., & Newport, E. L. (1989). Critical period effects in second language learning: The influence of maturational state on the acquisition of English as a second language. *Cognitive Psychology, 21*, 60–99.

Lovejoy, M., & Stone, P. (2012). Opting back in: The influence of time at home on professional women's career redirection after opting out. *Gender, Work, & Organization, 19*(6), 631–653.

Rose, S. J., & Hartmann, H. I. (2004). *Still a man's labor market: The long-term earnings gap.* Washington, DC: Institute for Women's Policy Research.

Solomon, C. R. (2014). "I feel like a rock star": Fatherhood for stay-at-home fathers. *Fathering, 12*, 52–70.

U.S. Census Bureau. (2013). *Facts for features: Father's day June 16, 2013.* Retrieved from http://www.census.gov/newsroom/facts-for-features/2013/cb13-ff13.html

U.S. Census Bureau. (2014). *Mother's day: May 11, 2014.* Washington, DC: U.S. Department of Commerce.

Vinkenburg, C. J., van Engen, M. L., Coffeng, J., & Dikkers, J. S. E. (2012). Bias in employment decisions about mothers and fathers: The (dis) advantages of sharing care responsibilities. *Journal of Social Issues, 68*, 725–741.

Wallace, K. (August 13, 2013). Moms "opting in" to work find doors shut. CNN website. Retrieved from http://www.cnn.com/2013/08/13/living/parents-mothers-opt-to-work/index.html

Warner, J. (2013, August 7). The opt-out generation wants back in. *New York Times Magazine.* Retrieved from http://www.nytimes.com/2013/08/11/magazine/the-opt-out-generation-wants-back-in.html?pagewanted=all

CHAPTER 7

WORKING PARENTS

Rebecca E. Michel and Eric J. Michel

CASE VIGNETTE: PHILIP AND LAURA

Driving home from work with great anticipation, Philip, a 38-year-old Caucasian male, could not wait to share his big news with his family. After graduating with a degree in business administration from Big State University, Philip began working as a management trainee at Roberts Automotive, a medium-sized organization in the aftermarket automotive supply industry. Over the past 16 years, Philip had steadily advanced through several positions of increasing responsibility but had yet to achieve his big break into middle management that would position him to ascend into upper management. Philip's fortunes changed today, as his manager, Jeff, informed him that he was recommending Philip to fill the open regional sales manager position.

Bursting with excitement, Philip gathered his wife, Laura, a 35-year-old Asian female, and their two 6-year-old twins, Ryan and Marissa, to share the big news. As Philip described the responsibilities of the regional sales manager position, a look of apprehension began to develop on Laura's face. Philip's current position did not require any travel, yet the regional sales manager position required considerable travel, potentially up to three nights each week out of town. Furthermore, since graduating from Big State University with a degree in communication, Laura has worked for a small, boutique advertising agency. For the past 6 years while the twins have been young, Laura passed up several promotions. Now, with the children in kindergarten, she had aspirations of advancing in her own career.

Laura raised these points to Philip and encouraged him to think about what kind of role he would like to play in the lives of the twins. She reminded him that his current job required him to work two weekends each month. As such, Philip was unable to coach the twins' t-ball team. At the time, several months ago, this conflict greatly pained Philip, and he and Laura spoke at length regarding the extent to which his work responsibilities were negatively impacting his family responsibilities. Philip had forgotten about the t-ball incident. Suddenly, Philip's radiant and optimistic perspective on the regional sales manager position had diminished.

Later that evening, Philip lay awake in bed thinking about the events of the day. Although he was initially taken aback by Laura's reaction to his big news, several questions began to swirl around his head: Would he be able to balance work and family responsibilities if he took the regional sales manager job? Was it fair for him to take this promotion given Laura had sacrificed her own career advancements to raise the twins? How should he and Laura prioritize each other's career objectives? He realized he and Laura would have much to talk about before he decided whether or not to interview for the regional sales manager position.

DESCRIPTION OF THE POPULATION

The situation encountered by Philip and Laura is common for a significant portion of working Americans. The conflux of economic, social, and technological trends in the United States has changed not only the composition of the workforce but the nature of work itself. Since the 1970s, American organizations have sought to meet challenges from the competitive global business environment by emphasizing lean and flexible organizational hierarchies (Friedman, 2006). This turbulent business environment has changed the nature of employer–employee relationships and, in turn, how working parents may experience and define careers. Many organizations have emphasized short-term employment contracts at the expense of long-term relationships with employees to be better equipped to handle market pressures.

When organizations emphasize short-term employment, there are several consequences. Employees are more prone to experience layoffs or contingent work relationships such as part-time, temporary, or contract employment (Feldman, 2006). Shorter organizational tenures mean fewer opportunities for upward mobility within one's immediate organization (King, Burke, & Pemberton, 2005) and individuals moving from one organization to assume employment in another (Valcour & Ladge, 2008). For working parents, the impact of the economic environment may be dramatic as layoffs, contingent work relationships, and relocations create hardships for both adults and children (Heymann, 2006).

Demographic figures suggest several social trends impacting the population of working parents in the United States. Recent employment figures from the Bureau of Labor Statistics (BLS, 2015) suggested that nearly 53 million working adults in the United States have one or more children younger than 18 years. However, parenthood impacts male and female workers differently. Striking differences exist between labor market participation rates of men and women. Among U.S. parents with children younger than 18 years, 70.1% of women and 92.8% of men are participating in the U.S. workforce. For U.S. parents who have at least one child younger than 6 years, 64.2% of women and 94.2% of men are participating in the U.S. workforce.

Parenthood also impacts earning potential, and research suggested significant variance in the earnings of fathers and mothers. The *motherhood wage penalty*, a term describing the negative relationship between motherhood and earnings, is a well-documented phenomenon (Anderson, Binder, & Krause, 2003). Avellar and Smock (2003) found that over time, each additional child had a further negative effect on a mother's wages. Although research suggested motherhood yields a wage penalty for women, fatherhood may yield a wage premium for men. Lundberg and Rose (2002) suggested men may garner up to a 7% increase in wages between the arrivals of their first and second children. Glauber (2008) suggested race may moderate the effects of the fatherhood wage premium; whereas Caucasian men may receive fatherhood premiums of up to 23%, African American men may receive fatherhood wage premiums of up to only 16%. These wage differentials impact the earning power of women and men. Finally, technological trends impact the experience of working parents. Developments in information technology have increased the extent to which work is portable. The rise of the Internet has allowed employees to work from home or other locations, but virtual work may be a double-edged sword, because it also demands many employees to remain connected to work at all times (Butts, Becker, & Boswell, 2015).

HISTORICAL OVERVIEW

A vast body of academic research addressing working parents has been completed in an attempt to understand how mothers and fathers approach responsibilities central to both work and family domains and how their perspectives impact career outcomes. Traditionally, research has relied on understanding how individuals characterize their work and family roles. Building on role theory (Kahn, Wolfe, Quinn, Snoek, & Rosenthal, 1964; Katz & Kahn, 1978), three related constructs offer a continuum to describe the relationship between one's work role and family role: role conflict between work and family, role balance between work and family, and role enrichment between work and family.

According to Kahn et al. (1964), role conflict is defined as the "simultaneous occurrence of two (or more) sets of pressures such that compliance with one would make more difficult compliance with the other" (p. 19). Role conflict between work and family may occur in two directions: work-to-family conflict or family-to-work conflict. Work-to-family conflict occurs when work responsibilities make it difficult for individuals to adequately perform family responsibilities, whereas family-to-work conflict occurs when family responsibilities make it difficult for individuals to successfully complete work tasks. For working parents, conflicts may become manifest through time-based, strain-based, or behavior-based conflicts (Greenhaus & Beutell, 1985). For example, work-to-family conflict may occur when parents have an inflexible work schedule (i.e., a time-based conflict) or when parents possess role ambiguity in their work role and are uncertain how to complete their job tasks (i.e., a strain-based conflict). In contrast, family-to-work conflict may occur when parents experience low spousal support or family conflict (i.e., strain-based conflicts) or when parents engage in openness and warmth, yet such behavior would be counterproductive at work (i.e., a behavior-based conflict).

Work–family balance results when "role-related expectations are negotiated and shared between an individual and his or her role-related partners in the work and family domains" (Grzywacz & Carlson, 2007, p. 458). Rather than an absence of conflict between work and family roles, work–family balance suggests individuals can socially negotiate role-related responsibilities within both personal and professional domains. Carlson, Grzywacz, and Zivnuska (2009) suggested work–family balance is performance neutral as, "work–family balance does not mean that an individual is a 'superstar' in both the work and family domains. Rather, upholding mutually agreed upon responsibilities is, in essence, meeting basic or core requirements of the role" (pp. 1463–1464). In this manner, work–life balance allows for an assessment of how working parents are able to meet demands at work and home.

In contrast to role conflict between work and family roles and distinct from role balance, role enrichment emerges when what occurs in one role improves the other role (Greenhaus & Powell, 2006). Work-to-family enrichment may occur when work tasks create confidence that in turn helps the individual be a better parent, when work puts an individual in a positive mood, or when individuals acquire skills or knowledge at work that helps the individual be a better parent. Family-to-work enrichment may occur when interactions with one's children create confidence that in turn helps the individual be a better employee, when family situations put an individual in a positive mood, or when family situations create a sense of urgency, thus helping the employee complete work tasks.

Over the past half-century, the stereotypical role of the father has shifted from financial provider to someone who is more involved in their children's lives (Burnett, Gatrell, Cooper, & Sparrow, 2011). Involved fathers take responsibility for their children's upbringing by engaging in their lives and remaining emotionally and physically accessible to their children (Pleck & Pleck, 1997). When these behaviors are applied to the father's work role, family-to-work enrichment may occur, resulting in the individual engaging in empathetic behaviors with colleagues or subordinates. Involved parenting also leads to positive work-related and personal outcomes, including increased job satisfaction, increased work–family enrichment, decreased work–family conflict, and decreased turnover intentions (Ladge, Humberd, Baskerville Watkins, & Harrington, 2015). However, despite some men wanting to be more involved in fatherhood, realities set in when family-friendly fatherhood policies are limited within work settings.

CAREER DEVELOPMENT NEEDS

Working parents experience a myriad of career development needs. Within the last three decades, the United States has witnessed a rise in the number of working mothers (BLS, 2015) and a shifting expectation that working fathers be more involved in their children's lives (Burnett et al., 2011). Working parents are encouraged to be both an ideal worker and an ideal parent (Hoobler, Hu, & Wilson, 2010). There are not enough hours in the day for working parents to live up to unrealistic demands, which can generate role strain and conflict within the work and family. Instead of succumbing to these ideals, working parents can benefit from developing realistic expectations about roles within work and family. Working parents experiencing role strain need to evaluate various aspects of their lives to determine the source(s) of the conflicts. Research suggests many antecedents to conflict between work and family including role overload (Byron, 2005), job stress (Ford, Heinen, & Langkamer, 2007), work demands and pressures (Butler, Grzywacz, Bass, & Linney, 2005), work role conflict, and occupational time demands (Michel, Mitchelson, Pichler, & Cullen, 2010). Working parents experiencing conflict within work and family also need to assess how the conflict is impacting their experiences in their career and at home. Specifically, they may need to focus attention on satisfaction within their job (Hoobler et al., 2010), marriage, and family (Carlson & Kacmar, 2000). Also, they may need to develop coping skills in order to manage symptoms associated with work–family conflict, including stress, somatic symptoms, physical health, and substance use (Allen, Herst, Bruck, & Sutton, 2000). Working parents can gain support from career counselors to address these issues.

Parents experiencing role enrichment may have many of their career development needs met. These working mothers and fathers exhibit high levels of life satisfaction (McNall, Nicklin, & Masuda, 2010) and mental and physical well-being (Hill, 2005), and it would be helpful for them to determine how to maintain these experiences. Several work factors enrich family, including income, supportive and flexible work environment, peer acceptance, job performance, opportunity to engage in meaningful work, and a family-friendly work culture (Greenhaus & Powell, 2006; Wayne, Randel, & Stevens, 2006). Working parents may also evaluate the degree to which career development needs are being met and find support systems to address any unmet needs.

CAREER DEVELOPMENT SUPPORTS

Supportive work environments and supervisors reduce work–family conflict for men and women (Thompson, Beauvais, & Lyness, 1999). Organizations provide various programs and policies to support working parents, including flexible work arrangements, compressed work weeks, flexible work hours, flexible work locations, child care, parental leave, and job sharing. However, work–family-friendly policies for fathers are still lagging behind support for working mothers (Rudman & Mescher, 2013), with only 15% of companies in the United States offering paternity leave (Harrington, Van Deusen, & Humberd, 2011). It appears that some organizations do not support flexible schedules for both working mothers and fathers and that societal norms still strongly encourage mothers to be primarily responsible for the family (Harrington & Ladge, 2009).

RELEVANT CAREER COUNSELING INTERVENTIONS

Career counselors supporting working parents must take a holistic approach (Whiston & Cinamon, 2015). Working parents may be experiencing successes and challenges in both careers and families, which can lead to further conflict or enrichment. For this reason, it is inappropriate to separate work and family from career counseling dialogue and interventions. Instead, all life roles and expectations must be explored within the career and family context to determine interventions to address the client's presenting concerns. In addition, working parents should decide for themselves what a positive family and work life looks like (Whiston & Cinamon, 2015).

Savickas's (2005, 2013) career construction theory and corresponding life design framework (Savickas, 2012) can facilitate meaning making among working parents. Career counselors could utilize the career construction interview (CCI; Savickas, 2011) or have clients complete a workbook entitled *My Career Story: An Autobiographical Workbook for Life-Career Success* (Savickas & Hartung, 2012). Both the interview and workbook prompt clients to answer a short series of questions and examine their narratives to conceptualize career issues and identify possible solutions. Through career construction, career counselors help clients discover their vocational personality, career adaptability, and life themes (Savickas, 2005). This can be particularly helpful for working parents experiencing conflict or enrichment between work and family (Whiston & Cinamon, 2015). See Appendix G for additional suggestions.

REVISITING THE CASE OF PHILIP AND LAURA

Philip's initial excitement regarding the potential promotion to regional sales manager was tempered by his wife's reaction. They decided it would be beneficial to obtain feedback and support from a career counselor who could help them evaluate options at this critical juncture. Each counseling session began and ended with a mindfulness exercise. The career counselor asked Philip and Laura to also practice mindfulness exercises at home to support their work–family balance. The counselor used career construction theory (Savickas, 2005) to encourage Philip and Laura to explore aspects of their home and work lives in a meaningful and supportive process. Phillip and Laura explained they were seeking counseling to determine whether Philip should pursue the position. They were both concerned if he took the position it would be challenging to balance career and family.

Philip and Laura shared and explored their narratives through the CCI. They recognized that so far in their lives together they had been extraordinarily adaptable and even used a mantra "not to bite off more than they could chew." On reflection, they had both passed up opportunities for career advancement throughout the years because they valued their relationship with one another and their children more than additional responsibility at work. Although Philip had experienced tremendous growth at the beginning of his career, since Ryan and Marissa were born, he adjusted his schedule and priorities so that he could be more involved with his family. This family involvement was not something Philip was ready to throw away. Rather than conceptualize himself as a "working man," Philip preferred the role of "coach." Together, they decided that Philip would not pursue the regional sales manager job.

Philip and Laura realized they could not do it all, but would continue to prioritize time with their family while the twins were still young. Throughout career counseling, Philip and Laura learned that they could keep working together to raise their children, support their partnership, and devote energy to both of their careers.

ADDITIONAL RESOURCE SUGGESTIONS

The Five Things Successful Working Parents Give Up to Reach a Work-Life Balance (www.forbes.com/sites/amymorin/2014/01/20/the-five-things-successful-working-parents-give-up-to-reach-a-work-life-balance)

Palmiter, D. (2011). *Working parents, thriving families: 10 strategies that make a difference*. North Branch, MN: Sunrise River Press.

Project Working Moms... and Dads too! (www.elearners.com/projectworkingmom)

White House Fact Sheet on Working Family Support (www.whitehouse.gov/the-press-office/2014/06/23/fact-sheet-white-house-summit-working-families)

Working Parents Magazine (workingparentsmagazine.com)

REFERENCES

Allen, T. D., Herst, D. E. L., Bruck, C. S., & Sutton, M. (2000). Consequences associated with work-to-family conflict: A review and agenda for future research. *Journal of Occupational Health Psychology, 5*, 278–308.

Anderson, D. J., Binder, M., & Krause, K. (2003). The motherhood wage penalty revisited: Experience, heterogeneity, work effort, and work-schedule flexibility. *Industrial & Labor Relations Review, 56*(2), 273–294.

Avellar, S., & Smock, P. J. (2003). Has the price of motherhood declined over time? A cross-cohort comparison of the motherhood wage penalty. *Journal of Marriage and Family, 65*(3), 597–607.

Bureau of Labor Statistics (BLS). (2015). *Employment characteristics of family summary.* Retrieved from http://www.bls.gov/news.release/famee.nr0.htm

Burnett, S., Gatrell, C., Cooper, C. L., & Sparrow, P. R. (2011). Fatherhood and flexible working: A contradiction in terms? In S. Kaiser, M. J. Ringlstetter, D. R. Eikhof, & M. Pina e Cunha (Eds.), *Creating balance? International perspectives on the work-life integration of professionals* (pp. 157–171). Berlin: Springer.

Butler, A. B., Grzywacz, J. G., Bass, B. L., & Linney, K. D. (2005). Extending the demands-control model: A daily diary study of job characteristics, work–family conflict and work–family facilitation. *Journal of Occupational and Organizational Psychology, 78,* 155–169.

Butts, M., Becker, W., & Boswell, W. (2015). Hot buttons and time sinks: The effects of electronic communication during nonwork time on emotions and work–nonwork conflict. *Academy of Management Journal, 58*(3), 763–788.

Byron, K. (2005). A meta-analytic review of work–family conflict and its antecedents. *Journal of Vocational Behavior, 67,* 169–198.

Carlson, D. S., Grzywacz, J. G., & Zivnuska, S. (2009). Is work–family balance more than conflict and enrichment? *Human Relations, 62*(10), 1459–1486.

Carlson, D. S., & Kacmar, K. M. (2000). Work–family conflict in the organization: Do life role values make a difference? *Journal of Management, 26,* 1031–1054.

Feldman, D. C. (2006). Toward a new taxonomy for understanding the nature and consequences of contingent employment. *Career Development International, 11*(1), 28–47.

Ford, M. T., Heinen, A., & Langkamer, K. L. (2007). Work and family satisfaction and conflict: A meta-analysis of cross-domain relations. *Journal of Applied Psychology, 92,* 57–80.

Friedman, T. L. (2006). *The world is flat [updated and expanded]: A brief history of the twenty-first century.* New York: Farrar, Straus and Giroux.

Glauber, R. (2008). Race and gender in families and at work: The fatherhood wage premium. *Gender & Society, 22*(1), 8–30.

Greenhaus, J. H., & Beutell, N. J. (1985). Sources of conflict between work and family roles. *Academy of Management Review, 10*(1), 76–88.

Greenhaus, J. H., & Powell, G. N. (2006). When work and family are allies: A theory of work–family enrichment. *Academy of Management Review, 31*(1), 72–92.

Grzywacz, J. G., & Carlson, D. S. (2007). Conceptualizing work–family balance: Implications for practice and research. *Advances in Developing Human Resources, 9*(4), 455–471.

Harrington, B., & Ladge, J. J. (2009). Work–life integration: Present dynamics and future directions for organizations. Org*anizational Dynamics, 38,* 148–157.

Harrington, B., Van Deusen, F., & Humberd, B. (2011). *The new dad: Caring, committed and conflicted.* Boston, MA: Boston College Center for Work and Family.

Heymann, J. (2006). *Forgotten families: Ending the growing crisis confronting children and working parents in the global economy.* Oxford: Oxford University Press.

Hill, E. J. (2005). Work–family facilitation and conflict, working fathers and mothers, work–family stressors and support. *Journal of Family Issues, 26,* 793–819.

Hoobler, J. M., Hu, J., & Wilson, M. (2010). Do workers who experience conflict between the work and family domains hit a "glass ceiling"? A meta-analytic examination. *Journal of Vocational Behavior, 77,* 481–494.

Kahn, R. L., Wolfe, D. M., Quinn, R. P., Snoek, J. D., & Rosenthal, R. A. (1964). *Organizational stress: Studies in role conflict and ambiguity.* New York, NY: Wiley.

Katz, D., & Kahn, R. L. (1978). *The social psychology of organizations* (2nd ed.). New York, NY: Wiley.

King, Z., Burke, S., & Pemberton, J. (2005). The "bounded" career: An empirical study of human capital, career mobility and employment outcomes in a mediated labour market. *Human Relations, 58*(8), 981–1007.

Ladge, J. J., Humberd, B. K., Baskerville Watkins, M., & Harrington, B. (2015). Updating the organization man: An examination of involved fathering in the workplace. *The Academy of Management Perspectives, 29,* 152–171.

Lundberg, S., & Rose, E. (2002). The effects of sons and daughters on men's labor supply and wages. *Review of Economics and Statistics, 84*(2), 251–268.

McNall, L. A., Nicklin, J. M., & Masuda, A. D. (2010). A meta-analytic review of the consequences associated with work–family enrichment. *Journal of Business and Psychology, 25*, 381–396.

Michel, J. S., Mitchelson, J. K., Pichler, S., & Cullen, K. L. (2010). Clarifying relationships among work and family social support, stressors, and work–family conflict. *Journal of Vocational Behavior, 76*, 91–104.

Pleck, E. H., & Pleck, J. H. (1997). Fatherhood ideals in the United States: Historical dimensions. In M. E. Lamb (Ed.), *The role of the father in child development* (3rd ed., pp. 33–48). New York, NY: Wiley.

Rudman, L. A., & Mescher, K. (2013). Penalizing men who request a family leave: Is flexibility stigma a femininity stigma? *Journal of Social Issues, 69*, 322–340.

Savickas, M. L. (2005). The theory and practice of career construction. In S. D. Brown & R. W. Lent (Eds.), *Career development and counseling: Putting theory and research to work* (pp. 42–70). Hoboken, NY: Wiley.

Savickas, M. L. (2011). *Career counseling*. Washington, DC: American Psychological Association.

Savickas, M. L. (2012). Life design: A paradigm for career intervention in the 21st century. *Journal of Counseling & Development, 90*, 13–19.

Savickas, M. L. (2013). Career construction theory and practice. In R. W. Lent & S. D. Brown (Eds.), *Career development and counseling: Putting theory and research to work* (2nd ed., pp. 147–183). Hoboken, NJ: Wiley.

Savickas, M. L., & Hartung, P. J. (2012). *My career story: An autobiographical workbook for life-career success*. Retrieved from www.vocopher.com

Thompson, C. A., Beauvais, L. L., & Lyness, K. S. (1999). When work–family benefits are not enough: The influence of work–family culture on benefit utilization, organizational attachment, and work–family conflict. *Journal of Vocational Behavior, 54*(3), 392–415.

Valcour, M., & Ladge, J. J. (2008). Family and career path characteristics as predictors of women's objective and subjective career success: Integrating traditional and protean career explanations. *Journal of Vocational Behavior, 73*(2), 300–309.

Wayne, J. H., Randel, A. E., & Stevens, J. (2006). The role of identity and work–family support in work–family enrichment and its work-related consequences. *Journal of Vocational Behavior, 69*, 445–461.

Whiston, S. C., & Cinamon, R. G. (2015). The work–family interface: Integrating research and career counseling practice. *The Career Development Quarterly, 63*, 44–56.

CHAPTER 8

MIDLIFE ADULTS: AT 40, THE EYES HAD IT, NOW AT 50, THE CAREER DOES! WHEN CAREER VISION BEGINS TO BLUR

Kevin B. Stoltz

CASE VIGNETTE: ZEK

Zek (Ezekiel) was a 51-year-old Black male who worked for several small companies as a mechanic. Most recently, he left his employer of 13 years due to a dispute concerning promised advancement and partial ownership in the business. He shared with his career counselor that he was feeling lifeless about his career and said that he could not see the future anymore. Zek said, "Life is a burden that is followed by more demands and less energy." In reminiscing, he recounted that he began working in the seventh grade as a mechanic's helper. He explained that he worked at home, as a young boy, helping his father fix things around the house and doing chores. In seventh grade, his father became ill and Zek went to work helping a local mechanic. He learned the trade and changed jobs a few times. This last one held promise that he could eventually own part of the business. When that fell through he left, and he now feels like he is starting over having nothing to show for his many years of work.

DESCRIPTION OF THE POPULATION

Middle Age: 20/20 or Blurred Career Vision

Middle-aged workers often experience Zek's predicament (Goodman, Schlossberg, & Anderson, 2006; Heppner & Heppner, 2005). Super, Savickas, and Super (1996) presented middle age, in the maxi-cycle of the work life span, as the maintenance stage. Before entering maintenance, individuals often reflect on career experiences and question whether engagement is sustainable for the future. If workers answer yes, then these individuals progress to developing in the career by increasing commitment and becoming innovators. If these individuals answer no, they must recycle through exploration and establish a new career identity. In addition, the concept of the traditional career perspective has declined in the global economy (Arthur & Rousseau, 1996; Hall, 2002; Hall et al., 1996; Savickas, 2011). The traditional perspective included the belief that employers dictated and controlled career growth and development. The traditional career path was planned and included predictable career transitions supported by employer training and other developmental opportunities. A person had to adhere to the developmental steps outlined for the career path. This model provided security and predictability to career progression. However, with the advent of the global economy, the social contract between workers and employers disappeared (Hall, 2002; Schein, 1964; Uchitelle, 2006). Employers no longer provided secure and stable lifetime employment and workers discovered freedom to pursue work unbounded by traditional beliefs and social constraints. From this new paradigm, career theories emerged highlighting opportunities for individuals and accounting for the stress and difficulties people encounter with the new responsibility to navigate their own careers.

The Protean (Hall, 1996) and the Boundaryless (Arthur & Rousseau, 1996) career concepts charge the worker with control of personal and professional development. This developmental process, referred to as midlife renewal (Engels, 1995), is an expected component in the life-span life-space approach (Super, 1957). In this developmental period, employees may benefit most from identity exploration and career education concerning the concepts of Protean and Boundaryless career attitudes. Individuals construct new career identities, recognizing career adaptabilities (Savickas & Porfeli, 2012) while drafting a story for a future that includes focusing on a meaningful work life.

HISTORICAL OVERVIEW

According to the Bureau of Labor Statistics (Sok, 2010), middle-aged workers older than 50 years experienced a sharp increase in unemployment. Additionally, 49% of persons older than 50 years were unemployed for an average of 27 weeks, longer than any group based on age demographics. According to Towner (2011), the number of persons older than 50 years changing jobs has increased from 20% in 1996 to 31% in 2011. Many reasons are cited for this phenomenon (e.g., career dissatisfaction; Brown, 1995; lack of challenge; Vander Zanden, 2000). According to Power and Rothausen (2003), middle-aged individuals often change jobs because they are no longer interested in learning about their present work outside of the requirements placed on them by the employer. This often triggers boredom and disengagement, which are a sign of the need to engage in career renewal.

From losing a position to voluntary transition, middle-aged workers are a specific demographic that may experience difficulty in navigating career change (Barclay, Stoltz, & Chung, 2011). Barclay et al. explained a process model of career change that is helpful in understanding the stages through which an individual may progress when undergoing a career transition. These authors outlined aspects of the client's narrative that indicate stages accompanied by specific processes. Each of the stages indicates client processes and counseling interventions that can promote transition to the next stage toward successful transition. Some of the client needs outlined by Barclay et al. are identifying sources of boredom or discouragement, letting go of an old work identity, expressing doubt and insecurity about possible selves, weighing the pros and cons of transition, and redefining new life roles. This approach integrates career and mental health functioning and extends the boundaries of traditional career counseling.

BARRIERS TO CAREER TRANSITION

Understanding that mid-career individuals may face several obstacles to career transition is an important aspect to consider. Bobek, Hanson, and Robbins (2013) posited three categories that all adult career changers face. These points are engaging in personal assessment of skills and abilities, acknowledging the need to develop career adaptability, and understanding the psychological and financial effects of transition. In the present work environment, continual skill development and a positive attitude toward acquiring new skills are employment imperatives (Bobek et al., 2013; Hall, 2002). Individuals must understand and identify what they bring to employment opportunities. Additionally, these individuals must express a willingness to engage in continual learning and skill development. The second aspect of 21st-century work life is developing career adaptability. Savickas (2011) outlined career concern, control, curiosity, and confidence as four dimensions of career adaptability. Concern represents a person's attention to career matters and opportunities. The ability to function well and meet socially prescribed behavioral and attitudinal expectations under the stress of career transition is the dimension of control. Exploratory behavior and attitudes of openness to new experiences are examples of curiosity. The last dimension, confidence, represents a person's beliefs in his or her abilities to execute plans and realize goals. These four dimensions form the basic skills, dispositions, and attitudes an individual uses to traverse career transitions, setbacks, and barriers. Finally, understanding the psychological and financial effects of transition is important. Alerting a midlife client to the financial resources and costs of transition is an area for concentration in counseling. Spending time planning and helping the client gain access to resources are activities appropriate in counseling.

The psychological aspects of career transition can be threatening and difficult to predict. When clients lose relationships due to transitions, they may lose connections to aspects of the self. Grief counseling is an important component of recognizing this loss (Bejian & Salomone, 1995; Salomone, 1988). In addition, when midlife clients engage in new activities, they may experience thoughts of being an imposter or feeling awkward in new roles. Helping clients navigate these new experiences and explore new dimensions of the identity is an important aspect to career counseling. According to Hall (2002), identity is a "metacompetency" (p. 32) that allows people to understand aspects of the self and acquire new skills and learning based on core identity aspects. Thus, engaging in exploration of identity with clients is a part of career counseling and is important with midlife career changers as they face threats and adjustments to their identity.

In addition to the obstacles concerning midlife transition, there are psychosocial needs that are important to the career counseling process. According to Levinson, Darrow, Klein, Levinson, and McKee (1978), midlife is an important developmental stage, which includes reflection on aging, reasons for life and future goals, identity, and relationships. When individuals engage in career transition, they may evaluate their overall success in life (Cochran, 2001). Using these constructs to help individuals reevaluate interpretations is essential when counseling midlife career changers. Other more typical needs addressed when working with midlife career transition include financial concerns, loss of security, loss of relationships, and general fear of the unknown (Newman, 1995). Newman viewed this as a stage of career renewal and urges counselors to encourage clients to explore ways to update skills, engage in career appraisal, and reorganize priorities.

RESOURCES FOR MIDLIFE TRANSITION COUNSELING

Various resources are available to help augment the career counseling process and assist the client in making a career transition. These resources are listed as activities to extend the concepts discussed in the counseling sessions.

- National Career Development Association: http://www.ncda.org/aws/NCDA/pt/sd/news_article/5232/_PARENT/layout_details_cc/false
  http://www.ncda.org/aws/NCDA/pt/sd/news_article/88749/_PARENT/layout_details_cc/false
- Public Broadcasting Systems (Producer). (2012). *Boundless potential: Reinvent your career in midlife and beyond* [DVD-AS]. Retrieved from teacher.shop.pbs.org/product/index.jsp?productId=18631766&cp=
- Johns Hopkins Job Transition Guide: hrnt.jhu.edu/tmod/career/JobTransition Manual.pdf
- My Career Story: An Autobiographical Workbook for Life/Career Success (Savickas and Hartung, 2012): vocopher.com/CSI/CCI_workbook.pdf
- *Self-Directed Search—You and Your Career* (Holland, 1994, form R, 4th ed.). This booklet can be used to help assemble a collection of objects that represent the various concepts and dimensions of the Holland coding system used to help clients discuss aspects of a personal career story (portrayed in the following).

MEETING THE CAREER TRANSITION NEEDS OF MIDLIFE CLIENTS

Glasses, Contacts, or Radial Keratotomy: Clarifying the Career Images

Although there are many resources, some clients may experience stress and confusion during the transition. Counselors can tailor interventions to meet the individual needs of the client. There are many well-known career interventions that address assessing interests, values, and skills. Although valuable, these constructs do not conceptualize the psychosocial assets and strengths a client brings to the transition process. Savickas (2011) conceptualized these psychosocial assets as career adaptability. Having interventions to help the client develop and use personal career adaptability is an important aspect of preparing clients for transition and helping them compete in the global economy. Savickas suggested the Career Construction Interview (CCI) to assist clients in narrating a career story that includes aspects of career adaptability and identity. The process helps clients perform an inventory of skills, interests, and abilities. In addition, the CCI helps the client identify personal images that give glimpses of the client's identity and personal striving toward significance. See Appendix H for additional suggestions.

REVISITING THE CASE OF ZEK

The construct of identity is a critical component to career intervention in the 21st century (Hall, 2002; Savickas, 2011). Until recently, career researchers focused little attention on assisting clients in making changes to their career identity. Emerging research (Hall, 2002; Porfeli & Savickas, 2012) is highlighting the importance of this construct in understanding and nurturing the evolution of a person's career identity. Thus, attending to Zek's evolving identity would be an appropriate intervention based on the particulars of the case and the emerging literature.

After encouraging Zek to express his grief and anger at being disappointed with his career, a next step would be to help Zek orient toward self-understanding. This would include a focus on his identity. Current research (McAdams & McLean, 2013) supports the use of narrative storytelling as a way of helping clients understand and discover personal identity. This narrative approach fits well with many interventions as story is a focal point in counseling.

For this intervention (Career Walkabout), the counselor needs to have objects and manipulatives that represent the six work environments (realistic, investigative, artistic, social, enterprising, conventional) theorized by Holland (1992). Additionally, the counselor will need a line of chairs for the client to sit on at various times during the intervention. The chairs represent the different jobs or positions that the client has held over his or her life span. The objects become the artifacts of the client's story. The artifacts or objects should represent the many aspects of the Holland codes (e.g., values, interests, attitudes, and rewards) and become tangible aspects of the client's story.

The client is asked to sit on one of the chairs and discuss aspects of the position or job. During the narrative, the counselor listens for Holland themes and selects objects that represent those themes. For example, as Zek discusses his first job when he was 13 years old, he tells about helping his boss, the mechanic. He cleaned tools, straightened and organized the shop, and assisted by holding parts during replacement or repair. These conventional and realistic activities were represented by a set of toy tools and a shop towel. As he talked about the job, Zek picked up the toy tools and handled them while discussing learning about use of the tools for different jobs (skills and interests). He also expressed how he looked up to his boss (image and identity) and thought that he wanted to be skilled like him and able to fix most anything (future image and identity). The counselor reflected these skills and interests and highlighted Zek's accomplishments in wanting to be like his role model. Zek was prompted to choose an object to represent his role model. Zek selected a toy fox figure and said he was sly and smart like a fox. All the items were placed in front of Zek as he talked more about this position. Zek reminisced that he learned so much from his first boss.

Moving to the next chair, Zek was instructed to collect all his artifacts and make the physical move to the next chair. Zek explored his next position of working for a popular chain store. Here, he performed standard maintenance functions such as oil changes and brake replacements. Zek said the work was too routine and did not take much thought or skill (anti-image). He confessed that it paid well, but he did not like the routine work (value). However, he did enjoy interacting with the customers (social). He built a loyal following of customers that would request his work. His most enjoyable aspect of this position was when a customer would have an unusual complaint or experience with the car and Zek would work with the customer to locate and complete the repair (investigative). The counselor placed a mechanical puzzle and a toy human figure in front of Zek, indicating the investigative and social nature that he was discussing. Zek explained that the personal challenge of understanding the mechanical process and finding the problem was the exciting and satisfying part of this job;"a little like Sherlock Holmes" he said (image). His face was noticeably happier as he smiled, talking about this ability to solve complex mechanical problems (skill and interest).

His next chair included a story of him working for a company that serviced equipment used to transport baggage at the airport. Here, he observed and talked with many different mechanics about all types of equipment. He especially enjoyed talking with and watching the jet engine mechanics. One of the airline companies was attempting to document how certain mechanics could be more productive in taking apart, servicing, and reassembling jet engines. Zek was fascinated with this process and learned that the company could not document the idiosyncratic movements of specific mechanics. This personal knowledge (called feel) was not comprehendible to the engineers and technical writers. Zek remembered being proud (value) that these mechanics' feel could not be portrayed in the writing of the technical service books. This helped him realize he too had specialized knowledge that could not be documented by engineers or technical writers. The counselor took a manual from the bookshelf and placed a post-it note on the cover. On the post-it note, the counselor drew a zero and struck a line through it, the symbol for no. Zek laughed and nodded his head yes. This was placed in the pile of objects by the chair.

As Zek worked his way through his various positions, the counselor continued to help him assemble objects that represented his experiences and accumulated knowledge. This helped Zek begin to see some of his collected knowledge and skills in tangible form. He stated, as he looked at the assembly of objects,"I suppose I do have some things to show for my years of work. I guess I am not starting over." The counselor took this to indicate that Zek was realizing he had accomplished some aspects of his life goals. He was becoming that man that could "fix almost anything." Zek smiled when he heard this quote from his first job experience. He explained how much his first boss had impressed him and that he was using him as an image or guide. His first boss owned his own garage and had a loyal following of customers. Zek realized how much he wanted to emulate his mentor, but he felt intimidated by the accounting and financial side of the business. He stated he was open to learning but did not know how to go about getting that type of experience. Furthermore, he said he did not know how to get financing for a business. He guessed he could do well, but he just felt overwhelmed thinking about starting his own business. The counselor reminded him of his accomplishments in school and that his testing indicated that he could learn the different aspects of business accounting and finance.

This latter part of the conversation began to lay the groundwork for Zek's future. The counselor took Zek to the last chair, the very front of the row. He asked Zek to look forward and describe what he could imagine as the next step now. Zek said that he could imagine having his own shop but that it was like stepping off a cliff. He was scared and did not know what to expect. He felt anxious, like he was on the edge. He explained that each time he made a job change previously, there was a secure position and vision (traditional career perspective). This time, everything seemed so insecure and unclear and everything relied on his abilities (Protean and Boundaryless career perspectives). The counselor drew Zek's attention to the former chair where he had talked about the inability of portraying specific mechanical procedures. He reminded Zek of his words: "I felt proud that the mechanics' feel could not be put into a manual." The counselor then related Zek's present situation as not fitting into the manual or routine. Zek smiled and said, "Yes, I see that. I like the safety of a defined position and routine, yet I value doing things that are not visible and I enjoy a challenge."

In this scenario, the counselor used a process allowing the client to account for his accumulation of skills and knowledge across the work life span. Additionally, by recounting this work history, the client began to learn he carried an image (identity) of what he wanted in his work life. He realized that he could learn, as shown by the accumulated skills of his career. He expressed belief that he could move toward his image of owning his own shop, being an independent business owner, and solving complex mechanical problems for his customers.

From this point, the counselor began to link Zek with resources to assist him in learning about starting a business. Zek even began to talk about attending a local community college concerning business courses, especially accounting and finance. Zek seemed poised to take the steps to move toward his personalized career image with more understanding of his skills, abilities, and personal identity.

ADDITIONAL RESOURCE SUGGESTIONS

AARP: http://www.aarp.org/?CMP=KNC-360i-google-dso-CPA&360cid=SI_824946799_58993300113_1&Google:%20gclid=CObzu5utmskCFYU9aQodd8oFSg

This association provides many resources for members older than 50 years. Resources include articles about employment, finance, balanced living, and many other topics related to midlife and beyond.

Federal Student Aid: studentaid.ed.gov

Operated by the U.S. government, this service supplies resources for acquiring loans to complete higher education and technical education in the United States.

Idealist Careers: idealistcareers.org

This organization provides resources and job search capabilities for individuals in career transition.

O*NET resource center: www.onetonline.org

Organized and provided by the U.S. Department of Labor/Employment and Training Division, this resource helps counselors and clients explore employment sectors with complete job information.

Senior Job Bank: www.seniorjobbank.org

This organization is focused on assisting older workers to locate employment opportunities.

Small Business Association: www.sba.gov/thinking-about-starting

Created by the U.S. government, this service provides resources and training opportunities concerning starting and operating a small business.

REFERENCES

Arthur, M. B., & Rousseau, D. M. (1996). *The Boundaryless career: A new employment principle for a new organizational era*. New York, NY: Oxford University Press.

Barclay, S. R., Stoltz, K. B., & Chung, Y. (2011). Voluntary midlife career change: Integrating the transtheoretical model and the life-span, life-space approach. *Career Development Quarterly, 59*, 386–399.

Bejian, D. V., & Salomone, P. R. (1995). Understanding midlife career renewal: Implications for counseling. *Career Development Quarterly, 44*, 52–63.

Bobek, B. L., Hanson, M. A., & Robbins, S. B. (2013). Counseling adults for career transition. In S. D. Brown & R. W. Lent (Eds.), *Career development and counseling: Putting theory and research to work* (2nd ed., pp. 653–682). Hoboken, NJ: Wiley.

Brown, D. (1995). A values-based approach to facilitating career transitions. *Career Development Quarterly, 44*, 4–11.

Cochran, S. V. (2001). Psychotherapy with men navigating midlife terrain. In G. R. Brooks & G. E. Good (Eds.), *The new handbook of psychotherapy and counseling with men: A comprehensive guide to settings, problems, and treatment approaches* (pp. 444–463). San Francisco, CA: Jossey-Bass.

Engels, D. W. (1995). Common themes in midlife career transitions. *Career Development Quarterly, 44*, 83–88.

Goodman, J., Schlossberg, N. K., & Anderson, M. L. (2006). *Counseling adults in transition: Linking practice with theory* (3rd ed.). New York, NY: Springer.

Hall, D. T. (2002). *Career in and out of organizations*. Thousand Oaks, CA: Sage.

Hall, D. T. (1996). *The career is dead, long live the career: A relational approach to careers*. San Francisco, CA: Jossey-Bass.

Heppner, M. J., & Heppner, P. P. (2005). Addressing the implications of male socialization for career counseling. In G. E. Good & G. R. Brooks (Eds.), *The new handbook of psychotherapy and counseling with men: A comprehensive guide to settings, problems, and treatment approaches* (pp. 172–185). San Francisco, CA: Jossey-Bass.

Holland, J. L. (1992). *Making vocational choice: A theory of vocational personalities and work environments* (2nd ed.). Odessa, FL: Psychological Assessment Resources.

Holland, J. L. (1994). *SDS self-directed search—You and your career* (form R, 4th ed.). Lutz, FL: Psychological Assessment Resources.

Levinson, D., Darrow, C., Klein, E., Levinson, M., & McKee, B. (1978). *The seasons of a man's life*. New York, NY: Knopf.

McAdams, D. P., & McLean, K. C. (2013). Narrative identity. *Current Directions in Psychological Science, 22*, 233–238.

Newman, B. K. (1995). Career change for those over 40: Critical issues and insights. *Career Development Quarterly, 44*, 64–66.

Porfeli, E. J., & Savickas, M. L. (2012). Career Adapt-Abilities Scale-USA Form: Psychometric properties and relation to vocational identity. *Journal of Vocational Behavior, 80*, 748–753. doi:10.1016/j.jvb.2012.01.009

Power, S. J., & Rothausen, T. J. (2003). The work-oriented midcareer development model: An extension of Super's maintenance stage. *The Counseling Psychologist, 31*, 157–197.

Salomone, P. R. (1988). Career counseling: Step and stages beyond Parsons. *Career Development Quarterly, 36*, 218–221.

Savickas, M. L. (2011). *Career counseling. Theories of psychotherapy*. Washington, DC: American Psychological Association.

Savickas, M. L., & Porfeli, E. J. (2012). Career adapt-abilities scale: Construction, reliability, and measurement equivalence across 13 countries. *Journal of Vocational Behavior, 80*, 661–673.

Schein, E. H. (1964). How to break the college graduate. *Harvard Business Review, 43*, 68–76.

Sok, E. (2010). *Record unemployment among older workers does not keep them out of the job market* (10–04, March 2010). Retrieved from http://www.bls.gov/opub/ils/summary_10_04/older_workers.htm

Super, D. E. (1957). *The psychology of careers: An introduction to vocational development*. Oxford, UK: Harper & Bros.

Super, D. E., Savickas, M. L., & Super, C. M. (1996). The life-span, life-space approach to careers. In D. Brown & L. Brown (Eds.), *Career choice and development* (3rd ed., pp. 121–178). San Francisco, CA: Jossey-Bass.

Towner, B. (2011). *Power of 50: 50 jobs for a second career*. Retrieved from http://www.aarp.org/work/working-after-retirement/info-06-2011/jobs-for-a-second-career.html

Uchitelle, L. (2006). *The disposable American: Layoffs and their consequences*. New York, NY: Knopf.

Vander Zanden, J. W. (2000). *Human development* (7th ed.). New York, NY: McGraw-Hill.

CHAPTER 9

OLDER ADULTS

Wendy K. Killam and Bill Weber

CASE VIGNETTE: JOHN

John is a former high school coach and history teacher. Now 65 years old, he had taken early retirement when he was only 58 years old but has quickly found himself needing to return to the workforce. He retired early to be closer to his grandchildren. When John retired, he took a partial lump-sum retirement package from the state teacher's retirement system, which lowered his monthly pension by a considerable amount. He also had to pay a considerable portion of the lump-sum in taxes; this could have been avoided if he had waited until he was 59 and a half years old to retire. Unfortunately, his decision was impulsive and motivated by pressure from his daughter who wanted him to move closer to be nearer to his grandchild. Rather than investing the money from the lump-sum and paying off his bills as planned, John and his wife Gina bought a new car, paid off their daughter's student loan from her graduate degree, gave their son Jake money for a down payment on a home, and bought an extravagant playhouse for their grandchild. The money that was intended to carry him into debt-free retirement was foolishly depleted.

John quickly realized that his monthly pension was not enough money for him to live the lifestyle he wanted, and he began to look for a job. He was able to secure a part-time job working at a private church school teaching physical education and coaching. However, after 3 years, the school was forced to make budget cuts and he found himself unemployed. John applied for several teaching jobs but was not hired. He blamed his advanced age and experience. The reality is that a recent college graduate could be paid considerably less than John due to the years of experience that would factor into his pay within a school system. Additionally, a recent graduate would possess much more current and up-to-date skills and knowledge. When asked questions about recent changes and the use of technology in interviews, John simply changed the topic to avoid answering them. This did not help his chances of being hired for a position in an educational setting.

Despite not being offered several full-time jobs for which he applied and interviewed within the public school system, John was able to secure a part-time school job as a basketball assistant coach after a year of unemployment. During the year in which he was unemployed, John borrowed money from his mother and younger brother to avoid foreclosure on his home and mowed lawns to make enough money to pay his bills. His part-time job allowed him to pay his current bills, but he has yet to repay family members. When he lost his part-time job after 2 years, he began looking once again for a teaching and/or coaching job but was unable to secure one. He was forced to sell his five-bedroom home and make significant changes to his lifestyle, which contributed to feelings of depression. His family is unwilling to loan him additional money and he is currently struggling to pay his bills. John is frustrated at his inability to find a job similar to the one he has held in the past and sees no other job options. He is unsure how he will be able to continue to meet his financial obligations despite having already downsized his lifestyle significantly.

DESCRIPTION OF THE POPULATION

By 2030, approximately 20% of the workforce will be comprised of older adults. Currently, roughly 13% of the workforce is older than 65 years (McGuire, 2009). The number of individuals working longer will continue to increase into the foreseeable future (Collins, Hair, & Rocco, 2009). Additionally, only 27% of adults between the ages of 50 and 70 years surveyed in a recent study believed that they would never work again (Kidahashi & Manheimer, 2009). People are delaying retirement and working longer for a number of reasons including such factors as significant changes in Social Security. Currently, full benefits are not available until age 67 years for many individuals, which encourages people to delay tapping into Social Security and working longer (Wenger & Reynolds, 2009). Some older workers simply cannot afford the decrease in income that comes with retirement. In fact, many well-qualified and well-trained older adults are typically well compensated for their unique skill sets (Sweet, 2007). Unfortunately, not every older adult holds a position that warrants competitive compensation. Those who lack specific or valuable skill sets may hold jobs that offer little opportunity for advancement.

HISTORICAL PERSPECTIVE

Throughout the 1950s and 1960s, many full-time employees worked in companies where highly specific on-the-job training offered little opportunity for advancement (Herr, 2001). During the 1970s and 1980s, jobs became increasingly more specialized, requiring additional training. The workforce in the 1980s and 1990s began to include more highly trained employees. An increasing number of jobs were created that required college degrees (Lord & Farrington, 2006). There was also significant job growth in the areas of science, technology, and social service. Thus, college, both 2- and 4-year degree programs, attracted new high school graduates as well as individuals of all ages who were already in the workforce. People today are increasingly willing to take part-time jobs (Wenger & Reynolds, 2009). However, part-time jobs often lack benefits and frequently offer lower pay. Unfortunately, employers are not especially accommodating to older workers regarding their need for flexible job schedules (Moen, 2007). This is a major consideration for many older adults who may want to have more time off for leisure pursuits or medical needs. Older adults who have specific job skills are often in high demand and are able to use their job skills as a bargaining tool to ensure greater flexibility in their work schedules. As the workforce ages, employers may be required to offer greater flexibility in order to attract well-qualified employees. It is somewhat ironic that inflexible employers perceive older adults as inflexible themselves in regards to their willingness to learn new skills. However, older adults have grown in their awareness of the need to be open to new knowledge in order to maintain their competitiveness for jobs.

CHALLENGES FACED BY OLDER WORKERS

An employer's perception of older adults as lacking flexibility in adapting to changes or learning new job tasks and skills can contribute to older adults being overlooked for promotions and advancement (Lord & Farrington, 2006). Ageism is still a significant negative force in the work world and is visible in hiring practices, promotion decisions, and terminations. Discrimination in the workplace can impact an individual's physical and emotional health (Chou, 2012). Even feeling that one is being discriminated against can negatively affect how a person relates to others in the workplace. A study in 2007 conducted by the American Association for Retired Persons (AARP) found that age discrimination is a barrier for individuals older than 50 years in the workplace. Another study found that inappropriate jokes, lack of respect, and assumptions concerning the health of older workers were a concern for 84% of employees older than 60 years (Roscigno, Mong, Byron, & Tester, 2007). In fact, studies have indicated that younger workers tend to perceive older workers as being frail and in poor health (Duncan & Schaller, 2009). The perception that other employees have regarding older adults can create issues that contribute to discrimination in a workplace setting. A common perception is that older adults are less capable than younger adults in handling issues due to physical decline. However, when looking at supervisory jobs, there are numerous studies that have found no significant difference in the work performance of older supervisors compared with younger ones. It is important to note, however, that older adults are less likely to be promoted and are often perceived by management as less capable and less productive than younger workers. These perceptions regarding performance can inhibit career opportunities for older adults (Lord & Farrington, 2006). As older adults remain in the workforce or reenter the workforce, these attitudes and beliefs may begin to change. As a larger proportion of the workforce is soon made up of older adults, who are living longer, perceptions may change due to the continued productivity and developing skills of older adult workers.

FUTURE TRENDS

With people living longer, they are also remaining active and productive well into older adulthood more so than in the past (Boswell, 2012). Given the economic trends, this indicates that many older adults will work longer than ever before. Traditionally, employers often encouraged older workers to retire in order to make room for younger workers who could be paid less. However, there are definitely fields in which experience is greatly valued (Brewington & Nassar-McMillan, 2000). One challenge often faced by this group is reentry into the workforce. In some cases, an individual is so focused on a specific job and work setting that the person is unaware of his or her full value and the transferability of his or her job skills. It is critical that one considers career adaptability. The idea of career adaptability can be defined as the readiness a person has to cope with changes in work and work conditions (Ebberwein, Krieshok, Ulven, & Prosser, 2004). See Appendix I for additional innovative suggestions on working with this population.

In addition to being able to recognize the value and transferability of job skills, there are other options for older adults. A growing number of older adults are going back to college. Their needs are often overlooked by an educational system that focuses heavily on traditional college-age students (Schaefer, 2010). Being open to learning can be beneficial for the employee. There is a perception and stereotype by employers that older workers are difficult to train, resent having to learn new ways of doing things, and struggle with new technology (McCann & Keaton, 2013). It is important to also note that many younger bosses fail to fully recognize the knowledge and experience older workers bring to the workforce (Wenger & Reynolds, 2009). It is therefore important for older adults to be unafraid to proactively describe the ways in which their knowledge and skills can be uniquely beneficial to an organization.

REVISITING THE CASE OF JOHN

John's primary care provider suggested that he seek counseling to address his feelings of depression when John came in for a checkup for hypertension. The doctor noticed that John appeared somewhat depressed and he successfully encouraged John to see a counselor. After the first meeting with John, the counselor opened up a discussion about John's employment issues. John revealed that he had never considered any other options beyond teaching and coaching. The counselor was able to use the Creating a Career Genogram Sandworld intervention to help John visualize the variety of jobs that have been held by his family members. In fact, he was able to describe the transition from education to private industry that some relatives had made in the past. The counselor assisted John in identifying several of his unique skills that were transferable to other jobs. One position that was mentioned was that of a restaurant manager, a position in which the employee is responsible for scheduling and motivating restaurant team members.

John broadened his job search and applied for several jobs in the private sector. He also practiced his interviewing skills with the counselor, who noted that John had a tendency to ignore questions that he felt uncomfortable answering. John was able to refine his interview skills through ongoing role play with his counselor. Within 5 months, John was hired full-time as an assistant manager at a major restaurant chain. Although the job is very different from what John had done previously, he enjoys working with his young team members and mentors them in a manner similar to how he mentored his high school basketball players as a coach. He is a positive role model for the young adult members of his team and believes that although his new position is not one he had ever expected to hold, his work and his life have meaning.

REFERENCES

Boswell, S. S. (2012). Old people are cranky: Helping professional trainees' knowledge, attitudes, aging anxiety and interest in working with older adults. *Educational Gerontology, 38*, 465–472.

Brewington, J. O., & Nassar-McMillan, S. (2000). Older adults: Work-related issues and implications for counseling. *The Career Development Quarterly, 49*(1), 2–15.

Chou, R. J. (2012). Discrimination against older workers: Current knowledge, future research directions and implications for social work. *Indian Journal of Gerontology, 2*, 25–49.

Collins, M. H., Hair, J. E., & Rocco, T. S. (2009). The older worker–younger supervisor dyad: A test of reverse Pygmalion effect. *Human Resources Development Quarterly, 20*(1), 21–41.

Duncan, L. A., & Schaller, M. (2009). Prejudicial attitudes toward older adults may be exaggerated when people feel vulnerable to infectious disease: Evidence and implications. *Analyses of Social Issues and Public Policy, 9*(1), 97–115.

Ebberwein, C. A., Krieshok, T. S., Ulven, J. C., & Prosser, E. C. (2004). Voices in transition: Lessons on career adaptability. *The Career Development Quarterly, 52*(4), 292–308.

Herr, E. (2001). Career development and its practice: A historical perspective. *Career Development Quarterly, 49*(3), 196–211.

Kidahashi, M., & Manheimer, R. J. (2009). Getting ready for the working-in-retirement generation: How should LLIs respond? *LLI Review, 4*, 1–8.

Lord, R. L., & Farrington, P. A. (2006). Age-related differences in the motivation of knowledge workers. *Engineering Management Journal, 18*(3), 20–26.

McCann, R. M., & Keaton, S. A. (2013). A cross cultural investigation of age stereotypes and communication perceptions of older and younger workers in the USA and Thailand. *Educational Gerontology, 39*, 326–341.

McGuire, J. (2009). Ethical considerations when working with older adults in psychology. *Ethic and Behavior, 19*(2), 112–128.

Moen, P. (2007). Not so big jobs and retirements: What workers (and retirees) really want. *Generations, 31*, 31–36.

Roscigno, V. J., Mong, S., Byron, R., & Tester, G. (2007). Age discrimination, social closure and employment. *Social Forces, 86*(1), 313–334.

Schaefer, J. (2010). Voices of older baby boomer students: Supporting their transitions back into college. *Educational Gerontology, 36*, 67–90.

Sweet, S. (2007). The older worker, job insecurity, and the new economy. *Generations, 31*, 45–49.

Wenger, J. B., & Reynolds, J. (2009). Older married workers and nonstandard jobs: The effects of health and health insurance. *Industrial Relations, 48*, 411–431.

CHAPTER 10

VETERANS

Wendy K. Killam, Bill Weber, Tony Michael, and Chad Luke

CASE VIGNETTE: MARK

Mark is a 33-year-old White male. He joined the army right after high school in 2004 with a desire to seek vengeance on those who harmed America during 9/11. He served three combat tours during Operation Enduring Freedom and on at least one occasion watched several members of his unit die in combat. He has been diagnosed with acute stress disorder and is on medication for depression from the U.S. Department of Veterans Affairs (VA). Mark is divorced and has two young children. He wants to make a better life for himself and provide for his children. His marriage could not withstand the stress and pressure of his frequent deployments. On return from his last combat tour, his wife indicated that he had changed too much. Mark has a hard time relating to others and often becomes anxious, agitated, and angry. He feels like no one understands the sacrifices made by those in the military and that people often are negative toward him because he is a veteran. He blames his wife for the divorce and feels that she was uncommitted to the relationship despite the fact that toward the end of the relationship there were reports of domestic violence. Mark has received treatment for excessive use of alcohol but continues to deny that he has a problem. He attended court-ordered anger management classes and parenting classes; he believes that they were a waste of time, but they were something he had to do in order to have unsupervised visitation with his children.

Mark left the military 2 years ago and has taken a few college courses but is unsure what he wants to do with his life. He knows he wants to make a difference but is unsure how he can. He lost sight in his right eye and lost his leg in an improvised explosive device (IED) explosion. At times, he has had a hard time adjusting to his new limitations. He becomes easily frustrated when things do not go his way and even had a few issues when he took a college class. He was unable to work with a group and the other students in the group felt he was demanding at times and he did not show up at other times. Mark believed that they were unorganized and simply would not commit to meetings that he scheduled or the way in which he broke up the project. He became highly upset when a group member was 30 minutes late to a meeting due to childcare issues and proceeded to yell at her when she showed up and called her uncommitted. Mark has low tolerance when people make mistakes and becomes highly agitated. This has caused him to have difficulty keeping a job. He has been fired from three jobs in the last year due to yelling at coworkers and customers. Like many former military personnel, Mark struggles with employment issues.

DESCRIPTION OF THE POPULATION

There are millions of unemployed veterans seeking employment. The military is still male dominated, with 86% of active duty members being male (Robertson & Brott, 2013). There are more than 22 million veterans in the United States, with 10% of all veterans having served during the Gulf War Era (Boutin, 2011). Although 10% might not seem high, this equates to roughly 1.7 million troops who were deployed to Operations Enduring and Iraqi Freedom (Berger, 2010). Additionally, the number of female veterans has increased. Disability is not uncommon among this population (Boutin, 2011). In fact, there are numerous disabilities among this population including both physical disabilities and psychiatric disabilities; posttraumatic stress disorder (PTSD) and traumatic brain injuries are among some of the more common disabilities (Boutin, 2011). About 30% of veterans with PTSD never recover (Graf, Miller, Feist, & Freeman, 2011). Disabilities may impact the way in which the veteran relates to others. Disabled veterans face challenges in relating to others and struggle with being in civilian culture.

The military has its own unique culture. Due to differences between the military and civilian life, many veterans struggle with understanding others in a work environment and adapting to changing demands (McAllister, Mackey, Hackney, & Perrewe, 2015). According to Clemens and Milsom (2008), veterans regularly entered the military just after high school and have not learned the skills necessary to productively engage the civilian job market. This stress of adjusting to a different work environment can be compounded when the individual has unresolved emotional issues. In fact, most veterans who need mental health treatment never seek it out. There continues to be a stigma regarding seeking out mental health services. In a study by Cornish, Thys, Vogel, and Wade (2014), the area in which most veterans struggled was relating to others after deployment. They also expressed concerns that civilians had no understanding of what they encountered and endured and thus often found civilians to be insensitive to their needs.

In addition to relationship issues, Cornish et al. (2014) found that veterans struggled with anxiety, anger, depression, and thoughts of suicide. Some veterans struggled with adjusting to physical limitations due to being injured and were generally more anxious; in a work situation, these traits could negatively impact performance. In Mark's case, he often became angry at coworkers and customers. For employers, a negative experience with a veteran could result in the employer choosing to hire nonveterans. In fact, the unemployment rate for veterans has been much higher than the national average, with some states reporting the unemployment rate for veterans as triple the national average (Robertson & Brott, 2013). A growing number of veterans who are unemployed may find themselves homeless. This is due to increased costs of housing as well as the delay in receiving benefits (Bullock, Braud, Andrews, & Phillips, 2009).

The numerous challenges faced by veterans in adjusting to civilian life are impacted by a loss of identity and the loss of support that one often receives in a military community (Robertson, 2013). The degree of support from family and friends can impact a person's ability to adjust to civilian life (Graf et al., 2011). About 44% of all veterans report having some type of issue integrating back into civilian life (McAllister et al., 2015). Although some may think that the challenges are new, on leaving the military individuals often struggle to find new career options. The challenge for counselors is helping younger veterans who are trying to find new career paths.

HISTORICAL PATHS AND CAREER CHALLENGES

Historically, most veterans leave the military considering career options. The age at which a person leaves the military differs, but has traditionally been in the 40s and 50s, which for many would be retirement (Robertson, 2013). Currently, male veterans between the ages of 18 and 24 years have the highest rate of unemployment among the veteran population (Boutin, 2011). In the past, there have been programs to assist veterans in securing employment or training for new employment. This dates back to the GI Bill of Rights that was signed into law in 1944. The law was updated in 2008 with provisions in place to encourage young veterans to attend college and earn bachelor's degrees (Boutin, 2011). Even with the opportunity to attend college and develop new career skills, the challenges can be overwhelming for some veterans.

Challenges faced by veterans include feeling a stigma if they seek out assistance of any type (Cornish et al., 2014). Some veterans have reported feeling uncomfortable working in civilian environments (McAllister et al., 2015). This discomfort could contribute to stressful relationships within work environments for veterans. Many combat veterans have reported having difficulty interacting with others (Graf et al., 2011). This can contribute to difficulties in the work environment. The challenges faced by veterans from the past are similar to those of today. The difference is that today there are more programs designed to help veterans' transition to civilian life.

EXPECTED CAREER DEVELOPMENT NEEDS

Today's veterans need compassion and understanding from family and friends. It is not uncommon for veterans to have difficulty talking about their experiences (Graf et al., 2011). In order to be able to move forward with a new career, veterans often need to process what has occurred. Around 6 million veterans in the United States struggle with integrating into civilian life (McAllister et al., 2015). These difficulties impact all areas of life and can lead to stressful situations. Difficulty finding work and adjusting to civilian life can lead to homelessness for some veterans (Bullock et al., 2009). Veterans need support to be able to move forward with their lives.

SUPPORTS IN PLACE

Currently, veterans can seek help from the VA; however, there is often a delay in receiving benefits and the process can be quite lengthy (Bullock et al., 2009). Being able to connect with other veterans can be beneficial in helping with adjustment (Graf et al., 2011). Some colleges have started veteran's centers on campus to help veterans have a place where they can connect with others who can relate to their unique challenges. Offering support can come in various forms, but it can be challenging for families and others who may not fully understand the unique needs of veterans. Another issue is that due to the stigma of seeking assistance, many veterans do not actively seek assistance to deal with their issues (Cornish et al., 2014). This is an area where the counseling profession needs to continue to work to make changes and to advocate for social programs that assist veterans with employment challenges.

In terms of career counseling interventions, there is a wealth of innovative techniques that are now being applied to this group. Understanding the unique transition needs of veterans allows counselors to tailor their counseling practice effectively to their needs. See Appendix J for a large group of innovative techniques.

REVISITING THE CASE OF MARK

Mark's challenges are not uncommon for veterans. At this point, Mark may feel alone and overwhelmed while trying to adjust. The anger and depression are issues the counselor will need to help him work through. He would benefit from learning new coping mechanisms. However, right now a pressing concern is helping him feel supported. The technique titled Who's Got Your 6, *which is included in Appendix J of this book, could be used to assist him in identifying not only career possibilities but also social support as he moves forward in life. The counselor could ask him questions regarding how he is coping with all of the changes he has been dealing with in recent months and help him to identify sources of support. This could be a way in which Mark begins to consider his current support system and ways to expand it.*

Another intervention that could be used would be the intervention On The Double: Developing a Job Interview Script. *This intervention could help Mark to look at his areas of strength and to build on them as he prepares for a job interview. The counselor might also work with Mark to role-play and practice his interviewing skills once he has considered his strengths. It can be highly beneficial to help a client focus on the positive aspects of his life and to take a strengths-based approach. Mark has numerous challenges and has faced quite a few changes in recent months, but by focusing on what he can control and helping him identify sources of support and his own skills, the counselor can encourage Mark as he continues on his career journey.*

REFERENCES

Berger, T. J. (2010). Testimony of Thomas J. Berger, executive director, Veteran's Health Council, regarding mental health & substance abuse issues facing returning veterans relating to criminal justice and alternatives to incarceration, *U.S. Sentencing Commission* May 17, 2010.

Boutin, D. L. (2011). Effective vocational rehabilitation services for military veterans. *Journal of Applied Rehabilitation Counseling, 42*, 24–32.

Bullock, E. E., Braud, J., Andrews, L., & Phillips, J. (2009). Career concerns of unemployed U.S. war veterans: Suggestions from a cognitive information processing approach. *Journal of Employment Counseling, 42*, 171–181.

Clemens, E. V., & Milsom, A. S. (2008). Enlisted service members' transition into the civilian world of work: A cognitive information processing approach. *Career Development Quarterly, 56*, 246–255.

Cornish, M. A., Thys, A., Vogel, D. L., & Wade, N. G. (2014). Post-deployment difficulties and help seeking barriers among military veterans: Insights and intervention strategies. *Professional Psychology, Research and Practice, 45*, 405–409.

Graf, N. M., Miller, E., Feist, A., & Freeman, S. (2011). Returning veterans' adjustment concerns: Family views. *Journal of Applied Rehabilitation Counseling, 42*, 13–23.

McAllister, C. P., Mackey, J. D., Hackney, K. J., & Perrewe, P. L. (2015). From combat to khakis: An exploratory examination of job stress with veterans. *Military Psychology, 27*, 93–107.

Robertson, H. C. (2013). Income and support during transition from a military to civilian career. *Journal of Employment Counseling, 50*, 26–30.

Robertson, H. C., & Brott, P. E. (2013). Male veterans' perception of mildlife career transition and life satisfaction: A study of military men transitioning to the teaching profession. *Adultspan Journal, 12*, 66–79.

CHAPTER 11

CAREGIVERS

Nakeshi L. Dyer and Jonie Oliver

CASE VIGNETTE: SHARON

Sharon is a 37-year-old African American female and a high school graduate. She does not have any siblings or children (though she has always hoped to have a son and a daughter), and she has never been married. Growing up, Sharon and her parents moved around quite a bit due to her father being in the military. When Sharon was 16 years old, her mother had a stroke, which impacted her speech and mobility to such a degree that she was no longer able to work but did qualify for disability benefits. After the stroke, Sharon became largely responsible for cleaning the house and helping her mother complete activities of daily living like dressing, cleaning, and cooking. During this time, Sharon worked sporadically (on a part-time basis) at a local fast food restaurant as a cashier and a line cook.

When Sharon was 19 years old, her mother was diagnosed with diabetes, and due to complications her right leg was amputated below the knee. Six months after the amputation, Sharon's parents divorced and she became her mother's full-time care taker. The divorce resulted in a significant decrease in the household income as well as help with caregiving duties. Although the family could use the money from Sharon's part-time job, she terminated her employment to care for her mother. When Sharon was 21 years old, she registered for classes at a local community college with hopes of becoming a registered nurse. She signed up for two online courses but found it difficult to keep up with the courses while caring for her mother. After one semester, she withdrew from school with below-average grades in her classes. Three months ago, Sharon's mother passed away from diabetes-related complications. She is seeking the help of a career counselor because she feels she has no marketable skills to support herself.

What Are Some of the Areas of Concern for Sharon?

Income, employment, education, housing, job training and experience, social support, counseling (grief/personal), and career counseling.

THE DIVERSE CAREGIVER POPULATION

Caregiving is the act of tending to the needs of children (minor or adult aged), elderly adults, or sick or disabled individuals. Most of the time, caregivers are family members who volunteer or are expected under the circumstances to take care of their children, parents, close relatives, or friends as they get older, develop health problems, or can no longer take care of themselves. Caregivers may perform duties such as cleaning, shopping, cooking, managing household finances, administering medication and other health care–related duties, and helping with activities of daily living (National Alliance for Caregiving in Collaboration With AARP, 2009).

It appears that more people are providing ongoing care to relatives and friends with disabilities, illnesses, and other special needs than ever before. In 2009, the National Alliance on Caregiving issued a report, which indicated that 28% of adults are providing regular help to another person. Most of this care is provided to older relatives, but the total also includes younger individuals like children with and without special needs and those with chronic mental and physical health concerns. Although there is an increase in the number of caretaking individuals, many families have fewer resources to assist in caring for their loved ones (Zarit, 2014). As a result, some caretakers have to relinquish some or all of their caretaking duties to find paid employment. Others have to find ways to balance work and caretaking responsibilities at home (Zarit, 2014). For women and men who have spent a significant portion of their life caring for family and home, returning to the workplace or entering it for the first time can be difficult. This is particularly true if the necessity to return to work is due to the loss of the family's main financial support or because of unexpected and urgent circumstances (Locke & Gibbons, 2008).

During the period from 2007 and 2009, and longer in some cases, many countries around the world experienced significant downturns in economic activity; this global fiscal slump was coined the "Great Recession" (Bureau of Labor Statistics, 2012; Sum & Khatiwada, 2010). During this time, many large industries such as the banking and automotive industries declared bankruptcy and depended on governmental "bailouts" to remain operational. A housing crisis resulted in numerous foreclosures for families unable to afford their mortgage payments. Unemployment rates soared as major corporations and businesses closed or laid off employees. The distribution of household incomes became even more unequal as more families in the working and middle classes struggled to meet their family's needs and/or sustain their current level of living (Sum & Khatiwada, 2010). The recession exhausted resources across many families (Mattingly & Smith, 2010), reducing the scope of the systems on which some depended for economic support. In order to provide for the needs of self and family during these macroeconomic concerns, some were forced to reenter or enter the workforce for the first time (Varmecky, 2012).

Factors other than the Great Recession have resulted in more caregivers entering the workforce. For instance, 2005 marked the first time in U.S. history that the majority of adult-aged women were living without spouses, with the proportion of unmarried women rising from 35% in 1950 to 51% in 2005 (Roberts, 2007). A few possible explanations for this significant change could be that women are choosing to marry later in life or are choosing to cohabitate versus entering into marriage (Roberts, 2007). Others who do decide to marry may outlive their spouses or their marriages may end through divorce (Appelbaum, 2011). According to the Centers for Disease Control and Prevention (CDC), a little more than half of all first marriages end in divorce (Centers for Disease Control and Prevention/National Center for Health Statistics, 2011). The divorce rates for second and third marriages are higher (Banschick, 2012). The end of significant relationships for those performing unpaid caretaking duties can create great economic hardships; these hardships often can force some caretakers to enter the paid job market (Amato, 2000).

TRADITIONAL CAREER PATHS

Caregivers develop a particular set of skills while caring for others. Like other skilled workers, they tend to use the skills and experience that they have when considering career options. Therefore, caregivers tend to look for other opportunities to provide care. Self-efficacy is developed as they become more confident in their skills and abilities. This self-efficacy gives them the confidence to seek other opportunities to hone their skills. Likewise, they may be lacking self-efficacy in other areas, such as academia or working in a more formal setting. This lack of self-efficacy may cause apprehension at the thought of venturing into new fields.

Caregivers attempting to make a change may face significant barriers. These barriers include lack of self-efficacy to venture into new fields, lack of clear pathways to other fields, lack of training to secure other employment, and the lack of resources to take time for sincere contemplation regarding career aspirations during the transition. Being a caregiver also is associated with societal stereotypes: It is viewed as not a "real job" or something done only by unskilled or uneducated people. This characterization may cause caregivers and others to devalue the work of caregivers. Using this societal stereotype to choose career goals may cause one to "set the bar too low." When faced with the commitment of time and money necessary to acquire new skills needed for "prestigious" careers, low self-efficacy and negative outcome expectations may convince caregivers that change is impossible.

Bandura's (1986) social cognitive theory posits that occupational choices are made over a span of time, not in one moment. Self-efficacy, perceived barriers, outcome expectations, and career goals (Gibbons & Shoffner, 2004) are the central tenets of the social cognitive career theory (SCCT), derived from Bandura's social cognitive theory. According to SCCT, individuals use self-efficacy and outcome expectations to make career choices and set career goals. Limited, and perhaps negative, experiences may cause caregivers to eliminate career options arbitrarily.

HISTORY OF CAREER OBSTACLES

The decision to enter or return to the paid workforce is sometimes a difficult one to make for caregivers. There are several personal, cultural, social, historical, environmental, and institutional obstacles to consider when transitioning from the role of unpaid worker in the home to paid worker outside of the home. The multifarious public and private responsibilities that some may value, gender-based complications, and internal and external beliefs about work can generate important challenges for caregivers transitioning to the workforce (Hackett, 1997). For women, these obstacles can be even more poignant when societal, familial, or personal views about gender roles are in conflict with working outside of the home. Although there are many challenges to take into consideration, just a few are briefly outlined as follows.

Perceptions of Family

Caregivers who must seek paid work outside of the home may be bombarded with feelings of guilt, shame, and worry due to having less time to tend to their families and homes. They may also face criticism or judgment from others about their work decision. For those whose identities are greatly defined by their caregiving roles, this can have a negative impact on well-being (Ronzio, 2011).

Disparate Treatment/Discrimination

Caregivers who work outside of the home may encounter conflict with work and family duties, which can limit opportunities for job advancement. They are more likely to face rigid work-related policies—like mandatory overtime—making balancing work and family responsibilities difficult. Family-related crises can lead to discipline or termination when a caretaker violates work policy to address caregiving responsibilities. Also, some caregivers entering the workplace may be older than the average employee, making them more vulnerable to workplace stereotypes and discrimination (Equal Employment Opportunity Commission [EEOC], 2007).

Assumptions/Perceptions of Potential Employers

Potential employers may view some applicants with caretaking responsibilities unfavorably merely due to gender-based assumptions regarding caretaking duties. It may be assumed that caretaking responsibilities will make female employees less dependable than male employees. These gender-based perceptions can also result in employers viewing men who perform caretaking duties as poor providers because their focus is not exclusively on paid labor. A potential employer may refuse to hire applicants providing care to sick family members or relatives with disabilities because it may be assumed that they will have unstable attendance (Ortiz & Roscigno, 2009; Schultheiss, 2009).

Uncertainty (Self-Efficacy)

Entering the workplace for the first time or after a significant break can be a daunting task, and caretakers in this position may feel ill prepared for the transition. It is important during this shift that caretakers learn about job-seeking skills such as creating resumes and interviewing skills, but it is just as important that they learn about and develop skills to enhance well-being, self-confidence, and resilience (Ronzio, 2011).

Experience (Too Much/Too Little)

Some caretakers entering the paid labor market may hear that they have too much or too little experience and be denied employment as a result. Caretakers reentering the market may apply for jobs for which their work histories exceed the qualifications; however, the jobs may allow space for more flexibility or offer quick solutions to financial crises. Others may apply for jobs that better match their current interests but their paid work histories may not meet the minimum qualifications for the job (August & Quintero, 2001).

Earning Potential

Caretakers returning to the workforce are often and rightfully concerned about their earning potential. Many, especially women, often accept jobs in sales or administrative positions (although their skills may match higher paying jobs) because these jobs provide greater flexibility to manage their home and work commitments. Others may doubt their ability to earn a decent income due to their limited work experiences outside of the home. It is important that caretakers in this dilemma highlight how their caretaking duties and skills may transfer to the paid labor market (Ronzio, 2011).

Interviewing Skills/Getting an Interview

One of the first steps to securing a job interview is to have a well-designed resume. There are various types of resume formats (e.g., functional, chronological, combination), and it is important to select a format that best suits one's experiences and the types of jobs sought. There are several resume examples and templates available online, as well as organizations that offer resume assistance to caretakers entering the job market. In addition to preparing the resume, caretakers should practice for the interview.

Learning about the organization's vision, management structure, and customer base and knowing what to wear, how to respond to certain questions, and what questions to ask the interviewers are important things to learn and rehearse beforehand. Postinterview etiquette (e.g., thank-you notes, follow-up phone calls/e-mails) is also important to consider. A simple web search will produce plenty of information on how to prepare and dress for interviews, questions that may be asked, and ways to respond to difficult questions. There are also local organizations available to help caretakers prepare for a successful interview (Appelbaum, 2011).

Affluence/Money for Now

Caretakers who have more educational, social, and financial commodities and support are better positioned to achieve occupational success and upward mobility in the workplace. They may have more latitude to pursue educational and training opportunities that can enhance their technical skills and job readiness. Conversely, caretakers who enter the job market with limited education and lower incomes often face unequal access to resources due to institutional inequities and lower quality education. They are more likely to be in serious financial crises and, as a result, may accept minimum-paying jobs with little opportunity for advancement even if their skill set exceeds the demands of the job. They are less likely to have time to pursue additional training to enhance their skill set and employability. Additionally, they may have limited knowledge and awareness about career enhancing opportunities and resources that are available to them. Because of these unique challenges, it is critical that career counselors be equipped and prepared to act as educators and advocates for equal employment opportunities (Ibrahimovic & Potter, 2013).

EXPECTED CAREER DEVELOPMENT NEEDS

Training is a particularly salient need. Whether seeking education, certification, or experiential learning, getting back into the labor market will require significant development. The logistics of enrolling in college and applying for financial aid may present a challenge. Workplace etiquette, an intangible quality, is developed over time and through multiple work experiences. A caregiver may have experienced significant disruption and/or stagnation in these areas. Thus, a caregiver may benefit from exploring career options, investigating the requirements of those options, locating training and education to fulfill those requirements, and securing funding to actualize the plan. Opportunities to learn new things and build self-efficacy before starting a job could increase openness to new opportunities (Ibrahimovic & Potter, 2013). Due to lack of exposure to work and educational opportunities, attention should be given to providing opportunities to experience and learn both personally and vicariously, raising awareness of different careers, and challenging clients' preconceived notions of barriers (Ibrahimovic & Potter, 2013).

SUPPORTS IN PLACE FOR CAREGIVERS RETURNING TO WORK

One important responsibility of career counselors is to be well acquainted with the local and national resources and supports available to help caretakers in occupational transition. These are just a few of the resources and types of services that may be useful for caretakers. Counselors should become familiar with and learn how to access similar resources in their local communities.

- *Child support enforcement office*: The Office of Child Support Enforcement website (www.acf.hhs.gov/programs/css) offers contact information for all local and tribunal child support offices.
- *Peer support groups*: There may be local or online support groups for caretakers entering the job market.
- *Ticket to Work program*: This program is offered through the Social Security Administration and supports career development for Social Security disability beneficiaries aged 18 to 64 years who want to work (www.socialsecurity.gov/work/).
- *Medicare information for caregivers*: This information is designed to help caregivers address challenging issues and work effectively with Medicare to ensure their loved ones receive the best possible care (https://medicare.gov/campaigns/caregiver/caregiver.html).
- *Career counseling*: This can help someone better cope with unforeseen career challenges and transition issues.

- *Career interest inventories*: These can be used to help clients uncover career interests and identify how they may relate to various occupations and careers.
- *Paid day care while interviewing*: Some states' displaced worker programs may cover day care costs while caregivers complete interviews or participate in workshops and training courses.
- *Displaced homemaker programs*: Many states and organizations offer assistance programs to train displaced caregivers and help them find work.
- *Job readiness/development services*: Several states offer workforce development initiatives that may include occupational assessments to determine job interests and marketable skills, help completing job applications, resume writing, and interviewing etiquette.
- *Legal aid*: Displaced caretakers who are unable to take care of themselves when they lose their partner's financial support may benefit from the services of their local legal aid.
- *Dress for success*: This promotes the economic independence of financially disadvantaged women by providing professional attire and a network of support and career development tools to help them thrive in work and life (www.dressforsuccess.org).
- *Grants for displaced workers*: There are local and federal grants available to help displaced homemakers return to school or afford specialized job training.
- *Educational attainment*: Some colleges and universities offer special grants to help displaced caretakers attend school; federal grants such as Pell grants may also help to fund educational pursuits.
- *Informational resources*: Many professional organizations offer a comprehensive list of resources and information for caregivers; one example is the "Resources for Caregivers of Diverse Populations and Specific Age Groups" provided by the American Psychological Association (APA; www.apa.org/pi/about/publications/caregivers/resources/populations.aspx).
- *Workforce or labor services department*: This department can provide information on the Workforce Investment Act and the Adult and Dislocated Worker Program (www.doleta.gov/programs/general_info.cfm).

RELEVANT CAREER COUNSELING INTERVENTIONS

A career counselor working with this population would do well to realize that encouraging one to gain new skills or get more education is a valid intervention. Feeling stuck in a career due to lack of education and training can cause issues with self-esteem. Encouragement and a step-by-step plan can be the catalyst to change. Using a client's past successes to build confidence and self-efficacy can provide him or her with the willingness to move forward.

It is essential for counselors to gain an awareness of real and perceived barriers that are causing clients' reticence (Ibrahimovic & Potter, 2013). Introduce resources to help minimize the effects of each, including talking through and redefining misconceptions. Job shadowing and meeting others who have overcome similar obstacles are interventions that can be arranged through community organizations and actualized through individual and/or group counseling sessions. See Appendix K for additional suggestions.

CONCLUSION

For those who have mostly or only performed unpaid caretaking duties, career transitions can be difficult to navigate. Caregivers who have to work outside of the home and maintain caretaking responsibilities are often perplexed by the logistics of balancing the two sets of competing responsibilities. Some caretakers may be at greater psychological risk due to the factors that triggered the need to seek employment along with the interruption this change may have on their identity. Career counselors are in a position to help caregivers traverse this new and unfamiliar occupational terrain. In order to be effective when working with this population, it is important that counselors recognize and be prepared to facilitate caretakers' movement through the myriad emotional, social, cultural, and institutional barriers that they may encounter.

REVISITING THE CASE OF SHARON

Sharon's counselor decided to integrate techniques from Motivational Interviewing (MI; Miller & Rollnick, 2002; Motivational Interviewing Network of Trainers [MINT], 2008) into their work together. This career intervention is modeled after major tenets and skills found in Motivational Interviewing and can be used with clients navigating career transition across all phases of career development. It can be a useful way to help clients enhance their sense of autonomy and self-efficacy, crucial tenets when working with clients like Sharon and other caretakers transitioning to the paid job market. It is important to note that there is no set order or time limit in which clients should resolve their issues or make progress and that Sharon fluctuated back and forth across stages frequently as she tried to solidify her career transition. Through consistent use of MI support and exploration, Sharon was able to determine that she would seek out positions that would allow her to use her love of caregiving and her desire to learn nursing skills. She loved helping those who were unable to help themselves, so she was excited to be offered an opportunity to work as she earned her Certified Nursing Assistant training. She recognized that this might be the first step on her journey to pursue the nursing career for which she had always longed.

REFERENCES

Amato, P. R. (2000). The consequences of divorce for adults and children. *Journal of Marriage and the Family, 62*, 1269–1287.

Appelbaum, E. (2011). *Women's employment in recession and recovery*. Retrieved from http://cepr.net/index.php/op-eds-&-columns/op-eds-&-columns/womens-employment-in-recession-and-recovery

August, R. A., & Quintero, V. C. (2001). The role of opportunity structures in older women workers' careers. *Journal of Employment Counseling, 38*, 62–81.

Bandura, A. (1986). *Social foundations of though and action: A social cognitive theory*. Englewood Cliffs, NJ: Prentice-Hall.

Banschick, M. (2012). The high failure rate of second and third marriages: Why are second and third marriages more likely to fail? Published in *Psychology Today*. Retrieved from https://www.psychologytoday.com/blog/the-intelligent-divorce/201202/the-high-failure-rate-second-and-third-marriages

Bureau of Labor Statistics. (2012). *The BLS spotlight on statistics: The recession from 2007–2009*. Retrieved from http://www.bls.gov/spotlight/2012/recession/audio.htm

Centers for Disease Control and Prevention/National Center for Health Statistics. (2011). *National married and divorce trend rates*. Retrieved from http://www.cdc.gov/nchs/nvss/marriage_divorce_tables.htm

Equal Employment Opportunity Commission. (2007, May 23). *Enforcement guidance: Unlawful disparate treatment of workers with caregiving responsibilities*. Retrieved from http://www.eeoc.gov/policy/docs/caregiving.html

Gibbons, M. M. & Shoffner, M. F. (2004). Prospective first generation college students: Meeting their needs through social cognitive career theory. *Professional School Counseling, 8*(1), 91–97.

Hackett, G. (1997). Promise and problems in theory and research on women's career development. *Journal of Counseling Psychology, 44*, 184–188. doi:10.1037/0022–0167.44.2.184

Ibrahimovic, A., & Potter, S. (2013). Career counseling with low income students: Utilizing social cognitive career theory and the theory of circumscription and compromise. *Career Planning and Adult Development Journal, 29*(4), 60–71.

Locke, W. S., & Gibbons, M. M. (2008). On her own again: The use of narrative therapy in career counseling with displaced new traditionalists. *The Family Journal, 16*, 132–138. doi:10.1177/1066480708314258

Mattingly, M. J., & Smith, K. E. (2010). Changes in wives' employment when husbands stop working: A recession-prosperity comparison. *Family Relations, 59*, 343–357. doi:10.1111/j.1741–3729.2010.00607.x

Miller, M., & Rollnick, S. (2002). *Motivational interviewing: Preparing people for change* (2nd ed.). New York, NY: Milford Press.

Motivational Interviewing Network of Trainers. (2008, June). Exercise adapted by C. Delos Reyes from the Ohio Motivational Interviewing Network of Trainers Training held in 2008.

National Alliance for Caregiving in Collaboration With AARP. (2009). *Caregiving in the U.S. 2009*. Retrieved from http://www.aarp.org/research/topics/care/info-2014/caregiving_09.html

Ortiz, S. Y., & Roscigno, V. J. (2009). Discrimination, women, and work: Processes and variations by race and class. *Sociological Quarterly, 50*, 336–359.

Roberts, S. (2007, January 16). 51% of women are now living without spouses. *The New York Times*. Retrieved from http://www.nytimes.com/2007/01/16/us/16census.html?_r=0

Ronzio, C. (2011). Counseling issues for adult women in career transition. *The Journal of Employment Counseling, 49*, 74–84.

Schultheiss, D. (2009). To mother or matter: Can women do both? *Journal of Career Development*, 36, 25–48. doi:10.1177/0894845309340795

Sum, A., & Khatiwada, I. (2010, November 1). The nation's underemployed in the "great recession" of 2007–2009. *Monthly Labor Review*, 3–15.

Varmecky, J. H. (2012). Learning for life transitions. *Journal of Adult Education, 41*(2), 1–11.

Zarit, S. (2014, June 9). As Americans age, caregiving challenges increase. American Psychological Association. Retrieved from http://www.apa.org/news/press/releases/2014/06/caregiving-challenges.aspx

CHAPTER 12

TEEN MOTHERS

Diandra J. Prescod

CASE VIGNETTE: WILHEL

Wilhel is a 16-year-old sophomore in high school who has a 2-year-old daughter and comes from a Puerto Rican background. Wilhel is being raised by her grandmother. Her father left when she was an infant, and her mother has been in and out of correctional facilities since she was a young child. Wilhel continues to attend school, but her attendance and grades have dropped since giving birth. After urging her to go for the past year or so, Wilhel's grandmother finally convinced her to see the school counselor, Ms. Johnson.

First, Ms. Johnson wanted to get to know Wilhel and asked her about her family and upbringing. Wilhel explained that her Hispanic heritage was a large part of who she is. Her grandmother, born and raised in Puerto Rico, raised Wilhel with strong family values. Wilhel was raised speaking both English and Spanish, predominately speaking Spanish with English spoken only in school. She explained that her grandmother was upset when she found out she was pregnant but has been supportive ever since. Her grandmother watches the baby while Wilhel is at school. When asked how she describes herself, Wilhel responded, "Well, I'm a girl with a baby (chuckle), I don't know what else to say."

MEETING THE CAREER COUNSELING NEEDS OF UNWED TEEN MOTHERS

Although the number of teen mothers is decreasing due to more widespread information regarding birth control, young women handling parenting responsibilities and school completion have unique career development needs. In this chapter, interventions that have a holistic focus on the client are presented to provide counselors with unique tools to realistically build a teen parent's career knowledge, resources, and aspirations.

Much misinformation and misconception surround the topic of teen pregnancy. Society tends to place a large amount of judgment on teens who become mothers. *Why would she do that? How can she possibly finish school now?* These are questions that certainly arise in conversations surrounding the topic. Parents urge their children not to become a person "like that." When speaking about the loss of respect and judgment from others, one teen described it like this:

> All the negative things people said about me, you know, they were like, "You're so young, you don't need to be pregnant," you know. They'd call me names, I think that was the hardest thing. (Brubaker & Wright, 2006)

Teen mothers face this type of judgment on a regular basis. It is also important to capture the scope of the concern before exploring the need for career counseling. The issue of teen pregnancy deserves attention, and systems need to be put in place that address the educational and career needs of this unique population. Following are important facts related to the demographics of this population:

1. Three in ten teen girls in the United States will get pregnant at least once before age 20 years. That is nearly 750,000 teen pregnancies every year.
2. Parenthood is the leading reason that teen girls drop out of school. More than 50% of teen mothers never graduate from high school. Aid young parents by starting a Babysitter Club so that they can take General Education Diploma (GED) classes.
3. About 25% of teen moms have a second child within 24 months of their first baby.
4. Less than 2% of teen moms earn a college degree by age 30 years.
5. The United States has one of the highest teen pregnancy rates in the Western industrialized world.
6. In 2011, the teen birthrate in the United States fell to the lowest level recorded in nearly 70 years of tracking teen childbearing.
7. In 2008, the teen pregnancy rate among African American and Hispanic teen girls, aged 15 to 19 years, was more than two-and-a-half times higher than the teen pregnancy rate among White teen girls of the same age group.
8. Eight out of 10 teen dads do not marry the mother of their child.
9. A sexually active teen who does not use contraceptives has a 90% chance of becoming pregnant within a year.
10. Almost 50% of teens have never considered how a pregnancy would affect their lives.
11. Teens had fewer babies in 2010 than in any year since the mid-1940s (dosomething.org, 2014).

The Centers for Disease Control and Prevention (CDC) has found that teenage birthrates have declined in recent years. From 1991 to 2012, the birthrate for teenagers aged 15 to 19 years declined from 61.8 births per 1,000 to a historic low of 29.4 births per 1,000. There was a significant decline in birth rates across all races and ethnic groups. For Black teens aged 15 to 19 years, the CDC reported that the teen birthrate declined from 118.2 per 1,000 in 1991 to 43.9 per 1,000 in 2012 (Martin, Hamilton, Osterman, Curtin, & Matthews, 2015). In comparison, the reported teen birthrate went from 104.6 to 46.3 for Hispanic teens and from 43.4 to 20.5 for White teens. Although the number of teen births is decreasing, the career paths of these young women still require focused attention.

The U.S. Department of Health and Human Services examined characteristics associated with adolescent childbearing. Adolescents who have a positive attitude toward school and engaging in after school activities are less likely to give birth to a child (Kirby & Lepore, 2007). Teens whose mothers were teens when they gave birth or whose mothers have only a high school diploma are more likely to give birth to a child in their teens than teens whose mothers have some college education. In addition, teens who live with both parents and who live in wealthier areas experience fewer incidences of teen births (Martinez, Copen, & Abma, 2011).

The CDC places the issue of reducing teen pregnancy among its top six priorities and describes the issue as a "winnable battle" (CDC, 2014). Perception of HIV risk, condom usage, communication with parents, and knowledge of sexual issues are all topics of importance to the CDC in examining teen pregnancy. Although it is very important to focus on reducing teen pregnancy, we cannot forget about aiding the teens who have already given birth. We know that teen mothers face a number of career obstacles due to the difficulties of caring for a child and remaining focused on receiving an education.

Historical Career Paths of Unwed Teen Mothers

> Sometimes I cannot cope.... My marks are dropping. (Bhana & Mcambi, 2013, p. 16)

> When I am absent, [my school friend] brings me handouts from teachers, takes down homework and informs me about the things that were happening at school. If it wasn't for her, I would be in trouble. (Bhana & Mcambi, 2013, p. 16)

These quotes describe the many challenges that teen mothers face on a regular basis. Young mothers who do not delay childbearing face a number of challenges including educational, economic, and career development difficulty. Graduating high school poses a challenge, and if teen mothers do not complete high school, significant economic challenges follow (Gyamfi, Brooks-Gunn, & Jackson, 2001; Rothenberg & Weissman, 2002). It is difficult to find well-paying jobs and career/vocational challenges often arise (Julian & Kominski, 2011). Let us explore the many educational, economic, and career development challenges faced by young, teen mothers.

Educational Concerns

Research has shown that primary and secondary interventions have been somewhat effective in schools, but research also illustrates the educational challenges that teen mothers face. Key, Gebregziabher, Marsh, and O'Rourke (2008) explored secondary pregnancy interventions for teen mothers that involved social workers and a home visitation model intervention. The results of the intervention revealed lower subsequent births in teen mother participants (17%) than in the comparison group (33%). It should also be noted that fewer subsequent births existed among participants who had greater participation in medical care and case management

(Key et al., 2008). These findings indicate that implementing a more holistic approach (including medical care and case management) was effective.

Encouraging students to finish school and enroll in higher education proves difficult in this population. Rothenberg and Weissman (2002) examined a program implemented at a large hospital in an urban area. The hospital created a program that stressed the significance of education and becoming a well-rounded teen parent. The teens entered the program pregnant and remained in the program until their babies turned 1 year old. There were 80 teens involved in the program with only 28% enrolled in a high school or GED program. Enrollment in a 2-year college was 13% and enrollment in a 4-year college was 0.03%. Even more disappointing, only 0.03% graduated from a 2-year college and 0.01% graduated from a 4-year college (Rothenberg & Weissman, 2002). A similar article noted that teen girls who were not academically successful before giving birth were even less successful after giving birth (Casserly, Carpenter & Halcón, 2001). These difficulties, in return, create economic challenges for young teen mothers.

When young mothers do not attend school, it makes it hard for them to provide for their children. Whether receiving public assistance or working, these young mothers face difficulties making enough money to provide for their families (Horton, 2006). Gyamfi et al. (2001) examined 188 single Black mothers either on welfare or employed but previously on welfare. The study discovered that employed mothers completed more years of school and had fewer children than unemployed mothers. Employed mothers also reported less parental stress and fewer depressive symptoms than unemployed mothers. The outlined research and information regarding teen mothers highlights the significant educational difficulties teen mothers face. In addition, we can see that educational attainment is tied to economic factors.

Economic challenges not only affect teen mothers, they also affect their children. Not being able to move on to higher education contributes to these economic difficulties; appropriate career interventions could have a positive impact on these issues. Connected to economic difficulties are career and vocational challenges. Teen mothers face educational obstacles that significantly impact their education and career goals. Sadly, only about 50% of teen mothers receive their high school diploma by the age of 22 years. This statistic is compared with approximately 90% of young women who delay childbirth until after adolescence (Perper, Peterson, & Manlove, 2010). Even though teen mothers do not always reach career success due to a variety of circumstances, many of them have the motivation to pursue these goals. Teen mothers have high aspirations for themselves, such as getting married, being financially stable, and having careers that will ensure stability for themselves and for their family (Klaw, 2008).

Teen mothers face many career development challenges that are hard to overcome. Career success takes much more than merely having the motivation to do well. Even though they may be motivated to complete their education, this becomes increasingly difficult when they must add child care expenses into their budgets (Smith-Battle, 2007). This may cause them to put a hold on their career goals. "It does affect their future a little bit because you have to put everything on hold and you have to rethink everything around your child" (Redwood, Pyer, & Armstrong-Hallam, 2012). That was one teen mother's statement about future aspirations. Factors including having mentors, support from parents/guardians, and current academic success are all crucial to young mothers feeling encouraged to achieve success in a career (Hellenga, Aber & Rhodes, 2002).

Zhan and Pandey (2004) explored the benefits of educational attainment for single mothers, including the life changes it brought about. Young mothers who had earned a college degree made money and owned homes with values significantly higher than young mothers who had not earned a college degree. Additionally, it was nine times more likely for educated teen mothers to live above the poverty level (Zhan & Pandey, 2004). The U.S. Census Bureau examined educational attainment and found that those without a high school diploma working less than full time earned around $11,000 per year compared with full-time individuals with professional degrees who made around $100,000 per year (Julian & Kominski, 2011). Education and salary are strongly correlated. When a young person pursues higher education, he or she is more likely to gain better employment and earn more in salary during his or her lifetime.

EXPECTED CAREER DEVELOPMENT NEEDS

Ettinger (1991) created a list of necessary life skills for teen parents to develop. Although created in 1991, this list is still valid for teen parents more than two decades later:

1. Building self-concept
2. Building support systems
3. Learning how to access available child care, transportation services, and other support services necessary to one's survival
4. Learning how to meet the challenge of combining work and family roles
5. Learning how to give and receive emotional support
6. Networking for work opportunities and connections
7. Enhancing interpersonal communication and relationships

Because these mothers are also young adults, career development needs coincide with growth into adulthood. Teen mothers want to be able to care for their children in every way they can, including economically. Financial pressures are strongly felt by teen mothers; this causes many of them to go to work after giving birth and forego educational pursuits. Career development needs include encouragement to continue their educations. In addition, they need help exploring their options and finding answers for questions such as these: *How can they receive money for school? Who will watch the baby during class? How will they juggle working, going to school, and caring for an infant? What will they major in?*

Turnage and Pharris (2013) discussed three issues that impact teen mothers: education, identity development, and maternal support. Before becoming mothers, these teens enjoyed being with peers their own age and enjoying age-appropriate activities. With the transition to parent, a teen's expected growth and development patterns change as she balances adolescence and motherhood (Prescod & Daire, 2013; Turnage & Pharris, 2013). Support is crucial during this time and many teen mothers look to their own mothers for guidance and knowledge. The teen's mother can help the teen identify "mother" as one of her roles and provide emotional support (DeVito, 2010). In many ways, education, identity development, and maternal support are all needed to effectively encourage career development for the teen mother.

Examples of Successful Programming

Pregnancy Assistance Fund (PAF). The Office of Adolescent Health (OAH) runs a $25 million grant program "to provide expectant and parenting teens, women, fathers, and their families with a seamless network of supportive services to help them complete high school or postsecondary degrees and gain access to health care, child care, family housing, and other critical supports" (U.S. Department of Health & Human Services, 2014). Grantees across the nation are doing very important work as it relates to teen parents. The PAF has clear goals that center on career development for teen parents. Supporting teen parents in the pursuit to finish high school and to move on to higher education is imperative.

Talking With Teens. This program addresses the need that teens have for information about sex that is often not effectively conveyed by their parents. Eighty-seven percent of teens said that postponing sexual activity would be easier if they were able to communicate more with their parent/guardian (Albert, 2012). Additionally, 38% of teens said that their parents influenced their decisions about sex the most, and 22% said that friends influenced their decisions about sex the most (Albert, 2012). Encouragement of parents to have these conversations with their adolescent children might have a significant impact on the reproductive and sexual activities of their children.

Talking With Teens outlines three things teens want to hear from their parents/guardians: (a) the reasons that teen pregnancy is not a good idea and discussion of future positive opportunities, (b) a parent's rationale for asking the teen not to have sex or to use contraception, and (c) for parents to accept that a teen's questions about sex or contraception do not imply that the teen is sexually active (U.S. Department of Health & Human Services, 2014). The program also outlines 11 key points to remember when communicating with teens:

1. Keep your composure
2. Be present
3. Be sympathetic
4. Stress safety
5. Provide the facts
6. Talk to them, instead of preaching
7. Have lots of discussions
8. Keep tabs on TV
9. Make media matter
10. Chat in the car
11. Text your teen

The Mothers of Mount Sinai (MOMS). MOMS is a program, based in New York City, that helps teens finish their education and find jobs (Swedish, Rothenberg,

Fuchs, & Rothenberg, 2010). This program has been effective in changing the direction of the lives of teen mothers. A small study examining the program's effectiveness showed that 45% of the women had become financially self-sufficient and that 74% of them did not become pregnant a second time (Swedish et al., 2010). The Mount Sinai Adolescent Health Center provided a variety of services to teens including primary care, sexual and reproductive health, counseling and mental health, and violence prevention and treatment, among many others.

Adolescent Girls and Parenting Education (AGAPE). AGAPE High School of the Saint Paul Public Schools in Minnesota prides itself on offering a holistic education for teen mothers including physical, emotional, and academic integrity; parental support; and postsecondary preparation (Saint Paul Public Schools, 2012). Goals include increasing reading and mathematics skills and better preparing students to take the American College Testing (ACT) examination. This program is specifically geared toward teen mothers and illustrates the importance that these educators place on high school graduation and matriculation into higher education.

Various programs have been implemented to increase the knowledge that teens have about sexual education and contraception. The CDC funds programs through the Community Coalition Partnership Programs for the Prevention of Teen Pregnancy (Shearer, Gyaben, Gallagher, & Klerman, 2005). Other programs include the Postponing of Sexual Involvement Program (PSIP) and the Youth Asset Development Program (YADP) (Yampolskaya, Brown, & Vargo, 2004). Many programs were also implemented to educate young people on the importance of completing their high school education. These programs include a home visitation model intervention and a hospital-based intervention program for pregnant and parenting teens (Key et al., 2008; Rothenberg & Weissman, 2002).

Relevant Career Counseling Interventions

When asked about professional treatment, one teen said, "It's harder for a young person possibly because, you know, they don't know what's going on and they haven't possibly got the professional help they need around them because the professionals look a bit funny at them, sort of 'Well it's your own fault' kind of attitude" (Redwood et al., 2012).

Many interventions related to teen pregnancy center around prevention; however, many key elements in preventative efforts are important in career counseling interventions. Advocates for Youth: Rights. Respect. Responsibility (2014) outlined eight principles important for implementing programs to prevent teen pregnancy. Although these are all rules for preventative programs, career interventions for teen mothers can follow the same ones. These are eight clearly thought-out goals that include short- or long-term goals, cultural appropriateness, and community involvement among other important aims. Programs and agencies wanting to create career interventions for teen mothers can use these eight principles as an outline for creating effective interventions, perhaps in the following way:

1. *Set clearly defined and realistic program goals and objectives*: Make sure you have a clear idea of what exactly your program or intervention should deliver. A career

intervention for young teens should focus on completing high school and moving on to higher education. Talk to teens about the change in identity and caring for an infant, all the while encouraging them to finish school and working with them on career plans.

2. *Encourage community collaboration*: Use the resources around you! Involve schools or universities in your area. Inquire about partnering with their career services, and work together to provide support for the teens. Think about involving churches, hospitals, and other people in the community.
3. *Involve youth in needs assessment, program design, implementation, and evaluation*: Ask the teens what they want or need in this type of program. Sometimes we see ourselves as experts and forget to go to the source. Involve the teens in program planning, and take their ideas into consideration.
4. *Create activities that are both age and developmentally appropriate*: Take into account who you want to serve. How old are they? What grade are they in? Try not to assume what the teens may or may not know and start from the beginning if you have to. Some of the teens might not know where to look for scholarships. Others might not know how to fill out a college application. Some might need help organizing their time during the week.
5. *Provide culturally appropriate program activities*: Talk to the teens and ask them questions about their background. This will provide insight into how they see the world and why they make certain decisions.
6. *Coordinate messages to target both young women and men*: This career intervention would be focused on teen mothers, but you can include young men in certain ways. Provide information for the teen mother that she can take home and share with her partner if she has one.
7. *Offer long-term and consistent support*: This is very important to keep in mind with teen mothers. Support should continue long term; even if that support turns into a text, a phone call, or an occasional home visit. Make your teen mothers feel supported and encouraged.
8. *Provide information on both abstinence and contraception and ensure access to contraceptive services*: A career intervention for teen mothers would focus more on contraception and access to contraception services. Educate the teens on contraception and reproductive health services.

Prescod and Daire (2013) created an intervention for unwed young Black mothers (UYBMs) combining Gottfredson's career theory (1981) and *The Diagnostic and Statistical Manual of Mental Disorders*, fourth edition's (*DSM-IV*; American Psychiatric Association, 1994) Outline for Cultural Formulation. Gottfredson's theory of circumscription and compromise explains how and why young adults are attracted to certain careers. Influences such as self-concept and environment can influence what career young adults want to pursue. The *DSM-IV*'s Outline for Cultural Formulation is used to aid clinicians in a multicultural setting. We used the *DSM-IV*'s outline along with the Byars-Winston's (2010) translation to create our own (Table 12.1).

Following this outline allows a clinician to explore various issues that might arise within the relationship along with allowing the professional and teen mother to get to know one another at a deeper level. Although this intervention is aimed at UYBMs, it is applicable to the wider population of teen mothers.

TABLE 12.1 ***DSM-IV*'s Outline for Cultural Formulation and 2013 Translation**

DSM-IV'S OUTLINE FOR CULTURAL FORMULATION	PRESCOD AND DAIRE'S TRANSLATION (2013)
1. *Cultural identity of the individual:* asking about the client's ethnic and cultural identity, what language the client speaks, and the client's involvement in his or her original culture and present culture.	1. Self and cultural identity; being a young Black mother
2. *Cultural explanations of the individual's illness*: identifying how the client and the client's community and family perceive/explain the illness, symptoms as described by the client, and previous experiences with mental health care or other professional care.	2. Self and cultural concept of career problems
3. *Cultural factors related to psychosocial environment and levels of functioning*: identifying the functioning levels of social stressors and accessible social supports, including religious network and family support.	3. Self in cultural context
4. *Cultural elements of the relationship between the individual and the clinician*: noticing differences between the client and clinician (i.e., culture and social status) and problems that may arise because of the differences (i.e., diagnosis and treatment).	4. Cultural dynamics in the therapeutic relationship
5. *Overall cultural assessment for diagnosis and care*: evaluating how cultural consideration influences diagnosis and care.	5. Overall cultural assessment for diagnosis

Incorporating technology into career interventions for teen mothers also proves to be useful. Katz et al. (2011) discussed the outcome of a counseling intervention that used cellular phones. The goal of the intervention was to decrease the incidence of subsequent pregnancies among teen mothers. The intervention involved weekly calls from a counselor for the first 6 months and biweekly calls for the following year. The study found that fewer subsequent births occurred for teen mothers in the intervention group. Using technology such as cell phones, iPads, laptops, and so on might make interventions more effective. Being able to send a text or FaceTime with a teen mother could be useful if they are not able to make it to a counseling session or simply to keep lines of communication open between the counselor and teen mother.

Meaningful and effective career development interventions should be holistic, comprehensive, and systematic (Niles & Harris-Bowlsbey, 2013). Taking into account the many aspects of identity assists the counselor in encouraging the teen to finish school and allows the counselor to use relevant interventions in the appropriate manner (Chablani & Spinney, 2011; Herrman & Waterhouse, 2011; Prescod & Daire, 2013). Herrman and Waterhouse (2011) found that students who lived in more urban areas had more positive views about teen parenting than teens in suburban areas. In addition, they found that Black and Latino students had more positive views about teen parenting than White students. In another study, researchers examined the effects of an intervention for "high risk" pregnant and parenting mothers who were in danger of dropping out of school and street or gang involved (Chablani & Spinney, 2011). The program, Circle of Care, offered transitional employment, parenting education, life skills and employment training, and placement, among many other things. None of these young women had participated in any type of parenting program previously; therefore, the program employees used a "relentless outreach" approach. They consistently worked to engage the young women through various means to keep them involved in the program. See Appendix L for additional suggestions.

REVISITING THE CASE OF WILHEL

We will now follow up with Wilhel, the client described at the start of this chapter:

Ms. Johnson asked Wilhel about her career goals. Wilhel explained that she wants to finish high school and be able to work full time to support her child and help her grandmother with bills. Ms. Johnson expressed her empathy for Wilhel's situation and said she understood why finances were a concern for her. Wilhel went on to explain that she has always been interested in architecture but admitted that it was a silly dream. "How could I even pay for all that? And plus, I don't know anyone who does that stuff," she went on to say. Ms. Johnson paused for a moment and thought about herself and her upbringing.

Ms. Johnson is a 32-year-old woman raised in Barbados. She came to the United States at the age of 17 years with her siblings and was raised by both of her parents who supported her throughout her schooling. She did not have to work until after she finished school and has no children. Ms. Johnson did not reveal all of these things to Wilhel but explained that her upbringing was a bit different from her own. They discussed having to put in extra effort to understand each other. Ms. Johnson realized that she had a number of issues to address in counseling: (a) being a teen mother and the challenges that come along with it, (b) not having the support of parents, and (c) rejecting architecture as a realistic career goal.

After a few weeks of counseling, Ms. Johnson helped Wilhel create a career action plan for herself. Wilhel's career action plan needed to consider her as a young teen mother with no other family support than her grandmother. Ms. Johnson suggested that Wilhel sign up for a local program aiding teen mothers. This program would give her classes in time management and child care, among others. Additionally, Ms. Johnson would help Wilhel apply for scholarships in hopes that she could take night classes and work during the day. Although apprehensive, Wilhel decided to sign up for the program and start researching scholarships.

This vignette shows a brief outline of how a clinician might aid a teen mother in her career development. Everyone's career path is different, and there simply is no one way of pursuing one's career. Wilhel needed a solution that would allow her to support a child and go to school. Not every young woman can go to school without working, especially in her situation. Therefore, it would not have been appropriate for Ms. Johnson to discourage Wilhel working. Looking at her situation realistically, it makes sense for her to work. Although Ms. Johnson came from a different upbringing, she remained empathetic and kept the lines of communication open with Wilhel. It was not necessary to judge or criticize Wilhel; it was important to meet her where she was and help her in the best way possible, considering every aspect of her situation.

In conclusion, it is suggested that we change our language to reflect a more positive perspective. Let teen mothers know that they can, instead of cannot. Do not reprimand them; support them and let them know they have someone to lean on. Remember that the young woman is so much more than a child with a child. She is a young adult with dreams and aspirations that should not fade away because she gave birth.

ADDITIONAL RESOURCE SUGGESTIONS

Centers for Disease Control and Prevention: www.cdc.gov/teenpregnancy/aboutteenpreg.htm
The National Campaign: www.thenationalcampaign.org/why-it-matters/teen-pregnancy
Sexuality Information and Education Council of the United States (SIECUS): www.siecus.org/index.cfm?fuseaction=Page.ViewPage&PageID=1190
U.S. Department of Health & Human Services: http://www.hhs.gov/ash/oah/oah-initiatives/tpp/

REFERENCES

Advocates for Youth: Rights. Respect. Responsibility. (2014). *Components of promising teen pregnancy prevention programs*. Retrieved from http://www.advocatesforyouth.org/publications/publications-a-z/514-components-of-promising-teen-pregnancy-prevention-programs

Albert, B. (2012). *With one voice: America's adults and teens sound off about teen pregnancy*. Washington, DC: The National Campaign to Prevent Teen and Unplanned Pregnancy. Retrieved from http://thenationalcampaign.org/resource/one-voice-2012

American Psychiatric Association. (1994). *Diagnostic and statistical manual of mental disorders* (4th ed.). Washington, DC: Author.

Bhana, D., & Mcambi, S. J. (2013). When schoolgirls become mothers: Reflections from a selected group of teenage girls in Durban. *Perspectives in Education, 31*(1), 11–19.

Brubaker, S. J., & Wright, C. (2006). Identity transformation and family caregiving: Narratives of African American teen mothers. *Journal of Marriage and Family, 68*, 1214–1228.

Byars-Winston, A. M. (2010). The vocational significance of Black identity: Cultural formulation approach to career assessment and career counseling. *Journal of Career Development, 37*(1), 441–464.

Casserly, K. R., Carpenter, A. S., & Halcón, L. (2001). Adolescent parenting: Relationship to school attendance and achievement. *The Journal of School Nursing: The Official Publication of the National Association of School Nurses, 17*(6), 329–335.

Centers for Disease Control and Prevention. (2014). *About teen pregnancy*. Retrieved from http://www.cdc.gov/teenpregnancy/aboutteenpreg.htm

Chablani, A., & Spinney, E. R. (2011). Engaging high-risk young mothers into effective programming: The importance of relationships and relentlessness. *Journal of Family Social Work, 14*, 369–383.

DeVito, J. (2010). How adolescent mothers feel about becoming a parent. *The Journal of Perinatal Education, 19*(2), 25–34.

Dosomething.org. (2014). *11 facts about teen pregnancy*. Retrieved from https://www.dosomething.org/facts/11-facts-about-teen-pregnancy.

Ettinger, J. M. (1991). *Improved career decision making in a changing world: Integrating occupational information and guidance*. Washington, DC: National Occupational Information Coordinating Committee.

Gottfredson, L. (1981). Circumscription and compromise: A developmental theory of occupational aspirations. *Journal of Counseling Psychology Monograph, 28*(6), 545–579.

Gyamfi, P., Brooks-Gunn, J., & Jackson, A. P. (2001). Associations between employment and financial and parental stress in low-income single Black mothers. *Women & Health, 32*(1–2), 119–135.

Hellenga, K., Aber, M. S., & Rhodes, J. E. (2002). African American adolescent mothers' vocational aspiration-expectation gap: Individual, social and environmental influences. *Psychology of Women Quarterly, 26*(3), 200–212.

Herrman, J. W., & Waterhouse, J. K. (2011). What do adolescents think about teen parenting? *Western Journal of Nursing Research, 33*(4), 577–592.

Horton, A. (2006). An American dilemma: Black teenage childbearing. *Journal of Human Behavior in the Social Environment, 13*(2), 15–34.

Julian, T. A., & Kominski, R. A. (2011). Education and synthetic work-life earnings estimates. *American Community Survey Reports*, ACS-14. U.S. Census Bureau, Washington, DC.

Katz, K. S., Rodan, M., Milligan, R., Tan, S., Courtney, L., Gantz, M., . . . Subramanian, S. (2011). Efficacy of a randomized cell phone-based counseling intervention in postponing subsequent pregnancy among teen mothers. *Maternal and Child Health Journal, 15*(Suppl 1) S42–S53.

Key, J. D., Gebregziabher, M. G., Marsh, L. D., & O'Rourke, K. M. (2008). Effectiveness of an intensive, school-based intervention for teen mothers. *The Journal of Adolescent Health: Official Publication of the Society for Adolescent Medicine, 42*(4), 394–400.

Kirby, D., & Lepore, G. (2007). *Sexual risk and protective factors: Factors affecting teen sexual behavior, pregnancy, childbearing and sexually transmitted disease*. Washington, DC: ETR Associated and the National Campaign to Prevent Teen and Unplanned Pregnancy. Retrieved from https://thenationalcampaign.org/sites/default/files/resource-primary-download/protective_factors_full.pdf

Klaw, E. (2008). Understanding urban adolescent mothers' visions of the future in terms of possible selves. *Journal of Human Behavior in the Social Environment, 18*(4), 441–462.

Martin, J. A., Hamilton, B. E., Osterman, M. J., Curtin, S. C., & Matthews, T. J. (2015). Births: Final data for 2013. *National Vital Statistics Reports: From the Centers for Disease Control and Prevention, National Center for Health Statistics, National Vital Statistics System, 64*(1), 1–65.

Martinez, G., Copen, C. E., & Abma, J. C. (2011). Teenagers in the United States: Sexual activity, contraceptive use, and childbearing, 2006–2010 National Survey of Family Growth: National Center for Health Statistics. *Vital Health Stat, 23*(31). Retrieved from http://www.cdc.gov/nchs/data/series/sr_23/sr23_031.pdf

Niles, S. G., & Harris-Bowlsbey, J. E. (2013). *Career development interventions in the 21st century* (4th ed.). Upper Saddle River, NJ: Pearson.

Perper, K., Peterson, K., & Manlove, J. (2010). *Diploma attainment among teen mothers. Child trends, fact sheet publication* #2010–01. Washington, DC: Child Trends.

Prescod, D. J.. & Daire, A. P. (2013). Career interventions considerations for unwed young Black mothers in the United States. *Adultspan Journal, 12*(2), 91–99.

Redwood, T., Pyer, M., & Armstrong-Hallam, S. (2012). Exploring attitudes and behaviour towards teenage pregnancy. *Community Practitioner, 85*(3), 20–23.

Rothenberg, A., & Weissman, A. (2002). The development of programs for pregnant and parenting teens. *Social Work in Health Care, 35*(3), 65–83.

Saint Paul Public Schools. (2012). *AGAPE: Adolescent girls and parenting education.* Retrieved from http://agape.spps.org/

Shearer, D. L., Gyaben, S. L., Gallagher, K. M., & Klerman, L. V. (2005). Selecting, implementing, and evaluating teen pregnancy prevention interventions: Lessons from the CDC's Community Coalition Partnership Programs for the Prevention of Teen Pregnancy. *Journal of Adolescent Health, 37*, 42–52.

Smith-Battle, L. (2007). "I wanna have a good future": Teen mothers rise in educational aspirations, competing demands, and limited school support. *Youth and Society, 38*(3), 348–371.

Swedish, K. A., Rothenberg, A., Fuchs, K., & Rothenberg, G. (2010). Successful life navigation by former participants in a group for pregnant and parenting teens. *Vulnerable Children and Youth Studies, 5,* 310–321.

Turnage, B. F., & Pharris, A. D. (2013). Supporting the pregnant adolescent. *International Journal of Childbirth Education, 28*(4), 72–76.

U.S. Department of Health & Human Services. (2014). *Trends in teen pregnancy and childbearing. Office of Adolescent Health.* Retrieved from http://www.hhs.gov/ash/oah/oah-initiatives/tpp/

Yampolskaya, S., Brown, E. C., & Vargo, A. C. (2004). Assessment of teen pregnancy prevention. Interventions among middle school youth. *Child and Adolescent Social Work Journal, 21,* 69–83.

Zhan, M., & Pandey, S. (2004). Postsecondary education and economic well-being of single mothers and single fathers. *Journal of Marriage and Family, 66,* 661–673.

CHAPTER 13

FORMERLY INCARCERATED INDIVIDUALS

Robert A. Dobmeier

CASE VIGNETTE: YVETTE

Yvette is a 43-year-old African American woman who is scheduled to be released on parole from state prison in 4 months. She has been incarcerated or in detention many times, starting in her early teens. Her current sentence is for check forgery, for which she has also served time in the past. At the time of her last arrest 2 years ago, she was diagnosed with a substance-use disorder. She admits to using many substances including alcohol, cocaine, barbiturates, heroin, and marijuana (pot). She also reports that she has been hospitalized more than once for depression and suicidal behavior. She was born into a poor family and has never met her father. As a young teen, she was expelled from school for fighting and for threatening a teacher. Yvette reports that she has four children aged 10 through 29 years. Yvette reports that she loves animals and would like to get a job with a veterinarian or at a zoo working with animals. She is not hopeful about her potential job opportunities due to her criminal history and lack of a high school diploma or GED. She has mixed feelings about reentering the community. Although she wants to see her children and her girlfriend (she reports that she is bisexual), she fears that she will fall back into her past risky and illegal behaviors. She said she dreams of just moving far away and starting over.

DESCRIPTION OF THE POPULATION

It can be challenging for formerly incarcerated individuals to find work (Chamberlain, Boggess, & Powers, 2014; Kerley & Copes, 2004; Nally, Lockwood, Ho, & Knutson, 2014; Pogrebin, West-Smith, Walker, & Prabha Unnithan, 2014). Securing employment is frequently challenging for parolees, with some studies finding unemployment rates as high as 70% (Travis, 2005). Potential employers may be hesitant to hire former inmates due to perceived risk of employment failure or business loss (Chamberlain et al., 2014; Holzer, Raphael, & Stoll, 2006). Formerly incarcerated persons may have spotty work histories and may have limited education and job training background (Tolbert, 2012; Uggen, Manza, & Thompson, 2006), creating further obstacles to gainful employment. These challenges to becoming employed are exacerbated when the escalating number of individuals released annually from prisons in the United States (Carson & Sabol, 2012), slumping national economy that hinders job creation (Nally et al., 2014), and high density of parolees and probationers in limited geographical areas (Chamberlain et al., 2014) are taken into account.

Incidence/Prevalence of Imprisonment, Release, and Rearrest

In the United States, imprisonment rates have increased from 300,000 in 1980 to more than 1.5 million in 2012 (Carson & Sabol, 2012; Chamberlain et al., 2014; Pogrebin et al., 2014; Wright, Zhang, Farabee, & Braatz, 2014). A result of this exploding prevalence of incarceration is the high number of prisoners released into the community on parole, most of them in search of employment. At the end of 2013, more than 850,000 individuals were on parole (Bonczar & Herberman, 2014). Furthermore, the number of adults on probation at the end of 2013 in the United States was estimated at 3,910,600. All of these individuals resided outside of local jails in community settings, most of them in need of employment.

Reentry, Employment, and Recidivism

Obtaining and keeping a job are closely tied to recidivism rates. Joblessness equates to lack of funds and too much free time, which increase the likelihood of reoffending or violating supervision; increased frequency of incarcerations and periods of unemployment decrease the likelihood of finding gainful employment (Chamberlain et al., 2014; Nally et al., 2014; Needles, 1996; Richmond, 2014; Uggen, 2000; Wang, Mears, & Bales, 2010). In one study, Duwe and Clark (2014) discovered that most offenders will eventually reenter society but more than one third will be convicted of a new felony within 3 years (Minnesota Department of Corrections, 2013). Nationally, within 3 years of release, approximately 68% of former inmates were rearrested and 47% were convicted of a new crime (Langan & Levin, 2002). Moreover, 52% were reincarcerated for a new crime or for a violation of supervision conditions such as not complying with a curfew (Langan & Levin, 2002).

Educational illiteracy, limited job skills and interpersonal skills, criminal history, and neighborhood settings have been cited as obstacles to employment as well as increasing risk for reincarceration (Nally et al., 2014). Lack of education and work experience have also been barriers for female offenders seeking employment and trying to start fresh in the community (Richmond, 2014). Travis (2005) advised that successful reentry into the community can be even more overwhelming when released individuals are denied eligibility for public assistance, education loans, driving privileges, public housing, and food stamps, which are often required for survival and for making progress in society.

Diversity Among Offender Populations

Formerly incarcerated individuals represent diverse groups, all of whom encounter higher unemployment and underemployment rates and higher proportions of arrests and imprisonment than those without a criminal record. Career trajectories are more severe for street-level offenders than for white-collar offenders (Klenowski, 2012). Individuals residing in urban neighborhoods, particularly African American offenders, regularly encounter a notable lack of jobs in their communities, violence, and high crime rates. Many female offenders are underemployed and work in low-skilled jobs that pay menial wages, resulting in some women participating in illegal means of earning income (Richmond, 2014). The number of older adult prisoners is growing. The number of prisoners 50 years and older nationally was twice as high in 2010 compared with 2001 and five times as high as it was in 1990 (Haugebrook, Zgoba, Maschi, Morgen, & Brown, 2010). For older individuals, the likelihood of finding employment on release depends in part on their employment history throughout adulthood. Two other factors that should be considered are substance-use disorders and mental illness. Both of these contribute to obstacles to employment and career development.

HISTORICAL CAREER PATHS/CHOICES AVAILABLE

Until the 1990s, manufacturing jobs in inner city areas were available to those with little education and to ex-offenders. However, a shift in the labor market away from manufacturing in the United States has eliminated many of these types of low-skill jobs (Chamberlain et al., 2014). Thus, it can be difficult for street-level offenders to be able to move into a self-sufficient existence. On the other hand, some research indicates that when white-collar criminals reenter the community they typically return to a job similar to one held before incarceration (Kerley & Copes, 2004). Female offenders become underemployed when they reenter the community, employed in low-skilled jobs making insufficient wages, resulting in some women seeking illegal sources of income (Richmond, 2014). However, prison industries, organized work performed by inmates while they are serving time, are intended to strengthen an inmate's employability by training for a specific vocation such as building furniture, digitizing documents, or sewing uniforms. Such prison-based work training provides the individual with real work experience and the opportunity to learn a trade, learn productive work habits, and develop a strong work ethic (Richmond, 2014).

HISTORY OF CAREER OBSTACLES

Formerly incarcerated individuals regularly encounter one or more obstacles in their attempts to develop a career. Some of the obstacles may be in the culture or community in which they reside, others may be institutional or regulatory in nature, and still others may be within themselves.

Geographical Hurdles

Many parolees live in the inner city, where nearby jobs are likely white-collar business and professional, which reflects the increased competition for low-skill jobs close to where the parolee lives. Thus, the individual would likely have to travel out of the neighborhood, often without access to a car, for each workday. This may be particularly true for African American parolees (Chamberlain et al., 2014). One study suggested that returning to a more disadvantaged baseline neighborhood (greater poverty, unemployment, and residential turnover) was associated with higher risks of absconding and returning to prison for a technical violation, higher risk of arrest, and more adverse labor market outcomes including less employment and lower wages (Morenoff & Harding, 2011). Returning to a more affluent baseline neighborhood (high education, high income, and professional/managerial occupation) was associated with a lower risk of being arrested, absconding, and returning to prison on a technical violation and more positive labor market outcomes including greater employment and wages.

Youths and Young Adults at Risk

A consistent finding is that arrests, convictions, and incarcerations among adolescents and young adults have significant negative effects for them on later economic outcomes such as income, wealth, employment stability, and occupational prestige (Duwe & Clark, 2014; Kerley & Copes, 2004; Western, 2002). Freudenberg, Daniels, Crum, Perkins, and Richie (2008) discovered that adolescent males released from New York City jails exhibited low employment rates, low incomes, and high rearrest rates. Importantly, youths who were able to find employment and health insurance were less likely to be rearrested and to use drugs.

Criminal Background Checks and Discrimination

Although background checks are used to protect the employer, customers, and the public from potentially harmful behavior, they also may cost an ex-offender the opportunity to use skills, knowledge, and experience that would benefit the employer, customers, and the public, along with the individual (Holzer et al., 2006). The reasons for the criminal history screening include the fact that certain occupations are closed to individuals with a felony conviction (Hahn, 1991; Holzer et al., 2006). In addition, in many states, employers can be held liable for the criminal actions of their employees (Bushway, Stoll, & Weiman, 2007). Finally, employers who need to fill positions where employee monitoring is imperfect may place a premium on trustworthiness and may have little confidence in ex-offenders and are less likely to hire people with criminal records (Carson, 2010). Carson proposed that the Equal Employment Opportunity Commission (EEOC) should revise its guidelines to prevent employers from relying on criminal records inappropriately to exclude applicants with a criminal record.

Factors that affect employment after incarceration include race, criminal family background, offender type, age of onset, number of prior arrests, and total time sentenced (Kerley & Copes, 2004). Significant relationships have also been observed between the offender's education and post-release employment with reincarceration (Nally et al., 2014).

White-Collar Crime and Finances

White-collar crime offenders often have exemplary personal histories in terms of mainstream society, are experienced in the ways of society, and have acceptable deportment. This social sensitivity may outweigh the social harms from incarceration and allow the offender to rebound from a fall from grace (Benson, 1984; Kerley & Copes, 2004). However, access to money can be an obstacle to career success for both white-collar criminals who have compromised ethical values in pursuit of financial success and for street-level criminals for whom access to even meager financial resources can be daunting. Search for employment stability can be particularly challenging for vulnerable offender groups in a recession economy where jobs are hard to come by for most people (Nally et al., 2004).

Employment Obstacles for Female Offenders

Low employment rates and high recidivism are twin problems for female offenders (Freudenberg et al., 2008). Lack of education and training (Richmond, 2014), stigmatization from reincarceration and low wages (Freudenberg et al., 2008; Harm & Phillips, 2001), and substance-use problems and child care responsibilities (Owen & Bloom, 1995) have been identified as the primary reasons why female offenders are not employed. In addition, Uggen and Kruttschnitt (1998) found that women reported that they could earn more money through crime than in legitimate employment. It is likely that to help women avoid reincarceration, simultaneous attention needs to be given to improving women's capacity to earn a living wage, care for children, be provided health insurance, and have access to effective substance-abuse treatment. Furthermore, Estrada and Nilsson (2012) completed a study and its findings suggested that higher rates of poverty, social isolation, and early mortality associated with criminal behavior of women might contribute to the high unemployment and stunted repressed career aspirations often seen among some groups of female offenders. It seems urgent that researchers and policy makers continue efforts to discover interventions that will help formerly incarcerated women to develop a holistic lifestyle comprised of health, productive relationships and child caretaking, career development, and adequate income.

Employment Obstacles for Aging Offenders

In addition to the common challenges to employment for aging persons such as physical changes to one's body and loss of partner and friends who have died, older adults who are imprisoned also face the stigma of incarceration, broken employment history, and often loss of support from family and significant others (Haugebrook et al., 2010). Moreover, there is a growing body of evidence that many older offenders have experienced trauma (Courtney & Maschi, 2013; Haugebrook et al., 2010). The cumulative effect of trauma and stress over a lifetime can contribute to anxiety, alienation, misuse of substances, and even depression (Courtney & Maschi, 2013), all of which undermine one's readiness for maintaining career objectives as high-order priorities. For incarcerated older offenders, Reimer (2008) advised modification of existing work and education programs to include health care education, preventive medicine, and counseling.

Substance-Use Disorders as an Obstacle to Employment

Many researchers have reported that alcohol and other substance-use problems create substantial challenges for former prisoners as they enter the labor market after incarceration (e.g., Gideon, 2010; Kemp, Savitz, Thompson, & Zanis, 2004; O'Connell, Enev, Martin, & Inciardi, 2007; Sung & Chu, 2011; Visher, Debus-Sherrill, Yahner, 2011); approximately 80% of parolees have a history of substance abuse and nearly all are unemployed following release from prison (Kemp et al., 2004). Statistics indicate that the unemployment rate consistently ranged between approximately 65% and 85% for persons who were using opiates, primarily heroin, just before their entry into a drug user treatment program (Koo, Chitwood, & Sánchez, 2007).

Mental Illness as an Obstacle to Employment

The U.S. Office of Justice Programs, taking a broad view of what constitutes a psychiatric problem, reported that at midyear 2005, more than half of all prison and jail inmates had a mental health problem, including 705,600 inmates in state prisons, 78,800 in federal prisons, and 479,900 in local jails. These estimates represented approximately 56% of state prisoners, 45% of federal prisoners, and 64% of jail inmates (James & Glaze, 2006). For individuals with serious mental illness, incarceration poses a greater risk of being raped or otherwise victimized, and they are disproportionately held in solitary confinement; these individuals also frequently attempt suicide. Because treatment of mental illness is often not available behind bars, symptoms often get worse, sometimes leading to self-mutilation (National Sheriffs' Association, Treatment Advocacy Center, 2014). Older inmates face a greater incidence of trauma-induced stress, from experiences in prison as well as the community, that need to be treated (Haugebrook et al., 2010).

Homelessness and co-occurring substance-use disorders contribute to commission of criminal acts that often result in incarceration. There is a tremendous need to address this problem given the risk of harm to this vulnerable mentally-ill population. Timely delivery of case management services at the time of release from prison or jail, mental health counseling in the community and in prisons and jails, and close coordination and communication between criminal justice and mental health systems are required (Freudenberg et al., 2008; Hawthorne et al., 2012; Veysey, Ostermann, & Lanterman, 2014).

EXPECTED CAREER DEVELOPMENT NEEDS

In light of the evidence from the professional literature, it seems that in order for parolees and other ex-offenders to succeed in establishing a traditional career, a range of needs must be recognized. Some of those needs will be addressed in this section—for example, education, housing, aftercare services, child care, social support, treatment, policy changes, employment support, and job training.

Education and Job Training

Often men and women with a history of street-level crime, many of whom are African American and reside in inner city neighborhoods, need job training in new kinds of industries such as information processing and medical technology. Many in these groups will need to complete a GED, and possibly college level preparation, in order to meet prerequisites for job training (Chamberlain et al., 2014; Nally et al., 2014). It can be mutually beneficial to the individual (young adult, female offender, substance user), the employer, and to society for inmates to have access to secondary and postsecondary education while serving time (Duwe & Clark, 2014). Further research into the needs of women beyond that of employment to avoid reincarceration is necessary. There is some evidence that treatment of drug addiction and assistance with childcare (Richmond, 2014) may be particularly important needs for female offenders. For a subgroup of women from highly impoverished backgrounds and with lifelong histories of criminal behavior (Estrada & Nilsson, 2012), counseling and therapeutic supervision may prove valuable.

Public Policy Changes

Freudenberg et al. (2008) reported that public policies on employment, drug treatment, housing, and health care often blocked successful reentry into society from jail for women and adolescent males, suggesting the need for new policies that support successful reentry into society. Carson (2010) advised that the Equal Opportunity Commission should revise its guidelines to prevent employers from relying on criminal records inappropriately. There is a need to develop public policies that strike a balance between ensuring the safety of the public and educating the public about the effectiveness of rehabilitation versus punishment of offenders. Rehabilitation programs need to educate offenders about how to present themselves in employment settings in ways that focus on their achievements, knowledge, and job skills.

The redirection of seriously mental ill persons from treatment settings to criminal settings needs to be addressed on a policy level by state governments and by the federal government (Hawthorne et al., 2012). There is a need for the criminal justice and mental health systems, including treatment of co-occurring substance-use disorders (Veysey et al., 2014), to work in an integrated way to ensure treatment and appropriate placement of mentally ill persons that is consistent with their level of risk to themselves and to society and with their treatment needs.

A New Setting With Accompanying Resources

A number of empirical studies have reported (Morenoff & Harding, 2011; Nally et al., 2014), and interviews with inmates corroborate, that the street-level offenders returning from incarceration to the very neighborhood where their criminal history started and developed often increases the likelihood of recidivism. People, places, and things that are known and readily accessible to the individual can make returning to criminal behavior very convenient, particularly when the basic needs of income for self and family, jobs, transportation outside of the neighborhood, and other resources are not available. It is beneficial when inmates released to the community from prisons and jails have options of living in other communities (Chamberlain et al., 2014; Morenoff & Harding, 2011; Nally et al., 2014).

Educating High School and College Students on Ethical Work Practices

The world of white-collar crime is uniquely challenging because the values that underlie many white-collar crimes are inherent to a culture that celebrates and rewards financial achievement, entrepreneurial spirit, assertiveness in business interactions, influence over people, and creativity. There is often a thin line between these work values in the marketplace and unethical behavior that harms others or illegal behavior that breaks the law. There is a need to sensitize workers about social and legal consequences to illegal and unethical business behavior (Benson, 1984; Kerley & Copes, 2004). Klenowski (2012) advocated for general education in high school and college of ethical behavior on the job.

SERVICES FOR INCARCERATED OLDER ADULTS

Rising numbers of adults in their last years of life remain in prison settings serving life sentences or sentences that will not expire before the onset of disabilities or even death. In a humane society, there is a need to provide medical care for those with a terminal illness and specialized long-term care for those with debilitating conditions (Haugebrook et al., 2010). The growing evidence that many older offenders have experienced a history of trauma that has created mental health problems such as anxiety, depression, and social isolation, sometimes preventing the individual from pursuing career-oriented activities in prison or in the community, needs to be met with the offer of mental health assessment and mental health counseling when indicated (Courtney & Maschi, 2013; Haugebrook et al., 2010).

CAREER COUNSELING INTERVENTIONS

Intervention strategies to assist formerly incarcerated individuals to get and keep jobs and to avoid reincarceration emerge from diverse models representing a range of offender needs. Examples include substance-abuse treatment (Kemp et al., 2004; National Sheriffs' Association, Treatment Advocacy Center, 2014; O'Connell et al., 2007; Sung & Chu, 2011); employer commitment to hiring offenders (Carson, 2010); continuity models (Lattimore & Visher, 2013; Veysey et al., 2014) matching prison and community services; comprehensive reentry strategies (Freudenberg et al., 2008; Kemp et al., 2004; Lattimore & Visher, 2013; Northcutt Bohmert & Duwe, 2012; Pogrebin et al., 2014; Travis, 2005) reflecting clustering of services to meet multiple reentry needs; single employment programs (Kemp et al., 2004; Northcutt Bohmert & Duwe, 2012; Uggen, 2000) evaluating stand-alone offender employment programs; neighborhood of parolee residence interventions (Morenoff & Harding, 2011; Nally et al., 2014); individual change (Lattimore & Visher, 2013; Wright et al., 2014) focusing on the inmate's motivation to change; and spirituality or religion as a resource to individuals as they face the stress of reentry and high performance expectations from family, guards and deputies, probation officers, the public, and themselves (Bakken, DeCamp, & Visher, 2014; Gockel & Burton, 2013).

At this time, there is no clear direction as to a single evidence-based intervention that can be used to ensure successful reentry and employment success on the one hand and prevent reincarceration on the other. The mixed findings of multiple outcome studies reflect the multidimensional nature of formerly incarcerated individuals' experiences with career development. Career is more than having a job or series of jobs. It entails the life context in which one's work takes place. Support from family, parole supervisors, employers, communities, government policies, and treatment providers, when appropriate, is essential. It seems that focusing on single interventions to achieve employment and a crime-free lifestyle, be they employment, job training, education, or neighborhood of residence is insufficient. A number of researchers are coming to the conclusion that it is necessary to provide an array of services around the individual based on need. Rather than being program centered, criminal justice, mental health, substance use, and other systems who work with ex-offenders need to be person centered (see Appendix M for additional information).

Services Based on Need

Successful reentry might be evaluated by multiple outcomes and not just reincarceration, for example, employment, substance use, health, and mental health (Lattimore & Visher, 2013). Parole officers could assist their cases with reading job listings in a newspaper or on a computer in a public library, making referrals to employment agencies, and linking parolees with employment centers to help with developing a resume. Assistance with learning basic life skills through courses in budgeting, parenting, and interviewing would be beneficial for some. Others will require help with finding safe housing, medical care, and mentoring with clergy (Veysey et al., 2014). Still others will need coaching and resources to relocate to a community that is conducive to finding social supports and legal economic opportunities (Morenoff & Harding, 2011). Other services that comprise a continuum of care from the institution to the community are education (GED and college; Duwe & Clark, 2014; Northcutt Bohmert & Duwe, 2012); health insurance for self and children (Freudenberg et al., 2008); assistance with meeting financial obligations (Pogrebin et al., 2014); group and/or individual counseling; and mental health services for those facing mental illness, substance abuse, or co-occurring disorders (Veysey et al., 2014; Wright et al., 2014).

A growing number of researchers are recommending that spirituality or religion, depending on the individual's beliefs, be recognized as assisting many offending individuals to cope with stress and social demands that usually accompany reentry to the community. Many individuals in the criminal justice system desire to start fresh and are in need of support and services to help them get started. It is possible that the financial resources currently spent on incarceration could be channeled into services that assist offenders to set out in a new direction to create or to strengthen their career trajectory.

REVISITING THE CASE OF YVETTE

Yvette has multiple needs requiring attention to get her life back on track. She is hoping that her parole officer can help her to work with the community organizations to get the specific services that she needs as indicated in the following. She has talked with her parole officer about moving into a new community if her children and girlfriend are able to live with her. She believes that being in a new setting will keep her away from the people and places that get her into trouble. She has started taking courses and plans to earn her GED before being released. She would like to go to the community college but states that she will need to find out about transportation and she needs to think about childcare for her daughter. She recognizes that using drugs has caused many problems for her and she would like to give them up, but feels she will need help from a chemical dependency provider. She continues to get depressed at times and when this has happened in the past, she "goes into herself" and will sleep for days at a time. She would like to see a counselor and to get medication for her depression. She has not been able to get medication for her depression in the prison. She also needs to make sure that she has Medicaid coverage for herself and her two younger children. She believes that the intensive supervision that she will receive on release will help her to start out in the right direction. She feels motivated to be successful this time because she does not want to cause more heartache for her children and her girlfriend. She also knows that she needs to take care of her health if she wants to be around to watch her children grow up. She thinks that counseling can help her to understand herself better and to get the strength to follow through on her plans. Eventually, she would like to be able to work with animals. She would like to start college coursework to pursue a career as a veterinarian. In the meanwhile, she will need money to supplement her girlfriend's paycheck. She is hoping that she can get public assistance and food stamps to help them out until she can get on her feet and get a job. She is also hoping that her parole officer and her college teachers can guide her regarding who to contact to work in a veterinarian's office.

ADDITIONAL RESOURCE SUGGESTIONS

ACLU Criminal Law Reform: www.aclu.org/criminal-law-reform

American Civil Liberties Union (ACLU) Coalition Letter to the House Over-Criminalization Task Force Regarding Immigration Prosecutions: www.aclu.org/sites/default/files/assets/14_5_5_coalition_letter_to_the_over-criminalization_task_force_re_immigration_prosecutions_final.pdf

Proactive Community Supervision in Maryland: Changing Offender Outcomes, February 2006, Prepared by a joint research team: Faye S. Taxman, PhD, Virginia Commonwealth University; Christina Yancey, MA, University of Maryland; Jeanne E. Bilanin, PhD, University of Maryland: www.dpscs.state.md.us/publicinfo/publications/pdfs/PCS_Evaluation_Feb06.pdf

SAMHSA NREPP Correctional Therapeutic Community for Substance Abusers: www.nrepp.samhsa.gov/ViewIntervention.aspx?id=338

SAMHSA NREPP Mendota Juvenile Treatment Center Program: www.nrepp.samhsa.gov/ViewIntervention.aspx?id=38

SAMHSA NREPP Moral Reconation Therapy: www.nrepp.samhsa.gov/ViewIntervention.aspx?id=34

SAMHSA NREPP: www.samhsa.gov/nrepp and www.nrepp.samhsa.gov

U.S. Department of Justice, Office of Justice Programs, Ready4Reentry Prisoner Reentry Toolkit for Faith-Based and Community Initiatives, United States Department of Labor, Center for Faith-Based and Community Initiatives: ojp.gov/fbnp/pdfs/R4W_toolkit.pdf

U.S. Department of Justice, Office of Justice Programs, Reentry Partnerships, and Innovative Resources Highlighted at the Second Chances and Safer Communities Conference: ojp.gov/newsroom/pressreleases/2012/ojppr052212.pdf

REFERENCES

Bakken, N. W., DeCamp, W., & Visher, C. A. (2014). Spirituality and desistance from substance use among reentering offenders. *International Journal of Offender Therapy and Comparative Criminology, 58*(11), 1321–1339.

Benson, M. L. (1984). The fall from grace: Loss of occupational status as a consequence of conviction for a white-collar crime. *Criminology, 22*, 573–593.

Bonczar, T., & Herberman, E. (2014). *Probation and parole in the United States, 2013*. Bureau of Justice Statistics. Retrieved from http://www.bjs.gov/index.cfm?ty=pbdetail&iid=5135

Bushway, S., Stoll, M. A., & Weiman, D. F. (2007). Introduction. In S. Bushway, M. A. Stoll, & D. F. Weiman (Eds.), *Barriers to reentry? The labor market for released prisoners in post-industrial America* (pp. 1–26). New York, NY: Russell Sage Foundation.

Carson, E. J. (2010). Off the record: Why the EEOC should change its guidelines regarding employers' consideration of employees' criminal records during the hiring process. *The Journal of Corporation Law, 36*(1), 221–237.

Carson, E., & Sabol, W. (2012). *Prisoners in 2011*. NCJ 239808. Washington, DC: U.S. Department of Justice, Bureau of Justice Statistics.

Chamberlain, A. W., Boggess, L. N., & Powers, R. A. (2014). The impact of the spatial mismatch between parolee and employment locations on recidivism. *Journal of Crime and Justice*, 1–23. Retrieved from http://dx.doi.org/10.1080/0735648X.2014.965264

Courtney, D., & Maschi, T. (2013). Trauma and stress among older adults in prison: Breaking the cycle of silence. *Traumatology, 19*, 73–81. doi:10.1177/1534765612437378

Duwe, G., & Clark, V. (2014). The effects of prison-based educational programming on recidivism and employment. *The Prison Journal, 94*, 454–478. doi: 10.1177/0032885514548009

Estrada, F., & Nilsson, A. (2012). Does it cost more to be a female offender? A life-course study of childhood circumstances, crime, drug abuse, and living conditions. *Feminist Criminology, 7*, 196–219. doi: 10.1177/155708511142978

Freudenberg, N., Daniels, J., Crum, M., Perkins, T., & Richie, B. E. (2008). Coming home from jail: The social and health consequences of community reentry for women, male adolescents, and their families and communities. *American Journal of Public Health, 98*(9 Suppl.), S191–S202.

Gideon, L. (2010). Drug offenders' perceptions of motivation: The role of motivation in rehabilitation and reintegration. *International Journal of Offender Therapy and Comparative Criminology, 54*(4), 597–610.

Gockel, A., & Burton, D. (2013). Can God help? Religion and spirituality among adolescent male sex offenders. *Journal of Child & Adolescent Trauma, 6*, 274–286. doi: 10.1080/19361521.2013.836584

Hahn, J. M. (1991). Pre-employment information services: Employers beware. *Employee Relations Law Journal, 17*, 45–69.

Harm, N. J., & Phillips, S. D. (2001). You can't go home again: Women and criminal recidivism. *Journal of Offender Rehabilitation, 32*, 3–21.

Haugebrook, S., Zgoba, K. M., Maschi, T., Morgen, K., & Brown, D. (2010). Trauma, stress, health, and mental health issues among ethnically diverse older adult prisoners. *Journal of Correctional Health Care, 16*(3), 220–229.

Hawthorne, W. B., Folsom, D. P., Sommerfeld, D. H., Lanouette, N. M., Lewis, M., Aarons, G. A., . . . Jeste, D. V. (2012). Incarceration among adults who are in the public mental health system: Rates, risk factors, and short-term outcomes. *Psychiatry Online, 63*(1), 26–32. Retrieved from http://psychiatryonline.org/doi/full/10.1176/appi.ps.201000505

Holzer, H. J., Raphael, S., & Stoll, M. A. (2006). Perceived criminality, criminal background checks, and the racial hiring practices of employers. *Journal of Law and Economics, 49*, 451–480.

James, D. J., & Glaze, L. E. (2006). *Mental health problems of prison and jail inmates*. Washington, DC: Bureau of Justice Statistics, Office of Justice Programs, U.S. Department of Justice. Retrieved from http://www.bjs.gov/content/pub/pdf/mhppji.pdf

Kemp, K., Savitz, B., Thompson, W., & Zanis, D. A. (2004). Developing employment services for criminal justice clients enrolled in drug user treatment programs. *Substance Use & Misuse, 39*(13–14), 2491–2511.

Kerley, K. R., & Copes, H. (2004). The effects of criminal justice contact on employment stability for white-collar and street-level offenders. *International Journal of Offender Therapy and Comparative Criminology, 48*(1), 65–84.

Klenowski, P. M. (2012). Learning the good with the bad: Are occupational white-collar offenders taught how to neutralize their crimes? *Criminal Justice Review, 37*, 461–477. doi: 10.1177/0734016812465874

Koo, D. J., Chitwood, D. D., & Sánchez, J. (2007). Factors for employment: A case-control study of fully employed and unemployed heroin users. *Substance Use & Misuse, 42*(7), 1035–1054.

Langan, P. A., & Levin, D. J. (2002). *Recidivism of prisoners released in 1994*. Washington, DC: Bureau of Justice Statistics. Retrieved from http://www.bjs.gov/content/pub/pdf/rpr94.pdf

Lattimore, P. K., & Visher, C. A. (2013). The impact of prison reentry services on short-term outcomes: Evidence from a multisite evaluation. *Evaluation Review, 37*(3–4), 274–313.

Minnesota Department of Corrections. (2013). *Performance report: Fiscal year 2012*. St Paul: Author. Retrieved from http://www.doc.state.mn.us/PAGES/files/large-files/Publications/legislative-reports/2012DOCPerformanceReport.pdf

Morenoff, J. D., & Harding, D. J. (2011). *Final technical report: Neighborhoods, recidivism, and employment among returning prisoners*. Washington, DC: U.S. Department of Justice. Retrieved from https://www.ncjrs.gov/pdffiles1/nij/grants/236436.pdf

Nally, J. M., Lockwood, S., Ho, T., & Knutson, K. (2014). Post-release recidivism and employment among different types of released offenders: A 5-year follow-up study in the United States. *International Journal of Criminal Justice Sciences, 9*, 16–34.

National Sheriffs' Association, Treatment Advocacy Center. (2014). *The treatment of persons with mental illness in prisons and jails: A state survey*. Retrieved from http://tacreports.org/storage/documents/treatment-behind-bars/treatment-behind-bars.pdf

Needles, K. E. (1996). Go directly to jail and do not collect? A long-term study of recidivism, employment, and earnings patterns among prison releases. *Journal of Research in Crime & Delinquency, 33*, 471–488.

Northcutt Bohmert, M., & Duwe, G. (2012). Minnesota's affordable homes program: Evaluating the effects of a prison work program on recidivism, employment and cost avoidance. *Criminal Justice Policy Review, 23*, 327–351. doi: 10.1177/0887403411411911

O'Connell, D. J., Enev, T. N., Martin, S. S., & Inciardi, J. A. (2007). Working toward recovery: The interplay of past treatment and economic status in long-term outcomes for drug-involved offenders. *Substance Use & Misuse, 42*(7), 1089–1107.

Owen, B., & Bloom, B. (1995). Profiling women prisoners: Findings from national surveys and a California sample. *The Prison Journal, 75*, 165–185.

Pogrebin, M., West-Smith, M., Walker, A., & Prabha Unnithan, N. (2014). Employment isn't enough: Financial obstacles experienced by ex-prisoners during the reentry process. *Criminal Justice Review, 39*, 394–410. doi:10.1177/0734016814540303

Reimer, G. (2008). The graying of the U.S. prisoner population. *Journal of Correctional Health Care, 14*, 202–208. doi:10.1177/1078345808318123

Richmond, K. M. (2014). The impact of Federal Prison Industries Employment on the recidivism outcomes of female inmates. *Justice Quarterly, 31*, 719–745. doi:10.1080/07418825.2012.668924

Sung, H. E., & Chu, D. (2011). The impact of substance user treatment participation on legal employment and income among probationers and parolees. *Substance Use & Misuse, 46*(12), 1523–1535.

Tolbert, M. (2012). *A reentry education model: Supporting education and career advancement for low-skill individuals in corrections*. Washington, DC: U.S. Department of Education, Office of Vocational and Adult Education. Retrieved from http://www2.ed.gov/about/offices/list/ovae/pi/AdultEd/reentry-model.pdf

Travis, J. (2005). *But they all come back: Facing the challenges of prisoner reentry*. Washington, DC: Urban Institute Press.

Uggen, C. (2000). Work as a turning point in the life course of criminals: A duration model of age, employment, and recidivism. *American Sociological Review, 65*, 529–546.

Uggen, C., & Kruttschnitt, C. (1998). Crime in the breaking: Gender differences in desistance. *Law & Society Review, 32*, 339–366.

Uggen, C., Manza, J., & Thompson, M. (2006). Citizenship, democracy, and the civic reintegration of criminal offenders. *The Annals of the American Academy of Political and Social Science, 605*, 281–310.

Veysey, B. M., Ostermann, M., & Lanterman, J. L. (2014). The effectiveness of enhanced parole supervision and community services: New Jersey's Serious and Violent Offender Reentry Initiative. *The Prison Journal, 94*(4), 435–453. doi:10.1177/0032885514548007

Visher, C. A., Debus-Sherrill, S. A., & Yahner, J. (2011). Employment after prison: A longitudinal study of former prisoners. *Justice Quarterly, 28*(5), 698–718. doi:10.1080/07418825.2010.535553

Wang, X., Mears, D. P., & Bales, W. D. (2010). Race specific employment contexts and recidivism. *Criminology, 48*(4), 1171–1211.

Western, B. (2002). The impact of incarceration on wage mobility and inequality. *American Sociological Review, 67*, 526–546.

Wright, B. J., Zhang, S. X., Farabee, D., & Braatz, R. (2014). Prisoner reentry research from 2000 to 2010: Results of a narrative review. *Criminal Justice Review, 39*, 37–57. doi:10.1177/0734016813501192

CHAPTER 14

LESBIAN, GAY, BISEXUAL, AND TRANSGENDER INDIVIDUALS

Jane Rheineck, Suzanna M. Wise, and Jakendra D. Williams

CASE VIGNETTE: DILLON

Dillon is a 45-year-old gay male whose employment was recently terminated. Due to downsizing, he was recently "let go" from his mid-management position at a financial institution. The company he worked for provided his full medical benefits for him, Dillon's husband, and their two children (aged 7 and 10 years). Dillon's partner is an artist and sells his work on consignment throughout the region, which places Dillon in the role of primary financial support and sole provider for medical benefits.

Dillon and Charlie have a "traditional" lifestyle. They are legally married in the state they reside in. Dillon and Charlie live openly in their current community and have created a community of family with their friends. The family of origin for both is limited, and they reside more than 1,000 miles away. Luckily, Dillon's skill set is strong enough to quickly earn him an interview at a corporation some distance away from their current home. Unsure how to weigh the various pros and cons of the offer, Dillon decides to seek career counseling. It is essential that the career counselor who is chosen fully understands the unique considerations and the basic needs of a gay couple and their children.

CAREER COUNSELING NEEDS WITHIN THE LESBIAN, GAY, BISEXUAL, AND TRANSGENDER (LGBT) COMMUNITY

The LGBT community has made tremendous legal, social, and political progress over the last two decades; yet, LGBT persons still encounter barriers and obstacles in ways that can be very different than their heterosexual counterparts. Although the implementation of laws and further social acceptance has occurred, facilitating a cultural shift, one can argue that workplace discrimination, employee benefits, and opportunities for advancement can still be limited, especially from state to state or from employer to employer. So, in addition to customary issues such as identity management and discrimination, the career development process and the barriers for LGBT individuals and families have also shifted. The implementation of civil rights laws has certainly had a positive impact, but the decision-making process for career choices presents some new and different challenges. Even with laws and public policies changing, attitudes have not always changed as quickly.

An increase in LGBT civil rights has led to new laws and protections never afforded to the LGBT community before; thus, it may be wondered why there is a need to discuss LGBT career issues as different or unique. Despite visibility and acceptance, marginalized groups, including LGBT persons, continue to face job discrimination (Pope et al., 2004). Sexual orientation continues to be a workplace issue because no federal laws protect LGBT individuals from employment discrimination (Human Rights Campaign [HRC], 2014). Research has shown that anywhere from 15% to 43% of lesbian, gay, and bisexual people have experienced discrimination and harassment in the workplace. Moreover, a staggering 90% of transgender workers report some form of harassment or mistreatment on the job (HRC, 2014). These workplace abuses pose a threat to the economic security of LGBT workers (Center for American Progress, 2011). Sexual orientation is invisible to most people because of heterosexual ubiquity; regardless of more social acceptance, the United States is divided on the social appropriateness of sexual or affectional affiliation.

HISTORICAL PERSPECTIVE

When exploring career options, there have been two areas of primary concern for the members of the LGBT community when navigating the workforce: (a) perceived and actual threats to employment achievement and security based on self-disclosure, and (b) the actual experience of discrimination based on sexual and gender orientation (Degges-White & Shoffner, 2002). House (2004) identified several barriers for LGBT individuals impacting career choices: (a) deciding whether or when to disclose sexual orientation, (b) lack of support from peers, (c) inability to be "open" about intimate relationships, (d) a hostile work environment, (e) harassment from employer, (f) retention discrimination, and (g) low self-esteem due to societal stigma regarding sexual orientation. Someone who identifies as LGBT may not encounter these barriers, but one has to consider them.

Members of the LGBT community may experience negative effects due to stereotypes, discrimination, and environmental barriers that may impede career development (Elliott, 1993; Fassinger, 1991; Hetherington & Orzek, 1989). For LGBT persons, coming out can be an ongoing process that has been reexperienced throughout their life span. Sexual minorities, much like other minority groups, are distinct from the majority simply because of the multiple institutional and individual forms of oppression inflicted on them.

Occupational Choices

Although occupational stereotypes can be harmful, members of the LGBT community feel less constrained by gender stereotypes (Pope et al., 2004). Lesbians in particular may venture into traditional male occupations because they do not feel the need to accommodate society's ideas of what women's roles are. Although the "helping professions" may be perceived as "women's jobs," 84% of lesbian respondents in one study (Rheineck, 2005) reported being employed in this sector.

Most of these women chose these professions because of feeling safe or wanting to give back.

Conversely, gay men struggle with male gender expectations. Many occupational fields, especially those that have been male dominated, are typified by the expectation that those who hold positions in these fields will typify strong masculinity and heterosexuality. These biases may interfere with career choices (Gedro, 2007; Miller, 1995). Gender socialization is predicated on success and achievement, and when gay men buy into those messages they may experience workplace harassment and prejudicial treatment because of their sexual orientation (Nam Can Tau & Cartel, 2004).

EXPECTED CAREER DEVELOPMENT NEEDS

LGBT individuals often reexperience the coming out process with every new employment experience. Managing career development and sexual identity development simultaneously can create a disconnect for the individual. Previous research found that developmental theory (Super, 1990) and career construction theory (Savickas, 2005) are relevant because sexual identity and social acceptance impact a person when implementing self-concept in career development (Schmidt & Nilsson, 2006). The identity development process occurs concurrently with career development. Providing support, identifying individual career needs, understanding the barriers and challenges, and helping to develop sexual identity for the LGBT community provide counselors with an operational framework.

Super's Life-Span Approach

Using Super's (1990) Life-Span Approach to career development, Dunkle (1996) explored its application to gay men and lesbians. Super attached chronological age to his stages of career development, but sexual identity development may not occur simultaneously to one's age. The *growth stage*, a time when an individual is developing interests, values, and beliefs, traditionally occurs in childhood. Although little was known about gay and lesbian identity development during this time, research indicated that lesbians and gay men experienced confusion and isolation from early childhood (Green, 1987; Sophie, 1985/1986). Schmidt and Nilsson (2006) reported that because of variables such as social oppression and sexual identity, LGBT youth may not be able to negotiate the career development process at the same time they are beginning to recognize and understand that their sexual identities are different. Sophie (1985/1986) also postulated that adults going through the coming out process will have similar experiences; many experience a "second" adolescence.

The *exploration stage* is identified as vocational maturity, the readiness to complete the various stage-related tasks. An individual at this stage is exploring the work environment and career choice becomes clearer. At the early stages of identity development, vocational maturity was very low due to internalized homophobia and a limited support system (Schmidt & Nilsson, 2006; Shidlo, 1994). The early stressors in sexual identity formation, as well as putting one's energy toward sexual identity development, make one's career development less salient, leading to difficulties making a career choice during the exploration stage (Dunkle, 1996; Schmidt & Nilsson, 2006).

It has been reported that a deeper commitment to career has been developed through the *establishment stage*. During this stage, the self-concept has become increasingly stable (Super, 1990). Dunkle (1996) postulated that vocational maturity has been quite low as individuals may not have completed the self-exploration of the previous stage. As a result, individuals may have chosen a career that was based on incomplete information about self (Dunkle, 1996).

The *maintenance stage* involves completing tasks such as attaining achievement, competing with younger people starting their careers, and developing creative ways to cope with changes in the workplace (Super, 1990). Finally, a reduction in work hours and the preparation for retirement has typically been characteristic of the *disengagement stage*. Berger (1982) argued that coming out for older adults may have been less stressful because of their lower dependence on financial and emotional support from family.

Coming out later in life may introduce other stressors such as discrimination (real or perceived), lack of familial support in securing adequate medical care, housing, spirituality, mental health, and social networks (Orel, 2014). This generation (older than 65 years) grew up in a time where homosexuality was illegal and often dangerous. They also may be more accustomed to the stigmatization and may have passed for many years as heterosexual.

In short, Hetherington (1991) theorized that LGBT individuals who are early in their sexual identity development put other aspects of development on hold to cope with confusion over sexual identity. Thus, she proposed "during the early stages [of sexual identity development], a bottleneck effect may disallow career exploration" (Hetherington, 1991, p. 134).

EFFECTIVE CAREER COUNSELING INTERVENTIONS

A model for effective practice, *Career Counseling With Under Served Populations (CCUSP)*, was developed by Dr. Mark Pope (2011) and was originally based on his earlier research in career development with LGBT individuals. The following list provides a summary of the 13 key components that provide culturally appropriate career services.

Key 1: Take responsibility for your biases and prejudices. This is the foundational key on which all the others are built and is critical for career counselors, vocational psychologists, and all career development specialists. Bias can affect the interventions that are selected as well as how such interventions are used.

Key 2: Cultural identity development. Cultural identity development is the one element consistently recommended in the research literature as a critical component in successful career counseling with culturally diverse adults.

Key 3: Know the special issues of specific cultures. This awareness is essential for career counselors to provide effective services.

Key 4: Directly address issues of discrimination. Addressing these issues and preparing clients to handle the manifestations of racism, sexism, heterosexism, and other forms of discrimination is a primary role of the career counselor.

Key 5: Group career counseling has a strong appeal to many racial and ethnic minority clients. Several characteristics of group-oriented or collectivist cultures—primacy of group survival over individual survival, interdependency, connectedness—make them especially suited to group career counseling.

Key 6: The role of the family. Family, defined as broad and extended, is extremely important in the delivery of career counseling to individuals from collectivist cultures.

Key 7: Special issues of dual-career couples.

Key 8: Special issues when using career assessment instruments with individuals from different cultural communities. Special procedures have been recommended for using formal assessment tools with diverse individuals.

Key 9: Assist clients in overcoming internalized negative stereotypes or internalized oppression. This is a critical role of the career counselor because such stereotypes or internalized oppression can provide significant barriers to successful outcomes.

Key 10: Coming out issues with clients whose cultural membership is not obvious. The issue of whether to disclose one's culture to others is a unique issue for some clients (e.g., gay/lesbian/bisexual/transgender, and multiple race/ethnicity). In the sexual minority counseling literature, this is termed as coming out and has been central for gay men and lesbians who are seeking career counseling.

Key 11: To overcome societal stereotyping as a limitation on occupational choice, use occupational role model and networking interventions. Such interventions are very important for special populations that have historically been limited in their occupational choices.

Key 12: Provide a supportive environment in your office. At the programmatic level, this is one simple and concrete way to inform others that a career counselor is supportive of the struggles of culturally diverse persons.

Key 13: Provide positive and social advocacy for your culturally diverse clients. Career counselors working with any special cultural group must be supportive, going beyond "do no harm" to encompass a positive advocacy for their clients and their rights.

Using these keys as guidelines, appropriate holistic career counseling is a likely outcome. An individual's identity development occurs at a highly individual rate, so there is seldom a one-size-fits-all intervention plan. Please see Appendix N for additional suggestions for working with diverse groups.

UNDERSTANDING THE UNIQUE NEEDS OF TRANSGENDER CLIENTS IN THE WORKPLACE

Transgender individuals face covert and overt discrimination in virtually every context of life, including the workplace, as they navigate the complex process of gender transition and identity development. Career decision making is uniquely affected by this process due to implications for obtaining, negotiating, and retaining employment; thus, it is essential for career counselors and other vocational professionals to be aware of and responsive to the distinctive needs of this population. Although social progress is clearly evident for sexual minorities with regard to marriage equality and increased visibility, individuals who do not fit the traditional gender binary continue to face myriad systemic and individual-based challenges. Nongender binary identified individuals experience a stark lack of privilege that *cis-normative* (birth gender is same as claimed gender) individuals take for granted on a daily basis, such as restroom selection, access to needed health care services, preferred pronoun usage, and job security (Killermann, 2013). Counselors must be advocates for social justice for multicultural clients, especially when they are at a high risk of harm like the current population of transgender individuals.

A widely cited Williams Institute (2011) report estimated the size of the transgender population at 0.3% to 0.5% of the population in the United States, and contributors to this and another (Williams Institute, 2014a) report pointed out that it is difficult to ascertain an accurate census for several reasons: problems of self-reporting, lack of inclusivity within the definition of the umbrella term *transgender*, simplistic construction of survey questions, or lack at all of a transgender selection on survey forms. Additionally, some individuals identify themselves as *stealth*, which indicates that they have completed their transition and do not continue to identify as transgender but as the gender to which they authentically belong. These individuals would not be counted among the transgender population. Another transgender identifier is *person with a trans history*. This term indicates that the individual acknowledges a gender transition as well as identifies as the new gender.

Despite the relatively small self-reported number of transgender individuals in the United States, the transgender community suffers discrimination, attempted suicide, and completed suicide at drastically higher rates than the general population. Another Williams Institute report (2014b) states that percentages of attempted and completed suicide within the transgender community are 10 times that of the general population. This statistic has clear implications for the transgender clients who present for career and/or personal counseling as the workplace is often a site of discontent and adults spend the majority of their time at work.

Dispenza, Watson, Chung, and Brack (2012) stated that "Transgender persons experience discrimination long before they are ever fired from a job or denied employment." Although the transgender population, as a group, suffers discrimination and violence at significantly higher rates than the general population, multiple and intersecting identities put transgender individuals at even greater risk of discrimination and harm. Male-to-female transwomen of color experience the most frequent amount of brutal violence and are murdered at higher rates than the transgender population as a whole (Meyers, 2015).

As many have cited (Brewster, Velez, DeBlaere, & Moradi, 2012; Budge, Tebbe, & Howard, 2010; Dispenza et al., 2012; Furbish, 2015; Pepper & Lorah, 2008; Sangganjanavanich, 2009, 2010, 2013; Singh, Meng, & Hansen, 2014), there is a dearth of literature and empirical research on the experience of transgender individuals in the workplace. These authors further state that while there has been more attention paid in general to this population in the last 10 years, there is a need for longitudinal study and experimental research. In terms of career counseling practice, assessment instruments have not been normed on LGBT populations and thus often produce inaccurate results for LGBT clients. Brewster et al. (2012) were one of the first to conduct a study with transgender individuals in the workplace, making modifications to three existing career assessments—the Workplace Heterosexist Experiences Questionnaire (WHEQ); the Lesbian, Gay, Bisexual, and Transgendered Climate Inventory (LGBTCI); and the Workplace Sexual Identity Management Measure (WSIMM)—in an attempt to gather relevant career data on this population. The researchers found "initially promising evidence for the use of these modified measures with transgender individuals" (Brewster et al., 2012, p. 67). Additional career-related assessment instruments adapted or created for the LGBT population are necessary to accurately reflect an individual's aspirations, interests, goals, abilities, and values.

TRANSGENDER CLIENTS' EXPERIENCES IN THE WORKPLACE

To be transgender in the workplace requires intricate and complex strategies of identity management, which is the practice of carefully crafting and maintaining one's public presence. Although all of us engage in this type of management to gain and sustain social approval to some extent, transgender individuals engage in these practices for additional reasons: in an attempt to hide how they actually identify in terms of gender, in navigating the process of transitioning in their place of employment while attempting to maintain a sense of safety, in going stealth posttransition and not publicly revealing their journey at all, or in starting over at a new workplace living as their new gender and leaving their previous gender identity behind. However, this last example creates a sort of double-bind: Switching jobs to protect the new identity means erasing the old identity and all the work experience that went with it; completely starting over means taking a huge risk with income and livelihood and being "outed" with the new employer.

Dispenza et al. (2012) further stated that "it is important for career counselors and interventionists to understand how multilayered experiences of discrimination may potentially affect transgendered persons" (p. 67). The types of workplace discrimination and other environmental discrimination transgender individuals face include physical, mental, and emotional abuse from hetero- and cis-normative individuals as well as horizontal oppression from the greater LGBT community. One reason for this discrimination might be that individuals who are transgender "force" others to investigate their own identity when transpeople come out. This compels those in the majority to face the embedded gender binary, which can be a highly threatening paradigm shift to some people.

The implications of being out as a transgender in the workplace are not the same for every individual. For some it is better and for some it is worse; thus, it is important for counselors to seek out their client's phenomenological experience and discover how he or she can be of assistance. Additionally, experiences are different for male-to-female (MTF) than female-to-male (FTM) individuals (Dispenza et al., 2012; Pepper & Lorah, 2008).

RECOMMENDATIONS FOR WORKING WITH CLIENTS WHO IDENTIFY AS TRANSGENDER

Brewster et al. (2012) and Furbish (2015) suggested that in career counseling with transgender individuals, interventions should rely on self-reported, subjective experiences in the workplace; perceptions of workplace environments; and social justice conversations about career transition, resume building, and mechanics of the job search (Brewster et al., 2012; Furbish 2015). Dispenza et al. (2012) further asserted that "Career counselors and other interventionists could provide educational services to supervisors, human resources personnel, and other workplace employees regarding transgender persons. Topics such as (a) how to appropriately communicate about the transition process with transgender persons, (b) how to address pronoun and name changes of transitioning employees, and (c) how to accommodate work schedules for individuals who are undergoing routine medical procedures." It was also noted that action research with these individuals in the workplace would be a valuable addition to the field (Dispenza et al., 2012; Furbish, 2015).

In an activity as seemingly routine as resume review, authors (Furbish, 2015; Pepper & Lorah, 2008) encourage career counselors to use counseling microskills to help transgender individuals craft a protective resume that helps them answer employment gap questions or missing historical work experience when they are moving from one job to another, especially when leaving the old gender behind for the new one. Sangganjanavanich (2013, p. 360) added to this guidance by stating that "Practitioners, when working with clients, should always maintain an attitude of dignity and respect regardless of their client's social identity. Providing a welcoming environment, acknowledging oppression, and using trans-affirmative language are ways that career development practitioners can exhibit an affirmative approach." Above all, counselors have an obligation to uphold the ethical standards of The American Counseling Association, as well as adhere to the guidelines set forth in Multicultural Counseling Competencies. Furthermore, the World Professional Association for Transgender Health provides extensive resources for working with the trans population in all areas of physical and mental health, as well as comprehensive standards of care.

Counselors employing a social justice framework "should consider macrosystem-level structures that operate to reinforce trans-prejudice (e.g., health care access challenges, employment discrimination, career fairs, legislative activism) and ask, '*What actions can be taken to alter oppressive systems of gender?*" (Singh et al., 2014, p. 217). Graduate programs that train career and other mental health professionals must make careful use of a social justice and multicultural emphasis throughout the coursework in order to provide culturally sensitive services to trans-identified clients (Troutman & Packer-Williams, 2014).

REVISITING THE CASE OF DILLON

Recently, Dillon was offered a position out of state where there is more bigotry and open heterosexism. Dillon is torn about the decision, as uprooting the children and potentially exposing them to discrimination and harassment are legitimate concerns. Dillon is also concerned how their overall lifestyle would be impacted, including social and religious activities. Would they have to go back in the closet? Would they feel isolated? How safe would they feel? The salary is very good; in fact, their financial security would not be impacted. Dillon did not come out during the interview process.

Dillon did receive a severance package that offered career counseling through the company's Employee Assistance Program. He has come to you to assist in the decision-making process. Charlie is supportive with whatever decision Dillon makes. Dillon is starting to feel anxious due to the responsibility weighing on him as well as knowing and the knowledge that the job market is tight. Certainly, all 13 keys are important to the process, but with Dillon, pay particular attention to his concerns surrounding his family. He has identified employee benefits and concerns over social acceptance vis-à-vis lifestyle.

Through the lens of Super's Lifespan Approach (1990), Dillon is now struggling with specific values, confusion, and self-concept as it relates to career development. What is important to him? What are his priorities? What can he live with? Will his family be socially impacted? Considering what we know about career development issues for LGBT individuals—that is, inferior civil rights—these are prudent questions. Dillon also struggles to some degree with some of the processes in the establishment (stability of self-concept) and maintenance (attaining achievement) stages. How does he integrate his personal self and his work self? How does he feel about potentially hiding his sexual identity (identity management)? Does he forgo personal integrity for financial stability? If he comes out, will he limit his professional goals? Or does Dillon decide to not "hide" and let the "chips fall where they may"? Through careful and intentional exploration, only Dillon can decide what is best for him. Dillon's career decision making and career exploration may not result in definitive answers, but it will allow him to gain confidence and clarity on what he may encounter. Regardless, a solid foundation and understanding of the challenges will assist Dillon in his decision-making process.

ADDITIONAL RESOURCE SUGGESTIONS

Human Rights Campaign: www.hrc.org
Lambda Legal: www.lambdalegal.org
National Center for Transgender Equality: www.transequality.org/
Transgender at Work: www.tgender.net
Transgender Law Center: www.transgenderlawcenter.org

REFERENCES

Berger, R. M. (1982). The unseen minority: Older gays and lesbians. *Social Work, 27*(3), 236–242.

Brewster, M. E., Velez, B., DeBlaere, C., & Moradi, B. (2012). Transgender individuals' workplace experiences: The applicability of sexual minority measures and models. *Journal of Counseling Psychology, 59*(1), 60–70. doi:10.1037/0025206

Budge, S. L., Tebbe, E. N., & Howard, A. S. (2010). The work experiences of transgender individuals: Negotiating the transition and career decision-making processes. *Journal of Counseling Psychology, 57*(4), 377–393. doi: 10.1037/a0020472.

Center for American Progress. (2011, June 2). *Gay and transgender people face high rates of workplace discrimination and harassment.* Retrieved from https://www.americanprogress.org/issues/lgbt/news/2011/06/02/9872/gay-and-transgender-people-face-high-rates-of-workplace-discrimination-and-harassment/

Degges-White, S., & Shoffner, M. F. (2002). Career counseling with lesbian clients: Using the theory of work adjustment as a framework. *The Career Development Quarterly, 51*, 87–96.

Dispenza, F., Watson, L. B., Chung, Y. B., & Brack, G. (2012). Experience of career-related discrimination for female-to-male transgender persons: A qualitative study. *The Career Development Quarterly, 60*(1), 65–81.

Dunkle, J. H. (1996). Toward an integration of gay and lesbian identity development and Super's life-span approach. *Journal of Vocational Behavior, 48*, 149–159.

Elliott, J. E. (1993). Career development with lesbian and gay clients. *Career Development Quarterly, 41*(3), 210–227.

Fassinger, R. E. (1991). The hidden minority: Issues and challenges in working with lesbian women and gay men. *The Counseling Psychologist, 19*, 157–176.

Furbish, D. S. (2015). Exploring social justice via resumes. *Journal of Employment Counseling, 52*(1), 36–47. doi:10.1002/j.2161–1920.2015.00055.x

Gedro, J. (2007). Conducting Research on LGBT Issues: Leading the Field All Over Again! *Human Resource Development Quarterly, 18*(2), 153–158.

Green, R. (1987). *The "sissy boy syndrome" and the development of homosexuality*. New Haven, CT: Yale University Press.

Hetherington, C. (1991). Life planning and career counseling with gay and lesbian students. In N. J. Evans & V. A. Wall (Eds.), *Beyond tolerance: Gays, lesbians and bisexuals on campus* (pp. 131–146). Alexandria, VA: American College Personnel Association.

Hetherington, C., & Orzek, A. (1989). Career counseling and life planning with lesbian women. *Journal of Counseling & Development, 68*, 52–57.

House, C. J. (2004). Integrating barriers to Caucasian lesbians' career development and Super's life-span, life-space approach. *The Career Development Quarterly, 52*, 246–255.

Human Rights Campaign (2014). *Employment Non-Discrimination Act*. Retrieved from http://www.hrc.org/resources/entry/employment-non-discrimination-act.

Killermann, S. (2013). *The social justice advocate's handbook: A guide to gender*. Austin, TX: Impetus Books.

Meyers, L. (2015, April). Embracing the ongoing push for progress. *Counseling Today, 57*(10), 27–33.

Miller, G. (1995). *The gay male's odyssey in the corporate world*. Binghamton, NY: Haworth Press.

Nam Cam Tau, R., & Cartel, C. (2004). One career, two identities: An assessment of gay men's career trajectory. *Career Development International, 9*(7), 627–637.

Orel, N. A. (2014). Investigating the needs and concerns of lesbian, gay, bisexual, and transgender older adults: The use of qualitative and quantitative methodology. *Journal of Homosexuality, 61*(1), 53–78. doi:10.1080/00918369.2013.835236

Pepper, S. M., & Lorah, P. (2008). Career issues and workplace considerations for the transsexual community: Bridging a gap of knowledge for career counselors and mental health care providers. *The Career Development Quarterly, 56*(4), 330–343. doi: 10.1002/j.2161–0045.2008.tb00098.x.

Pope, M. (2011, December). The career counseling with underserved populations model. *Journal of Employment Counseling, 48*, 153–155.

Pope, M., Barret, B., Szymanski, D. M., Chung, Y. B., Singaravelu, H., McLean, R., & Sanabria, S. (2004). Culturally appropriate career counseling with gay and lesbian clients. *The Career Development Quarterly, 55*, 22–37.

Rheineck, J. E. (2005). Career decision self-efficacy of lesbians throughout the lifespan. *Adultspan, 4*, 79–91.

Sangganjanavanich, V. F. (2009). Career development practitioners as advocates for transgender individuals: Understanding gender transition. *Journal of Employment Counseling, 46*(3), 128–135. doi:10.1002/j.2161–1920.2009.tb00075.x

Sangganjanavanich, V. F. (2010). Workplace aggression: Toward social justice and advocacy in counseling for transgender persons. *Journal of LGBT Issues in Counseling, 4*(3–4), 187–201. doi:10.180/15538604.2010.524844.

Sangganjanavanich, V. F. (2013). Facilitating career development concerns of gender transitioning individuals: Professional standards and competencies. *Career Development Quarterly, 61*(4). 354–366. doi: 10.1002/j.2161–0045.2013.00061.x.

Savickas, M. L. (2005). The theory and practice of career construction. In D. Brown & R. W. Lent (Eds.), *Career development and counseling* (pp. 42–70). Hoboken, NJ: Wiley.

Schmidt, C. K., & Nilsson, J. E. (2006). The effects of simultaneous development processes: Factors relating to the career development of lesbians, gay, and bisexual youth. *The Career Development Quarterly, 55*, 22–37.

Shidlo, A. (1994). Internalized homophobia: Conceptual and empirical issues in measurement. In B. Greene & G. M. Herek (Eds.), *Lesbian and gay psychology: Theory, research, and clinical applications* (pp. 176–205). Thousand Oaks, CA: Sage.

Singh, A. A., Meng, S. E., & Hansen, A. W. (2014). I am my own gender: Resilience strategies of trans youth. *Journal of Counseling and Development, 92*(2), 208–218. doi:10.1002/j.1556–6676.2014.00150.x

Sophie, J. (1985). A critical examination of stage theories of lesbian identity development. *Journal of Homosexuality, 12*(2), 39–51.

Sophie, J. (1985/1986). A critical examination of stage theories of lesbian identity development. *Journal of Homosexuality, 12*(2), 39–51.

Super, D. E. (1990). A life-span, life-space approach to career development. In D. Brown, L. Brooks, & Associates (Eds.), *Career choice and development* (pp. 197–261), San Francisco, CA: Jossey-Bass.

Troutman, O., & Packer-Williams, C. (2014). Moving beyond CACREP standards: Training counselors to work competently with LGBT clients. *Journal for Counselor Preparation and Supervision, 6*(1). doi:10.7729/61.1088

The Williams Institute. (2011). *How many people are LGBT?* Retrieved from: http://williamsinstitute.law.ucla.edu/wp-content/uploads/Gates-How-Many-People-LGBT-Apr-2011.pdf

The Williams Institute. (2014a). *Best practices for asking questions to identify transgender and other gender minority respondents on population-based surveys.* Retrieved from http://williamsinstitute.law.ucla.edu/wp-content/uploads/geniuss-report-sep-2014.pdf

The Williams Institute. (2014b). *Suicide attempts among transgender and gender non-conforming adults.* Retrieved from http://williamsinstitute.law.ucla.edu/wp-content/uploads/AFSP-Williams-Suicide-Report-Final.pdf

CHAPTER 15

CULTURALLY DIVERSE WOMEN

Ricardo Phipps

CASE VIGNETTE: JACKIE

Jackie is a 30-year-old African American female who currently works as a phlebotomist at a large Catholic hospital. She has worked in that capacity for the last 8 years. Soon after graduating from high school, she began a romantic relationship with a man who was 5 years older than her. They had a child together and separated soon afterward. Jackie worked in retail for a few years to support herself and her son. Her mother and grandmother helped her with childcare. She decided to enter a phlebotomy-training program after talking to a friend of hers who worked in the allied health field in a hospital. Jackie was searching for more fulfilling work and better compensation. While in her training program, she met and started dating a fellow student. After both of them completed the program, they decided to live together and eventually had a child together. The relationship ended after about 5 years. Jackie's partner wanted to marry her, but she felt dissatisfied in the relationship. Jackie admitted to herself that she had experienced attraction to and romantic feelings toward other women ever since adolescence. At present, she has decided to place her relationship needs and questioning on hold because of her children's needs and also because of the conservatism of her family of origin and of her work environment. Since the end of her romantic relationship with her younger child's father, Jackie has immersed herself in work, even taking a second job to relieve some of the pressure of supporting her family largely on her own. Lately, Jackie has been frustrated by her job as a phlebotomist. She wants to be able to help people at a different level. She would like to go to nursing school or even medical school but does not see this as a viable option as a mother of two children, now aged 10 and 7 years. Jackie decides to see a counselor through the employer assistance program at the hospital to discuss her work frustration, financial pressures, and loneliness due to her decision not to explore possibilities for romantic companionship. What does career counseling have to offer this African American mother of two who is experiencing a hunger to reach for a more fulfilling level in her career and also questioning her sexual orientation identity?

Career counseling in the United States has developed and traditionally been practiced with a bias toward addressing the needs of European American males (Cook, Heppner, & O'Brien, 2002). Scholarly attention to the unique needs of women in preparing to enter and succeed in various careers only began to emerge in the 1960s and 1970s (Fitzgerald & Crites, 1979). Of particular interest in recent years is the career counseling needs of culturally diverse women, namely, women of color, women of nonmajority religious backgrounds, nonheterosexual women, and women with disabilities. Beyond having to combat male privilege, culturally diverse women confront White privilege, heterosexual privilege, Christian privilege, and/or able-bodied privilege in the workforce. Sexism has been emphasized considerably in the workplace without consideration of other forms of discrimination (Jackson, Esses, & Burris, 2001). European American females often focus exclusively on sexism in the White male-dominant workplace, whereas women of color face "gendered racism" in which it is difficult to distinguish the effects of different aspects of their intersecting identities (Blake, 1999). Ethnicity and gender complexities result in distinct challenges for women of color who attempt to rise in organizational hierarchies (Reuther & Fairhurst, 2000). Besides navigating through sexist systems, culturally diverse women also face racism, xenophobia, linguistic discrimination, homophobia, and disability-based discrimination as they secure their places in the workforce and assert their abilities to make unique contributions. Effective career counseling for culturally diverse women must include consideration of these unique issues.

This chapter explores the unique experiences of various groups of culturally diverse women who work in the United States and highlights common barriers faced by all culturally diverse women. Two career counseling theories, social cognitive career theory (SCCT) and narrative career counseling theory, are presented as possible orientations career counselors may use to empower clients. Finally, specific techniques and resources that might be beneficial to the career development of culturally diverse women across theoretical approaches are proposed.

CAREER DEVELOPMENT OF WOMEN OF COLOR

In spite of the many obstacles faced by culturally diverse women in the workplace, women of color have a long history of working outside the home, often due to financial necessity (Reid & Comas-Diaz, 1990). The labor force participation of immigrant women (first from Europe and later from Latin America and Asia) was constrained by employer discrimination, immigration policies that made employment status uncertain, and attitudes within their own cultures that restricted some married immigrant women to home-based outsource work, family-operated enterprises, or industries that employed family-based groups (Padavic & Reskin, 2002). Poverty and discrimination combined to concentrate immigrant women in particularly exploitative jobs in domestic work, migrant agricultural labor, and low-wage manufacturing. By the early 20th century, for example, women from southern and eastern Europe dominated the garment industry, laboring for low pay in factories, sweatshops, or crowded, urban workplaces (Kessler-Harris, 1982).

Even as the social and political dynamics of the United States changed and descendants of immigrants of European descent who were previously marginalized integrated into the mainstream majority culture, women of non-European backgrounds still faced tremendous obstacles in the workforce. African American women continued to face oppression and discrimination in the workplace that mirrored the practice of segregation and racism in larger U.S. society.

African American Women

Enslaved women of African descent were brought to the Americas to work as free laborers, regularly engaging in heavy field labor as well as performing most of the domestic labor of cooking, cleaning, and caring for children. Since the late 19th century, African American women have participated in the labor force at a rate higher than that of any other group of American women (Reid & Comas-Diaz, 1990). As late as 1997, 51% of African American women worked full time, compared with 42% of European American women and 35% of Latina women in the United States (Boydston, 2001). Not until World War II did African American women make significant headway in gaining industrial jobs, and only in the late 20th century did they make progress in gaining employment in large numbers in professional occupations other than teaching and nursing (Gordon, 2002).

As early as 1886, Spelman College in Atlanta began the first training program for African American female nurses and teachers (Gordon, 2002). Other training schools targeting African American women emerged in other urban centers around the nation in the late 19th and early 20th centuries, paving the way for small numbers of African American female nurses, teachers, and entrepreneurs. Accompanying the rise of these historically Black educational institutions was the founding of various Black Greek-letter sororities: Alpha Kappa Alpha Sorority in 1908, Delta Sigma Theta Sorority in 1913, Zeta Phi Beta Sorority in 1920, and Sigma Gamma Rho in 1922 (Breakfield, 2010). Seeking to promote community service, these sororities also fostered racial pride and sisterhood.

Along with the rise of limited opportunities in education for African American women, an increasing divide developed between lower socioeconomic status African American women who worked menial, blue-collar jobs just to support themselves and their families and those African American women who were able to direct their career paths in at least some limited sense. The desegregation efforts of the 1950s and 1960s eventually led to African American women being able to attend predominantly European American institutions, where they had access to educational programs beyond teacher training programs and nursing programs, to which African American women had been traditionally encouraged (Gordon, 2002).

African American women face unique career-related challenges. According to Allen (2002), little attention is given in the social science literature about the experiences of African American women negotiating multiple identities. According to recent research, African American women tend to revere those who are older (Allen, 2004), an important consideration in the building of mentorship relationships, and tend to have strong social networks and group loyalty (Arminio et al., 2000), often mobilizing their communities to social and political action through church and community groups (Parker, 2001). In the current career climate, lighter complexioned African American women still encounter preference over darker complexioned African American women in terms of hiring practices (Wade, Romano, & Blue, 2004). Career counselors should be attuned to these cultural strengths of

African American women as well as aware of within-group conflicts, such as skin color division.

Latina American Women

In the 20th century, a growing Latina workforce, both U.S. born and immigrant, was concentrated in migrant labor, food processing, industrial sweatshops, and domestic work (Reid & Comas-Diaz, 1990). Growing access to educational opportunities is changing that dynamic, but obstacles still exist in the workforce for Latina women in the United States, particularly the issue of reconciling family life and values with career ambition. Traditionally, Latina women have rejected feminism, claiming that seemingly "anti-men" and "anti-family" sentiments contrast with their traditions and cultural values (Holvino, 2010). A Latina feminist scholar and activist argues that Latina women face exclusion and rejection in the work world because their loyalty to the job is questioned in light of their loyalty to family needs (Hurtado, 1996).

Although the educational achievement levels of Latinas have risen in recent years, they are still significantly lower than those of European American women, with college graduation rates of Latinas at 31.3% in 2008 as opposed to 45.8% for European American women, according to the Center for American Progress (Jackson, 2013). Only 3% of Latina women work in science, technology, engineering, and mathematics (STEM) fields, while women in total make up 24% of the STEM workforce. As of 2013, Latinas owned about 1 out of every 10 women-owned businesses in the United States even though they make up a much larger segment of the female population. Latina women own 36% of all companies owned by minority women in America. Latina women make 88% of their male counterparts' annual full-time earnings. In Latino households, about 4 in 10 working wives were the primary breadwinners for their families, according to a 2010 Center for American Progress report, doubling the rate from 1975 (Jackson, 2013). Career counselors should be sensitive to the tension some Latina women may feel in balancing family obligations with career life.

Asian American Women

Asian men began to migrate to the United States in significant numbers in the early 1800s, primarily as cheap labor alternatives to Black slave and free labor (Min, 2006). Few Asian women accompanied these male workers for many years because American employers targeted single men, and married laborers preferred to send money to their families rather than transport them to a foreign environment with questionable safety. As a result of the gender imbalance that issued from Asian men typically migrating to the United States alone, Asian women were brought to the United States largely for sex-trafficking purposes, and many were forced to work as indentured prostitutes (Min, 2006). Discriminatory immigration policies limited the migration of Asian women to the United States for many years. Asian women typically worked as unskilled laborers and often were taken advantage of as sexual objects (Min, 2006).

The Civil Rights movement in the United States occasioned a reexamination of antiquated immigration laws affecting migration of Asians to the United States (Ng, Lee, & Pak, 2007). New immigration laws gave preference to Asian immigrants with specialized occupational skills needed in the labor market in the United States (Min, 2006). Large numbers of Asian immigrants, men and women, migrated to the United States in the late 1960s and early 1970s, largely to assume jobs in medicine, the hard sciences, and the engineering fields. As conversations swelled in the United States about the disadvantages that ethnic minorities faced, the notion of Asian Americans as the model minority also arose. The model minority "myth" originated during the late 1960s amid the Civil Rights movement when the racial tensions between racial minority groups and the majority White population were highest (Cao & Novas, 1996). Some Asian American studies researchers have proposed that this myth was utilized as a means to strip away the minority status of Asian Americans, as well as a means to politically separate Asian Americans from other communities of color (Cheng, 1997; Ng et al., 2007). This model minority myth largely ignores the within-group differences among Asian Americans. Many Southeast Asian Americans came to the United States as political refugees with few financial resources and little formal education and still experienced tremendous limitations in academic and career pursuits (Ngo & Lee, 2007).

The term *bamboo curtain* has been used to describe discrimination Asian American women experience in receiving promotions in their areas of work over and above discrimination experienced by Asian American men (Tan, 2008). Asian American women endure harsh stereotyping in many work sectors, being portrayed as subservient (Shi, 2008), cooperative, hardworking, willing to work for less (Hossfeld, 1994), and unambitious in terms of promotions (Allen, 2004). The number of Asian Americans, women and men, in the highest executive levels in the United States is very low, with some believing that this cultural group has poor managerial potential (Woo, 2000). Because Asian American women typically value the success of the team or the group over the individual, they are often taken advantage of and passed over for promotions (Tan, 2008). The career success of Asian American women suffers from these lingering stereotypes. Career counselors should be sensitive to the interplay between collectivist values and the values of the contemporary work culture in the United States. Career counselors may explore potential models of assertiveness with Asian American female clients who feel hindered by stereotyping but are at times hesitant to advocate for themselves.

CAREER DEVELOPMENT OF RELIGIOUS MINORITY WOMEN

Religion is another cultural factor that can greatly affect the career development and life of women in the United States. The United States has traditionally supported a Judeo-Christian majority culture, with the Jewish component being largely overshadowed by Christian culture. Changing demographics has created an emergence of Hindu, Muslim, Sikh, and other non-Judeo-Christian groups in the U.S. workforce. Women who identify themselves as spiritual, agnostic, or atheist are also present in the U.S. workforce and have their own career counseling needs. This chapter explores some unique career counseling issues of Muslim women in the

United States. Career counselors should educate themselves on the intersection of gender and religion in the workforce in other cultural contexts.

Muslim American Women

Career counseling for Muslim American women must include considerations for the great amount of diversity that exists within Islamic culture. Muslim women living in the United States may trace their lineage to Arabic or Persian countries in the Middle East, such as Egypt, Saudi Arabia, or Iran. However, large numbers of Muslim women in the United States also have family ties to countries in South Asia or Sub-Saharan Africa. The practice of Islam is also very prevalent in traditionally African American communities in the United States, creating the need for attention to the intersectionality of religion, gender, and race/ethnicity in the case of career counseling with African American, Muslim women. In summary, country of origin is a critical factor in working with Muslim American women in the context of career development.

Muslims living in the United States confront rampant stigmatization, especially since the September 11, 2001 terrorist attacks, which have resulted in people with Arab, Middle Eastern, and some outward Muslim characteristics, especially men, being unjustly associated with terrorism (Nassar-McMillan & Zagzebski-Tovar, 2012). Muslim women in the United States experience various types and levels of stereotyping. Domestically and abroad, Muslim women have been portrayed as the recipients of unequal treatment, oppressed by patriarchal family systems (Bartkowski & Read, 2003). Contrary to this belief, American Muslim women are more likely than their male counterparts to have college and postgraduate degrees; are more highly educated than women of other religious groups, except Jews; and report incomes more nearly equal to men than women of other religious traditions (Goodstein, 2009, p. 11).

Although Muslim American women have found some success in various career areas, attention must be given to the challenges they face in the workplace. Religious background can be an invisible cultural factor if an individual chooses not to disclose this information (Reeves & Azam, 2012). In the case of Muslim women who opt to wear the hijab, a traditional Islamic headscarf, in their place of work, their religious identity is revealed, making them vulnerable to stereotyping. In a study conducted by Reeves and Azam (2012) of Muslim American women working in the health care profession, the researchers found that many women choose to wear the hijab in environments where they expect to encounter some resistance from patients. According to the researchers, these women are most likely to do so if they feel that there is an atmosphere of institutional support in their work environment and if they have not experienced any grave acts of anti-Muslim discrimination in the past. Pasha-Zaidi, Masson, and Pennington (2013) conclude from an experimental study about perceptions of employability that potential employers may find women who wear the hijab as less employable in the United States. Consequently, wearing the hijab is an act of religious disclosure, a statement about women's previous experiences with discrimination, as well as a possible risk factor in gaining employment. Thus, career counseling with Muslim American women is deeply connected to cultural identity development.

Ethnic groups in the United States that are largely Muslim tend to espouse collectivist views. Muslim culture itself supports patriarchy and the importance of the family as a source of security and support for women. Career counselors may find Muslim women exhibiting a high level of anxiety about the opinions of family members in terms of career development (Nassar-McMillan & Zagzebski-Tovar, 2012). Although Muslim culture does not outwardly disparage counseling and psychotherapy, there is a typical cultural reticence about revealing intimate details of life to those outside the family circle. Career counselors may notice signs of other mental health issues. Career counseling may be viewed as a safe topic with which to begin the personal exploration process. It is important for career counselors to have information for appropriate referrals to community resources.

CAREER DEVELOPMENT OF WOMEN WITH DISABILITIES

The 2010 U.S. Census indicates that 56.7 million persons in the United States have disabilities, with women constituting a significantly larger number of these individuals than men (Brault, 2012). Guralnik et al. (1997) hold that women have a larger chance of becoming physically disabled as they age than men. Women with disabilities in the workplace may encounter discrimination, architectural impediments, attitudinal barriers, and income disparity. Gill (1997) reports that women with disabilities are often stereotyped in the workplace as dependent, childlike, incompetent, and powerless and that women with disabilities are often devalued and treated as if they are invisible, all leading to low self-esteem and stress. These experiences may vary according to whether persons develop their disabilities later in life or were born with them (Enright, Conyers, & Szymanski, 1996).

Career counselors should take intentional steps to better understand the discriminatory experiences faced by women with disabilities as well as to understand the supports and protections available through the disability rights movement, which can help women with both personal and career development (Noonan et al., 2004).

CURRENT CHALLENGES FACED BY CULTURALLY DIVERSE WOMEN

Underrepresentation in Career Fields

Many career areas in the United States are still characterized by gender imbalance. The number of females and underrepresented minorities is low in both college-level STEM degrees and in the national STEM workforce (Tate & Linn, 2005). According to the National Science Board (2008), women make up 46% of the total workforce, but hold only 28% of jobs in technical or STEM fields. African Americans and Latinos each comprise 13% of the total workforce, but only 3% of the technical workforce. Multiple avenues are needed to increase interest in STEM careers among culturally diverse women so that their potential contributions can be actualized. Generally, parents and educators in conservative communities of color are less likely to encourage girls to enter STEM fields, but their encouragement is critically important to changing the current trend (Alliman-Brissett, Turner, & Skovholt, 2004; Ian, 2014).

Multiple Roles

The issue of whether culturally diverse women can be successful in both careers and motherhood is not an issue unique to culturally diverse women (Cheung & Halpern, 2010); however, culturally diverse women experience a slightly different dynamic than majority-culture women. The concept of voluntary childlessness has been studied as a trend by which many women choose not to have children or to delay motherhood for career, financial, relationship, or other reasons (Kelly, 2009). Given that almost half of all women in the United States who earn more than $100,000 annually have no children (Hewlett, 2002), it appears that voluntary childlessness may have certain advantages along with the obvious disadvantages. Mason and Goulden (2004) argue that a double standard exists in the workplace, given that having children signals stability and responsibility for men, but seems to have the opposite effect among employers for women. African American women are voluntarily childless significantly less than European American women (Heaton Jacobson & Holland, 1999). European American women are more likely to be childless than African American women or Latina women (Kelly, 2009). Career counselors working with culturally diverse women must address with their clients the issue of negotiating multiple roles as career person and as family person. Clients may feel that they are not able to have a family and a successful career simultaneously. Counselors may point to models who defy these stereotypes.

Wage Differentials

Women earned wages at the rate of 78% of what men earned in the United States in 2007 (Arons, 2008). The gap between the salaries of culturally diverse women and European American males is on average larger than the gap between salaries of European American women and their male counterparts. In 2009, Latina women and African American women earned 62% and 71%, respectively, of what men earned, while Asian American women earned 95% of what men earned (Department of Labor, Bureau of Labor Statistics, 2010). Women with disabilities, especially those with children, often live in poverty due to low wages and underemployment (Noonan et al., 2004). These wage differentials can cause culturally diverse women to question their own ability or potential (Cook et al., 2002). Lower salaries also affect issues such as childcare, transportation, and wardrobe, all of which are connected to career success.

Career counselors working with culturally diverse women may help women feel empowered to negotiate for more just salaries and refrain from internalizing lower pay as indicative of lower levels of competence. Counselors may encourage clients to look for and identify careers and work environments that do not practice wage discrimination (Cook et al., 2002).

THEORY AND TECHNIQUES IN CAREER COUNSELING WITH CULTURALLY DIVERSE WOMEN

The use of SCCT has been shown to be effective for career counselors working with culturally diverse women (Lent et al., 2005). SCCT is rooted in social cognitive theory, credited to Bandura (1986). SCCT focuses on how the academic and career interests of individuals form, develop, and mature, which fosters better understanding of how career choices are made and actualized. SCCT relies heavily on the constructs of self-efficacy, outcome expectations, and goal setting (Lent, Brown, & Hackett, 1994).

In SCCT, the key constructs of self-efficacy, outcome expectations, and goals drive how people are attracted to or become disinterested in certain careers. Self-efficacy refers to attitudes people have about their ability to be successful at a particular undertaking. Self-efficacy generally forms out of personal performance experiences and social dynamics associated with performing particular tasks (Lent et al., 1994). In SCCT, outcome expectations refer to what people believe about the results or consequences of their own performance of certain tasks. Goals are seen in SCCT as plans or decisions to begin a particular activity. A core belief in SCCT is that people develop lasting interests in activities when they experience high self-efficacy and positive outcomes (Lent et al., 1994). Career counselors can help culturally diverse women entering or making transitions in the work world by providing activities and interventions to increase self-efficacy and belief in the attainability of desired outcome expectations. Supporting goal setting and planning is another critical resource career counselors may offer.

In working with culturally diverse women, career counselors may choose to begin with assessing level of career self-efficacy of clients. Data from the completion of assessment instruments such as the Career Decision-Making Self-Efficacy Scale (CDMSE; Taylor & Betz, 1983) or the New General Self-Efficacy Scale (NGSE; Chen, Gully, & Eden, 2001) may be helpful to career counselors. The instruments can be used to help career counselors to identify the negative messages to which culturally diverse women are subjected that negatively affect their self-efficacy in terms of careers that are not traditionally held by culturally diverse women.

Narrative Career Counseling

Narrative career counseling modalities have arisen as a way of accommodating the new reality of ever-changing career trajectories in the current information-based economy (Niles & Hartung, 2000). Based on social constructivist theory, which is rooted in the core belief that people make meaning and construct their social and psychological worlds through social interactions (Young & Collin, 2004), narrative approaches to career counseling allow individuals to construct their own selves and career paths according to changing values and changing sense of self that arise through changing relationships (Brott, 2005). In narrative career counseling, individuals write their own life stories, integrating aspects of life from outside of work and taking into account their roles as family member, worker, and member of their community. One of the strengths of narrative career counseling is that it addresses the stress individuals may experience when their desired career path takes them outside the realm of societal or family expectations, which often happens with culturally diverse persons and with women (Clark, Severy, & Sawyer, 2004). Savickas (2005) advocates for the use of career *storying*, by which individuals explore the relationship between the self they knew in the past and the self they know in the present with the self they want to become in the future.

Narrative career counseling typically involves the counselor engaging the client in a very collaborative fashion in which the counselor relinquishes the role of expert. Three basic phases characterize the helping process (Locke & Gibbons, 2008). First, the coconstruction phase involves the counselor and client uncovering the life story of the client and the overarching themes that create personal meaning for the client. Second, the deconstruction phase involves exploring different viewpoints and different possibilities in the search for the preferred way of being of the client. The third and final phase involves constructing a future story based on the identified values and meanings individual clients would like to have guiding their future. This process is very focused on making unique meaning of the life experiences of all clients, which makes its relevant for people of varying cultural backgrounds (Sharf, 2006). Locke and Gibbons (2008) present narrative career counseling as especially beneficial for culturally diverse women who have had to make radical shifts in their career and work life due to divorce or death of their partner.

Narrative career counseling may resonate highly with clients who have cultural backgrounds that hold storytelling very precious (Stebleton, 2007). For example, a storied approach to career counseling for women of African ancestry and culture allows individuals to tell their personal stories, whether in an individual or a group counseling setting (Maree, Ebersöhn, & Molepo, 2006). Success has been documented using the Career Construction Interview with lesbian women in the construction of life portraits, which facilitated an enhanced sense of self and a heightened sense of personal authorship (Maree, 2014). An assessment tool available to career counselors using narrative approaches is the Future Career Autobiography (FCA; Rehfuss, 2009), developed to measure qualitative change in occupational narratives as a result of career interventions. Specifically, the instrument is designed to measure change or lack of change in the occupational narrative of an individual over time. Narrative career counseling is most effective when counselors are not limited by strict time constraints. The goal is to facilitate empowerment in clients so that they feel free to travel career paths beyond those imposed by the expectations of others.

Mentoring

Mentoring relationships in the work setting are relationships between persons new to a job or disciplinary field and persons who are more experienced, in which the more experienced person provides support to the novice in assuming new responsibilities and new career identity (Gayle-Baugh & Sullivan, 2005). Research has validated the positive effects of mentoring relationships on career satisfaction, job satisfaction, career commitment, and expectations for advancement (Allen, Eby, Poteet, Lentz, & Lima, 2004), suggesting that mentoring can foster positive affective reactions to the work environment and positive psychological feelings toward career choices. For culturally diverse women, mentorship can be a very valuable resource in maintaining high career and job satisfaction, commitment, and hope for promotion. The career training aspect of mentorship can be effectively provided by various persons in the same field or work setting, but the psychosocial aspects of mentoring may best be provided by persons with whom the mentored person can identify. In the case of culturally diverse women, this may entail the deliberate building of relationships with more senior culturally diverse women in the same work setting. Given the relatively small number of culturally diverse women in certain career fields, creative ways are needed to facilitate these relationships. Mentorship relationships that arise in educational programs may need to be sustained even after both parties no longer have an academic connection. Mentorship relationships may arise through liaisons that originate at professional conferences, workshops, and other such training and development programs. Matching experienced and novice culturally diverse women in the same field creates the likelihood that the external psychological and social pressures that these women may encounter will be understood by mentors, who can in turn share coping strategies that worked successfully for them. Mentorship of culturally diverse women by other culturally diverse women can positively influence self-efficacy by providing role models with whom these individuals can relate in order to enhance feelings of being able to surmount obstacles that present in the work world (Lent et al., 2005).

Role of Spirituality

Culturally diverse women have reported the use of spiritual resources as helpful in navigating through career decisions and transitions to varying degrees according to cultural background. Much of the research on spirituality in culturally diverse women in general has focused on African American women. In a study of 119 African American women in the Northeast, Harris-Robinson (2006) concluded that African American women often use spiritual-focused coping as a first response to stress, with the likelihood of identifying spirituality as the most helpful coping mechanism varying positively with age. Lower socioeconomic African American women in the midst of career transitions indicate that spirituality is a critical source of resilience for them (Banerjee & Pyles, 2004).

Prayer, meditation, and spiritual reading may be recommended by career counselors to clients who indicate openness to using these resources as a means to cope with career-related stress. Spiritual outlets, such as church attendance or mediation groups, may also create the forum for clients to build support network relationships that will help them beyond the realm of counseling.

Techniques

Other career counseling techniques that are embedded in social constructivist or narrative approaches include life–role circles, lifelines, goal maps, and life space maps (Brott, 2005). Also helpful are career-o-grams, charts used to outline family and historical influences in career discernment (Thorngren & Feit, 2001). Similarly, Gibson (2005) advocates for the use of genograms in career counseling with some younger clients. These strategies foster discussion about career and life-related topics, including struggles related to navigating through multiple identities and confronting discriminatory behaviors. See Appendix N for additional suggestions for relevant interventions for culturally diverse clients.

Early Interventions for Culturally Diverse Girls

Given the adamant research supporting that parental support produces positive effects in the self-efficacy of girls (Alliman-Brissett et al., 2004), school counselors have a unique opportunity to advocate for empowerment of culturally diverse women by working with them as girls and adolescents. School counselors are in a unique position to provide career information to parents and girls, facilitate early mentorship and role modeling relationships, teach coping skills for managing discrimination-related stress, and model and encourage perseverance. For many culturally diverse groups, making career development a collective, family experience creates the needed atmosphere for success, even when cultural norms are being crossed in other ways. School counselors can initiate these types of conversations among parents and their culturally diverse daughters.

CONCLUSION

Many culturally diverse women will experience injustices that are due to racism, discrimination, oppression, sexism, and heterosexism. Pope et al. (2004) argued that career counselors have an ethical responsibility to address these issues with their clients even if they have to initiate the conversation. Savickas (2000) urged career counselors to consider the role of work in relation to other life roles, including a focus on how family roles may intersect with career and work roles. In the case of culturally diverse female clients, career counselors may validate the unpaid work done, such as childrearing and household responsibilities (Stebleton, 2007).

Career counselors may prepare clients for multiple potential obstacles by helping clients develop contingency plans and coping skills. Pryor and Bright (2006) refer to this approach to career counseling as the chaos theory of careers. Stead (1996) suggests that negative, unplanned events can be turned into positive work opportunities that result in desirable outcomes. In conclusion, career counselors working with culturally diverse women have the capacity to be agents of social change. These professionals contribute to the creation of a career demographic in the United States that is representative of the actual makeup of the nation by helping culturally diverse women anticipate possible challenges and construct proactive coping strategies. The focus of this type of career counseling is empowerment of clients so that culturally diverse women are free to self-determine their career identities just as others in U.S. society do.

REVISITING THE CASE OF JACKIE

Jackie is questioning in terms of sexual orientation and is apprehensive about revealing her questioning due to fear of family disapproval and workplace discrimination. The counselor might encourage Jackie to consult with human resources about the hospital's policies about discrimination. The counselor may invite Jackie to brainstorm about her reactions to the potential outcomes that may follow from disclosing her sexual orientation questioning to her family. A reminder that the decision to disclose this belongs to Jackie may be helpful to her.

Childcare is an issue that Jackie must address as she considers returning to school to further her career. Her mother and grandmother have helped her before. Perhaps after-school programs, such as school-based tutoring, church-based programs, Boys and Girls Club, or YMCA, can be utilized to supplement the childcare provided by family. The counselor may encourage Jackie to think of positive aspects of returning to school while her children are young, such as giving a positive example about the importance of education.

Jackie is struggling to make a decision about advancing her career. The possibilities she is considering will involve additional formal education. Exploring how she succeeded in the phlebotomy training program may calm apprehensions she has about returning to life as a student again, that is, reflecting on her past accomplishments can heighten self-efficacy in Jackie. The counselor may invite Jackie to reminiscence about personal and academic struggles she overcame as a student in the past.

The counselor may find it beneficial to invite Jackie to create a career timeline. As she has primarily worked as a phlebotomist, the timeline might be used to facilitate introspection about the different phases of her career as a phlebotomist. What was she seeking as a phlebotomy student? What fulfilled her as a novice phlebotomist? What is different about her identity now that she is more experienced in the field? Stories that illustrate the responses to these timeline questions could be solicited. The counselor could then encourage Jackie to tell a story of the person she aspires to be in 10 years.

The counselor might consider helping Jackie network with a mentor or support group. Perhaps there are other women who returned to school later in life with whom Jackie can be connected to learn their stories and to receive encouragement, particularly other African American women. The counselor might invite Jackie to reflect on the benefits of entering a nursing program that has large numbers of nontraditional students who complete the program. Because Jackie has thought of going to medical school, the counselor might suggest that Jackie begin to investigate the prerequisite coursework for medical school, the financial and time investment, as well as the rewards based on what is most important and valuable in having a meaningful life for Jackie.

REFERENCES

Allen, B. J. (2002). Goals for emancipatory communication research on Black women. In M. Houston & O. I. Davis (Eds.), *Centering ourselves: African American feminist and womanist studies of discourse* (pp. 21–34). Cresskill, NJ: Hampton Press.

Allen, B. J. (2004). *Difference matters: Communicating social identity*. Long Grove, IL: Waveland Press.

Allen, T. D., Eby, L. T., Poteet, M. L., Lentz, E., & Lima, L. (2004). Career benefits associated with mentoring for protégés: A meta-analysis. *Journal of Applied Psychology, 89*, 127–136.

Alliman-Brissett, A. E., Turner, S. L., & Skovholt, T. M. (2004). Parent support and African American adolescents' career self-efficacy. *Professional School Counseling, 7*(3), 124–132.

Arminio, J. L., Carter, S., Jones, S. E., Kruger, K., Lucas, N., Washington, J., . . . Scott, A. (2000). Leadership experiences of students of color. *NASPA Journal, 37*(3), 496–510.

Arons, J. (2008). Lifetime losses: The career wage gap. Center for American Progress. Retrieved from https://www.americanprogressaction.org/issues/women/report/2008/12/08/5343/lifetime-losses-the-career-wage-gap/

Bandura, A. (1986). *Social foundations of thought and action*. Englewood Cliffs, NJ: Prentice Hall.

Banerjee, M. M., & Pyles, L. (2004). Spirituality: A source of resilience for African American women in the era of welfare reform. *Journal of Ethnic and Cultural Diversity in Social Work, 13*(2), 45–70.

Bartkowski, J. P., & Read, J. N. G. (2003). Veiled submission: Gender, power, and identity among evangelical and Muslim women in the United States. *Qualitative Sociology, 26*(1), 71–92.

Blake, S. (1999). At the crossroads of race and gender: Lessons from the mentoring experiences of professional Black women. In A. J. Murrell, F. J. Crosby, & R. J. Ely (Eds.), *Mentoring dilemmas: Developmental relationships within multicultural organizations* (pp. 83–104). Mahwah, NJ: Lawrence Erlbaum.

Boydston, J. (2001). Women in the labor force. In S. Boyer (Ed.), *The Oxford companion to United States history*. New York, NY: Oxford University Press. Retrieved from http://www.anb.org/cush_wlabor.html

Brault, M. W. (2012). *Americans with disabilities: 2010*. Current population reports, P70-P131, Washington, DC: U.S. Census Bureau.

Breakfield, F. A. (2010). *Encircled by sisterhood: Mentoring experiences of African American women in Delta Sigma Theta sorority* (unpublished doctoral dissertation). Statesboro, GA: Georgia Southern University. Retrieved from http://digitalcommons.georgiasouthern.edu/etd/531/

Brott, P. E. (2005). A constructivist look at life roles. *The Career Development Quarterly, 54*(2), 138–149.

Cao, L., & Novas, H. (1996). *Everything you need to know about Asian Americans*. New York, NY: Penguin Plume.

Chen, G., Gully, S. M., & Eden, D. (2001). Validation of a new general self-efficacy scale. *Organizational Research Methods, 4*(1), 62–83.

Cheng, C. (1997). Are Asian American employees a model minority or just a minority? *The Journal of Applied Behavioral Science, 33*(3), 277–290.

Cheung, F. M., & Halpern, D. F. (2010). Women at the top: Powerful leaders define success as work + family in a culture of gender. *American Psychologist, 65*(3), 182–193.

Clark, M. A., Severy, L., & Sawyer, S. A. (2004). Creating connections: Using a narrative approach in career group counseling with college students from diverse cultural backgrounds. *Journal of College Counseling, 7*(1), 24–31.

Cook, E. P., Heppner, M. J., & O'Brien, K. M. (2002). Career development of women of color and White women: Assumptions, conceptualization, and interventions from an ecological perspective. *The Career Development Quarterly, 50*(4), 291–305.

Department of Labor, Bureau of Labor Statistics. (2010). Median weekly earnings of full-time wage and salary workers by selected characteristics. Retrieved from www.pay-equity.org/PDFs/ProfWomen.pdf

Enright, M. S., Conyers, L. M., & Szymanski, E. M. (1996). Career and career-related educational concerns of college students with disabilities. *Journal of Counseling & Development, 75*(2), 103–114.

Fitzgerald, L., & Crites, J. (1979). Career counseling for women. *The Counseling Psychologist, 8*(1), 33–34.

Gayle Baugh, S., & Sullivan, S. E. (2005). Mentoring and career development. *Career Development International, 10*(6/7), 425–428.

Gibson, D. M. (2005). The use of genograms in career counseling with elementary, middle, and high school students. *The Career Development Quarterly, 53*(4), 353–362.

Gill, C. J. (1997). The last sisters: Disabled women's health. In S. B. Ruzek, V. Olesen, & A. Clarke (Eds.), *Women's health: Complexities and differences* (pp. 96–112). Columbus, OH: Ohio State University Press.

Goodstein, L. (2009). Poll finds U.S. Muslims thriving, but not content. *New York Times*, March 2, p. 11.

Gordon, L. D. (2002). Education and the professions. In N. A. Hewitt (Ed.), *A companion to American women's history* (pp. 227–249). Hoboken, NJ: John Wiley.

Guralnik, J. M., Leveille, S. G., Hirsch, R., Ferrucci, L., & Fried, L. P. (1997). The impact of disability in older women. *Journal of American Medical Women's Association, 52*(3), 113–120.

Harris-Robinson, M. (2006). The use of spiritual-focused coping among working-class black women. *Journal of Religion & Spirituality in Social Work: Social Thought, 25*(2), 77–90.

Heaton, T. B., Jacobson, C. K., & Holland, K. (1999). Persistence and change in decisions to remain childless. *Journal of Marriage and the Family, 61*(2), 531–539.

Hewlett, S. (2002) *Baby Hunger: The new battle for motherhood.* London: U.K., Atlantic Books.

Holvino, E. (2010). Intersections: The simultaneity of race, gender and class in organization studies. *Gender, Work & Organization, 17*(3), 248–277.

Hossfeld, K. J. (1994). Hiring immigrant women: Silicon Valley's "simple formula." *Women of color in US society*, 65–93.

Hurtado, A. (1996). *The color of privilege: Three blasphemies on race and feminism.* Ann Arbor, MI: University of Michigan Press.

Ian, M. (2014). Can parents influence children's mathematics achievement and persistence in STEM careers? *Journal of Career Development, 41*(2), 87–103.

Jackson, L. M., Esses, V. M., & Burris, C. T. (2001). Contemporary sexism and discrimination: The importance of respect for men and women. *Personality and Social Psychology Bulletin, 27*(1), 48–61.

Jackson, M. (2013). Fact sheet: The state of Latinas in the United States. Center for American Progress. Retrieved from https://www.americanprogress.org/issues/race/report/2013/11/07/79167/fact-sheet-the-state-of-latinas-in-the-united-states

Kelly, K. R., Gunsalus, A. J. C., & Gunsalus, R. (2009). Social cognitive predictors of the career goals of Korean American students. *The Career Development Quarterly, 58*(1), 14–28.

Kelly, M. (2009). Women's voluntary childlessness: A radical rejection of motherhood? *WSQ: Women's Studies Quarterly, 37*(2), 157–172.

Kessler-Harris, A. (1982). *Out to work: A history of wage-earning women in the United States.* New York, NY: Oxford University Press.

Lent, R. W., Brown, S. D., & Hackett, G. (1994). Toward a unifying social cognitive theory of career and academic interest, choice, and performance. *Journal of Vocational Behavior, 45*(1), 79–122.

Lent, R. W., Brown, S. D., Sheu, H. B., Schmidt, J., Brenner, B. R., Gloster, C. S., . . . Treistman, D. (2005). Social cognitive predictors of academic interests and goals in engineering: Utility for women and students at historically Black universities. *Journal of Counseling Psychology, 52*(1), 84–92.

Locke, W. S., & Gibbons, M. M. (2008). On her own again: The use of narrative therapy in career counseling with displaced new traditionalists. *The Family Journal, 16*(2), 132–138.

Maree, J. G. (2014). Career construction with a gay client: A case study. *British Journal of Guidance & Counselling, 42*(4), 436–449.

Maree, K., Ebersöhn, L., & Molepo, M. (2006). Administering narrative career counselling in a diverse setting: Trimming the sails to the wind. *South African Journal of Education, 26*(1), 49–60.

Mason, M. A., & Goulden, M. (2004). Marriage and baby blues: Redefining gender equity in the academy. *The Annals of the American Academy of Political and Social Science, 596*(1), 86–103.

Min, P. G. (2006). Asian immigration: History and contemporary trends. In P. G. Min (Ed.), *Asian Americans: Contemporary trends and issues* (pp. 7–31). Newbury Park, CA: Pine Forge Press.

Nassar-McMillan, S., & Zagzebski-Tovar, L. (2012). Career counseling with Americans of Arab descent. *Career Planning and Adult Development Journal, 28*(1), 72–87.

National Science Board. (2008). *Science and engineering indicators 2008.* Retrieved from http://www.nsf.gov/statistics/seind08/tables.htm

Ng, J. C., Lee, S. S., & Pak, Y. K. (2007). Contesting the model minority and perpetual foreigner stereotypes: A critical review of literature on Asian Americans in education. *Review of Research in Education, 31*(1), 95–130.

Ngo, B., & Lee, S. J. (2007). Complicating the image of model minority success: A review of Southeast Asian American education. *Review of Educational Research, 77*(4), 415–453.

Niles, S. G., & Hartung, P. W. (2000). Emerging career theories. In D. A. Luzzu (Ed.), *Career counseling of college students: An empirical guide to strategies that work* (pp. 23–41). Washington, DC: American Psychological Association.

Noonan, B. M., Gallor, S. M., Hensler-McGinnis, N. F., Fassinger, R. E., Wang, S., & Goodman, J. (2004). Challenge and success: A qualitative study of the career development of highly achieving women with physical and sensory disabilities. *Journal of Counseling Psychology, 51*(1), 68–80.

Padavic, I., & Reskin, B. F. (2002). *Women and men at work* (2nd ed.). Thousand Oaks, CA: Sage Publications.

Parker, P. S. (2001). African American women executives' leadership communication within dominant-culture organizations. *Management Communication Quarterly, 15*(1), 42–82.

Pasha-Zaidi, N., Masson, T., & Pennington, M. N. (2013). Can I get a job if I wear hijab? An exploratory study of the perceptions of South Asian Muslim women in the US and the UAE. *International Journal of Research Studies in Psychology, 3*(1), 13–24.

Pope, M., Barret, B., Szymanski, D. M., Chung, Y. B., Singaravelu, H., McLean, R., & Sanabria, S. (2004). Culturally appropriate career counseling with gay and lesbian clients. *The Career Development Quarterly, 53*(2), 158–177.

Pryor, R. G., & Bright, J. E. (2006). Counseling chaos: Techniques for practitioners. *Journal of Employment Counseling, 43*(1), 9–17.

Reeves, T. C., & Azam, L. (2012). To wear hijab or not: Muslim women's perceptions of their healthcare workplaces. *Journal of Business Diversity, 12*(2), 41–58.

Rehfuss, M. C. (2009). The future career autobiography: A narrative measure of career intervention effectiveness. *The Career Development Quarterly, 58*(1), 82–90.

Reid, P. T., & Comas-Diaz, L. (1990). Gender and ethnicity: Perspectives on dual status. *Sex Roles, 22*(7–8), 397–408.

Reuther, C., & Fairhurst, G. T. (2000). Chaos theory and the glass ceiling. In P. Buzzanell (Ed.), *Rethinking organizational & managerial communication* (pp. 236–253). Thousand Oaks, CA: Sage Press.

Savickas, M. (2000). Renovating the psychology of careers for the twenty-first century. In A. Collin & R. A. Young (Eds.), *The future of career* (pp. 53–68). New York, NY: Cambridge University Press.

Savickas, M. (2005). The theory and practice of career construction. In S. D. Brown & R. W. Lent (Eds.), *Career development and counseling: Putting theory and research to work* (pp. 42–70). Hokoben, NJ: John Wiley.

Sharf, S. (2006). *Applying career development theory to counseling.* Belmont, CA: Thompson.

Shi, Y. (2008). The formation of a Chinese immigrant working-class patriarchy: Reinventing gendered expectations within the structural confines of US society. *Meridians: Feminism, Race, Transnationalism, 9*(1), 31–60.

Stead, G. B. (1996). Career development of Black South African adolescents: A developmental-contextual perspective. *Journal of Counseling & Development, 74*(3), 270–275.

Stebleton, M. J. (2007). Career counseling with African immigrant college students: Theoretical approaches and implications for practice. *The Career Development Quarterly, 55*(4), 290–312.

Tan, J. (2008). Breaking the "bamboo ceiling" and the "glass ceiling": The experience of women entrepreneurs in high-tech industries in an emerging market. *Journal of Business Ethics, 80*(3), 547–564.

Tate, E. D., & Linn, M. C. (2005). How does identity shape the experiences of women of color engineering students? *Journal of Science Education and Technology, 14*(5–6), 483–493.

Taylor, K. M., & Betz, N. E. (1983). Applications of self-efficacy theory to the understanding and treatment of career indecision. *Journal of Vocational Behavior, 22*(1), 63–81.

Thorngren, J. M., & Feit, S. S. (2001). The career-o-gram: A postmodern career intervention. *The Career Development Quarterly, 49*(4), 291–303.

Wade, T. J., Romano, M. J., & Blue, L. (2004). The effect of African American skin color on hiring preferences. *Journal of Applied Social Psychology, 34*(12), 2550–2558.

Woo, D. (2000). *Glass ceilings and Asian Americans: The new face of workplace barriers*. Lanham, MD: Rowman & Littlefield.

Young, R. A., & Collin, A. (2004). Introduction: Constructivism and social constructionism in the career field. *Journal of Vocational Behavior, 64*(3), 373–388.

CHAPTER 16

CULTURALLY DIVERSE MEN

Anne G. Morring, Andre Joachim, Beheshteh Abdi, Wendy K. Killam, and Suzanne Degges-White

CASE VIGNETTE: REGGIE

Reggie, a 19-year-old African American male, is a college sophomore who has not declared a major because he is still trying to figure out what career he wants to pursue. Reggie is a commuter student living at home with his married parents, Bonnie and James, and his three younger siblings, Christina, Jenny, and Mike. His mother runs a day care center out of their home, and his father has been working two part-time retail jobs since Reggie started college. Both parents are extremely supportive and proud of Reggie, who is the first man in their families to pursue a college education. When he began college, Reggie thought about pursuing a science degree, but the math and writing prerequisites were challenging for him. He grew frustrated and is ready to switch majors, but he is unsure of his career. His academic counselor encouraged Reggie to visit the Career Center on campus and, in addition to looking at the information at the Center, Reggie scheduled his first appointment with a career counselor.

CAREER COUNSELING CONSIDERATIONS FOR AFRICAN AMERICAN MEN

According to the 2010 U.S. Census Brief, African Americans were defined as Americans with ancestors from either Sub-Saharan Africa or Afro-Caribbean countries (Rastogi, Johnson, Hoeffel, & Drewery, 2011). The 2013 U.S. Census found people who identified solely as African Americans made up 13.2% of the total population in the United States (U.S. Census Bureau, 2015b); when accounting for identification within multiple racial identities, the percentage increased to 15.2% of the population (Office of Minority Health & Health Equity [OMHHE], 2015), which translated to 45 million individuals (U.S. Census, 2015a). The South had the highest proportion of African Americans within the total population of the geographical region at 20%, compared with 13% in the Northeast, 11% in the Midwest, and 6% in the West regions (Rastogi et al., 2011). The 2013 Census estimated the African American population would grow to 74.5 million people by 2060. Regarding financial circumstances, African Americans fare poorly. The national annual median income was $51,939, but the median income for African American households was only $34,598 (U.S. Census, 2015a), reflecting a significant disparity. Also, the poverty rate for African American families was 27.2%, almost twice the national rate of 14.5% (U.S. Census, 2015a).

Historical Career Paths and Available Choices

Employment for African Americans traditionally has fallen into a few specific job sectors and industries, specifically local government agencies, public employment, and unionized manufacturing jobs historically held by middle-class African Americans before the recession of the late 2000s (Asante-Muhammad, Chase, & Richardson, 2015). Since the recession, the two fields employing the most African Americans are the health care and retail industries. Health care offers African Americans better wages and benefits than retail, but African Americans are more likely to be employed as home health or nursing aides, which offer little opportunity for advancement and are not the highest paid positions. The Institute for Diversity in Health Management reported minority board members at 14% and minority executive positions at 12%, which were unchanged from the 2011 report, but the percentage of first- and mid-level management positions held by minorities increased two percentage points to 17% (American Hospital Association and Institute for Diversity in Health Management, 2012).

In terms of retail jobs, African American males have faced unequal treatment. Although African Americans comprised 11% of the retail labor force, the majority held cashier positions, which have the lowest wages (Ruetschlin & Asante-Muhammad, 2015); in terms of management positions, only 6% were held by African Americans. Also, African American males were often paid between 75% and 90% of wages Caucasians earned, which ranged from $1,850 to $7,500 a year in lost wages (Ruetschlin & Asante-Muhammad, 2015); lost wages have also resulted in many African American males working multiple jobs to support their families (Ho, Rasheed, & Rasheed, 2004). African Americans working in retail positions were more likely to have jobs involving schedules that were either unpredictable, unstable, or on-call, further intensifying both the racial wage divide and occupational segregation (Ruetschlin & Asante-Muhammad, 2015).

CAREER BARRIERS

African American males face significant challenges within American society (Franklin & Boyd-Franklin, 2000). Interpersonal and systemic discrimination are still prominent in society (Smith & Roysircar, 2010), leading to elevated social and health risks for African American males (Gordon, Gordon, & Nembhard, 1994; Leary, 1996). The National Association for the Advancement of Colored People (NAACP, 2015) reported that nearly 1 million of 2.3 million incarcerated Americans were African Americans. If current trends continue, one in three African American males could experience time in prison. Many African American males lack access to networking opportunities, negatively affecting their knowledge about career options and employment opportunities (White & Cones, 1999). Racial slights and microaggressions can affect the psychological well-being of individuals, leading individuals to feel a lack of worth (Franklin & Boyd-Franklin, 2000). The experiences of racism can cause African American males to be reluctant to seek out or participate in counseling (Patterson, 1996; Ridley, 1984).

The narrative surrounding African American males and education has focused on academic failure, low-test scores, underrepresentation within gifted education programs, and high dropout rates (Bennett et al., 2004), which are factors influencing career paths. Unequal opportunities, academic disparities, and unjust treatment based on socioeconomic status and race hinder African American males from achieving educational goals and career paths (Flowers III, 2015). As of 2013, 83.7% of African Americans who were 25 years or older held at least a high school diploma, but only 19.3% held a bachelor's degree or higher (U.S. Census Bureau, 2015a). When focused on science, technology, engineering, and mathematics (STEM) degrees, 8% were conferred on African American students (both male and female), whereas 77% were either Caucasian or Asian American (Stolle-McAllister, Sto. Domingo, & Carillo, 2011). Ethnic minorities enrolled in STEM programs at the same rate as Caucasian students, but were more likely to switch to a nonscience major (Tsui, 2007).

Although more African Americans enrolled in college in 2013 compared with previous years, only 1.7 million African Americans held an advanced degree (U.S. Census Bureau). Flowers III (2015) noted how African American male students viewed their academic abilities and identities played a part in their education; African American males may be more likely to disengage from academics due to a lack of identification within the current education system (Whiting, 2006). African American men were hired less often for positions within higher education compared with Caucasian males (Jackson, 2008). Several studies within the past decade (Cuyjet, 2006; Flowers III, 2015; Harvey, 2008; Moore & Owens, 2008) indicated the needs of Black male students have not been supported within the education system. When recognized for academic achievement, young African American men developed more self-esteem, more confidence in academic endeavors, and stronger self-concepts (Garibaldi, 1992), furthering academic success.

EXPECTED CAREER DEVELOPMENT NEEDS

Career development needs fluctuate based on the occupational market and societal needs. In the past, early childhood development, socioeconomic status, and gender were viewed as key influences on one's career (Osipow & Fitzgerald, 1996), reinforcing stereotypes about minorities. Observations about occupational demographics and barriers experienced by others affected congruence between perceived abilities and actions taken toward achieving career goals (Lent, Brown, & Hackett, 1996, 2000; Perrone, Sedlacek, & Alexander, 2001). Studies (Feij, Whitely, Peiro, & Taris, 1995; Miller & Jablin, 1991) have shown a connection between workers seeking help at new jobs and career enhancement within that job, but African American men are less likely than Caucasian men to seek help (Perrone et al., 2001). The perception that African American males were hired within fields employing few minorities based on their race rather than qualifications still exists (Leong, 1995); thus, unfamiliar occupational fields can propel African American men into unknown situations and hostile environments (Leong, 1995). Self-perceptions about self-efficacy, goal setting behavior, and expectations of outcomes shape actions and performances taken within one's career (Perrone et al., 2001).

The Casey Foundation and PolicyLink outlined four ways to foster economic and job-creation growth within communities of color: (a) promote industries that provide jobs for people without college degrees; (b) work with large anchor institutions, such as health facilities and schools, to provide occupational opportunities within low-income communities; (c) aid the start and expansion of minority-owned businesses by removing barriers hindering growth; and (d) ensure public money and investments for low-income communities to create opportunities and jobs (Gilliam, 2014). This model works with individuals at their current level, such as promoting jobs for people without college degrees, as well as advocating for businesses to come to areas where minorities live, rather than forcing minorities to travel great distances to get to their jobs.

Supports in Place

One of the main supports for African American males is the family. Smokowski, Reynolds, and Bezruczko (1999) found social and academic development grew out of parenting styles, attitudes, behaviors, and values. Moore (2006) found when parents conveyed the importance of education and their expectations for academic success, their sons were positively influenced; when families motivated and encouraged their sons to participate in science programs, African American students succeeded at higher levels compared with less supported students (Russell & Atwater, 2005). Parents who may have had little education will need support and help from their children's teachers, schools, and their community at large to help their children succeed academically (Garibaldi, 1992). As students succeed at school tasks, they are more likely to believe in their abilities to complete more difficult challenges, which further builds their self-efficacy (Kiran & Sungur, 2012) and has implications for their future career paths.

The most racially diverse organizations often have people of color in senior leadership positions (Asante-Muhammad et al., 2015). Mentoring or coaching can provide individually tailored and focused programs to promote growth in future business leaders (Asante-Muhammad et al., 2015). The U.S. Department of Education has a webpage devoted to scholarship opportunities for minority students (U.S. Department of Education, 2015). Numerous scholarships specifically for African American students are available, but a significant amount of scholarship monies are returned to the organizations from a lack of applicants (Tuskegee University, 2015). In 2014, President Obama launched *My Brother's Keeper Initiative,* aimed at partnering businesses and foundations with communities of color to mentor, build networks, and teach skills for occupations and education, as well as decrease neighborhood violence and improve nutrition and overall health for people of color (Office of the Press Secretary, 2014).

CAREER COUNSELING CONSIDERATIONS FOR LATINO MEN

As the United States expands in population, changes will occur in how people work, think, and interact with each other. The U.S. Census Bureau (U.S. Census, 2015b) estimated there will be more than 420 million people residing in America by 2060. This will impact careers, education, health care, and overall living. Latino Americans will surge as the largest minority group, accounting for more than one fourth of the population. Hispanic and/or Latino origins can be viewed as the heritage, nationality group, lineage, or country of birth of the person or persons' parents and ancestors before their arrival in the United States (Centers for Disease Control and Prevention [CDC], 2015). For the purposes of this chapter, readers should note that Hispanic and Latino are being used interchangeably.

The Office of Management and Budget explained that Hispanic populations are made up of people of Mexican, Puerto Rican, Cuban, Central or South American, and Spanish descents (persons from Spanish-speaking origins despite race). The CDC estimated current Hispanic populations in the United States totaled around 53 million in 2012 and are expected to be more than double by 2060, with a projected outlook of 128 million. This impending population increase will continue to influence the U.S. economy, careers, education, and Latino American males' perspectives and choices. Career counselors and advocates must remember that Latino Americans face some of the same barriers other minority populations have faced, such as conflicting familial expectations, negative stereotypes, educational oppression, marginalization, and lack of sociopolitical resources.

Occupational Outlook

Teranishi, Suarez-Orozco, and Suarez-Orozco (2011) explained that Latino immigrants are paid lower wages compared with native-born workers. This puts added stress on Latino males to contribute to their family's income by placing work above other pursuits. Latino American males make up about half of all farm workers, laborers, grounds maintenance workers, construction, and warehouse workers. Portes and Rivas (2011) found that the majority of manual laborers working in the United States come from Mexico and Central American countries. Lichter (2012) noted that "the so-called spatial assimilation model suggests that immigrants become integrated residentially with natives as they become economically assimilated. In the Hispanic case, however, the work available in rural labor markets typically comprises low-wage, low-skill jobs" (p. 16) with limited upward mobility. This trend can also be observed in urban areas. This phenomenon may be explained by the need for basic-needs income, resulting in the neglect of secondary education. This can lead to an unbreakable cycle in which Latino men rely on unskilled and low-wage jobs to support their family and the cycle continues for generations. The U.S. Bureau of Labor Statistics (BLS; 2010) explained that Latino men comprise the majority of service workers, construction workers, and maintenance workers in the workforce. Another trend in this report was that of all the minority races, both men and women, Latino men account for the smallest number of individuals working in management and professional career industries. Data gathered by the Pew

Hispanic Center (PHC, 2009) showed that even though Hispanic men represent a smaller percentage of students in the education system, they show a proportionally strong presence in the workforce, with undocumented workers making up the majority of the labor force. The PHC report is reflective of the career counseling challenges related to educational attainment, language barriers, family influences, or social perceptions of Latino men.

Career Barriers

Education and career barriers are associated with the decision made by many Latino males to disengage from postsecondary institutions in order to find work that will offer short-term gains. These short-term gains may assist the household income but may not be beneficial to the long-term stability of Hispanic males who desire thriving career options rather than the life-sustaining low-wage jobs that are customarily accessible to this population. This perpetual dynamic of career and self-actualization limitations can also be attributed to biases on macro and micro levels of the American labor force.

Biases

Hispanic males face unique barriers, both intentional biases and unintentional systemic biases that arise as a result of stereotypical beliefs. Some of the stereotypes against which they must fight include those related to dependability, industriousness, self-control, and intelligence (Luksyte, Waite, Avery, & Roy, 2013). Some of the earliest introductions of discrimination for Hispanic males are usually perpetrated in educational institutions during day-to-day interactions through the use of microaggressions that influence students' sense of self-efficacy as well as how they feel they are perceived by teachers, staff, and peers. Solorzano, Ceja, and Yoso (2000) explained microaggressions as affronts directed toward minorities, which can be intentional or unintentional, and are not always blatant discrimination. Microaggressions that stem from Latino "stereotypes include mistaking a Latino man for a janitor or being surprised when a Latino adolescent does well in school" (Huynh, 2012, p. 832). Schools are often organized to perpetuate ethnic inequalities through academic tracking, cultural biases against Hispanic cultures or individuals who speak Spanish as a primary language, and legacies of ambiguous relations between the academic institution and the community members (Luna & Revilla, 2013).

Language Barriers

Other barriers Latino males face are language barriers or English literacy deficits. Teranishi et al. (2011) explained that students in community colleges face many challenges surrounding verbal and written communication with faculty. Of the various immigrant populations in recent U.S. history, "Hispanics in particular have arrived in such large numbers in concentrated parts of the country that they are not inclined to acculturate" (Portes & Rivas, 2011, p. 222). Clark, Ponjuan, Orrock, Wilson, and Flores (2013) suggested that parental guidance is influential, but there can be additional hindrances with school–home communications when sending home letters in English to Spanish-speaking parents. These challenges can extend to how much or what types of familial support young Latino males have when it is time to consider postsecondary education opportunities, specifically, higher education institutions. Teranishi et al. (2011) explained that community colleges are in dire need of English as a Second Language (ESL) faculty to help students and their families experience increased connectedness, comprehend U.S. cultural expectations in schools and professional fields, and to help open up previously unconsidered opportunities to Latino males and their families through multifaceted career counseling. As noted by Lichter (2012, p. 217),

> This barrier can be attributed to immigrant parental members who migrate to the U.S. Children of immigrants, even if they are citizens of birth, face obvious challenges of having parents who may not speak English well, who are poor, and who are often less educated themselves.

Family Influences

Raque-Bogdan, Klingaman, Martin, and Lucas (2013) described how parental support is influential on children's self-efficacy in pursuing educational and career options. In an ever-changing job economy, family influences can become problematic when the cost of education compromises an individual's ability to sustain the family infrastructure. "An essential aspect to understanding Latino male achievement is the influence of *familismo*—a concept of Latino cultural norms that involves the strong identification and attachment to immediate and extended family" (Clark, Ponjuan, Orrock, Wilson, & Flores, 2013, p. 459). Family dynamics have strong influences on how Latino American men choose career paths. Although Latino families place high value on education, there is still pressure on Latino males to contribute to family financial stability by taking jobs and contributing other supports to the overall household (Clark et al., 2013). Educational aspirations can seem unimportant when factoring the need for financial support for everyday needs or collective family betterment over the expected cost of secondary education for one family member.

Needed Resources

Latino males are considered a marginalized population. Collaborating agencies should be aware of special concerns and/or circumstances that limit the career success of Latino males including meeting needs in terms of mental health, educational, and career counseling services.

Mental Health

Research highlighted that Latino men's job outlooks have dropped in recent years, which can have negative impacts on their families and/or their self-efficacy. Vasquez, Gonzalez-Gurada, & De Santis (2011) suggested Latino men's mental health concerns are neglected due to the lack of knowledge by clinicians regarding diversity issues. According to Rogers-Sirin and Gupta (2012), Hispanics experience a higher prevalence of depression due to issues related to assimilation and acculturation.

Educational Institutions

Parents of Latino males are less likely than parents in other groups to have earned a high school diploma and the least likely to have attained a bachelor's, master's, or a professional degree out of any other race. This report reflects the gap that needs to be closed in ensuring that Latino males are provided with the support necessary to successfully matriculate and complete 4-year degrees. Hispanics face unusually high dropout rates, which effectively limit their socioeconomic mobility and full participation in American society (Lichter, 2012). Research conducted by Clark et al. (2013) revealed through a study of four high schools and one community college that there was a significant lack of awareness of any specific support programs directed toward addressing issues or problems of Latino males.

Career Development Needs

For Latino men, educational attainment is correlated with career success. Program development should include family and community involvement, mentoring and role modeling, and supporting services and programs that encourage Latino male students to formulate and carry out educational goals (Clark et al., 2013). According to Rhodes, Daniel, Song, Alonzo, Downs, and Reboussin (2013), social support needs to encompass a number of areas, including emotional, instrumental, informational, and appraisal issues. Rogers-Sirin and Gupta (2012) found that clinicians should be more influential in fostering connections with peers and adults of the same ethnic group. Findings from these studies indicated there is a reoccurring theme that parental figures have more of an impact outside of educational institutions or mentors when assisting Latino males who invest in career or educational attainment. Family support for the education of young Hispanic males should be a key target for anyone providing career counseling.

Existing Programs and Initiatives

Community Programming

Encuentros Leadership: encuentrosleadership.org/
Fathers Active in Communities and Education: star.tamucc.edu/face.html
Hispanic Scholarship Fund: hsf.net/
Latino College Dollars Foundation: www.latinocollegedollars.org/

College-Level Programming

Lambda Upsilon Lambda Latino at Cornell University: http://www.launidadlatina.org/

Project MALES: ddce.utexas.edu/projectmales
The Clave Latino Male Empowerment Program: www.edexcelencia.org/our-work
Workforce Diversity Network: www.workforcediversitynetwork.com/index.aspx

CAREER COUNSELING CONSIDERATIONS WITH ASIAN AMERICAN MEN

Description of the Population

The number of Asian Americans in the United States has increased by more than 46% from 1990 to 2000, and they are the second fastest growing minority group in the United States (Kim & Atkinson, 2002). By the year 2050, Asian Americans will make up more than 9% of the U.S. population. Currently, they comprise just less than 5%, and there are more than 13.5 million Asian Americans living in the United States (Kelly, Gunsalus, & Gunsalus, 2009). It is, however, important to note that the term *Asian Americans* refers to a very diverse group that includes more than 24 different heritages or distinct groups. Thus, the term *Asian American* does not take into account the differences of all of these distinct groups, and these groups speak numerous languages based on different countries of origin (Kelly et al., 2009).

Similarities among cultures exist; for example, a focus is placed on the importance of the needs of the family, and decisions are typically made based on the best interests of the family rather than of the individual. These decisions include both career decisions and occupational choice (Lowe, 2005). This reflects the perception that a child serves as an extension of parents in many cases. Additionally, a mother is expected to raise her children, and the relationship between parent and child is perceived as the most powerful and valuable within the family, over and above the marital relationship. Given this construct, it makes sense that mothers are extremely involved in the college and career choices of their children (Dundes, Cho, & Kwak, 2009).

Historical Perspective

Asian American men immigrated to the United States in the mid-1800s seeking jobs to escape the severe economic problems in their native countries. This continued into the early 1900s as Asian men worked on plantations as well as on railroads. They also worked in the timber industry and in agricultural fields (Shek, 2006). Employers preferred to hire Asian American males over other groups because they could pay them lower wages. Additionally, due to language barriers, Asian Americans were not working in jobs where they could reach their full potential (Kelly et al., 2009). Furthermore, Asian males were often viewed as a threat to the majority group, and disturbing stereotypes developed. Legislation limiting immigration of Asians was passed in the late 1800s and early 1900s. After the bombing of Pearl Harbor, the negative stereotypes persisted. However, changes to immigration laws occurred in the 1960s, resulting in an influx of Asian males to the United States (Shek, 2006).

In the 1960s, the research and development field gained momentum, and there was an abundance of resources and professional opportunities. There was a high value placed on scientific excellence, and this professional environment benefited Asian Americans (Chen, Ren, & Reo, 2013). It was in the 1970s that the stereotype of Asians being the *model minority* developed with a large number of highly skilled and educated Asian males entering the U.S. workforce. This trend has continued, as has the model minority myth, and it continues to create challenges and negative perceptions for Asian males as they pursue their career aspirations (Shek, 2006).

Current Trends

The belief that one can cope and adjust plays a key role along with family support in terms of the ability of Asian Americans to succeed in their career goals (Taque-Bogdan, Klingaman, Martin, & Lucas, 2013). Kelly, Gunsalus, and Gunsalus (2009) indicated that when it comes to career choices, Asian Americans tend to select careers in computer science, biological science, and engineering fields. In fact, more Asian Americans earn both bachelor's degrees and master's degrees in these areas than any other racial or ethnic group in the United States. They found that 76% of master's degrees in computer science and 51% of master's degrees in engineering were earned by Asian Americans. The selection of occupations by Asian American men is dependent on several factors including family expectations and gender-role expectations.

Researchers have argued that there are several influences, such as enculturation, on the career choices of Asian American men (Kim, 2007; Liu, 2012; Song & Glick, 2004). The term *enculturation* refers to the idea that Asian American men's career-related decisions are often influenced by the internalization of gender-role expectations and the acceptance of occupational stereotypes (Kwan & Mutow, 2010). Parental expectations are another important aspect of decision-making processes in the lives of Asian Americans (Liu, 2012; Qin, 2010; Shen, 2015). This often results in Asian American males selecting certain college majors and ultimately occupations that best match with what will be most beneficial for their families rather than with their own personal interests and desires. In a recent study, Shen (2015) found that a family's support, but not pressure, about choosing specific majors was correlated with more stereotypical major choices. Stereotypes continue to impact Asian Americans in the workforce as well, and they often have to contend with the model minority myth.

Challenges

The model minority myth has been a main topic of many studies of Asian Americans; they are stereotypically represented as ready and able to overcome virtually any obstacle to ensure that they bring pride to their families, that their children are well educated (Sakamoto, Takei, & Woo, 2012), and that they will earn higher-than-average salaries compared with other groups (Kim & Zhao, 2014; Sakamoto, Goyette, & Kim, 2009). According to Kim and Zhao (2014), these beliefs are myths and they serve to hinder, rather than aid, the career success of these individuals. In fact, Kim and Sakamoto (2010) revealed that native-born Asian American men actually earn 8% less than White males.

Language barriers and the challenges inherent in learning how to navigate politically charged work environments where scientists are competing for limited research funding can create obstacles. Although discrimination based on national origin is illegal, it continues to occur (Chen et al., 2013). Kim and Zhao (2014) indicated that despite average equality in income with Whites, Asian American men still experience barriers and discrimination in the labor market and poor access to managerial and leadership positions in the labor market. Asian Americans are also less likely to obtain management positions or be offered opportunities to advance. They are often perceived as competent but cold (Hom, Ellis, & Robertson, 2008). The lack of warmth may be one factor that limits their opportunities for advancement. However, there is also a perception within the corporate world that Asian Americans lack leadership skills (Sy et al., 2010). All of these factors combine to create a very different set of career challenges than other diverse populations may face. It is a unique set of circumstances in which perceptions and stereotypes include an unexpected mix of strengths coupled with temperament inadequacies.

CAREER COUNSELING INTERVENTIONS AND TECHNIQUES FOR DIVERSE MEN

African Americans and other minorities are less likely than Caucasians to seek out counseling, but it is important to note that African Americans have been found to be more likely than their Caucasian peers to seek out career counseling services within their university or college (Greenhaus & Callanan, 2006). Career counselors should proactively reach out to minority communities and design career centers to be open and welcoming environments (Perrone et al., 2001). Career counseling centers should advertise their services directly to minority populations, as well as offer a variety of services such as career-related workshops, career fairs, and training for career-related computer programs (Perrone et al., 2001). African American men are cognizant of the ways in which race, gender, and skin color affect possible career paths (Walsh, Bingham, Brown, Ward, & Osipow, 2000), and career counselors can help prepare these clients to develop plans for coping with potential barriers by identifying previous barriers they have faced and overcome (Sedlacek, 1998). It is important for counselors to have strong levels of cultural awareness and knowledge regarding stress relief practices and issues related to overall health (Bowman, 1993). Ideally, career counseling centers have diverse staffs to meet the needs of their diverse clientele (Floyd, 1996), and interventions chosen should be appropriate for African American men (Hawks & Muha, 1991).

One model of career development that Cheatham (1990) called "Africentricity" focused on the interplay of both African and American cultures with specific attention given to the effect of familial obligations on decisions about careers (Pearson & Bieschke, 2001). The African American family can include relations by blood, marriage, informal or formal adoption, appropriation, and shared social networks and residential areas, which can form an extremely strong and resilient foundation and support for African American males (Billingsley, 1992; Ho et al., 2004). Parham and Austin (1994) also focused on the collectivistic way many decisions have been made within African American families and how that collaboration has influenced career choices.

Creative career interventions could be beneficial for African American males. Narrative therapy allows clients to tell their unique stories to counselors open to learning new contexts and ways of dealing with challenges and problems within the clients' realm of possibilities (Richert, 2003). The RESPECTFUL model (D'Andrea & Daniels, 1997, 2001) addresses the need for a counseling model that encompasses the wide variety of human experiences. More research and development of career interventions are needed to best serve African American male clients.

Counselors using career counseling strategies should remember the unique needs of the populations with which they are working. For instance, Latino men have a strong sense of family obligation, and it is important to help them focus on the long-term gains and success that might accompany investing into long-term education goals.

Feminist Approach

Using interventions aligned with feminist theory principles and Savicka's career-style interview model can have a positive effect on the career success of Latino men. Taber, Hartung, Briddick, Briddick, and Rehfuss (2011) explained that Savicka's career-style interviewing model assists counselors in learning about the client's worldview, which is important in finding out the individual's interest for different career pathways. Feminist theory has been extremely useful in working with marginalized populations, and this orientation can be expanded by the use of relevant career assessments. Counselors can facilitate the empowerment process by using feminist theory to assist their clients in developing new strengths, knowledge, and abilities (Crethar, Rivera, & Sara, 2008). Counselors who desire to take on an advocacy role as part of this approach should be mindful of including clients' families in career-related decisions due to the strong family obligations held by Latino men.

Asian Americans often encounter counselors who promote individualism and focus on the needs of the client without consideration for the impact on the family (Lowe, 2005). This is in direct opposition to traditional Asian values in which the needs of the family supersede the needs of the individual. Meyer, Zane, and Cho (2011) found that if a client and counselor were of the same ethnicity, a better treatment outcome results. Unfortunately, within the counseling field there are proportionally few minority counselors. This is especially troublesome as Asian Americans tend to terminate counseling prematurely at a much higher rate than their White counterparts. Counselors should be proactive in using culturally competent strategies that encourage client self-disclosure while respecting a client's cultural differences, including the need for clients to save face (Zane & Ku, 2014). Additionally, when Asian American males are considering career options, counselors need to develop individual and group career interventions in order to address gender roles and stereotypes that push Asian American men into traditional careers (Liu, 2012). See Appendix N for additional suggestions for working with diverse populations.

REVISITING THE CASE OF REGGIE

Reggie's counselor invited Reggie to speak about what motivated him to seek career counseling. Reggie opened up about achieving good grades throughout his education up through high school but that his college math and writing classes were more difficult than he had previously encountered. Reggie revealed that he felt like a failure for struggling in those classes until he discussed the issue with his parents, who supported his decision to pursue a different major. Reggie's counselor had him draw out a lifeline, which illustrated important events and moments in his life. As Reggie discussed his lifeline, themes of family, children, and education emerged. Reggie's counselor directed him to sources of additional information and resources for careers that addressed those themes and encouraged Reggie to discuss with his family their work together and his possible future career plans.

Reggie was initially hesitant to share with his parents that he had sought help from a counselor, especially when he reflected on career paths that actually held interest for him. As Reggie opened himself up to new career possibilities, he considered becoming an elementary school teacher, although he was unable to think of any other African American man in his life who was a teacher. Reggie was concerned that his friends might give him grief for pursuing that career. When Reggie finally spoke to his parents about his idea of becoming an elementary school teacher, they discussed the issue at length. His mother was very supportive as she had seen how much Reggie enjoyed helping her with the day-care center during the summertime. Although his father was surprised, he was impressed by his son's interest in serving as a role model and mentor for other African American children. In a follow-up session with the counselor, Reggie expressed greater confidence in his choice to pursue teaching, and the counselor was able to help Reggie lay out the necessary steps for achieving his educational and career goal.

REFERENCES

American Hospital Association and Institute for Diversity in Health Management. (2012). *Diversity and disparities: A benchmark study of U.S. hospitals.* Retrieved from http://www.hpoe.org/diversity-disparities

Asante-Muhammad, D., Chase, D., & Richardson, J. (2015). *NAACP opportunity & diversity report card: The health care industry.* Retrieved from http://action.naacp.org/page/-/economic%20opportunity%20documents/OpportunityDiversityReportCard-2015.pdf

Bennett, A., Bridglall, B., Cauce, A., Everson, H., Gordon, E., Lee, C.,...Stewart, J. (2004). All students reaching the top: Strategies for closing academic achievement gaps. A report of the national study group for the affirmative development of academic ability. Closing the achievement gap. Retrieved from http://files.eric.ed.gov/fulltext/ED483170.pdf

Billingsley, A. (1992). *Climbing Jacob's ladder: The enduring legacy of African-American families.* New York, NY: Simon & Schuster.

Bowman, S. L. (1993). Career intervention strategies for ethnic minorities. *The Career Development Quarterly, 42*, 14–25.

Centers for Disease Control and Prevention. (2015). Overview of race and Hispanic origin: 2010. Retrieved from http://www.census.gov/prod/cen2010/briefs/c2010br-02.pdf

Cheatham, H. E. (1990). Africentricity and career development. *Career Development Quarterly, 38*, 334–346.

Chen, C. C., Ren, I. Y., & Reo, A. (2013). Glass ceiling for the foreign born: Perspectives from Asian-born American R&D scientists. *Asian American Journal of Psychology, 4*, 249–257.

Clark, M. A., Ponjuan, L., Orrock, J., Wilson, T., & Flores, G. (2013). Support and barriers for Latino male students' educational pursuits: Perceptions of counselors and administrators. *Journal of Counseling & Development, 91*(4), 458–466.

Crethar, H. C., Rivera, E., & Sara, N. (2008). In search of common threads. Linking multicultural feminist, and social justice counseling paradigms. *Journal of Counseling & Development, 86*(3), 269–278.

Cuyjet, M. J. (2006). African American college men: Twenty-first century issues and concerns. In M. J. Cuyjet (Ed.), *African American men in college* (pp. 3–46). San Francisco, CA: John Wiley.

D'Andrea, M., & Daniels, J. (1997, December). RESPECTFUL counseling: A new way of thinking about diversity counseling. *Counseling Today, 40*(6), 30, 31, 34.

D'Andrea, M., & Daniels, J. (2001). RESPECTFUL counseling: An integrative model for counselors. In D. Pope-Davis & H. Coleman (Eds.), *The interface of class, culture and gender in counseling* (pp. 417–466). Thousand Oaks, CA: Sage.

Dundes, L., Cho, E., & Kwak, S. (2009). The duty to succeed: Honor versus happiness in college and career choices of East Asian students in the United States. *Pastoral Care in Education, 27*, 135–156.

Feij, J. A., Whitely, W. T., Peiro, J. M., & Taris, T. W. (1995). The development of career enhancing strategies and content innovation: A longitudinal study of new workers. *Journal of Vocational Behavior, 46*, 231–256.

Flowers, A. M., III (2015). The family factor: The establishment of positive academic identity for Black male engineering majors. *Western Journal of Black Studies, 39*(1), 64–74.

Floyd, C. (1996). Achieving despite the odds: A study of resilience among a group of African American high school seniors. *Journal of Negro Education, 65*, 181–189.

Franklin, A. J., & Boyd-Franklin, N. (2000). Invisibility syndrome: A clinical model of the effects of racism on African-American males. *American Journal of Orthopsychiatry, 70*(1), 33–41. doi:10.1037/h0087691

Garibaldi, A. M. (1992, winter). Educating and motivating African American males to succeed. *The Journal of Negro Education, 61*(1), 4–11.

Gilliam, F., Jr. (2014). Race for results: Building a path to opportunity for all children: Policy report. Retrieved from http://www.aecf.org/m/resourcedoc/AECF-RaceforResults-2014.pdf

Gordon, E. T., Gordon, E. W., & Nembhard, J. G. (1994). Social science literature concerning African American men. *Journal of Negro Education, 63*, 508–531.

Greenhaus, J. H., & Callanan, G. A. (2006). *Encyclopedia of career development* (2nd ed.). Thousand Oaks, CA: Sage.

Harvey, W. B. (2008). The weakest link: A commentary on the connections between K-12 and higher education. *American Behavioral Scientist, 51*, 972–983.

Hawks, B. K., & Muha, D. (1991). Facilitating the career development of minorities: Doing it differently this time. *The Career Development Quarterly, 39*, 251–260.

Ho, M. K., Rasheed, J. M., & Rasheed, M. N. (2004). *Family therapy with ethnic minorities* (2nd ed.). Thousand Oaks, CA: Sage.

Hom, P. W., Ellis, A. D., & Robertson, L. (2008). Challenging conventional wisdom about who quits: Revelations from corporate America. *Journal of Applied Psychology, 93*, 1–34.

Huynh, V., (2012). Ethnic microaggressions and the depressive and somatic symptoms of Latino and Asian American adolescents. *Journal of Youth & Adolescence, 41*(7), 831–846. doi:101007/s150964–012-9756–9

Jackson, J. F. L. (2008). Race segregation across the academic workforce: Exploring factors that may contribute to the disparate representation of African American men. *American Behavioral Scientist, 51*, 1004–1029.

Kelly, K. R., Gunsalus, A. C., & Gunsalus, R. (2009). Social cognitive predictors of the career goals of Korean American students. *The Career Development Quarterly, 58*, 14–28.

Kim, B. S. K. (2007). Acculturation and enculturation. In F. T. L. Leong, A. Ebreo, L. Kinoshita, A. G. Inman, L. H. Yang, & M. Fu (Eds.), *Handbook of Asian American psychology* (2nd ed., pp. 141–158). Thousand Oaks, CA: Sage Publications.

Kim, B. S. K., & Atkinson, D. R. (2002). Asian American client adherence to Asian cultural values, counselor expression of cultural values, counselor ethnicity, and career counseling process. *Journal of Counseling Psychology, 49*, 3–13.

Kim, C., & Sakamoto, A. (2010). Have Asian American men achieved labor market parity with White men? *American Sociological Review, 75*(6), 934–957.

Kim, C., & Zhao, Y. (2014). Are Asian American women advantaged? Labor market performance of college educated female workers. *Social Forces, 93*, 623–652.

Kiran, D., & Sungur, S. (2012). Middle school students' science self-efficacy and its sources: Examination of gender difference. *Journal of Science Education and Technology, 21*, 619–630. doi:10.1007/s10956–011-9351-y

Kwan, K.-L. K., & Mutow, J. E. (2010). Career development of Asian American men: Stereotyping influences of being Asian American, a man, and 'me'. In W. M. Liu, D. K. Iwamoto, & W. Chae (Eds.), *Culturally responsive counseling with Asian American men* (pp. 171–190). New York, NY: Routledge/Taylor & Francis Group.

Leary, W. E. (1996, October 24). Discrimination may affect risk of high blood pressure in Blacks. *New York Times*, p. A20.

Lent, R. W., Brown, S. D., & Hackett, G. (1996). Career development from a social cognitive perspective. In D. Brown, L. Brooks, & Associates (Eds.), *Career choice and development* (3rd ed., pp. 373–421). San Francisco, CA: Jossey-Bass.

Lent, R. W., Brown, S. D., & Hackett, G. (2000). Contextual supports and barriers to career choice: A social cognitive analysis. *Journal of Counseling Psychology, 47*, 36–49.

Leong, F. T. L. (1995). *Career development and vocational behavior of racial and ethnic minorities*. Mahwah, NJ: Lawrence Erlbaum.

Lichter, D. T. (2012). Immigration and the new racial diversity in rural America. *Rural Sociology, 77*(1), 3–35.

Liu, J. (2012). *A social cognitive examination of East Asian American career development: Contextual factors influencing career choice*. Milwaukee, WI: The University of Wisconsin-Milwaukee, Press.

Lowe, S. M. (2005). Integrating collectivist values into career counseling with Asian Americans: A test of cultural responsiveness. *Journal of Multicultural Counseling and Development, 33*, 134–145.

Luksyte, A., Waite, E., Avery, D. R., & Roy, R. (2013). Held to a different standard: Racial differences in the impact of lateness on advancement opportunity. *Journal of Occupational and Organizational Psychology, 86*(2), 142–165.

Luna, N., & Revilla, A. (2013). Understanding Latina/o school pushout: Experiences of student who left school before graduating. *Journal of Latinos & Education, 12*(1), 22–37. doi:101080/15348431.2012.734247

Meyer, O., Zane, N., & Cho, Y. (2011). Understanding the psychological processes of the racial match effect in Asian Americans. *Journal of Counseling Psychology, 58*, 335–345.

Miller, V. D., & Jablin, F. M. (1991). Information seeking during organizational entry: Influences, tactics, and a model of the process. *Academy of Management Review, 16*, 92–120.

Moore, J. L., III. (2006). A qualitative investigation of African American males' career trajectory in engineering: Implications for teachers, school counselors, and parents. *Teachers College Record, 108*, 246–266.

Moore, J. L., III, & Owens, D. (2008). Educating and counseling African American students: Recommendations for teachers and school counselors. In L. Tillman (Ed.), *The Sage handbook of African American education* (pp. 351–366). Los Angeles, CA: Sage.

National Association for the Advancement of Colored People. (2015). *Criminal justice fact sheet*. Retrieved from http://www.naacp.org/pages/criminal-justice-fact-sheet

Office of Minority Health & Health Equity. (2015). Black or African American populations. *Minority Health.* Retrieved from http://www.cdc.gov/minorityhealth/populations/REMP/black.html

Office of the Press Secretary. (2014). *Fact sheet: Opportunity for all: President Obama launches My Brother's Keeper initiative to build ladders of opportunity for boys and young men of color.* Retrieved from https://www.whitehouse.gov/the-press-office/2014/02/27/fact-sheet-opportunity-all-president-obama-launches-my-brother-s-keeper-

Osipow, S., & Fitzgerald, L. (1996). *Theories of career development* (4th ed.). Boston, MA: Allyn & Bacon.

Parham, T. A., & Austin, N. L. (1994). Career development and African Americans: A contextual reappraisal using the nigrescence construct. *Journal of Vocational Behavior, 44,* 139–154.

Patterson, C. H. (1996). Multicultural counseling: From diversity to universality. *Journal of Counseling and Development, 74,* 227–231.

Pearson, S. M., & Bieschke, K. J. (2001). Succeeding against the odds: An examination of familial influences on the career development of professional African American women. *Journal of Counseling Psychology, 48*(3), 301–309. doi:10.1037/0022–0167.48.3.301

Perrone, K. M., Sedlacek, W. E., & Alexander, C. M. (2001). Gender and ethnic differences in career goal attainment. *The Career Development Quarterly, 50,* 168–178.

Pew Hispanic Center. (2009). Social and economic characteristics. Retrieved from http://www.pewhispanic.org/2009/04/14/iv-social-and-economic-characteristics/

Portes, A., & Rivas, A. (2011). The adaptation of migrant children. *The Future of Children, 21*(1), 219–246.

Qin, X. (2010). *Family impact on Asian American's career choice* (Doctoral dissertation). Retrieved from ProQuest Dissertations & Theses (PDQT). 3452104.

Raque-Bogdan, T. L., Klingaman, E. A., Martin, H. M., & Lucas, M. S. (2013). Career-related parent support and career barriers: An investigation of contextual variables. *The Career Development Quarterly, 61*(4), 339–353.

Rastogi, S., Johnson, T. D., Hoeffel, E. M., & Drewery, M. P., Jr. (2011). *The Black population: 2010: 2010 census briefs.* Retrieved from http://www.census.gov/prod/cen2010/briefs/c2010br-06.pdf

Richert, A. J. (2003). Living stories, telling stories, changing stories: Experiential use of the relationship in narrative therapy. *Journal of Psychotherapy Integration, 13*(2), 188–210. doi:10.1037/1053–0479.13.2.188

Rhodes, S.D., Daniel, J., Song, E.-Y., Alonzo, J., Downs, M., & Reboussin, B.A. (2013). Social support among immigrant Latino men: a validation study. *American Journal of Health Behaviors, 37,* 620–628.

Ridley, C. R. (1984). Clinical treatment of the non-disclosing Black client. *American Psychologist, 39,* 1234–1244.

Rogers-Sirin, L., & Gupta, T. (2012). Cultural identity and mental health: Differing trajectories among Asian and Latino youth. *Journal of counseling psychology, 59*(4), 555.

Ruetschlin, C., & Asante-Muhammad, D. (2015). *The retail race divide: How the retail industry is perpetuating racial inequality in the 21st century.* Retrieved from action.naacp.org/page/-/economic%20opportunity%20documents/Retail_Race_Divide_Rename.pdf

Russell, M., & Atwater, M. (2005). Traveling the road to success: A discourse on persistence throughout the science pipeline with African American students at a predominately White university. *Journal of Research in Science Technology, 42,* 691–715.

Sakamoto, A., Goyette, K. A., & Kim, C. (2009). Socioeconomic attainments of Asian Americans. *Annual Review of Sociology, 35,* 255–276.

Sakamoto, A., Takei, I., & Woo, H. (2012). The myth of the model minority myth. *Sociological Spectrum, 32*(4), 309–321.

Sedlacek, W. E. (1998). Admissions in higher education: Measuring cognitive and noncognitive variables. In D. J. Wilds & R. Wilson (Eds.), *Minorities in higher education 1997–1998: Sixteenth annual status report* (pp. 47–71). Washington, DC: American Counselor Education.

Shek, Y. L. (2006). Asian American masculinity: A review of the literature. *The Journal of Men's Studies, 14*, 379–391.

Shen, F. C. (2015). The role of internalized stereotyping, parental pressure, and parental support on Asian Americans' choice of college major. *Journal of Multicultural Counseling and Development, 43*, 58–73.

Smith, M. L., & Roysircar, G. (2010, October). African American male leaders in counseling: Interviews with five AMCD past presidents. *Journal of Multicultural Counseling & Development, 38*(4), 242–255.

Smokowski, P., Reynolds, A., & Bezruczko, N. (1999). Resilience and protective factors in adolescents: An autobiographical perspective from disadvantaged youth. *Journal of School Psychology, 37*, 425–448.

Solorzano, D., Ceja, M., & Yosso, T. (2000). Critical race theory, racial microaggressions, and campus racial climate: The experiences of African American college students. *Journal of Negro Education, 69*, 60–73.

Song, C., & Glick, J. E. (2004). College attendance and choice of college majors among Asian-American students. *Social Science Quarterly, 85*, 1401–1421.

Stolle-McAllister, K., Sto. Domingo, M., & Carrillo, A. (2011). The Meyerhof way: How the Meyerhof scholarship program helps Black students succeed in the sciences. *Journal of Science Education & Technology, 20*(1), 5–16. doi:10.1007/s10956-010-9228-

Sy, T., Shore, L. M., Strauss, J., Shore, T. H., Tram, S., Whiteley, P., & Ikeda-Muromachi, K. (2010). Leadership perceptions as a function of race-occupation fit: The case of Asian Americans. *Journal of Applied Psychology, 95*, 902–919.

Taber, B. J., Hartung, P. J., Briddick, H., Briddick, W. C., & Rehfuss, M. C. (2011). Career style interview: A contextualized approach to career counseling. *Career Development Quarterly, 59*(3), 274–287.

Taque-Bogdan, T. L., Klingaman, E. A., Martin, H. M. & Lucas, M. S. (2013). Career-related parent support and career barriers: An investigation of contextual variables. *The Career Development Quarterly, 61*, 339–353.

Teranishi, R. T., Suárez-Orozco, C., & Suárez-Orozco, M. (2011). Immigrants in community colleges. *The Future of Children, 21*(1), 153–169.

Tsui, L. (2007). Effective strategies to increase diversity in STEM fields: A review of the research literature. *Journal of Negro Education, 76*(4), 555–581.

Tuskegee University. (2015). *List of scholarships for African American students.* Retrieved from http://www.tuskegee.edu/academics/academic_services/career_development/list_of_scholarships_for_african_american_students.aspx

U.S. Bureau of Labor Statistics. (2010). Earnings and employment by occupation, race, ethnicity, and sex, 2010. Retrieved from http://www.bls.gov/opub/ted/2011/ted_20110914.htm

U.S. Census Bureau. (2015a). *Facts for features: Black (African-American) history month: February 2015.* Retrieved from http://www.census.gov/newsroom/facts-for-features/2015/cb15-ff01.html

U.S. Census Bureau. (2015b). U.S. Census Bureau: State and county quick facts. Retrieved from http://quickfacts.census.gov/qfd/states/00000.html

U.S. Department of Education. (2015). Scholarship opportunities for minority students! *White House initiative on historically Black colleges and universities.* Retrieved from http://sites.ed.gov/whhbcu/2013/11/21/scholarship-opportunities-for-minority-students/

Vasquez, E. P., Gonzalez-Guarda, R. M., & De Santis, J. P. (2011). Acculturation, depression, self-esteem, and substance abuse among Hispanic men. *Issues in Mental Health Nursing, 32*(2), 90–97.

Walsh, W. B., Bingham, R. P., Brown, M. T., Ward, C. M., & Osipow, S. H. (Eds.). (2000). *Career counseling for African Americans.* Mahwah, NJ: Taylor & Francis.

White, J. L., & Cones, J. H., III. (1999). *Black man emerging: Facing the past and seizing a future in America.* New York, NY: Routledge.

Whiting, G. W. (2006). Promoting a scholar identity among African American males: Implications for gifted education. *Gifted Education Press Quarterly, 20*(3), 2–6.

Zane, N., & Ku, H. (2014). Effects of ethnic match, gender match, acculturation, cultural identity, and face concern on self-disclosure in counseling for Asian Americans. *Journal of Psychology, 5*, 66–74.

APPENDIX A

INTERVENTIONS FOR HIGH SCHOOL GRADUATES

BRANCHING OUT ON THE FAMILY TREE OF CAREERS

Barb C. Wilson

This activity can be used with a variety of populations and is grounded in family systems. It can also be modified for use with adolescents and adults. Through this activity, participants explore the career history of their families using a family tree. Clients gain insight into patterns and options that may have not otherwise been considered.

Materials Required: Writing instruments, paper.

Preparation Needed: Before completing this activity with the client, the counselor should have a clear understanding of the family dynamics. This activity may not be appropriate for someone who is going through difficult family issues. The counselor should discuss the activity in advance so that the client can do some family research before the activity.

Activity Directions:

1. The client should write his or her name at the bottom of a blank page. This activity may be completed as a genogram.
2. Starting at the client's location within the family tree, ask the client to draw siblings, parents, then grandparents, and so on, continuing to a level of comfort and awareness.
3. After the client has completed several family placements, have the client write each person's career under his or her name on the paper. If a person was not employed, then have the client write a descriptive word (i.e., homemaker, disabled, etc.).
4. Next, ask the client to look for patterns or comment on anything that stands out. Is one side of the family grouped into a career cluster? Are there any gender differences?
5. After a complete discussion about trends, patterns, and notable characteristics of the family tree, ask the client what he or she would like to place under his or her own name for a career choice or interest.

BRIDGE OF LIFE: CREATING A CAREER PATH

Montserrat Casado-Kehoe

This activity can be helpful with high school students who are in search of direction in terms of determining a career path and what it may take to pursue that career. This is a guided imagery and visual arts exercise that encourages self-direction and potential career paths.

Materials Required: White or colored paper, colored pencils, crayons and markers, or paints. Relaxing music can also be used to facilitate creativity.

Preparation Needed: None.

Activity Directions:

1. Ask clients to close their eyes and focus on their breathing. Focus on relaxation for several minutes. Ask the clients to visualize a bridge that represents their life, noting where they are on their bridge now and where they are headed career-wise. Once the clients have a picture in their mind, ask them to open their eyes.
2. Ask clients to draw a picture of their bridge on a piece of paper. You can tell them that this bridge will represent their life and, in particular, you will use it to think of their potential path to follow as you explore a career.
3. Ask them to use a variety of colors and textures using the colored pencils, crayons and markers, or paints.
4. After they have drawn the bridge, ask them to place themselves somewhere on this bridge that they will need to cross as they pursue a new career.
5. Next, ask the clients to focus on the pillars that help support the bridge. They can then add the different work or volunteer experiences they have had, and what the job required of them in terms of skills, to the pillars of their bridge.
6. Ask the clients to focus on the career that they would like to pursue and to draw it at the end of the bridge. Instruct them to reflect on the skills that they will need for that vocation.
7. After the clients have identified a career, ask them to look at their bridge and draw, along the bridge, the steps they will need to take to pursue that dream career that stands at the end of the bridge. The clients can write on their drawing or use symbols and draw.
8. Process the drawing and ask the clients to tell you what it means. Use the following questions to facilitate discussion: *Tell me about your drawing. What is your dream career? What steps will you need to take to pursue this career? What skills or work experiences have helped you so far that may help you pursue this career? As you travel across your Bridge of Life, what will help you accomplish this career dream? As you travel through your Bridge of Life pursuing your career, what reminders may help you when things become challenging? What could you tell yourself that would help you cross the bridge and achieve your career dream?*

CAREER TREE

Hewitt B. Rogers and Bethany Kennedy

This activity works best in individual counseling but can be modified for use with small groups. The goal of this activity is to provide direction for adolescents and young adults who face challenges when choosing a career path. Specifically, the exercise promotes career discovery by allowing the client to develop and explore a career path. The client begins by planting the career seed, making choices to help that career seed develop strong roots, and taking the necessary steps to ensure that it matures into a thriving career tree. When used in groups, clients are able to strategize and collaborate on career paths and scenarios that will help a client determine whether the career will be a good fit.

The career tree helps facilitate exploration and discovery of career choices based on client interests. The activity is meant to be completed indoors and used by individuals or small groups. Although this exercise can be done individually, several benefits are present when administered in a group setting, including peer support and collaborative career exploration.

Materials Required: Tape or glue, construction paper, multicolored note cards, scissors, easel or presentation board, and writing utensils.

Preparation Needed: The counselor will place the outline of a tree trunk on a presentation surface so it is ready for the client to place the career paths (branches) and note cards (leaves) to build his or her career tree. Multicolor leaves can represent emotions or feelings pertaining to career choices.

Activity Directions:

1. Before the activity begins, it is important to talk with the client about possible feelings associated with career exploration. At times, the client can become more anxious, confused, and discouraged throughout the process, and it would be beneficial to encourage that person to continue through the journey of career discovery. Once the client acknowledges the condition, proceed with the activity. Research before, during, or after the activity can benefit the client and should be encouraged. This research can help the client understand the options offered and provide knowledge pertaining to the given career path. This is an effective way to assign the client homework and allow the client to discover distinctive data.
2. The career tree is cut and placed on the presentation surface. During this time, the client will begin to make choices based on his or her interests. Depending on the client's age, you can ask questions about the likelihood of attending college. Based on the client's answer of "college," "vocational schools," or "no college," the client will attach a branch to the tree trunk by writing the answer on the note card (leaf) and placing it on the career tree.
3. Depending on the answer, you may want to pursue this line of thought by asking more questions. Some examples are as follows: *Tell me more about your decision and how you were led. Are there any previous or current family indications in deciding? What is it that excites you about the choice? Based on your decision, tell*

me your strengths/weaknesses, likes/dislikes about this choice. Do you have any experience working within this field (i.e., internship, school-based programs, or shadow programs)?

4. If the client is currently in college, move to the next step in the activity. The next step will allow the client to further explore the decision that was made previously. Depending on the answer, ask the client about possible career interests, hobbies, and majors. The client will pick three areas of career exploration that sparked interest. The client will write the career choice on a multicolored note card (leaf) and place it on a branch from the career tree. At this point, the client should have a trunk, top of tree, three branches, and three leaves. After each leaf is placed on the tree, allow the client to explore the reasons behind each one. The note cards (leaves) can be cut in half, and the client can write the reasoning on the card (leaf) and place it on the branch of the career tree. Encourage questions, and give the client time to reflect and explore.
5. The career tree can take several weeks to complete. It can be limited with the number of career choices; however, it is important to allow the client to fully explore and discuss different paths. The goal is to allow the client to consider all options in a safe, nonjudgmental environment. It is crucial to build trust and rapport within the relationship and to encourage, support, and challenge the client's career discovery.

Suggested Modifications: This activity works particularly well for expressive clients but might be challenging for others. Counselors can modify as needed and leave out the artistic element. Using lines to connect note cards and taking a more rudimentary approach can still allow clients to explore different career paths.

Evaluation Plan: Counselors should evaluate the client's motivation, engagement, decision-making skills, and ability to adapt before, during, and after the exercise.

COMPUTER-GENERATED CAREER TRADING CARDS: ENVISIONING GOING PRO

Katrina Cook, Suzanne Mudge, and Laurel Malloy

This activity is designed for small group counseling settings but can be adapted for individual counseling and classroom guidance. The goal is to facilitate the exploration of specific careers. Clients develop visual images of relevant career goals or aspirations.

Materials Required: Computer, Microsoft Word, a photo editing program, a baseball card template (e.g., teacherspayteachers.com, appollostemplates.com, etc.), printer, and paper. Also, sample career trading cards should be available for the clients to review.

Preparation Needed: Have some sample completed career trading cards available for the clients to review.

Activity Directions:

1. Introduce the session by saying: *For today's activity in career exploration, you will identify possible factors that you are looking for in a job. From that information, you will identify careers that best represent your preferences.*
2. Ask the clients to reflect on what career-related activities they like or think they would like. Encourage the clients to jot down their ideas on paper.
3. Show clients a sample of the career trading card template and explain that each client will be creating three cards representing selected careers.
4. Then, show samples of previously made career cards. Ask the clients to identify an activity represented by each card.
5. Then, give each client three paper career card templates. Ask each client to review his or her preferred activity list and select three activities that he or she will connect with potential careers.
6. Say to the clients: *Looking at each of your cards, can you think of a job which involves that activity? In pencil, write that job on the back of the paper template.*
7. Each client will choose one template for sharing. Ask the following questions: *What job and activity are represented by this card? How are the job and activity related? Can anyone think of any other jobs related to these activities?* (Encourage clients to jot additional jobs in pencil on the back of the card.) *What other activities might someone interested in those jobs do?* Then ask the original client to circle the job that he or she is most interested in getting more information on. Repeat with all clients. As time permits, allow the clients to process the other two cards.
8. Clients will prepare the text for the cards along with a photo image for the card. Encourage clients' creativity in creating their career photos. Clients can then print out their completed cards or save the images as photo collages.

THE KEY TO YOUR TREASURE BOX

Vincent D. Hinton and LaWanda S. Edwards

The purpose of this intervention is to help clients explore various career choices. The use of this intervention is designed to help them think outside of the "ideal" treasure box (career) in selection of a career and think of other related careers associated with their choice. For example, if a client expresses a desire to play in the National Football League (NFL) as a career, this choice and other related career choices would be explored, such as coach, physical therapist, marketing director, and so on.

Materials Required: Images of a treasure box (*each treasure box is labeled as a career choice*), drawings or cutouts of keys (*each key will demonstrate what the client thinks it would take to unlock the treasure box/career choice*), pens, markers, and paper.

Also Recommended: Counselors may elect to use actual keys and have an actual treasure box featuring a lock. For example, the counselor may have several keys (different sizes, colors, shapes, patterns) in a clear plastic container or clear bag; a client will then select a key to actually open the lock. Each key would represent the necessary step to reach the career choice.

Preparation Needed: Gather materials and have knowledge of career options.

Activity Directions:

1. To begin this exercise, explain to the client that the treasure box represents his or her selected career option(s). As a team, you will work together to explore what that career choice means and the potential steps to reach that career option. If the client selects two treasure boxes, you will explore both career choices with the client. This intervention may be implemented in one session or could be used over the course of several sessions.
2. You may begin with the treasure box; get to know more about the client and his or her career choice by asking any of the following: *Tell me a little more about this particular career choice and some of the reasons it is important to you. What are some of your influences in making this selection? In what ways is this career choice influenced by your family and/or friends? How successful have you been in the past with the work toward this career selection? How committed are you in working through the process of this career selection?*
3. Invite the client to cut out several "keys", and ask the client to select the number of keys he or she thinks would be necessary to reach the career choice (the client may have a number of options to explore; as the counselor, be mindful of your time and what's appropriate for the client).
4. Once the number of keys has been selected, have the client write on each key what would be needed (or steps needed) to actually be in that particular career choice. Remember, the key is to help the client think both inside and outside of the treasure box (anything is considered an option for this activity).

5. The next step (for you as the counselor) is to begin the process of opening the treasure box by having the first key. Although this key is not the key to the client's career choice, it is the key that starts his or her journey. You may explain to the client that you may provide him or her with keys throughout the exercise; however, your key will not open the treasure box; it simply gives the client an option to look at a different key and find out what it may offer. For example, you may explain to the client that it is almost like if you were to get ready to grab your key to start your car or the key to open the door to your house, but you realize you grabbed the wrong key, so you **S**top, **R**eflect, **A**ssess, and **C**ontinue (SRAC). You stop what you are doing to reflect, assess your thoughts, and continue with what you think is the best option. As the counselor, you may offer the client opportunities to stop, reflect, assess, and continue on with the task.
6. As you continue, ask the client to place the keys in a particular order (the least challenging to most), or simply ask the client to select a key based on where he or she would like to start the exploration.
7. Once a client selects a key, it is important to process his or her thoughts and explore the potential values, barriers, and options for each key. Throughout this process, the client may decide to keep a key or give you a key to discard or to hold and discuss at a later date. For homework, *if necessary*, the client may select to work on a task until the next visit or session. For each key, you may ask the client any of the following questions: *Tell me a little more about what this key means to you and how what is written on the key is needed to help you reach your career goal. What special skills may be necessary to use this key (education, skill set, etc.)? What challenges (barriers, obstacles) may you face in completing this task on your key? How committed are you to working on this key (the step toward reaching their goal or career choice)? Is this a key you would like to keep or one to discard (as the counselor you would maintain a list of the keep and discard keys, almost like a pros/cons list for the client)?*
8. *Goal setting*: Once you have completed the process of exploring the thoughts of the client centered on the treasure box and reviewing each key of the client, process each key by asking probing questions; ask the client to determine what he or she is committed to working on, and establish his or her goals and/or homework assignments. Over a period of time or even in one session, the client should have clearer steps toward his or her career choice and the necessary steps to reach a career choice that is best for him or her.
9. *Session summary*: As the counselor, you may decide to end the session or intervention by asking the client any or all of the following questions: *What did you learn about yourself as a result of completing this exercise? What would be the next step for you on your journey of seeking the best career option?*
10. *Reflection summary*: As the counselor, you may elect to provide a reflection and allow the client to share his or her thoughts and reflections and how this activity may influence the client's career path or journey.

THE ROAD TO SUCCESS

LaWanda S. Edwards and Vincent D. Hinton

Clients are better able to overcome career barriers when they have support, and this activity allows clients to identify and discuss barriers experienced while trying to reach career goals. The goal of this intervention is to prepare clients to overcome their identified barriers.

Materials Required: Paper, markers, crayons/colored pencils.

Preparation Needed: Before meeting with the client, the counselor should draw a box in the bottom left corner of the paper and write "Start" in the box. The counselor should then draw another box in the upper right corner of the paper, then draw a road from the bottom left corner to the top right corner of the paper. The road should be winding, not straight.

Activity Directions:

1. Invite the client to identify his or her career goal and write it in the box in the upper right corner of the paper.
2. Using the metaphor of the "road to success," discuss the possibility of roadblocks and other obstacles that might delay or obstruct the client's achievement of a career goal. Ask the client to imagine and draw in the potential obstacles to his or her career success.
3. After the client completes the drawing, ask the client to identify each roadblock in succession and brainstorm ideas for removing or overcoming the roadblock. As the client discusses how to remove each of the roadblocks, identify words that describe the characteristics the client would be displaying (perseverance, determination, grit, diligence, dedication, punctuality, responsibility, etc.).
4. When the client gets to the goal in the upper right corner, encourage the client to remind you of some of the characteristics that are necessary to reach the career goal. Encourage the client to journal about these qualities and ways in which they can be developed or strengthened along the road to success.

APPENDIX B

INTERVENTIONS FOR COMMUNITY COLLEGE GRADUATES

THE CAREER JAR

Corie N. Schoeneberg, Nancy L. A. Forth, Atsuko Seto, and Penny Dahlen

This activity is helpful for clients who are in the initial stages of their career exploration and who are unsure of which career clusters and/or professional characteristics might be a desirable and appropriate fit for them.

Materials Required: Paper, large-mouth jar, and writing materials (optional).

Preparation Needed: Prior to the session, the counselor will create prepared slips of paper of at least 20 to 50 various professions from each of the career categories, such as elementary school teaching aid or building construction site manager. Lists of occupations can be found on www.onetonline.org/. Each slip of paper should contain one career title and is then folded in half, concealing the title. Once folded, all slips of paper are placed in a large-mouth jar so that the client can reach into the jar.

Activity Directions:

1. Introduce the session to the client by explaining the rationale of identifying his or her personal interests, values, and possible career aversions as a way of beginning the initial phases of career exploration.
2. Present the jar of the pre-labeled careers, and then instruct the client to select one of these slips of paper without looking at the profession.
3. Once the client has selected a slip of paper, instruct the client to read the profession and ask the client to provide his or her general perception of this job, details regarding the tasks and environment of this profession, and feelings regarding personally working within this career. In some cases, the client will state that this career is not for him or her due to factors such as an undesirable salary or negative perception of the tasks involved. However, upon further discussion, the client may find some elements of the profession that are of interest. For example, a client may quickly respond that she does not want to

be a retail sales worker but enjoys the idea of working with people. The client has the opportunity to learn as much about himself or herself when drawing a career slip that he or she does not gravitate to as when drawing ones ones that immediately spark interest.

4. Additional processing questions may include:
   a. *What specific aspects of this job do you think you might enjoy? What might you dislike and why?*
   b. *Do you have any past experiences that connect you with this profession?*
   c. *What do you know about the work environment of this job? What parts of it fit you and what aspects of it do not and why?*
   d. *What skills do you believe are involved in this job and how do these skills match up with your experience and strengths?*
   e. *What additional information would you like to know about this profession?*
   f. *What feelings come up for you when you imagine working within this specific profession?*
   g. *Who (family members, close friends, etc.) would support you in pursuing this specific profession and why? Who would be opposed to it and why? How do you feel about their reactions to your decision?*
   h. *What other jobs can you think of that have similar skills, goals, work environment, career aspects, or connections that interest you?*
5. As the client discusses the selected profession, assess the client's knowledge base surrounding this job as well as general career familiarity; listen for the client's interests, values, curiosities, and concerns; and note any patterns.
6. At the close of the session, summarize the client's personal discoveries, interests and disinterests, notable values and feelings, and identified questions or *wonderings,* and then collaborate with the client on creating a plan for the next step to take in the career process.

THINK TANK

Katherine M. Hermann and Alyce R. Clark

This activity is designed to help clients handle the transition from community college into either the workforce or a 4-year university. Occupational exploration for these individuals is unique given that they are confronted with both a range of opportunities and challenging stressors. The activity encourages a focus on both of these while building the client's confidence. Attention to personal development may be important as these clients transition from what may be perceived as a protected environment into a larger and possibly more intimidating one. This activity uses metaphor and the creative process to explore this life transition and helps clients explore what it is like to go from being a big fish in a little tank to a little fish in a big tank.

Materials Required: Two containers, one smaller and one larger (fishbowls are ideal, but other containers can work), colored construction paper (red, blue, green, yellow, brown, purple, orange, black, white), and a pen or pencil.

Preparation Needed: Gather materials and cut construction paper into eight rectangular strips.

Activity Directions:

1. Ask the client to imagine that the community college experience is a fish tank, and he or she has been a fish swimming in it over the past years.
2. Instruct the client to think about all the elements of the community college experience, both positives and obstacles. Create a list of these elements. Brainstorming and discussing during this phase can help the client consider how the environment, schedule, activities, community, friends, course materials, finances, professors, and so on contributed to the experiences.
3. After the client develops a list of elements, ask him or her to choose a color to represent each element (i.e., blue, like water, could be environment; brown, like gravel, could be an unenjoyable element; green, like plants, could be fun activities or finances; red, like food and the feeding schedule, could be routine; yellow, like some fish, could be friends; orange, like other fish, could be family).
4. Instruct the client to write important parts of each element on a strip of construction paper (use the color of construction paper that coincides to the selected element) and place it into the fishbowl. For example, if yellow is friends, he or she would write the name of each of his or her friends on a yellow strip of paper.
5. Process with the client what it is like to see different aspects of this experience. He or she may find it helpful to discuss things that were intimidating that later became a welcome part of the experience.
6. Next, ask the client to move the elements (pieces of paper) that he or she would like to have in the next phase of life into the larger fishbowl. Ask questions to help process the experience, such as: *What do you want to leave behind?*

What do you think you will need more of in the future? In addition to moving existing elements, allow the client to introduce new colors to identify possible wants or needs for this next phase of life.

7. Process this new fish tank as a way to help the client clarify what is important for the next phase of life, discuss possible options, and build on strengths. The following list of questions may be helpful:
    a. *What are the immediate differences you notice looking at the larger fishbowl?*
    b. *In what ways is this new tank different/alike?*
    c. *In what ways is the larger tank a new adventure?*
    d. *What are some things you would like to take with you into the larger tank?*
    e. *What kinds of fish do you need in your new tank (guppies, sharks, and clown fish)?*
    f. *What kind of fish will you be in the new tank?*
    g. *What is it like to go from being in a little tank into the larger tank (anxious, excited, nervous, regretful, or hopeful)?*
    h. *What will you miss about the smaller tank? Who will be joining you in this move to the larger tank?*
    i. *What was it like to enter the smaller tank? How did you overcome the challenges in the smaller tank?*
    j. *What challenges will you face in the larger tank? What can you do to overcome these challenges?*
    k. *What are some of the strengths that helped you survive and thrive in the smaller tank? How can you implement these strengths in the larger tank?*

YOU'VE GOT SKILLS! MAKING THE MOST OUT OF THE SKILLS YOU POSSESS

Bridget Tuohy Helms

This activity encourages clients to recognize the transferable skills that they possess. Therefore, this activity emphasizes the matching of skills to a career path to help clients find meaningful and fulfilling careers. Transferable skills are also called employment skills. In this intervention, individuals or groups will assess the skills they possess and evaluate which skills will transfer to potential career pathways. Individuals will explore a career path to ascertain if the skills they possess are compatible with desired career objectives.

Materials Required: Career Map (Figure B.1), Map About Me (Figure B.2), pen or pencil.

Recommended: Computer for additional research, if needed.

Preparation Needed: None.

Activity Directions:
Instruct client(s) to follow the following directions:

1. On the Career Map, write your desired profession in the top box.
2. On the Career Map, write "Yes" or "No", depending on whether or not you feel the skill listed is needed for that profession.
3. In the same box, evaluate if this skill is:
   a. *Very Important*
   b. *Somewhat Important*
   c. *Not Important*
4. If you are unsure whether or not the skill is needed for that profession, use the Internet to research what skills are needed for the desired profession.
5. Using the Map About Me, evaluate your skill levels.
   a. For each skill listed, write "Yes" or "No" depending on whether or not you possess this skill.
   b. If so, evaluate whether your skill level is:
      1. *Advanced*
      2. *Proficient*
      3. *Basic*
   c. *If no, is this something you can actually work toward? Yes or No?*
6. Next, compare your desired profession with your current skill level. Following are suggested questions for processing this activity:
   a. *What did you learn about yourself by doing this activity?*
   b. *What was easy and/or difficult about doing this activity?*
   c. *What did you learn from this activity that you didn't know before?*
   d. *Explain why it is important to think through and evaluate how your skills match up with a desired profession and the skills needed for that profession.*

e. What were the surprises you discovered, if any?
f. What are the changes or improvements you can make to help you obtain your desired profession?
g. What are your top three transferable skills?
h. What are your three weakest transferable skills?
i. How could you highlight and make the most of your top three transferable skills?
j. What could you do to improve your three weakest transferable skills?

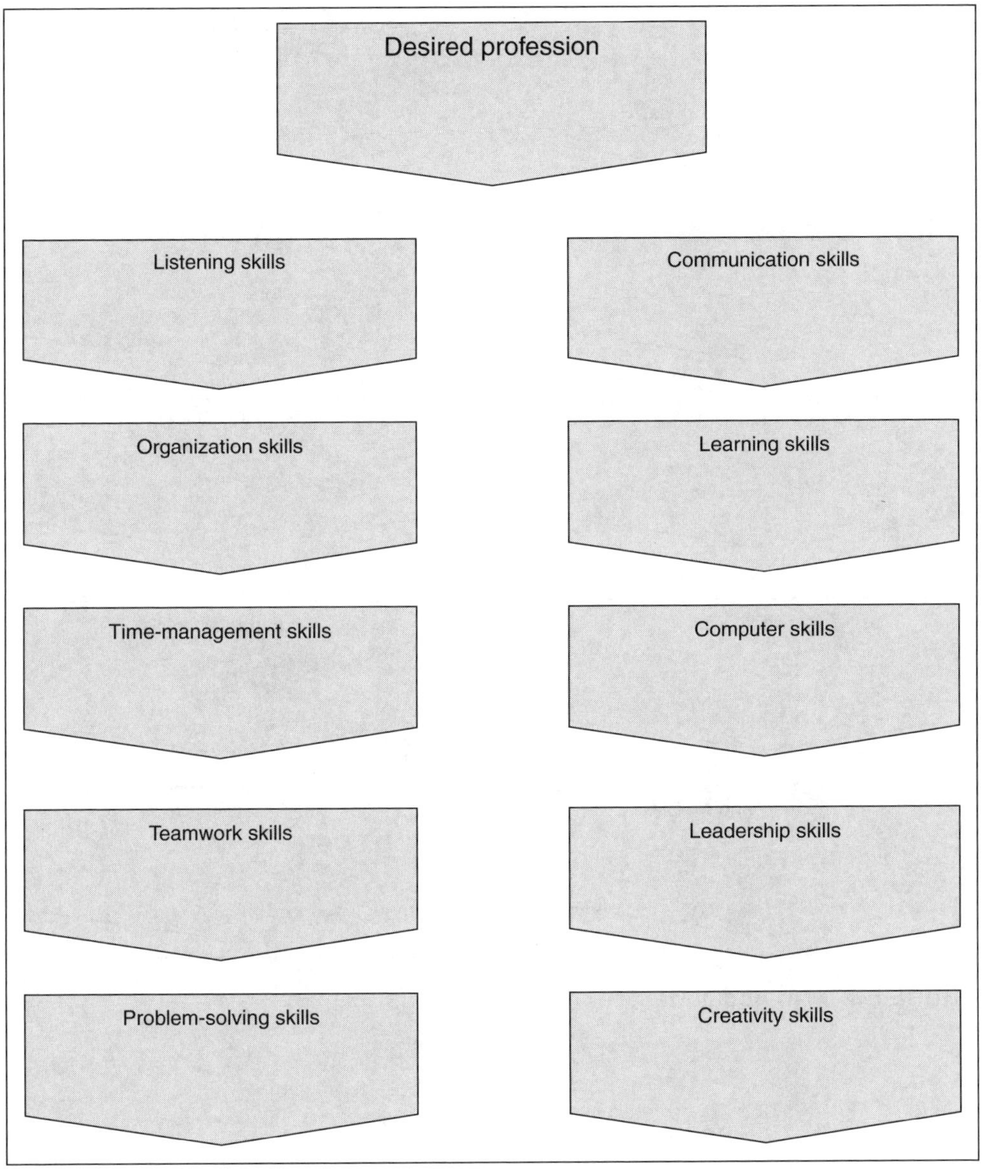

FIGURE B.1 Career Map.

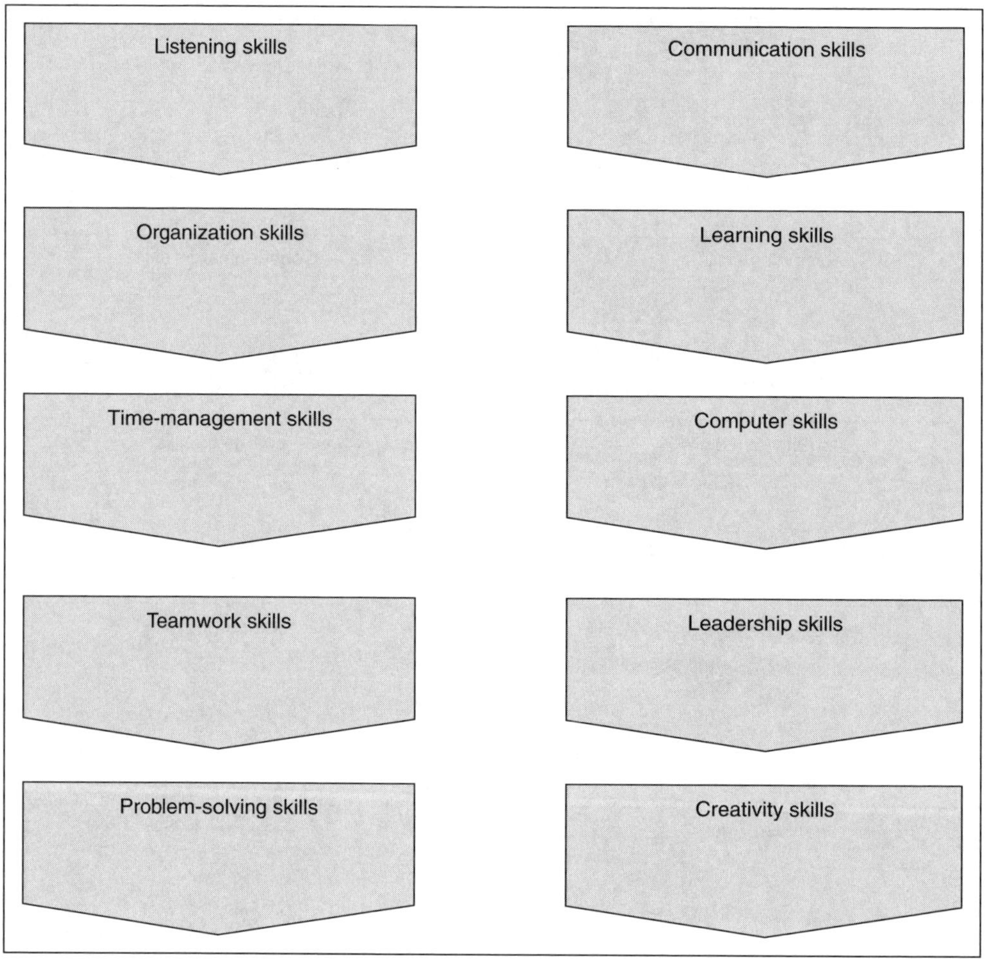

FIGURE B.2 Map About Me.

APPENDIX C

INTERVENTIONS FOR TRADITIONAL COLLEGE GRADUATES

CARNATION CAREER COLLAGE

Lucy Parker

The career collage activity emphasizes individual need, attention, and expression that prospective workers are looking for when determining their next career move. This task is beneficial as it provides meaning to construction with an open-ended question of what clients' values, strengths, and experiences are, intrinsically. The career collage can facilitate clients' meaning making about both direct and indirect variables that will influence their interests and/or disinterest in various careers. This activity also facilitates further insight into oneself, which may assist in the meaning-making process of finding one's ideal career. This collage activity can also serve as a resource that clients can use to externalize their possible uncertainty, ambiguity, and/or anxiety about their career indecision.

Materials Required: Pencil, Carnation Career Collage (Figure C.1), scissors, tape, magazines.

Preparation Needed: It is recommended that the counselor provide a model of a Career Collage. This model should not be shown as an expectation to meet, but rather an ideal option as the counselor uses this model to demystify this activity and to use himself or herself as a therapeutic model and tool (Yalom, 2002).

Activity Directions:

1. Introduce the activity to the client at the start of the individual career counseling session. For example, you may introduce the career collage by stating: *We are going to co-construct a picture of a carnation, which represents your values, strengths, interests, and experiences regarding your career interests and history. In this activity, I will assist you in finding various meanings about you and your thoughts about your past careers and your career dreams.*
2. Provide a pencil and the forms for this collage (Figure C.1) to the client. The client can choose to write in adjectives, draw symbols, and/or cut and tape

pictures from magazines onto the form. If the client uses magazines, provide tape/glue and scissors.

3. Before the actual collage is generated, you and the client will begin a discussion about the client's career thoughts. Introduce the client to this activity, and, preferably, show the client an example of a collage pertaining to the counselor's career and interests.
4. With the client, discuss the items listed on the carnation picture. These will include:
   A. The Carnation Leaves—Client's Experiences and Knowledge:
   You may use questions to ask the client about his or her experience. For example: *As we continue to create a flower that symbolizes you and your career interests, what are some past jobs you have worked at? What are some volunteer experiences you have had? What are your educational experiences? What about your professional trainings?*
   B. The Carnation Stem—Client's Strengths:
   Then you may use questions and/or linking from previous sessions to inquire about the client's strengths. The client may also initially generate these on his or her own if this client is more active in the therapeutic session.
   C. The Carnation Core—Client's Values and Interests:
   You may ask the client what he or she values. For example: *I know we have talked about your family meaning a lot to you... thus, do you want a career that allows you to be close to your home? You mentioned in previous sessions that you like to work with children.... Are you a caretaker? Do you like to teach?* The client may also autonomously write his or her most salient interests on this piece of the collage (without the initial counselor's scaffolding).
   D. The Carnation Petals—Client's Prospective Job or Career Considerations:
   The client may write his or her prospective jobs or careers on the petals independently or in facilitation with you. Once these are written, the client may conceptualize the entire flower. You can also help. For example, incongruences and congruences may also help to guide the client in determining his or her career preferences. For example, you may ask: *You mention you like children and put a prospective career of teaching on your petal section. How much have you considered teaching? What grade levels would you consider teaching?*
5. There are many potential varying interpretations and associations to this activity. For example, members can see for themselves their own holistic conceptualization of a career and all of their inner dialogue about both their personal and professional interests. This activity may also help you, as the counselor, to better understand the client.
6. At the end of this collage, you and the client can use this activity as a dialogue to further create career decisions. Some process questions to use in the discussion may include: *Tell me about your carnation. What is the most powerful theme about your flower? What feelings did you experience when filling in each section of your flower? What did you enjoy about constructing this flower? What are some uncertainties and/or struggles you experienced while completing your flower? What else did you learn about yourself in the process of creating your flower? Were*

there any new insights about yourself after creating this activity? Were there any new insights about your career options after creating this activity? From this experience, what will you take with you as you continue and/or enter into the workforce? Is there any other important message or discussion point you can think of after creating this carnation? How can I make this activity more meaningful for you in your career considerations?

7. This client can then take this activity home so that he or she has a tangible resource later that can remind the client of the intrapersonal conceptualizations that were constructed during this activity.

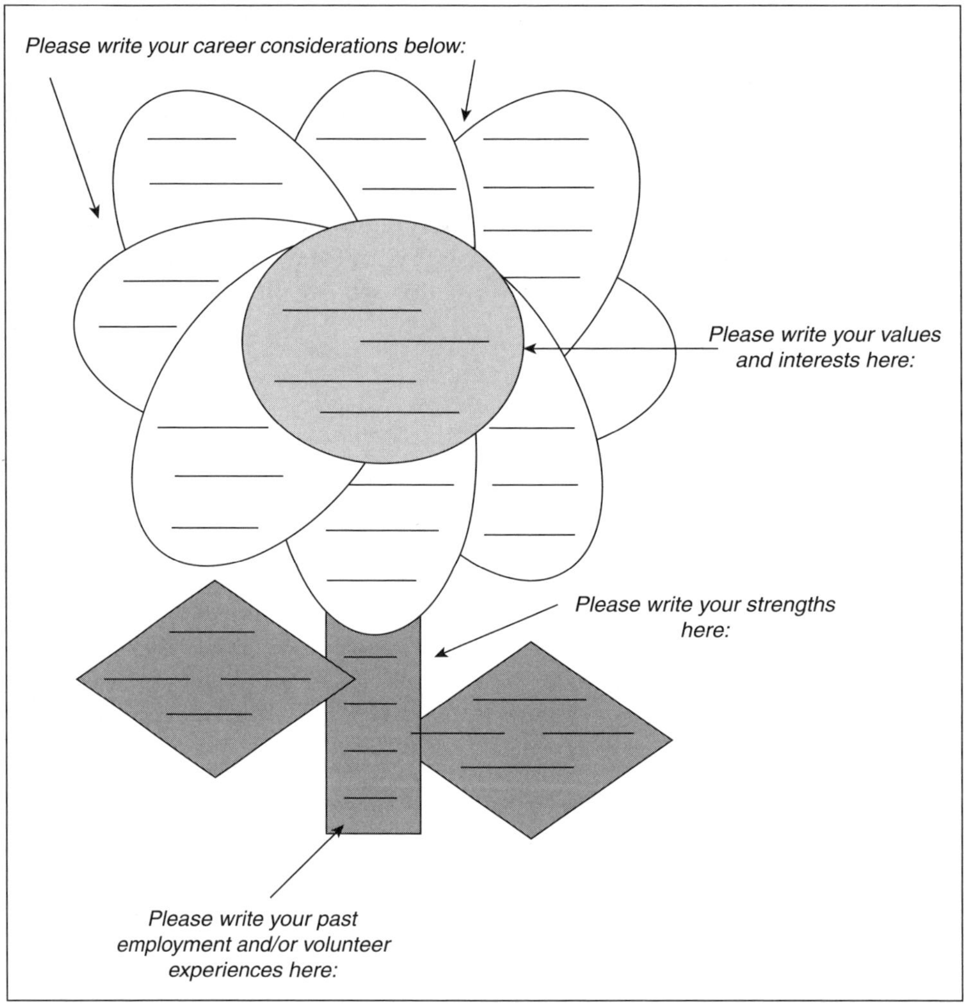

FIGURE C.1 Carnation Career Collage.

READING BETWEEN THE LINES

Melissa A. Wheeler and Sandra Logan

This activity is designed for clients with minimal work experience or career changers who have difficulty analyzing a job posting to identify what employers are looking for, whether or not they meet qualifications, and what experiences they have that relate to a particular posting. Adults and late adolescents will learn how to analyze a job posting and use this analysis to begin crafting a cover letter.

Materials Required: Highlighters, pen, client's resume, one to two printed job postings, paper, Post-It notes (one color for every job position held by client), index cards, tape, a flat space for working.

Preparation Needed: The client should be instructed to find one or two job postings to which he or she is interested in applying for employment. These postings should be printed out and brought to the meeting. Alternatively, the counselor can have a hard copy of the classifieds at hand or work with the client in the office to identify a job posting that is of interest.

Activity Directions:

1. With the client, choose a job posting from the options presented by the client to develop a cover letter for use in the office.
2. Discuss with the client that employers put clues in postings to let potential hires know what they want. It is up to the jobseeker to translate this code to develop a resume and cover letter that matches what the employer wants with the experience that he or she has.
3. Both you, as the counselor, and the client should read over the job posting chosen for this activity. Both of you should identify key skills and experiences desired by the employer based on the wording of the job posting. The client will highlight the keywords in the posting. Explain to the client that he or she will now "read between the lines" of the job posting.
4. Once the key skill and experience words are highlighted, ask the client what he or she thinks that the employer wants. Assist the client in "translating" what the employer wants. Take notes on the job posting or index card if additional clarification of the wording of a job posting is needed or has been provided.
5. On index cards, write the keywords/experiences highlighted in the job posting. Use one card for each job posting experience or skill that is highlighted.
6. Place the index cards on the flat surface (or use tape to place them on the wall) in a row. Allow room to place sticky notes underneath each index card.
7. Ask the client to review his or her resume to see what positions the client has held, and align them with the employer's desired skills or experience. The client can highlight positions or bullets on his or her resume that match an employer-desired skill or experience.

8. Discuss with the client any additional experiences in the positions not listed on the client's resume that match what the employer desires. Ask the client to write these on his or her resume under the corresponding experience.
9. Assign a sticky note color to each position the client has held that aligns with a desired element of the job posting.
10. Methodically work through each index card of keywords, matching job experiences to the index cards. Write the job bullet/experience on the Post-It note color that corresponds with the job position that your client gained the experience under.
11. Once this has been done for every index card, the client will copy the graph created with index cards and Post-It notes onto a sheet of paper.
12. You and the client will talk through how to take each column of the graph and craft sentences to address how the client meets each job posting keyword/experience with his or her previous work experience.
13. Once the sentences have been crafted, work with the client to combine this information into a cover letter that best matches the job posting and the client's prior experience.

APPENDIX D

INTERVENTIONS FOR NONTRADITIONAL HIGHER EDUCATION STUDENTS

GETTING A LIFE!

Susan R. Barclay

This activity is useful for clients who are interested in pursuing additional education, yet lack clarity as to which educational areas to pursue; for clients who desire a career change; or for clients who lack satisfaction, meaning, and fulfillment in their current work lives. The goal is to help clients author, deconstruct, and reauthor their story, and assist them with making vocational choices that will guide them to more meaningful and satisfying work lives.

Materials Required: Whiteboard, flip chart, or large sheets of paper (e.g., newspaper end rolls); a copy of the Career Construction Interview (CCI) questions.

Preparation Needed: None.

Activity Directions:

1. Ask the client to explain how you (the counselor) can be helpful to him or her.
2. Work through each of the CCI questions.
3. Record client responses on the whiteboard. If using a flip chart or large sheets of paper, you might tape these to the wall to create a continuous sheet.
4. As the client responds to each CCI question, ask for clarity or explore responses as needed to understand how the client has made vocational decisions in the past, what his or her preoccupation is that is creating barriers (derived from early recollections), and the client's self-advice (derived from the motto). Continue until the client has responded to every CCI question.
5. Ask the client to help identify themes in the CCI responses recorded on the board/paper. Facilitate this process and make tentative guesses as to the connection of the themes to how the client stated you could be helpful.
6. You and the client work collectively and collaboratively to use patterns in explaining past decisions and unconscious roadblocks constructed by the client. By dismantling the barriers, clients experience freedom to re-author their story and move forward in making more meaningful and fulfilling career decisions.

GETTING SMART: SETTING SMART GOALS IN CAREER EXPLORATION

Ryan Day and Michael A. Keim

This activity allows the counselor and the client to collaborate and explore careers by assisting clients to develop clear and concise SMART goals along with choosing careers that are aligned with personal values. SMART goals are those that are SPECIFIC, MEASURABLE, ACHIEVABLE, REALISTIC, and TIMELY, which are key in assisting clients to set effective career goals and objectives. A worksheet is provided that briefly defines SMART goals and provides guidance to the client in order to develop a list of goals in a step-by-step manner.

Materials Required: *SMART Goals Worksheet* (Figure D.1), pen or pencil.

Preparation Needed: Prepare copies of the worksheet.

Activity Directions:

1. State for the client:
   The following are components of an effective goal—one that describes performance standards that will tell us what good behavior looks like. The SMART acronym can help us remember these components:

***S**pecific*	*The goal should identify a specific action or event that will take place.*
***M**easurable*	*The goal and its benefits should be quantifiable.*
***A**chievable*	*The goal should be attainable given available resources.*
***R**ealistic*	*The goal should require you to stretch some, but allow the likelihood of success.*
***T**imely*	*The goal should state the time period in which it will be accomplished.*

2. Discuss some of the following tips for setting effective goals with the client:
   - Create a list of several goals on a separate sheet of paper. A list of five to seven goals gives you several things to work on over a period of time.
   - State goals as declarations of intention, not items on a wish list. "I want to apply to three schools" lacks power; "I *will* apply to three schools" is intentional and powerful.
   - List objectives that support your goals and interests. Explore options that align with your vision statement and confirm your goals.
   - Attach a date to each goal. State what you intend to accomplish and by when. A good list should include some short term and some long-term goals. You may want a few goals for the year and some for 2- or 3-month intervals.
   - Determine the steps necessary in reaching your goals. Please be specific. "To find a career" is too general; "to find and research five career options before the end of the month" is better. Sometimes a more general goal can become the long-term aim.
   - Evaluate your options and eliminate any uncertainty/doubt (be honest with yourself).

- Write down your goals and put them where you will see them. The more often you read your list, the more results you get.
- Review and revise your list. Experiment with different ways of stating your goals. Goal setting improves with practice, so play around with it.

3. Present the client with the *SMART Goals Worksheet* and collaboratively work through the goal-setting process. Help the client to be sure he or she meets the requirements for a SMART goal.
4. Assist the client in identifying a first step toward accomplishing his/her primary goal.
5. Set a clear date for the client to return to check on progress toward the completion of goals.
6. Continue to assess the client's progress and assist him or her to address expected or emergent barriers to success and explore possible alternatives to overcoming these barriers.
7. Lastly, have the client complete the remaining questions listed on the *SMART Goals Worksheet*, and then discuss them openly in session.

(Specific, Measurable, Achievable, Realistic, Timely)

Goal Statement:	Accomplishment Date:
Where am I now in reaching my goal?	
Current Barriers:	New Alternatives:
1.	1.
2.	2.
3.	3.
4.	4.

How will I know when I have accomplished my goal?

Steps to accomplish goal:

1.
2.
3.

What/Who are my resources?

What are three things that I can do today to work toward my goal?

1.
2.
3.

FIGURE D.1 SMART Goals Worksheet.

HOW DO YOU LIKE YOUR Ps AND CARROTS?

James R. Huber

This versatile, two-part activity offers a creative structure and a supportive process to clarify professional interests and personal motivations. The goal of this activity is to "think and link" diverse interests and influences in exploring career choice.

Materials Required: Paper and pencil, flipchart/whiteboard and markers (for groups), cans of peas, and a bag of fresh carrots (optional).

Preparation Needed: Handouts with the prompts in Part One and Part Two may be printed.

Activity Directions:

Part One: The Ps (Professional Interests)

1. Give clients paper and pencils.
2. Ask clients to fold the paper into four even columns lengthwise.
3. Instruct clients to label each column with the following headings from left to right:
   Professions *Populations* *Problems* *Places*
4. Starting with the first column, ask clients to brainstorm specific professions they may be interested in and list them in that column (e.g., teacher, counselor, nurse, etc.). Encourage them to think freely and write down any occupation or job of interest. For larger groups, create the same four headings on the board and record some of their interests there as examples for all to see.
5. For the second column, ask clients to list any specific populations they might like to work with in their careers (e.g., older adults, lesbian, gay, bisexual, and transgender [LGBT] individuals, veterans, children, etc.). Again, encourage them to think freely and write down any group of people in any order regardless of what they wrote under professions in column one.
6. For the third column, ask clients to list any specific problems that they would like to help people with in their careers, and write them down in any order under that heading (e.g., depression, drug abuse, bullying, disabilities, etc.).
7. Finally, in the fourth column, ask clients to record any specific places where they might like to work in their careers (e.g., hospital, school, clinic, newsroom, etc.). Encourage them to freely think of work settings without regard to any interest listed in the first three columns.

8. Using the example written on the board/flipchart, point out that the interests in the four columns need not connect in any logical way in rows from left to right. For example:

Professions	*Populations*	*Problems*	*Places*
Teacher	Older Adults	Depression	Hospital
Counselor	LGBT	Drug Abuse	School
Nurse	Veterans	Bullying	Clinic
Writer	Children	Disabilities	Newsroom

9. When the clients have completed their four lists, instruct them to circle their top choice or ideal interest in each column and share the resulting four-interest combination with the group (e.g., teacher, LGBT, bullying, and school).
10. Ask clients to describe any new career interests, insights, or ideas based on their circled combinations or any other possible combinations of preferred Ps.
11. To enhance client engagement and to emphasize the importance of a positive attitude, consider presenting each client with a small can of peas after the activity, saying: *Remember, career success comes in cans, not cannots!*

Part Two: The Carrots (Personal Motivation)

1. Tell clients that in addition to their Ps, or professional interests, their career choices are often influenced by their personal motivations or "carrots."
2. Explain the traditional metaphor for motivation as "the carrot dangled in front of the horse to make it move forward."
3. Using a prepared handout, facilitate a discussion of the following questions:
    a. *What do you notice/like about the combination of the four Ps you have circled?*
    b. *How might this combination provide you with some specific career direction?*
    c. *Who do you know who is currently working in any of your circled preferences?*
    d. *What family members, relatives, or friends do you know in any of your interests?*
    e. *How have the persons mentioned earlier influenced your interest in that preference?*
    f. *How has your gender, age, race, religion, ethnicity, and so on, influenced your interests?*
    g. *What obstacles do you think might challenge your pursuit of your interests?*
    h. *What work or volunteer experience do you already have in any of your interests?*
    i. *Who is already supportive or unsupportive of your career interests?*
    j. *What do you still need to know about any of your four preferred Ps?*
    k. *What could you do to learn more about one of your specific interests?*
    l. *What do you think is the next step you need to take to pursue your interests?*
4. To enhance client engagement and enjoyment, and to encourage everyone to speak, consider passing around a large carrot for each speaker to use as a "microphone," and then give everyone a carrot to eat or keep when the activity is completed.
5. Before clients leave, make a photocopy of their four-column professional interest worksheet for individual follow-up as needed and continuity in career counseling.

APPENDIX E

INTERVENTIONS FOR DUAL-CAREER COUPLES

POWER COUPLES: UNITE!

Samantha Barbieri, Michelle Cap, and Marion Cavallaro

This activity helps dual-career couples become aware of conflicts that may occur while managing work and partner roles. The activity assists couples in identifying and using communication strategies to understand individual, work, and relationship needs and stresses. Dual-career couples will have an opportunity to understand each other and develop a plan to reduce stress and conflict in their lives. Through the use of a fantasy exercise and a discussion of dual-career couple scenarios, participants will be encouraged to share their concerns with one another and develop realistic plans to manage conflict and enhance their relationship.

Materials Required: Dual-Career Couples Scenarios sheet.

Preparation Needed: Copy the "Dual-Career Couples Scenarios" sheet for program participants.

Activity Directions: Inform participants that the program will consist of two exercises: a "Fantasy Life" Guided Imagery and a Dual-Career Couples Scenarios Discussion.

"FANTASY LIFE" GUIDED IMAGERY

1. Guided Fantasy
   - Inform participants that they will be working independently for the first part of this activity.
   - Instruct participants to "forget" their current lives and imagine what their "fantasy life" would be like. Lead participants in this fantasy with the following instructions:
   Who would be present in their fantasy life?

What would their family life be like? For example, how much time would they spend with the significant people in their lives? When would they see these important people? What would they be doing together? On evenings? On weekends?
What career would they have? How much time would they spend on their career in the evenings and on weekends? What kind of travel would be required?
What role would they play at home regarding home and family responsibilities?
What role would their partner play?

2. Partner Discussion
   - Ask participants to share their fantasy life with their partners and discuss:
   Similarities and differences between each of their fantasy lives.
   What elements of their fantasy lives they would incorporate into their real lives.
   What they would have to do make this happen.
3. Group Discussion
   - Using the following processing questions, lead participants in a discussion about any conflicts that arose and ways in which they could resolve their conflicts:
   What was it like to "forget" your current life?
   What did you initially feel as you were imagining your fantasy life?
   While you were imagining your fantasy life, what stood out to you?
   What did you notice?
   How is your real life similar to your fantasy life? How is it different?
   How was it to discuss your fantasy life with your partner?
   What conflicts came up? How were you able to resolve them?
   How did you feel after your discussion (inspired, discouraged, optimistic, hurt, angry, excited)?
   What can you do to help yourself and your partner resolve any negative feelings?
   Is your fantasy life, in any way, attainable?
   What aspects of your fantasy life do you like that you can incorporate into your real life?

DUAL-CAREER COUPLE SCENARIOS

1. Partner Discussion
   Distribute the "Dual Career Couples Scenarios" sheet and select a scenario to discuss that reflects some of the issues that occur in their lives. With their partners, clients discuss the processing questions listed following the scenarios.
2. Group Discussion
   - For each of the scenarios, ask couples to share their responses to the processing questions and then discuss:
   What are some effective strategies to help couples understand their partners' stressors and needs?
   What are the common barriers to communication? What are the ways couples can reduce these barriers in their relationship?

What are some practical next steps couples can take to reduce stress in their lives and work toward a common goal?

3. Instruct couples to select one of the following cases:

Scenario One

Dan is a financial planner, and his wife, Kim, is a middle-school teacher. They both work jobs that require a 40-hour-week schedule, though Kim is required to attend faculty meetings, teacher workshops and conferences, and come in after hours for parent–teacher conferences. Dan holds traditional values and the view that the woman should take care of the house, which includes cleaning and cooking. Kim does the cleaning and cooking so that it gets done but feels that they should share the workload at home because they both work full-time jobs.

Scenario Two

Steve and Sandy have been married for 4 years and have three children together. Steve stays at home and takes care of the children while Sandy works in the public relations industry. Sandy travels a great deal for work. Steve and Sandy are experiencing conflict within their relationship because Steve feels that Sandy should lessen her workload so she can spend more time at home with their family.

Scenario Three

Diana and Ingrid have been together for 15 years and are both dedicated to their professional careers. Recently, Diana has been offered a high-level management position in her company that will require later hours and frequent travel. Although Ingrid is happy for Diana that she is being recognized for this promotion, she is worried about the impact of Diana's increased workload on their lives. Thus far, the couple has enjoyed a fairly regular schedule that has allowed them ample time to relax, dine out, and travel together.

4. Discuss the following:

   What is the initial reaction to the scenario?
   What conflicts are present in this scenario?

   a. Communication:
      - *Which communication barriers could interfere with the couple resolving the conflict?*
      - *Which communication strategies could help this couple resolve their conflicts?*

   b. Individual/Work/Relationship needs and stresses:
      - *What stressors are present in this scenario?*
      - *Can you relate to these stressors?*
      - *What are some stressors in your relationship?*
      - *Are you/is your partner aware of the significance of stressors in your life?*

c. Gain understanding about each other:
   - *What are some strategies that could help you and your partner understand each other's perspective?*

d. Develop a mutual plan to reduce stress and conflict:
   - *How would you help this couple create a plan to reduce stress and conflict?*
   - *Do you/your partner have a "game plan" for how to reduce/mediate stress/conflict?*

Practical Solutions

What are some practical steps that this couple could take to communicate, achieve compromise, and work toward a common goal? What are some steps you and your partner could take as well?

NAVIGATING MILITARY CULTURE WHILE RETAINING A SENSE OF "I"

Katherine M. Wix and Erin N. Friedman

Military-connected families face unique challenges, especially when it comes to career aspirations. Some of the most pressing concerns facing this population are mobility, transition, career network, and portability of career skills and knowledge (Saltzman et al., 2011). Military families move approximately every 2 to 3 years (National Military Family Association, 2015), often leaving military spouses unable to find suitable employment, let alone fulfilling careers. Saltzman et al. (2011) stressed the importance of weighing career options due to transitions, mobility, portability, and lack of access to relevant career networks. Thus, family-centered initiatives are necessary in career exploration. This activity attempts to increase military spouses' awareness of military values and individual values, identify career goals, and find careers congruent with individual needs. Many military spouses are ill-prepared to enter fulfilling careers and often lack self-efficacy in regards to career potential. With appropriate career exploration and training, military spouses can factor in the unique demands of military life and personal fulfillment. Barriers to career fulfillment include environmental as well as relational challenges. Additionally, providers can assist clients by becoming well-informed and knowledgeable of military culture, local resources, and career advancement concerns for military-connected families (Murphy & Fairbank, 2013). Objectives for this activity include reframing military spouses' beliefs about career abilities, visualizing integration of community and military networks for career opportunities, and recognizing how military strengths translate to civilian traits.

Materials Required: List of process questions/lesson plan, Values Sort Indicator (Figure E.1), Values Sort Cards (Figure E.2), scissors, and list of community and military resources (optional).

Preparation Needed: Prepare Values Sort indicator.

Activity Directions:

1. The *Navigating Military Culture While Retaining a Sense of "I"* career activity is broken into two phases to foster increasing levels of depth that counselors can use with clients to further explore military spouses' personal career goals and self-efficacy. Both phases of *Navigating Military Culture While Retaining a Sense of "I"* center on creating career goals and aspirations through processing reflective questions. Counselors may want to incorporate conversations previously held with other military spouses regarding self-concept, career goals, and the union of military culture and individual aspirations in an attempt to reduce stigma and introduce dialogue regarding common experiences.

First Phase

The counselor will spend time processing specific questions with the client in order to help differentiate between the client's career goals and the reality of living within the military family or values instilled within military culture. The counselor will listen to client responses while helping to maintain focus on client's personal beliefs and aspirations—trying to separate those from the reality of military lifestyle. Phase one focuses on the client's perceptions and career aspirations. Counselors can help clients map out career paths and, as they encounter obstacles, work to process the client's feelings and reactions to obstacles.

First Phase Process Questions

How does your spouse's military affiliation affect your day-to-day life?
How does your spouse's Military Occupational Specialty (MOS) impact your career goals or aspirations?
How has being married to a service member impacted your career?
How do you work with that?
How does your service member support your career?
How do you and your spouse negotiate deployment or mobility/transition?
How do you renegotiate if circumstances change?

Follow-up questions to client responses:

If you could do anything, what would you do?
What is stopping you from pursuing __________?
What can you do to change ___________?

Counselor awareness and considerations: Military Occupational Code or Specialty (MOS code) is a code used to identify a specific job assigned to each service member (Rand, 1992). Counselors also need to be aware of and be sensitive to service member assignments overseas as these may include living apart from the family unit. Additionally, counselors may inquire about service member's combat experience in order to learn if family is receiving support for loss of limb(s), mental or physical impairment, grief, loss, or death.

Second Phase

In the second phase, clients will identify values or "non-negotiable wants" of a career as well as ideal preferences. Values are beliefs that influence behavior and decision making. The purpose of implementing the Values Sort activity is to help clients clarify and prioritize individual values. Clients can discuss values and overcoming obstacles with the support of their counselor. Collaboratively, clients and counselors will work to identify careers that encompass individual client values to achieve new career hopes and goals. New careers may be self-identified or prompted by counselors, who will challenge clients to problem solve and find ways to create space for their career aspirations. Counselors will help encourage clients to identify and process values by asking questions pertaining to strengths and career goals. The Values Sort activity will help military spouses identify personal values to develop a sense of empowerment through career exploration.

Second Phase Instructions

1. Counselors will provide clients with the Values Sort Cards (Figure E.2). If time allows, counselors will have cut-out cards ready to use. If cards are not separated, the counselor should ask the client to cut out each card.

2. Counselors will lay down two laminated headings labeled, "Nonnegotiable/ Deal Breakers" and "Ideal Preferences" (Figure E.1).
3. Counselors will ask clients to identify five nonnegotiable factors wanted in a career, and five to ten ideal preferences. Counselors will remind clients to pay particular attention to cards that they cannot do without. Careful selection of cards highlights important personal values that clients will consider when choosing career options, which may mean that clients have to make difficult decisions.
4. When finished, clients will put aside cards that did not make it into either category.
5. Counselor and client will discuss each value placed in the "Nonnegotiable/ Deal Breaker" category and then also discuss values placed in the "Ideal Preferences" category to highlight careers that embody shared values.

Counselors can encourage clients to identify values and strategies to overcome military lifestyle obstacles in order for spouses to seek career goals. Counselors will lead discussion on how knowing individual values can assist in fulfilling career aspirations and will also discuss how some values and job requirements may be in opposition. For example, you cannot take a job that requires 60-plus hours per week if one of your values is having time to spend with your family. Clients may look to incorporate personal strengths and strategies to overcome military lifestyle or cultural barriers. Clients will complete phase two by verbalizing an in-depth concept of career goals and the ability to discuss specific strategies to implement when barriers threaten career goals.

Second Phase Process Questions

1. *What are some of your strengths?*
2. *What do you do well?*
3. *How have those strengths helped you?*
4. *What can you honestly see yourself doing and enjoying? What are some changes you are excited about making?*
5. *What are your thoughts on portability?*
6. *How has, or will, moving impact you and your career goals?*
7. *Can you list several specific and important values?*
8. *How were these values developed?*
9. *How have some of your values changed over time? Talk to me about the importance of these values and how each value resonates with you.*
10. *How might it be beneficial to create possible plans that you could employ if necessary?*
11. *For instance, what supports will you need to have in place if your spouse is deployed? Some ideas to ponder may consist of the following:*
    Assistance with childcare
    Carpool options
    Afterschool activities
    Emotional support
    Time for yourself

**If clients struggle to respond, engage in a discussion of ingrained values and automatic responses.

Nonnegotiable/Deal Breakers	Ideal Preferences

FIGURE E.1 Values Sort Indicator.

Variety and change at work	Have control/power/authority	Be active in your community
Be an expert	Travel often	Live simply
Work on the frontiers of knowledge	Be rewarded monetarily	Live close to sports/recreational facilities
Help others	Be an entrepreneur	Entertain at home
Help society	Work as a team	Have access to educational/ cultural opportunities
Experience adventure/excitement	Have regular work hours	Vacation
Feel respected for your work	Set your own hours/have flexibility	Save money
Compete with others	Be wealthy	Be involved in politics
Take risks/have physical challenges	Work in a fast-paced environment	Spend time with family
Have lots of public contact	Have prestige or social status	Live in a big city
Influence others	Have intellectual status	Live abroad
Engage in precision work	Have recognition through awards/ honors/bonuses	Have time for spirituality/personal growth
Gain a sense of achievement	Wear a uniform	Be a homeowner
Opportunities to express your creativity	Work in an aesthetically pleasing environment	Live in a rural setting
Work for a good cause	Work on the edge, in a high-risk environment	Have fun in your life and work

FIGURE E.2 Values Sort Cards.

Military Values/Strengths	Civilian Values/Strengths
Camaraderie—Unit cohesion and teamwork	Friendships and teamwork
Alertness—Vigilance or watchful	Mental vision or administrative preparedness
Armed for combat	Creation of safe environments, protector
Emotional control—esp. under pressure	Calm, cool, collected
Disciplined, commanding presence	Confidence, assurance

FIGURE E.3 A Comparison of Military and Civilian Values.

WHAT'S YOUR TEMPERATURE?

Katherine M. Hermann and Zach J. Hebert

The "What's Your Temperature" activity builds on the idea that every couple has an ideal thermostat temperature setting, which must be negotiated to keep both partners comfortable and content. Using the thermostat analogy, a therapist can help a dual-career couple find similar equilibrium and balance as they explore their respective careers within the strictures of their relationship. In addition to career exploration, the activity also allows a counselor to model and teach positive communication strategies, encourage perspective taking, facilitate effective problem solving, and foster individual and cooperative values exploration.

Materials Required: Unmounted white board, drawing paper, a marker, 30 glass pebbles (15 in each of two colors).

Preparation Needed: Before beginning the session, the counselor will use a ruler to create a set of lines on the white board, leaving space between each to comfortably fit a row of glass pebbles.

Activity Directions:

1. To prepare for the activity, have each of the clients briefly discuss his or her respective career and/or educational histories and aspirations.
2. Using the analogy of the thermostat, explain that, as with the temperature within a home, in order for a relationship to be most successful, both partners must be willing to negotiate and compromise to find a balance that is comfortable for everyone.
3. Next, use the white board to facilitate a brainstorming session wherein the couple develops a list of potential value areas that may impact their career decisions. You may find it necessary to facilitate this process by offering examples such as the following: finances, time constraints, sharing of household responsibilities, the building of a family, flexibility, career versus job, and so on.
4. Once the couple has created an exhaustive list (about 8–10 value areas), give the couple the glass pebbles. Allow each client to choose a color to represent his or her "votes."
5. Have the clients look over the list and internally prioritize some or all of the items, then take turns placing pebbles down next to the items on the board that are most important to them, with a single pebble representing something a little important, two pebbles representing something fairly important, and three pebbles or more for something very important, and so on. By the end of the process, neither client should have any pebbles left.
6. Process with the clients how they made their decisions. You may find it helpful to initiate this conversation with a discussion of shared values to facilitate collaboration. Help the couple to safely discuss and negotiate thoughts and feelings about the values that are not as important to each partner, modeling good communication skills and helping the couple recognize any blind spots.

The couple should feel free to move and reassign their pebbles during this stage of processing.

7. After the discussion is complete, tally up the total number of pebbles in each row, then order the listed values from most to least important on a separate sheet for the clients to keep.
8. Reflect with the clients on the list created, highlighting common values and eliciting suggestions on potential goals for both of them, individually and as a couple.
9. Next, facilitate a discussion linking how the values relate to career options and opportunities. Ask the couple questions to foster a discussion on the relationship between the values and career choices, job prospects, possible decisions, and future plans.
10. Finally, discuss the skills the couple used when negotiating their values and how these same skills can be applied to other decisions they will face as a couple in the future.

Variation: This activity can be done more than once, even in a single session, to reflect life changes, such as having children or having children move away, or simply to plan for the future (*This is where you are now, but how do you think that might change in five years? How about ten?*).

APPENDIX F

INTERVENTIONS FOR STAY-AT-HOME MOTHERS RETURNING TO WORK

LYRICS OF MY LIFE

Sandra Logan and Carly Heckathorn

This activity is designed for young adult mothers who are having difficulty envisioning their career path. By identifying meaningful songs, clients will explore how lyrics can represent the story of their lives. Utilizing narrative theory (White & Epston, 1990), counselor and client will discuss relevant themes and identify the client's beliefs about his or her own self-efficacy. Following these revelations, clients will construct their own lyrical story that demonstrates their desired career path.

Materials Required: Pen/pencil, paper, computer with Internet access and speakers.

Preparation Needed: Prepare a list of songs or themes to serve as an example for the client.

Activity Directions:

1. Ask the client to identify songs with lyrics that represent his or her goals, career, and/or future.
2. The client writes a list of song titles and respective lyrics that he or she finds representative of his or her life. You can collaboratively research songs with the client, if desired.
3. Prompt the client to identify a narrative. Song selections are reviewed together to determine themes and the client's beliefs (e.g., does the client feel in control of her future? Does she feel that her status as a young mother has limited her career plans?).
4. With the client, deconstruct the client's narrative by identifying any beliefs that the client would like to change.
5. With the client, reconstruct a new narrative based on the client's previous answers and his or her stated values.

6. The client is instructed to create a playlist with the new narrative in mind. A possible adaptation for a clients who is more creatively inclined may be for him or her to write his or her own lyrics as well.

Activity Adaptation: For clients who are more visual and/or kinesthetic learners, you may elect to have them use note cards to document their beliefs and narratives from steps 3 to 5.

MAXIMIZING UNEMPLOYMENT: EMPOWERING FEMALES FOR WORKFORCE REENTRY

Patrick D. Murphy, Steven D. Wright, and Amanda M. Evans

The number of women entering the workforce has increased, but women are more likely to exit and reenter the workforce due to competing personal responsibilities including, but not limited to (a) child birth/child rearing, (b) divorce/relationship changes, (c) accepting caregiving responsibilities for older relatives, and so on (Alonso-Almeida, 2014). Women who reenter the workforce report challenges including rebranding themselves and adjusting to work–life balance issues (Chae, 2002). Literature has suggested that self-confidence, self-image, and self-esteem are all considered to impact women's perceptions of themselves as they make decisions regarding reentry to the workplace (Ericksen et al., 2008). Thus, it is important for counselors to explore these self-perceptions with clients. The purpose of this activity is to challenge the clients' negative perceptions and to reflect on their unique skills. Focus on managing multiple identities, such as caregiver, mother, and partner, is incorporated. The goal is to explore the transferability of traits and skills to potential work environments.

Materials Required: Index cards, pens or pencils, a copy of the group member's resume, and list of adjectives used to describe employable skills.

Preparation Needed: Ideally, this group activity should be introduced with a group in the transition or working stage because it involves discussing group member vulnerabilities. Following a discussion on the member's reasons for an absence from the workforce, fears associated with reentering the workforce, and casual factors, the facilitator could use this intervention to transition the clients from problem identification to problem solving. Group members will be encouraged to bring an updated resume and/or cover letter to the group meeting.

Activity Directions:

1. Group members will be directed to review their resumes. Process questions following this review might include: *(a) What are you thinking when you look at your resume? (b) Are there gaps in your resume? (c) How do you think potential employers perceive these gaps?*
2. After a discussion of each member's professional documents, say: *Let's think about those gaps in your resume: (a) What was your life like during those gaps? (b) What was added and/or subtracted from your life in those gaps? (c) What did you learn about life and yourself in those gaps?*
3. Following this time for members to self-reflect and consider their entry and absence from the workforce, provide each member 10 blank index cards.
4. Ask each group member to list 10 (or as many as possible) positive aspects or skills about himself or herself obtained during the gap of employment.
5. If a group member is unable to list 10 positive aspects or skills on his or her own, you, as the facilitator, and the other group members will work together to help him or her identify aspects or skills.

6. When all group members have identified skill sets, members will rejoin the group to present and discuss what they have learned.
7. With the group members, discuss some of the following questions:
   a. *How can you use the skill sets you have obtained during your gap in employment to help you obtain employment?*
   b. *How can you rebrand yourself using what you have learned about life, employment, and the other group members to reach your goal?*
   c. *Do you see ways in which the positive aspects you identified can help you succeed?*
   d. *How can this particular skill help you be successful in a different role?*
   e. *Of the positive aspects about yourself you listed, which do you believe would be the most beneficial in a new work environment?*
   f. *What are ways in which leaving the workforce has prepared you to do well in a new work environment?*
   g. *How could you adjust the words on your cards to make them more congruent with career-based terminology?*
8. Group members will then transition to discussing the entire intervention and their continued needs of the group regarding workforce reentry.

APPENDIX G

INTERVENTIONS FOR WORKING PARENTS

GIVE ME FIVE

Diane M. Dryja

The purpose of this counseling intervention is to help clients improve their overall quality of life by being able to identify past satisfying experiences, greatest challenges, and strengths and values that may affect the quality of work–life balance. This will help the client make more informed decisions about future plans, leading to a more satisfying, purposeful, balanced life. This activity utilizes elements of visualization, mindfulness, and cognitive behavioral processes.

Materials Required: Paper or copy of the handout supplied here (Figure G.1), pencil or pen, crayons, markers, or colored pencils.

Preparation Needed: Gather the materials listed earlier. The client can trace his or her own hand onto a sheet of paper or use a therapist-provided copy of the handout supplied here.

Activity Directions:

1. State the Purpose: Let the Client Know…
   This activity is designed to help identify where areas of strengths, interests, and values are in order to assist them in making career decisions that make sense for this point in their life. During this activity, they will be closing their eyes from time to time and using their breath to relax and help them recall events.
2. Setup: Using the Handouts
   Simply give each client a handout and ask the client to assign a color to each number on the number line for use later in the activity. Let the client know that the color he or she assigns to 1 will represent the worst or least satisfying and that the color he or she assigns to 5 will represent the best or the most satisfying.

3. No Handout Option
   Have the client trace his or her hand on a sheet of paper, then draw a number line from 1 to 5 underneath the hand, having the client assign a color to each number in the same manner as indicated when using the handouts.
4. Now you are ready to guide the client through the following process:
   a. Ask the clients to close their eyes and take a few deep relaxing breaths and think of past careers, experiences, or jobs they have had (allow each client some time to process). Let them know that they may be surprised at particular emotions this may stir up but that these emotions will help them to further identify what has worked for them in the past and what may no longer be serving them now. Then have each client write down one thing that comes to his or her mind on each finger on the handout.
   b. Ask the clients to close their eyes again and think about the skills they learned, performed, or observed during the course of these five past events.
   c. Ask the clients to write these down on each matching finger. Using the scale, have them color each finger with the color that identifies the most satisfying to the least satisfying experience.
   d. Ask the clients to notice any areas where the skill sets or experiences overlap in any way and to write these items in the webbing between the fingers of the hand.
5. Exploring Challenges and Strengths:
   a. Ask the clients to close their eyes, take a deep breath in and out through the nose, and then gently allow the breath to soften and bring their attention to things that challenge their ideal work/life balance.
   b. Ask the client: *Where are those challenges coming from? Are some internal? For example, are you experiencing automatic negative thoughts or struggling with staying positive?* (Allow the client some time to process.) *When you are ready, write on the palm of the hand the internal challenges that came up for you. Are some external? If external challenges came to your mind, such as coworkers, homelife disruptions, work schedule, or environment, write them down beside the palm of the hand.*
   c. Repeat the process, only this time ask the client to focus attention on strengths and/or positive resources. Give examples of internal and external strengths and/or resources, like having a good memory (internal) and having a good support network (external).
6. Direct the client: *Take a moment now to look at what has come to your conscience awareness; notice if you see any connections, patterns, or any sense of significant meaning in any way. Then close your eyes, take a few deep breaths, and allow yourself to meditate for a few moments on five things that are truly important, meaningful, and purposeful to you right now. Your deep breathing will help you let go and enter into a state of relaxation, which will give your thoughts permission to surface. When you feel ready, release them onto the paper, writing them above each finger.* Encourage the client to take some time here to simply study the hand he or she created.
7. Ask the client: *Have you found parts of your hand are serving your work–life balance needs appropriately right now? Close your eyes, letting the breath relax and deepen.*

Ask yourself if you were to assign a color to how well you are playing your hand at this point, what color would you use? Color the palm of the hand that color.

8. Closing: Close the activity by asking the client what he or she has discovered by using a variety of open questions. The questions should address what the client needs to accept, choose, and/or take action on in order to improve his or her work–life balance. This will help the client to be able to map out a plan to create a more positive, satisfying, and rewarding hand, one that will assist the client in making good decisions about changing careers or making his or her current career more meaningful and hopeful at this time in the client's life.

Scale: ____

1 Worst/Least	2	3	4	5 Best/Most

The number 1 represents the worst or least satisfying and 5 represents the best or most satisfying.
Assign a color to each number by placing a dot of that color underneath each number.
Identify five careers, experiences, jobs (fingers).
Explore five skill sets from each (fingers).
Notice where the skill sets interconnect (webbing between fingers).
Note five challenges (internal palm of hand/external outside of the hand).
Note five strengths (internal palm of hand/external outside of the hand).
Note five things that are meaningful or important to you. (One above each finger). How do you think all of these factors influence your current career choice?

FIGURE G.1 Give Me Five Activity Page.

SHARING RECIPES FOR SUCCESS

Laura Bruneau and Lori Notestine

This intervention was originally designed for stay-at-home mothers who are weighing the decision to return to work. Many women faced with this decision often face anxiety and challenges related to self-image. This activity, however, could easily be adjusted for counseling working parents. Using myriad interventions in a group setting, clients will create recipe jars for success utilizing inspirational objects and messages to self. Drawing upon a relational cultural paradigm (Schultheiss, 2007), the goal of this activity is for women to co-construct meaning and reimagine themselves as they reflect on mattering, as women, mothers, and professionals.

Materials Required: Mason jars, strips of paper, tag/label, colored pencils, markers, ribbon (and other optional craft supplies) for each group participant.

Preparation Needed: None.

Activity Directions:

1. Introduce the activity toward the end of the first group session. For example, you might say: *We are going to create recipe jars over our group sessions. You may have received a recipe jar as a gift at some time in your life* (share photo of a recipe jar). *We won't be putting food ingredients in these jars, however. Instead, you will be putting in a variety of inspirational objects and written messages to yourself. These objects and/or written messages are intended to support and encourage you as you journey back into the workforce* (self-disclose an example or two). *You will be adding to your recipe jar between sessions and you will share your completed recipe jar with the group at our final session.*
2. Give the basic materials to each group member, including the mason jar and the strips of paper. The members then choose a variety of craft materials, such as colored pencils, ribbons, markers, tags, and so on, to decorate the jar.
3. Before the first group session closes, have each member write down an inspirational message to include in the recipe jar. For example, a member might write, "I am a strong woman—I can be a good worker and a good mom."
4. As homework, and between each subsequent group session, ask members to consider inspirational objects that they may include in their jar. For example, a member may include a wrist watch as a reminder of the importance of time management. Members can also write down ideas, strategies, and/or messages to self.
5. There are many potential variations to this activity. For example, members can include messages to self at the end of each group session in addition to out of session activities. In addition, at the end of the group sessions, members can share a message or idea with the group members sitting next to them. Finally, this activity may be modified with props such as a toolbox with which working fathers may more readily identify.
6. At the culminating group session, members will present and share their recipe jar for success. Members should prepare for this activity by selecting themes from their jar and/or the top three most important objects/ messages.

Facilitate a dialogue with the group member and the group about the experience of creating the recipe jars.

7. Process questions to use in the discussion include: *Tell us about your recipe jar. What is the most powerful theme, object, or message? What was it like to create the jar? What did you enjoy about the process? What were some struggles you faced in creating the jar? What did you learn about yourself in the process of creating the jar? From this experience, what will you take with you as you enter the workforce?* And to the group: *What feedback do you have for this group member about his or her experience?*
8. Ask group members for feedback about how to improve the activity for future groups.
9. In addition, this activity could be implemented in an individual counseling setting with the client completing the recipe jar in and out of session.

APPENDIX H

INTERVENTIONS FOR MIDLIFE ADULTS

CAREER WALKABOUT

Kevin B. Stoltz

Clients in middle life often possess an understanding of personal values, skills, and interests. Evaluating and reaffirming or rejecting aspects of the self is an important aspect of midlife career changers (Cochrane, 2001; Motulsky, 2010; Super, 1957). In career counseling, helping clients understand and account for life changes, events, and adjustments is a central focus in facilitating assessment of meaning and purpose in life trajectories. This intervention facilitates the client's sojourn into significant career events, providing space and time to further explore, inventory, and understand the transitioning self and evolving career identity (Hall & Murvis, 1995) accompanied by this life stage. Walkabout *is a term assigned to the Australian Aboriginal ceremonial phenomena of leaving life (e.g., family, home) for a short time during adolescence, by going into the outback exploring spiritual and ancestral roots (Merriam-Webster, 2005). This journey is usually spontaneous and unplanned. In this intervention, personal wanderlust and self-discovery are used, during the midlife career transition, to symbolize the return to self-discovery and identity evolution of early life stages. The goal of this intervention is to allow the client to reflect and reexperience significant career events, constructing a story used to integrate the many incidents and experiences along the client's lines of career development. This story is used to understand the self and pen future chapter outlines for the client to use as a guide for continuing to construct a meaningful life; the return from Walkabout.*

Materials Required: The materials for Career Walkabout can be vast and varied. Foundationally, artifacts that represent the six Holland (1992) themes are needed to represent values, attitudes, interests, and skills. The items can be represented by many common office items, however, some intentional objects may need to be purchased and present to offer the client a wide range of artifacts to collect during the Career Walkabout. For example, with realistic career themes, the counselor may need to purchase toy tools to represent specific activities or skills. Additionally, sporting toys (e.g., toy football, soccer ball) may assist clients in discussing physical activities. Play money can represent monetary compensation and other symbols can be used to represent the various dimensions mentioned by Holland. In addition, Holland discussed values of realistic individuals. Holland included practicality, adventurous, strength, and productivity as the important values, and these can be represented by many artifacts (e.g., compass for adventurous, small hand weight for strength). Counselors are encouraged to collect artifacts that represent all six aspects of the Holland coding themes and accompanying rewards, values, and other dimensions referenced by Holland (1994). Because this is a process that uses personal narrative to construct stories, many artifacts may take on individualized meaning, similar to the use of toys in play therapy (Landreth, 1991). Having a large supply of artifacts for the client to manipulate and accumulate will help the client to construct more complete and meaningful career life stories. Another aspect of this intervention uses movement and location to help the client shift when telling stories accounting for career transitions. This physical relocation is believed to help the client view completed transitions from one or more vantage points. To accomplish this, counselors need an array of chairs for the client to arrange and occupy when telling specific stories. Chairs may be different sizes and have a specific characteristic that is important to the client (e.g., armchairs may signify positions of authority or leadership). The arrangement of the chairs is best left to the client, but some suggestions include rows for similar careers and broken rows and clusters for careers that demonstrate several transitions or interruptions. The counselor can be a key element in helping the client to construct a geography of chairs that represents the client's story, similar to family sculpting. Additionally, having a few other sitting items (e.g., stools, pillows) that may represent temporary assignments or limited times of employment may be helpful in constructing the individualized Careersculpts. As a way to express themes and recognize emotional or significant events, counselors should have art materials and the supplies for the client to create signage for aspects of the narrative. Paper, colored pencils, materials for collages, clay, and other creative materials are important so that the client can construct artwork that represents emotions and thoughts related to the stories. The counselor is often the catalyst for engaging the expression of themes and stories from clients. Freeing the self from prescripts for objects and artifacts is an important aspect of this intervention. Counselors are encouraged to enter the client's world and help the client express and explore detailed aspects of the Career Walkabout.

Preparation Needed: As Career Walkabout is considered an intense and detailed intervention, the therapeutic relationship between counselor and client should be strong. This intervention is intended for use with clients with whom the therapeutic alliance is considered strong. Clients should be given a brief description of the intervention and understand that eliciting former memories and retelling events with movement and artifacts may provoke emotional responses. The counselor explains that Career Walkabout is an intervention that helps clients to understand life events that coalesce into general life themes. Within life, themes are the skills, values, interests, and attitudes that an individual uses to navigate life tasks and socially imposed developmental milestones. By creating and telling stories of past career experiences, the counselor and client gain insights into important factors to include when deliberating and determining future steps in addressing the client's concerns with career transitioning. The goal of the intervention is not simply about recounting the events but that all behavior has a purpose and the purpose relates to personal goals, meaning, and satisfaction. By assembling these artifacts, the intervention is designed to accentuate life themes that the client hopes to realize in all behaviors, including work-focused ones.

Activity Directions:

Introduction

1. Explain to the client that understanding interests, values, and attitudes is one important step to career counseling, but further exploration is optimal to understand the relationships and dimensions of how these personal elements culminate to create a career identity.
2. Perhaps share an example from your own life, using artifacts to give reality to the illustration.
3. Reassure the client that this may feel uncomfortable at first, but the intervention is usually effective in helping individuals understand important elements of meaning in career and life.
4. This intervention may take several sessions to complete based on the number of jobs the client reported or the detail within jobs. Thorough exploration is a key element in this intervention so the client can gain insight into career attitudes, behaviors, and emotional responses to career events.

Arranging the Career Walkabout Landscape

5. Take one or two chairs and ask the client to arrange them as representations of his or her first experiences with working. Many clients may refer to working at home as children or their first jobs in high school. This should be up to the client to choose and you will follow this decision by prompting the client to talk about the experience.
6. As the client describes the experience, you may retrieve an item and ask the client for permission to place the item near him or her and explain the significance. Any items placed by you need to be reflective of the client's story (e.g., content, feeling). This may go on for one or two more times, and then you can invite the client to select items. Each time the client selects an artifact, you may respond with a reflective statement (e.g.: *You've chosen the Post-It notes to represent the duties you had for taking inventory and making lists*). This technique acknowledges the client's intentions.

Exploring and Interpreting the Terrain

7. Once the client has completed the Careersculpt (artifacts and chair positioning of one job or work experience), prompt the client to move to a neutral chair to view and talk about the Careersculpt from an outside perspective. You may also move closer to the client to see the view from his or her perspective.
8. From the new vantage point, help the client glean themes and meaning from the artifacts. Exploratory questions help to facilitate this process. Examples

include: *Which of these items, attitudes, values, behaviors, and so on, did you take with you to your next job? Which of these items, attitudes, values, behaviors, and so on, did you want to leave behind?*

9. A few salient themes should arise in this conversation; you or the client can create signage to place in the chairs or among the surrounding artifacts to represent those themes.
10. Next, the client is prompted to move to another salient job and begin the process again. Repeating all the steps and exploring each job thoroughly is important. Even if the client dismisses the position as unimportant or transitional, exploration may uncover important values or experiences. Additionally, asking how the client maintained life and emotional control during times of transition may help to expose coping and stress reduction skills used by the individual. These can be highlighted and strengthened for use in future sessions.

Geographic Elements: Acknowledging Themes

11. On completing the various Careersculpts, you and the client can begin to view the accumulation of artifacts and suggest client meaning. The artifacts represent the various aspects and dimensions of the client's career and are used to create the grand career narrative (Super, Savickas, & Super, 1996). In narrating this story to the client, use each job as a chapter and explain the salient learning and experiences taken forward. In addition, you may explain the challenges that seem to be relevant across all of the Careersculptps. These life theme challenges are often troublesome for clients and, when uncovered, can have a cathartic and moving effect. During this process, you are enlisting the help of the client to story and restory these events to demonstrate client strengths and Career Adapt-Abilities (Savickas & Porfeli, 2012). Ultimately, the story leads to a personal identity and how the individual moves through and perceives life experiences.

Storying the Future

12. Once all jobs are explored and salient themes are acknowledged and embraced by the client, place the client in a new chair, surrounding the client with salient artifacts from the Career Walkabout, recognizing the accumulated skills, talents, and burdens that the client brings to the current career transition. This step is where the client is asked to narrate a career story using the artifacts and is directed specifically to narrate the next chapters in the client's career progression. Both the positive and negative aspects are used to narrate a story.

Returning to Life: Goal Setting and Next Steps

13. Once the new story chapter is outlined and the client is exhibiting readiness to engage in action, goal setting can occur. Goal setting includes establishing short- and long-term goals that include measurable steps to create self-efficacy in moving toward established goals.

14. You are encouraged to allow clients to create artifacts that represent salient aspects from the Career Walkabout. These artifacts can be carried with the client and placed in important locations in the client's Lifescape (a simile for all the client's life roles, similar to a home landscape with specific elements designed to create a complete theme and impression). Pictures of client's various Careersculpts can be recorded as a reminder for the client to use during stressful periods of the transition. In addition, therapeutic notes (notes penned by the client during the sessions as self-encouragement) and other mementoes can be sent to the client in the e-mail to follow up on the progress and prompt memories of goals, strengths, and successes.

Lifescapes: Integrating Careersculpts and Walkabout in a Narrative Landscape

Although described as a career-specific intervention, the Career Walkabout can be altered for other life roles to construct stories for detailing life themes with strengths, successes, and burdens. Careersculpts are used to create scenery for the Career Walkabout. The Career Walkabout includes several Careersculpts to create themes and perceptions of accumulated skills, values, and abilities. The counseling sessions may end here, or the client and counselor may combine other life challenges into separate walkabouts (e.g., walkabout for relationships). Combining these walkabouts into a complete canvas is the basis for forming a garden of personal growth: a Lifescape. The Lifescape construct includes Super's (1990) concept for integrating all the life roles. Symbolized with a gardening simile, the client's life becomes a plot of ground, ripe for cultivation. The individualized scenes (Careersculpts) become cultivated stories (Walkabouts), which are combined to create a complete Lifescape for the person, accounting for the individual's abilities to adapt and pursue growth across all life dimensions.

LOST IN TIME

Penny Dahlen, Nancy L. A. Forth, Atsuko Seto, and Corie N. Schoeneberg

This activity is helpful for clients who would like to use their passions in a career. The exercise is a visualization walking clients through stages of their development to identify times where they were engaged in a passion and/or deep purpose. The purpose is to help clients clarify times when they were fully engaged in their passion and help them to identify how they can turn this passion into a career path.

Materials Required: Paper and colored pens or pencils.

Preparation Needed: Have the supplies available for clients.

Activity Directions:

1. Introduce the session to the client by asking whether the client would be willing to do a visualization about his or her life path.
2. Once the client agrees, say (slowly): *Close your eyes and get comfortable, take a deep breath. If you aren't comfortable closing your eyes, find something you can gaze upon for a few moments. Now go back in time to when you were a little child, about 3 to 5 years old. Recall a time where you were engaged in an activity where you were having fun and lost track of time* (pause for 30 seconds). *Remember what you were doing and how it felt. Now go to when you were 7 to 10 years old; recall again a time in your life where you were engaged in something where you were having a great deal of fun and lost track of time. What were you doing, where were you, and how did it feel?* (Pause for 45 seconds.) *Next, recall a time during your preteen years where you were doing something fun. Who were you with and what were you doing?* (Pause for 45 seconds.) *Let's move to your teenage years; recall a time or two where you were engaged in something you really enjoyed where you weren't worried about time. What were you doing? How did it feel? Who were you with? Sit with this experience for a moment* (pause for 45 seconds to a minute). *When you are ready, come back to the room here.*
3. Provide paper and pencils and ask the client to draw one horizontal line and one vertical line so the client has four boxes. In the box to the upper left, he or she draws a picture of the image recalled from ages 3 to 5. In the box on the upper right, he or she draws the image from the visualization from age 7 to 10. In the box on the lower left, the client draws an image from the preteen year's visualization. In the box on the lower right, he or she draws an image that captures the image from the visualization from the teenage years.
4. After the client draws the pictures, ask what comes to him or her from the visualization and drawn images about who he or she is and what his or her purpose is in the world.

5. Additional processing questions may include: *How might these images together represent work or career possibilities? What other skills might you need to turn this passion into a career? What feelings come up for you when you imagine doing this image for a profession?*
6. As the client discusses the images and helps to turn passion into a profession, listen for self-defeating thoughts that might keep the client from pursuing his or her passion.
7. At the close of the session, ask what stood out about the session work for the client and what next steps the client can take to turn the passion toward a career.

APPENDIX I

INTERVENTIONS FOR OLDER ADULTS

CAREER TIMELINE: HIGHS AND LOWS

Gail K. Roaten and Elsa Soto Leggett

This activity was adapted from an activity titled "Career Services I Needed" (Minor & Celotta, 2000). The objective of the activity is to assist clients reflect on their career development history, noting career highs and lows, reflecting on times they needed assistance, and focusing on the type of career assistance they are currently seeking. The counselor assists the client in assessing the impact of previous career development history, both positive and negative, on the client's current status. The counselor and client may then work together to formulate client goals.

Materials Required: Large manila/newsprint drawing paper, colored pencils/crayons/markers.

Preparation Needed: None.

Activity Directions:

1. Ask clients to draw a timeline of their life from birth up to the present. Do not provide too much direction, but rather encourage the client to be as creative or simple as he or she may wish.
2. Instruct the client to use symbols and/or pictures to note important and salient life events—those that have impacted him or her. In addition, ask the client to include personal milestones and include all jobs he or she has held. You may need to process that this activity is not about the "quality" of the artwork, but rather about the process.
3. After clients finish drawing, ask them to go back over the timeline and denote career *highs* with a "+" and *lows* with a "–."
4. Then ask clients to recall times they could have used, or did gain, career assistance. Note these places with an arrow pointing to that time on their line.
5. Begin to process the times the client needed or could have benefited from career assistance by asking the client to share about these times. Have the client focus on the areas with the arrows. Ask the client the following questions: *When you look at these times in your career, did you receive any career assistance or*

guidance? If not, why do you think you did not? Do you think you could have benefitted from some career assistance or guidance? If you did receive some career assistance, how did that work for you? How did you go about getting that assistance? Do you think not having or having that career assistance influenced your career situation or status?

6. Ask the client to share about *low* periods or times. Ask the client to reflect and share how these experiences have impacted his or her career status. Questions can include: *When you look at those low periods or experiences, how did you feel? What was happening that made this a "low" for you? What could you control in that situation, and what was out of your control? How did this impact other life roles at that time? If career assistance had been available to you, what would it have looked like? What other support systems were available to you during this time? How do you think this event or period has influenced your current career situation or status?*
7. Repeat this exercise with client highs periods: *When you look at those high periods or times when your career was what you wanted for yourself, what was happening that made you feel it was a high period in your career? What was happening that made it a "high"? How did this impact other life roles at that time? Did you have any assistance along the way with this period or situation? What support systems were available to you during this time? How do you think that event or period has influenced your current career situation or status?*
8. Process and review with the client the impact of the past on the client's current functioning. Transition from this discussion to helping the client(s) formulate goals for therapy and future careers. Prompts that can be used include: *How do you think your previous "lows" have impacted where you are today? What about the "highs"? In light of what you have discovered through your career timeline, what are some things you have recognized that work for you and do not work for you? Now looking forward, what are some goals you have for yourself with regard to your career? What are some steps you could take toward reaching those goals? Do you think you will need some career assistance with those? What are current support systems and resources available to you? What will that assistance look like? Where will you find it?*

Processing is critical to the process, and additional questions or revision of questions correlated with a specific theoretical approach might be used. If this activity is used with high school students or counselor education students, a few tweaks will be necessary. The instructor needs to emphasize using this activity with future clients seeking career counseling.

EMOTIONALLY FOCUSED CAREER PORTFOLIO PROCESSING INTERVENTIONS FOR MATURE ADULTS

Sabina R. de Vries, Katrina Cook, and Mary Mayorga

This intervention is for older adults who find themselves out of work and struggling to find employment. Anxiety, stress, depression, grief/loss concerns, and relationship strain can impact self-esteem, coping skills, and sense of control. Problems arise when clients, through their existential angst, are overly focused on "doing" at the expense of processing emotions. As an adaptation of emotion-focused therapy by Greenberg (2004), the therapist assists with emotional processing and generation of alternative emotional responses to a career crisis. Although it is important to process feelings around the loss of career/employment, it is also important to honor a client's need to "do something." This type of client often has difficulty searching for employment. The client's job searching skills are often outdated, and the loss of employment occurred suddenly and unexpectedly. A career portfolio is a great tool to organize job search efforts and provides opportunities for processing emotions regarding loss of employment. Clients can also be asked to journal about portfolio items as well as job search and interview experiences.

Materials Required: Folder, paper, tabbed dividers, computer, printer, web access.

Preparation Needed: None.

Activity Directions:

1. Ask the client to collect information pertaining to unemployment benefits and the local unemployment office and other community resources.
2. Have the client prepare a resume listing personal information, education, knowledge, skills, accomplishments, and the like. There are a number of great resume writing resources available online (i.e., www.quintcareers.com). Frequently, local community service organizations offer free resume writing workshops.
3. Remind the client that the resume should be adjusted to conform to a variety of job applications or career fields.
4. Ask the client to complete free career assessment tools such as O*NET Interest Profiler, O*NET Ability Profiler, O*NET Work Importance Locator, and O*NET Work Importance Profiler (available at www.onetcenter.org) to be included in the career portfolio.
5. Ask the client to complete the Holmes and Rahe Stress Scale (available at en.wikipedia.org/wiki/Holmes_and_Rahe_stress_scale).
6. Ask the client to complete a free version of the Kersey Personality Inventory (available at www.keirsey.com).
7. Offer couple's or family counseling, if necessary. Unemployment can be stressful for the entire family and can lead to conflict. The client and his or her family might need assistance with coping under these high-stress conditions.

8. Provide the client with instructions for grounding exercises such as deep breathing or meditation. Remind the client of the need to also focus on self-care.
9. In order to foster autonomy and self-efficacy, assist the client in brainstorming about other materials that should be included in the portfolio.

APPENDIX J

INTERVENTIONS FOR VETERANS

CAREER GENOGRAM

Chad Luke and Tony Michael

This activity expands the traditional genogram, or family tree, to include educational and vocational information of veterans' families. What typically emerges from this intervention is thoughts and attitudes regarding the world of work, educational attainment, and quality-of-life issues. Often it is the first time that veterans (or clients in general) have made connections between family cultural messages regarding work and education and how their current perspectives are shaped by those relationships. It also highlights how veterans' military experience may have shaped their view of family vocational values and interests. The emphasis is on process and awareness, not completeness of information or thoroughness of charting.

Materials Required: Drawing paper (preferably large sheets of newsprint or butcher block paper), colored pencils, markers.

Genogram Symbols: Sites like Wikipedia have a great user-friendly chart like these (retrieved from en.wikipedia.org/wiki/Genogram, January 7, 2015).

Preparation Needed: None.

Activity Directions:

1. Ask clients to create a typical genogram using basic symbols for fundamental relationships (this is not an exercise where absolute precision or detail is expected or necessary).
2. Ask them to add in educational level and career or job types.
3. Ask them to share aloud their work, prompting where necessary to explore attitudes, meanings, and messages that emerge for them as they reflect.
4. Process questions that can be used include the following: *What values were conveyed about education and work? How does the information on the page aid your understanding of your decision to pursue military service, and then inform what*

your next steps might be? What questions would you like to ask their family members (living and accessible or not) about that person or persons' education and work life? What themes emerged from your genogram? What would you like to maintain; what would you like to change? How did the relationships with each individual impact the messages you received regarding work and career?

CAREER STRATEGY AND TACTICS-PLANNED HAPPENSTANCE

Chad Luke and Tony Michael

This activity is based on social learning theory, developed by Krumboltz (2009). It is based on the principle and empirical findings that many successful people attribute at least part of their success to luck or unforeseen positive events. In planned happenstance, the goal is to help the clients to prepare themselves for serendipitous events, relationships, or circumstances in order for them to effectively respond. We do not literally "make our own luck," but we can strategically position ourselves to increase the likelihood that positive things will come our way and be ready to take advantage of the opportunity.

Materials Required: Questions for Reflection handout.

Preparation Needed: Create Questions for Reflection handout from the following:

- When is the last time I allowed my **Curiosity** to guide my exploration of new learning opportunities?
- How **Flexible** am I in exerting effort despite setbacks?
- What do I do to maintain **Optimism** through changing attitudes and circumstances?
- To what extent am I cultivating **Persistence** through viewing new opportunities as possible and attainable?
- In what ways am I willing to take action in the face of uncertain outcomes? **Risk-Taking**.

Activity Directions:

Briefly describe the theory to the client(s). Once they have a quick overview, discuss the five domains or qualities that promote planned happenstance: Optimism, Curiosity, Persistence, Risk-Taking, and Flexibility. The first area for reflection is how these five areas may have presented themselves during the individual's military experience. Next, discuss how those qualities may have resulted in unexpected opportunities or successes within the military. Now that you have established a type of precedent of planned happenstance qualities in a military context, guide the discussion toward how it would look in civilian life to exhibit these qualities for career development.

Process Items:

1. Veterans already possess many skills and qualities necessary for planned happenstance; they need to see them for what they are.
2. The qualities identified earlier are transferable from military life to civilian life; career counseling helps veterans make these connections.

COUNTERINTELLIGENCE: CAREER MYTHS FOR VETERANS

Chad Luke and Tony Michael

One of the underlying difficulties for veterans in particular, and people in general, in career development is the admixture of misinformation, faulty assumptions, and "word on the street" information. Career and work myths can limit veterans' beliefs in opportunities available to them, stifling initial efforts as well as persistence, which are both critical factors in career success.

Materials Required: The list of career myths in the Activity Directions section.

Preparation Needed: None.

Activity Directions:

Use the following list of career myths to generate a conversation regarding beliefs about work and career opportunities for veterans. Brainstorm alternatives to these beliefs, along with resources for debunking them.

- All military personnel are angry and aggressive—they have to be—and therefore so are veterans.
- All veterans have posttraumatic stress disorder (PTSD) and are therefore likely to "go off" at work.
- All veterans have trouble reintegrating back into civilian life and therefore back into the workplace.
- The skills needed to be successful in the military are vastly different than the skills needed to succeed as a civilian employee.
- All veterans are "high maintenance" in that they have a lot of physical and mental issues to contend with.
- You can be successful without good people skills.
- There is a perfect job waiting out there for you.
- Working hard and keeping your nose clean will guarantee success.

Process Questions:

How have misinformation and faulty assumptions hurt you in the past? What did you do in the past to resolve discrepancies between the faulty and accurate information? How might maintaining faulty beliefs about career development pay off for you?

CREATING A "SOUP SANDWICH" OUT OF CAREER EXPLORATION

Tony Michael and Chad Luke

This career counseling intervention is based on cognitive therapy. Using the concept of cognitive distortions (Leahy, 1996), veterans are asked to reflect on what thoughts are inhibiting their progress in career exploration.

Materials Required: Pen and paper.

Preparation Needed: None.

Activity Directions:

1. Begin the session asking the client if he or she is familiar with the military metaphor of a "soup sandwich." Spend time discussing the idea with the client. Ask him or her to picture eating a sandwich full of soup. Imagine how messy and disorganized it would be.
2. Use the visualization to transition into the topic of the client's career exploration. Ask your client how he or she has made exploring a new career messier or more disorganized than it needs to be. Make a list of comments made by the client for future conversations.
3. Provide the following information from Leahy (1996) to your client:
   Cognitive Distortions
   1. *Mind reading*: You assume that you know what people think without having sufficient evidence of their thoughts.
   2. *Fortune telling*: You predict the future—that things will get worse or that there is danger ahead.
   3. *Catastrophizing*: You believe that what has happened or will happen will be so awful and unbearable that you will not be able to stand it.
   4. *Labeling*: You assign global negative traits to yourself and others.
   5. *Discounting positives*: You claim that the positives that you or others attain are trivial.
   6. *Negative filter*: You focus almost exclusively on the negatives and seldom notice the positives.
   7. *Overgeneralizing*: You perceive a global pattern of negatives on the basis of a single incident.
   8. *Dichotomous thinking*: You view events, or people, in all or nothing terms.
   9. *Shoulds*: You interpret events in terms of how things should be rather than simply focusing on what is.
   10. *Personalizing*: You attribute a disproportionate amount of the blame to yourself for negative events and fail to see that certain events are also caused by others.
   11. *Blaming*: You focus on the other person as the source of your negative feelings, and you refuse to take responsibility for changing yourself.

12. *Unfair comparisons*: You interpret events in terms of standards that are unrealistic—for example, you focus primarily on others who do better than you and find yourself inferior in the comparison.
13. *Regret orientation*: You focus on the idea that you could have done better in the past, rather than on what you can do better now.
14. *What if?*: You keep asking a series of questions about "what if" something happens and fail to be satisfied with any of the answers.
15. *Emotional reasoning*: You let your feelings guide your interpretation of reality.
16. *Inability to disconfirm*: You reject any evidence or arguments that might contradict your negative thoughts.
17. *Judgment focus*: You view yourself, others, and events in terms of evaluations of good/bad or superior/inferior rather than simply describing, accepting, or understanding. You are continually measuring yourself and others according to arbitrary standards, finding that you and others fall short. You are focused on the judgments of others as well as your own judgments of yourself (Leahy, 1996).

4. Ask the clients what cognitive distortions most commonly affect their career decision making. How do the cognitive distortions contribute to the client making a "soup sandwich" (i.e., disorganized mess) of finding a new career? What specific effects have these cognitive distortions had on the client's past (and present)? What changes does the client think need to be made in order to meet his or her goals in the future? How does the client think he or she can accomplish these changes? What support system or resources are available?

FLAGGING THE CAREER MINEFIELD

Chad Luke and Tony Michael

This activity is drawn from the work of Alfred Adler (as described in Erford, 2014) and addresses how we often encounter unexpected setbacks and barriers that in most cases can be predicted. In fact, many of the barriers we face in our lives follow a pattern of sorts, in terms of how we think, feel, act, and relate. The same is true for veterans, and possibly to a greater extent, given the transitions associated with military to civilian work culture. Flagging the minefield gives veterans an opportunity to anticipate unhelpful, unhealthy attitudes and behaviors and both become alert to and aware of those before they happen and modify those attitudes and behaviors before they derail their career path.

Materials Required: Drawing paper, colored pencils, markers.

Preparation Needed: None.

Activity Directions:

1. One creative variation on this activity when using it with clients is to ask them to create a battlefield map with their current vocational situation on one side, their career goals on the other side, and room in the center to plant their flags.
2. Ask them to draw icons or images that represent mines in career development. Examples to get them started might include: beliefs about negative perceptions of veterans leading to defensiveness in the veteran; memories of past failures or lack of success in attaining goals; wrestling with veteran-related issues such as traumatic brain injury (TBI), PTSD, or other adjustment disorders; and self-defeating behaviors such as avoidance of job searches, proactivity, follow-up calls, and so on.
3. Process their work, attending to the following guidelines: provide an opportunity for clients to "sit with" their project in order to be available for whatever emerges; attend to affect and body language as they explore and engage in the process; explore the source of these "mines" for underlying causes or precipitating factors that could create ongoing problems; and brainstorm solutions, work-arounds, "minesweepers," and the like to assist in preempting and then moderating the potential negative effects of these mines.

"FLIGHT SIMULATED" JOB INTERVIEW

Tony Michael and Chad Luke

This intervention is based on experiential learning and psychodrama, using role-playing to prepare veterans for upcoming job interviews. The technique can also help the veterans to gain awareness of the positions of others and help them to understand how others see them and improve the veteran's confidence. Caveat: Keep in mind that role-playing is beneficial for highly motivated and intelligent individuals; if a veteran currently experiences symptoms or characteristics associated with PTSD or TBI, this technique may not be as worthwhile.

Materials Required: None.

Preparation Needed: None.

Activity Directions:

1. Ask the client what the purpose of flight simulation (or boot camp training) is. Use the metaphor of a flight simulation (or boot camp training) to talk about the importance of preparation and rehearsal for better performance in job interviews.
2. Spend a few sessions advising the client on what valuable information should be within their resume, how to respond to questions with directness but not frigidity, and how to extenuate specific interpersonal skills during a job interview.
3. Inform the client that the next counseling session will be a role-play where he or she should wear, talk, and do what he or she would at an upcoming interview.
4. At the next counseling session, role-play as an interested employer who has a job opening. This session can also be recorded to provide additional feedback to the client if desired. Ask for the client's resume and ask typical questions like: *Tell me about yourself. What are your strengths and weaknesses? Why do you want this job? Where would you like to be in your career five years from now? What's your ideal company? What attracted you to this company? Why should we hire you? What did you like least about the military (or last job)? When were you most satisfied in the military (or last job)? What can you do for us that other candidates can't? What were the responsibilities of your last position? What do you know about this industry? What do you know about our company? Are you willing to relocate? Do you have any questions for me?*
5. If it is beneficial for the individual, also ask career development, salary, or behavioral interview questions. These may include: *What are you looking for in terms of career development? How do you want to improve yourself in the next year? What kind of goals would you have in mind if you got this job? If I were to ask your last supervisor to provide you additional training or exposure, what would she suggest? What salary are you seeking? What's your salary history? What was the last project you headed up and what was its outcome? Give me an example of a time that you felt you went above and beyond the call of duty at work. Can you describe a time*

when your work was criticized? Have you ever been on a team where someone was not pulling his or her own weight? How did you handle it? Tell me about a time when you had to give someone difficult feedback. How did you handle it? What is your greatest failure and what did you learn from it? What irritates you about other people and how do you deal with it?

6. After the interview, have the client make notes about his or her performance on the interview that lists strengths and things to work on.
7. Provide constructive feedback that highly emphasizes optimism for the client on his or her simulated interview. If the session was recorded, highlight specific instances to watch together that reveal enthusiasm, confidence, and poise. Remember to acknowledge not just verbal communication but also the nonverbal communication (e.g., body language).
8. If needed, repeat the process as a means for growth and development.

ON THE DOUBLE: DEVELOPING A JOB INTERVIEW SCRIPT

Tony Michael and Chad Luke

The following intervention is based on narrative therapy and cognitive processing and is designed to help veterans learn appropriate, thoughtout responses for upcoming job interviews.

Materials Required: Pen and paper.

Preparation Needed: None.

Activity Directions:

1. Have clients prepare a script that includes the information they want to convey in an upcoming job interview. Provide a pen and paper for them to write down their thoughts.
2. Begin by having clients discuss their past experiences and proven success in a few sentences. Provide the following for them as an example to quickly foster thoughts:
   "I have been in the military for the past 5 years. My most recent experience has been as a technical engineer in the United States Army. One reason I particularly enjoyed this job, and the challenges that went along with it, was the opportunity to make a practical impact in society. In particular, I had opportunities to help conduct land surveys, make maps, and prepare detailed plans for construction projects that improved people's daily lives."
3. Next, have the clients write their strengths and abilities:
   "My real strength is my attention to detail. I pride myself on my reputation for following through and meeting deadlines. When I commit to doing something, I make sure it gets done, and on time."
4. Have the client provide a conclusion with a statement about his or her current situation:
   "What I am looking for now is a company that values work ethic, where I can join a strong team and have a positive impact on the company and customers."
5. Provide some time to process the script with the client. What part(s) of the script did the client think were strong? What part(s) of the script did the client think needs to be improved? Offer unconditional positive regard and optimism to your clients regardless of the content.
6. Have clients refine and practice with their script until they feel confident about what they want to emphasize. Remind them that their script should help them stay on track, but they should not worry about memorizing it, as they do not want to sound stiff and rehearsed. It should sound natural and conversational.

REFRAMING YOUR CAREER HOUSE

Michael A. Keim and Ryan Day

Military veterans returning from deployment or ending their terms of service and reentering the civilian workforce possess extensive training, leadership experience, and many skills that would enable them to be successful in diverse work environments; however, many of these veterans may not have the experience or guidance while in the military to translate those skill sets and work descriptions into terms that are more recognizable and understood by most employers. It is also important to assist veterans to understand the value of the skills and experience they possess that can apply to civilian jobs. The following activity is designed to meet both of these career objectives.

Materials Required: Paper, craft sticks, markers, cellophane tape, construction paper.

Preparation Needed: If the career counselor is not already familiar with civilian equivalencies for skills, training, and experience gained by service members in the military, some research will be required. A good place to start is O*NET Online, which is sponsored by the U.S. Department of Labor and contains detailed descriptions of current occupations.

Activity Directions:

1. Ask the clients to briefly list the types of training, leadership experiences, and skills they developed while in the military on a piece of paper.
2. Explain that you are going to do an activity together to help them better understand how employers understand these skills and what terms they use for the same experiences.
3. State for the client: *If you think of developing your career like building a house, you already have a strong foundation of training that prepared you for your military occupation. The framework of that house was built with skills and experiences that are particular to military service, and therefore you use military terms to describe what you did. Let's use these sticks to represent the frame of the house—its walls, supports, and roof. Label each of the main skills that you demonstrated in your military position on one side of each stick.*
4. When this part of the activity is completed, assist the client to identify similar terms used in the civilian world to describe the experience or skill set described on each of the sticks.
5. The client would then label the stick on the opposite side with the civilian term. Putting these together by taping them to a piece of paper in the shape of a house, the client can then see how he or she has "reframed" the career house that the client has already made in his or her own life. The client can then see it literally from the employer's perspective, as well.
6. These new terms for military skills and experiences can be used to assist the client to develop a resume that fits civilian job expectations and descriptions.

"SEMPER FI-ABLE" TRAITS

Tony Michael and Chad Luke

Semper fidelis *is a Latin phrase that means "always faithful" or "always loyal." The term is well-known in the United States as the motto for the U.S. Marine Corps (i.e., commonly shortened to* semper fi*). Using the meaning of the* semper fi *term, this technique challenges veterans in reflective thinking to examine what personal skills or traits can be extended across career occupations.*

Materials Required: Pen and paper.

Preparation Needed: None.

Activity Directions:

1. Begin the session by asking the client if he or she is familiar with the term *semper fi*. Provide the following definition to help guide the career counseling intervention: *Semper fidelis*—a Latin phrase that means "always faithful" or "always loyal."
2. Ask the client what comes to mind when he or she hears the word *semper fi*.
3. Transition the conversation toward the client's career exploration. What career skills or personality or occupational career characteristics does the client consider "always faithful" for him or her regardless of the environment or situation?
4. Make a list of these skills and characteristics. What is it about these skills or characteristics that the client appreciates? Depending on the client, you could have him or her rank the skills or characteristics that are most valued to help provide additional reflective thinking.
5. Spend time discussing with the client how he or she could integrate these *semper fi* traits into resumes, future applications, and future career interviews.

THE "SQUARED AWAY" RESUME

Chad Luke and Tony Michael

Two main challenges face many, if not most, individuals when creating a resume, and veterans are no different in this respect: bragging about oneself on one hand and not valuing and/or articulating one's experience on the other. As such, there are two main process tasks that are essential in creating a resume: (a) recognizing the value of one's experiences and presenting them, as in the case of veterans, unapologetically and with confidence and clarity; and (b) to create a plan or vision for the future. This resume approach attempts to accomplish both at the same time. It merges the traditional resume with what might be an ideal resume.

Materials Required: Drafting paper, writing implements.

Preparation Needed: None.

Activity Directions:

Use a blank version of the Today Resume/Ideal Resume (Figure J.2) to direct clients toward owning their experience and embracing it without making excuses for perhaps not having more civilian education or experience. The point is to help make the connections of transferability.

Process questions may include:

- *What can you do (demonstrably), or have you done, that no one else (or few) can do?*
- *How do you approach tasks in novel ways?*
- *How can we quantify your learning experiences in the military that generalize to skills employers are looking for?*
- *Emphasize qualities that employers are looking for that might be emphasized in the military: self-sufficiency, teamwork, communication, problem solving, and so on.*

Traditional—Where You Have Been	Ideal—Where You Want to Go (5 Years)
Education • Include any and all learning/training modules associated with service. • High school, college, technical.	Education • What do you want this section to say about your education in 5 years? • High school diploma? Certificate? BA? • What steps are necessary to move toward that happening?
Experience • Military experience counts! • What did you bring to the task that was qualitatively different from what another might bring? • What did military experience teach you that can be applied to civilian life?	Experience • Rather than apologize for lack of experience, gain it! • In 5 years, what would you like to have in this spot? • Consider internships, volunteering, part-time work, job shadowing, and informational interviews.

FIGURE J.2 Today Resume/Ideal Resume.

WHO'S GOT YOUR 6?

Tony Michael and Chad Luke

This technique is derived from a constructivist and systems theory framework. The intervention focuses on the importance of veterans identifying their own career narrative and how other individuals have assisted in a particular sequence of connectedness in determining their vocation. Veterans are also challenged to reflect on what current career vocations may have their back or be veteran friendly.

Materials Required: Paper and pen.

Preparation Needed: None.

Activity Directions:

1. Have the client list all of his or her previous career vocations. Write down the experiences shared. Ask the client how he or she found these previous jobs. What influenced him or her toward particular previous experiences?
2. Discuss with the client the concept of "got your 6." In military terms, the slang "got your 6" typically refers to "got your back." This phrase is a foundational principle in the military.
3. Ask the client about the first time he or she heard the phrase "got your 6" in the military. Furthermore, ask the client what the significance of the principle is to him or her.
4. If applicable, transition the discussion by having the client identify what non-military individuals in his or her life may have provided vocational support. How did these individuals provide him or her support? How did the support impact the client?
5. Have the client list common descriptors of these individuals. If applicable, discuss with the client the value of having a strong support system in finding a new vocation.
6. Discuss with the client how some vocations may be more supportive to veterans than others. In addition, discuss with the client how he or she needs to be in a work environment that helps in the transition of post military and fosters his or her vocational skills. Furthermore, discuss with the client the importance of allowing others to stand beside him or her and get his or her back in finding a new vocation.

APPENDIX K

INTERVENTIONS FOR CAREGIVERS

A PLAYLIST FOR EMPOWERMENT: SONGS IN THE KEY OF YOUR LIFE

Cynthia B. Greer

This two-session workshop integrates the concepts and understanding that, as human beings, we are always in "transition." This workshop will use music therapy as a modality to provide a sense of empowerment for people who are primarily in the second phase of transition. The "songs in the key of your life" is based on Stevie Wonder's album (1976) Songs in the Key of Life. *This workshop is for men and women in their 50s and older, who are considered as the "Baby Boomer" generation, and who are in "transition." The goal is increased understanding of the phases of transition and exploration of past identities through music and development of a new playlist that will foster a sense of empowerment for the future.*

Materials Required: The counselor/facilitator should have a copy of the book *Transitions: Making Sense of Life's Changes* by William Bridges (2009), a CD of Stevie Wonder's *Songs in the Key of Life*, a sound system, copier and copies of the lyrics of some of the selected songs on the CD, computer/laptop with access to the Internet, notebook paper, pen/pencils, and large writing pad and markers. Participants should be encouraged to bring or have access to their own laptop, MP3 player, and smartphone. It would be helpful if participants had their own copy of the Bridges book, but it is not required.

Preparation Needed: Read the Bridges (2009) book and prepare a handout defining transitions and giving a brief description of the three phases. Review the theoretical constructs of career and lifestyle development as a lifelong process. Revisit the theories of Donald Super and Sunny Hansen and her Integrative Life Planning (ILP) construct. Listen to the Stevie Wonder CD and pay specific attention to the following songs: "As," "I Wish," "Have a Talk With God," and "Pastime Paradise." Also, access the YouTube video of Chuck Brown's song "Beautiful Life." Provide written copies of the playlist assignment to participants. Ethical guidelines for confidentiality in a group situation need to be reviewed. Review, online, Steven Covey's information about writing a personal mission/purpose statement.

Activity Directions:

Session 1

1. Introduce yourself and have the clients introduce themselves. Explain the purpose and goals of the workshop, discuss confidentiality guidelines, and review the discussion guidelines. Explain the need for the group to be a safe place for discussion and that people will be sharing personal information. It should be stressed that no one should dominate a discussion and that there is a need for brevity.
2. Introduce the concept of transition by defining the term and explaining the phases of transition. You can use the handout as a resource.
3. Clients will be asked to share what stage of transition that they believe they are in and briefly explain why they believe that they are in that phase.
4. You should paraphrase each client's perspective and give a summary of the perspectives with the purpose of transitioning to the introduction of Stevie Wonder's CD, *Songs in the Key of Life*. Ask clients if they know who Stevie Wonder is, what they know about him, and whether they have listened to his music.
5. Play select songs from the CD, such as "Pastime Paradise"—about people who live in the past and have little hope for the future—or the songs "I Wish" or "Have a Talk With God." A hard copy of the lyrics can be made available to the clients.
6. Encourage clients to give their perspective of the songs in terms of Wonder's values, beliefs, and possible challenges.
7. For the homework assignment, request that clients develop their own playlist. Each client should have at least one song in the following four categories that: (a) describes the major challenges in his or her life; (b) describes the client's current phase in his or her transition; (c) provides motivation, inspiration, and strength; and (d) describes the future and/or purpose. Clients should come to Session 2 prepared to share their playlist. The written instructions should explain how the playlists can be downloaded/recorded.
8. End the first session with Chuck Brown's YouTube video, "Beautiful Day," as an example of a song that describes choice, attitude, purpose, and possibly a new beginning.

Session 2

1. Remind everyone about confidentiality and the guidelines for discussion.
2. Give a brief overview of Session 1 and restate the homework assignment and the purpose.
3. Request that the clients discuss the process and success of putting their playlists together. Ask about the challenges the clients encountered and request that they reflect about what they learned from the process. Summarize the reflections.
4. Ask the participants the names of the songs that they chose in the four categories. Request for a volunteer to write the songs on the writing pad

while the clients call out the names of the songs. Post the lists of songs on the wall.

5. Based on the available time and number of clients, ask for at least two or three volunteers to share their playlists with the group and give a brief explanation of their song choices. Group members are encouraged to ask questions of clients about their past successes, their core values, their contributions, and their future goals. The playlist should not only serve as inspiration, but the process of putting the playlist together should provide a sense of empowerment to move forward from phase 2 toward phase 3, a new beginning, by reflecting about their successes based on their challenges, their contribution, their values, and their goals. These are the components to developing a personal mission or purpose statement.
6. As the workshop concludes, use the playlist as a metaphor to replace the old tape of confusion that has resided in the client's brain to the new playlist that allows him or her to develop a new purpose and mission for a new beginning.
7. As the workshop concludes, congratulate the clients on their new playlists and give the clients a one-page handout on writing a personal/mission statement that they take with them.

FROM REPORTING TO RESUMES

Melissa A. Wheeler and Sandra Logan

This activity was developed while working with midlife adults who were forced career changers but also works well with anyone who has difficulty taking his or her job narratives and turning them into effective resume bullet points. The goal of this activity is to help clients who struggle with resume writing in developing a clear, effective resume while allowing the space for clients to share and reflect on their job narratives.

Materials Required: Paper, pencils, three highlighters—one green, one blue, and one yellow.

Preparation Needed: None.

Activity Directions:

1. Discuss with the client that creating a resume from scratch can be difficult without a starting point or a direction in mind. It can also be hard to condense the roles, responsibilities, and skills used in a lifetime of jobs into a clear, concise resume. Resumes need to be attention grabbing and highlight the important parts of one's job; this activity will help the client to develop his or her job story and pick out the attention-grabbing headlines.
2. In this activity, you will be assisting the client in writing the story of his or her jobs. You will serve as the client's recorder/reporter while allowing your client the freedom to express his or her job narratives. Ask the client to tell you the story of his or her jobs.
3. As the client narrates these stories, take notes on the paper. Use a different sheet for each job the client discusses. Try to capture as much of the client's story as possible. The client may need prompting in order to get started or may need additional prompting to provide the details needed to help in resume writing. Ask questions such as: *What did you do every day? How long/when did you hold this position? What were some of your greatest accomplishments? What did you gain from this experience: skills, knowledge, and recognition? What did you like and not like about this position?*
4. Once the client has given a clear story of each job, review what you heard by going through your notes with the client one job at a time. Ask the client to read through and add to or edit the job stories.
5. Ask the client to highlight keywords in the story. Together, you are trying to pick out the headlines to be showcased in the client's resume. Highlight skills in yellow, accomplishments in green, and responsibilities in blue.
6. Begin the first step in creating the resume by writing each job position on one single piece of paper with enough space between jobs for your client to write three to four bullet points under each job title.
7. Ask your client to go through each job story with highlighted words to choose the top three or four from each job he or she would like to be "headlines" for each position.

8. After your client has created the job headlines list, work with him or her to make each bullet point best represent what the client is trying to convey. Discuss the power of using action verbs, showcasing quantity, and communicating accomplishments as ways to catch the attention of employers in the same way a catchy headline captures attention in a news article.
9. At this point, you can ask your client to take the completed list to reflect on and edit further. Once the client feels the list is accurate and best represents his or her condensed job stories, the client is ready to construct the rest of the resume. The client can refer to his or her whole job story to create other parts of the resume as needed.

Adaptations: This activity can be adapted depending on your client's needs and the time allotted for your meeting. Possible adaptations include providing the client with the story directions and prompting questions in office and asking the client to type up his or her story at home to discuss in your next meeting. Another adaptation could include the counselor typing the job stories once narrated for use in the next meeting with the client.

This activity can also be used as a way for a client to reflect on his or her past career story while working to identify a trajectory for the new story. To accomplish this, ask the client to highlight job likes in one color and dislikes in another color. Place the likes and dislikes in separate lists and ask the client to reflect on what he or she sees. Ask the client to write a job story based on what he or she would like to see represented (or write the headlines for his or her dream job).

GETTING RID OF GHOSTS

Margo D. Sutorius-Milano and Charles E. Myers

Childhood and family experiences influence career choices, decisions, and success (Saka, Gati, & Kelly, 2008; Slaten & Baskin, 2014). Research strongly points to the influence of relational variables on career outcomes (Slaten & Baskin, 2014). Specifically, parents or primary caregivers are the most used relationship in making career-related decisions, and many individuals report making choices to maintain a sense of belonging to please caregivers (Amundson, Borgen, Iaquinta, Butterfield, & Koert, 2010; Slaten & Baskin, 2014). Although many career counselors ignore the influence of relationships on career choices (Schultheiss, Kress, & Manzi, 2001), exploring the role of early relationships on career choice can be helpful. This activity facilitates clients' exploration of the role of past relationships on career choices. Increased awareness of true career aspirations and familial influences on career decision making can empower clients to reevaluate career direction and goals.

Materials Required: Client choice of crayons, markers, colored pencils, paint, paintbrushes, and paper.

Alternative Material Options: Digital materials via searching the web for pictures and images.

Preparation Needed: None.

Activity Directions:

1. Orient the client to the proposed session content—specifically, the role that past experiences and relationships may have had in influencing career decisions and choices. Conduct a brief relaxation exercise.
2. Give the following directions:
   Let's think about your family (or primary caregivers) growing up and now.
   I would like for you to think about your sense of feeling cared for by your family (or primary caregivers) and really belonging with them as you grew up. Take your time to think about this with sincere reflection.
   As you were growing up, what did you learn from your caregivers about careers for you?
   What differences did you perceive between you and your parents and/or family? How did that affect your choice of ________ (classes/major/career)?
   Did you feel supported or discouraged in your career aspirations?
   How did those differences influence your perception of you and what you can do?
   Using the materials we have here, I would like you to somehow depict what has been brought into your life and career path now that you would like to change or eliminate.
   Were you told that you could not do or be something? Or that you have to be or do something specific, like follow the family business? Or did you sense that from others?

Did you make choices that you might not have made if you were living in a different life? What are those? Which do you want to get rid of?

Were their messages, instructions, or rules that you had to follow that you did not agree with?

Was a trait or characteristic developed, like nervousness, low self-esteem, or lack of confidence, in the past that is affecting you now in school or work?

Draw that entity in any way you imagine it to look like. It can be a literal picture, like an overbearing mom you can never please. It can be a symbolic illustration, like a large rock sitting on someone's shoulder. Any way you perceive the entity is perfectly fine.

Give time for the client to draw, paint, or search the web.

3. As the client is drawing or searching, instruct him or her to write a statement underneath the pictures: *I would like you to write a very brief, one sentence statement to the entity. Feel free to be unedited. For example, 'Get the hell out of here.' Or 'Just trust the process!' Write it as you feel best depicts what you want to tell the entity to go or what to do.*
4. After the client has completed his or her work, invite the client to share the drawings with you or the group.
   a. Process the meaning of the picture using some of these points and questions: *Tell me about your picture. Where did ______ come from? How did that happen and what or who did it involve? What other places in your life does it emerge? How can we ask it to leave? What can we change? How so?*
   b. Ask the client to describe the statement at the bottom of the picture: what it means and how she or he imagines saying it (tone, cadence, inflection, volume, etc.).
   c. For an individual: *I will count to three, and we will say [the statement] to [the entity] together exactly as you wish it spoken (e.g., yell it, sing it, use sarcasm).* For a group: *We will count to three, and as an entire group, we will speak [the statement] to [the entity] together exactly as [the individual member] wishes it spoken. For example, we will yell it, sing it, or use sarcasm, exactly as requested.*
   d. Ask the client what he or she wishes to be done with the picture. Some choose to crumple it up and throw it out. Others choose to keep their picture for inspiration. Some clients may cut off certain parts of the picture and keep the rest. You can offer different options.
5. Use this activity as a starting point for more substantive career counseling and planning or as an intervention to move past a sticking point in process. *Getting Rid of Ghosts* may also stimulate the emergence of family-related issues and topics that are best discussed in individual or family counseling; thus, a referral may be necessary.

APPENDIX L

INTERVENTIONS FOR TEEN MOTHERS

CONQUERING CHOICES AND CHALLENGES: CAREER MAP COCONSTRUCTION

Diandra J. Prescod and Lucy Parker

The technique of mapping allows the clinician or school/career counselor to explore various issues that might arise in the teen mother–counselor relationship, along with allowing the counselor and teen mother to get to know one another at a deeper level. Specifically, career map creation is meaningful and is a holistic, comprehensive, and systematic intervention (Niles & Harris-Bowlsbey, 2013) for clients, especially teen mothers. The following mapping exercise emphasizes the resilience and autonomy that many future clients, especially teenage mothers, will need in order to successfully pursue various careers (Brown & Associates, 2002; White, 2007).

Materials Required: Career Map printout (Figure L.1), journal, pencil.

Preparation Needed: Copies of Career Map available.

Activity Directions:

1. Begin phases of the Career Map and processing:
   a. *Co-construction phase*—This involves you and the teen mother uncovering the (mother's) client's career and the overarching themes that create personal meaning for her (i.e., those that will be incorporated in this map).
   b. *Deconstruction phase*—This involves exploring different viewpoints and different possibilities in the search for the preferred career as is written and mapped out by the client/teenage mother.
   c. *Future career path construction*— This is based on the identified concepts that individual clients (mothers) compose in their maps. This process is very focused on making unique meaning of the life experiences of all clients.
2. Using the map(s):
   The worksheet is considered a technique to empower a young mother when conceptualizing her career journey, including her career challenges, aspirations, and conceptualizations. In addition, the Career Map is adapted using both Brown and Associates's (2002) model and White's (2007) mapping techniques.

This Career Map is used to assess thoughts on prestige, gender roles, and societal pressures on young mothers in regard to careers.

3. Counseling dialogue following map creation:
   With the client, you may process this career map construction using various questions and dialogue, including: *Which careers are seen as being predominantly male careers? Which careers are seen as being predominantly female careers? What is the most powerful theme about your map during this dialogue? What feelings did you experience when completing your map? What did you enjoy about constructing this map? What are some uncertainties and/or struggles you experienced regarding career choice and/or this map creation? What else did you learn about yourself in the process of constructing your career map? Were there any new insights about you after constructing this map? Were there any new insights about your career options after constructing this map? From this experience, what will you take with you as you continue and/or enter into the workforce? Is there any other important message or discussion point you can think of about your career journey and/or map? How can I make this activity more meaningful for you in your career considerations?*
4. Remember to also facilitate and discuss the following factors, including those from Ettinger's (1991) skills concepts, when processing about the client's constructed career map (Form A): *Self-concept, support systems, access to available childcare, transportation services and other support services necessary to one's survival, the challenge of combining work and family roles, emotional support, networking for work opportunities and connections, interpersonal communication and relationships, clearly defined and realistic program goals and objectives, and community collaboration.*
5. Themes to remember in regard to map creation include the following:
   a. Let teenage mothers know that they can, instead of can't.
   b. Do not reprimand teen moms, despite the technique used.
   c. Remember to let teen moms know that they have someone to lean on using our core counseling skills.

(High) **Prestige** (Low)	
Please write any societal pressures or stereotypes associated with the above occupations that you feel/have felt may impact your career decision(s). →	Masculine Feminine

Place the occupations (listed below) on the map where you think they should be placed in order from most prestigious to least prestigious.

Manicurist Accountant Journalist Engineer Professor	Photographer Mechanic Stock Broker Historian Athlete	Counselor Librarian Electrician Psychologist Teacher	Politician Biologist Pilot Physician Zoologist

FIGURE L.1 Form A: Career Map.

Source: Adapted from Brown (2002) and White (2007).

RECONCEPTUALIZING CAREER IDENTITY: UTILIZING STRENGTHS TO TRANSCEND DOMAINS

Erin N. Friedman and Katherine M. Wix

This career exploration intervention is designed for individuals who are specifically struggling to identify their skill sets. Through guided reflection, counselors can help clients to develop their self-efficacy by identifying areas of success, despite those areas initially appearing unrelated to larger career goals, and drawing attention specifically to clients' strengths. This activity's goal is the transformation of the client's perceptions of his or her ability and to discover the client's underlying universal core skill sets. Lastly, with this renewed sense of self, clients will develop ownership over their career goals and generate attainable career options based on individual strengths that are transferable to other domains (see Figure L.2 for a visual representation of the intervention). The objectives for this activity include client identification of areas of strength, transferable strengths, clear and distinct goals, and new self-efficacy beliefs.

You and your client will be creating a portfolio to expand client self-efficacy by identifying and gathering individual achievements in one place. Once the portfolio has been created, the client will explore the various documents making up the portfolio and will work to identify themes. Underlying core themes are identified through processing questions with the end goal of creating a comprehensive profile. The client will use the comprehensive profile to recognize the culmination of personal skill sets and experiences in an attempt to identify a new sense of sense of self or new self-concept. This new self-concept, which is comprehensive and strengths-based in nature, will be used to create career goals as well as evaluate the client's outcome expectancies, addressing any fears that may act as barriers to the client's newly invented strengths-based self-concept.

Materials Required: Binder or portfolio, paper and writing utensil, dry-erase board (optional), dry-erase markers (optional), and generic list of skills (optional).

Preparation Needed: None.

Activity Directions:

1. First Phase—Client Identification of Skills:
   Begin the intervention by asking the client to reflect and list or cocreate a list of specific skills, strengths, or areas of known competency. You can elicit these ideas through the use of open-ended questions (provided in the following). Ideally, you will begin by writing down accomplishments on a dry-erase board or another medium so the client has a visual representation of accomplishments. You will stress the importance of identifying ALL accomplishments (it does not have to relate to employment or career). If the client needs help or encouragement to begin brainstorming accomplishments, you can inquire about various areas of life by asking the following questions:
   a. *Can you tell me a little about yourself?*
   b. *What are your interests?*
   c. *What do you enjoy doing?*
   d. *How do you spend your time?*

If able, the client should identify skills he or she uses when engaging in hobbies/interests. If unable, you can use a scaffold approach and help the client to identify underlying skills inherent in those interests or hobbies. For example, you can ask: *What do you have to do to be good at ______?* Your goal is to draw attention to universal underlying skill sets the client uses during these activities. Using a strengths-based approach, you should elicit a plethora of the client's interests, hobbies, or moments of success that naturally branch into other life accomplishments.

2. Second Phase—Create Your Personal Portfolio:
   Ask the client to insert at least one page for each skill set or accomplishment listed or discussed earlier. Note that the client must come up with at least 10 different skills or accomplishments. Once each skill set or accomplishment has been added to the portfolio, lead a discussion to explore emerging themes and underlying strengths. You can also encourage deeper discussion by asking specific questions pertaining to the client's fine motor, interpersonal, analytical, administrative, and innovative skills/abilities. The goal of this activity is to form a new way for the client to begin perceiving himself or herself, which may also lead to the client experiencing a new and improved self-concept. Begin this intervention with the more traditional talk therapy approach and initiate a discussion with the client, focusing on summarization of identified skill sets and accomplishments. Work with clients to discover new insights achieved through an expressive arts process, which will help to lead the client to a new career self-concept. The new self-concept summary can be done in a multitude of ways. For example, the client may choose to write a narrative summary or a poem, create or draw a diagram, or create another visual representation. The client should be allowed the freedom to express this new self-concept in whatever way resonates the most with him or her. Process the union of the skills and accomplishments mentioned with the new self-concept themes that emerged throughout the expressive arts intervention. Finally, when this new perspective has been processed and created, the client will generate a new self-concept summary on the page entitled, "Who I Am," which will become page 1 of the portfolio.

   Suggested Counselor-Directed Process Questions:

   When you review your portfolio, what strengths stand out?
   What strengths were less visible before the activity?
   How do you see yourself incorporating these strengths in moving forward?
   Talk to me about your new skill set or learned abilities (self-efficacy).

   Summary of Portfolio Contents:
   - Who I am: A culmination of strengths (new self-concept).
   - Things that make up me: A tribute to my skills and accomplishments. (Note to counselors: This particular section will vary in page length depending on how many skills and accomplishments the client is able to recall. When the client shares a specific skill or accomplishment, a new sheet of paper should be included in the portfolio and the skills or accomplishment should be listed on the top of the page.)
   - Goals—How can I make this a reality (addressed in phase three)?

3. Third Phase—Goal Setting:
   Once the client has created his or her personal portfolio and processed reflective questions, you can help the client to see how skills transcend from areas of interest to career domains. You will spend time with the client brainstorming possible career goals that incorporate interests, as well as skills previously identified in the client's portfolio. You can use a variety of practices to facilitate this activity (e.g., wordweb, linear map, and road map). Creativity allows the client the freedom to express himself or herself; thus, brainstorming becomes a natural part of the process in which the generated ideas will be used to identify and create attainable goals. These goals cement the client's new sense of identity rooted in strengths and possibility. This stage can also be used to encourage the client to develop higher levels of self-esteem and agency by having self-generated goals. Once the client has created goals based on the new self-concept, you and the client can continue this journey by making goals a reality. You can help to target the client's expectancy beliefs and can work together to deconstruct fears and create a plan so the client feels empowered and can see that success is possible.

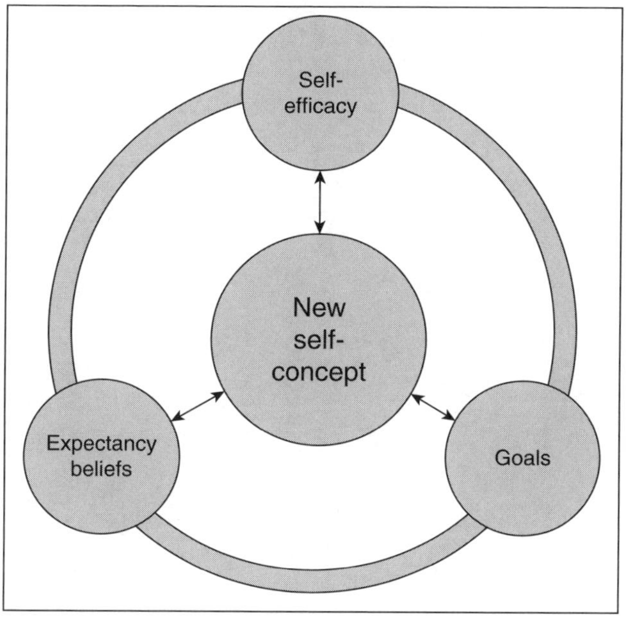

FIGURE L.2 Visual Representation of the Intervention.

APPENDIX M

INTERVENTIONS FOR FORMERLY INCARCERATED INDIVIDUALS

THE ROAD NOT TAKEN: EXPLORING CAREER JOURNEY AS LIFE STORY

Karen J. Haas

This intervention is beneficial to adolescents or adults who are in the process of exploring their identity, seeking purpose in life, and looking for a career that is meaningful to them as individuals. This intervention can be especially powerful for those clients who view themselves as unsuccessful or as having no particular talents or skills because they define themselves by their past life stories. The theoretical orientation centers on the narrative or storied approach to career counseling. Narrative counseling is used here as a means of helping the client to discover how life stories define him or her and how to move past these stories to reauthor a more powerful and positive narrative (Nafziger & DeKruyf, 2013; Rehfuss, 2009; Thomas & Gibbons, 2009). Through a series of activities, the counselor and client work together to co-construct or uncover and explore the client's life story and then to deconstruct or explore unproductive themes and patterns in the individual's life strategies. The counselor follows this interactive exploration of the client's story with an exercise to determine client values. In the final phase, the counselor helps the client to reauthor and construct a new, more productive story built on dignity and competence. The session activities conclude with the counselor and client teaming to develop steps toward achieving the client's career goals. With modification, this intervention can also be delivered in a small group format.

Materials Required: Sheets of paper, colored pencils or markers, pens/pencils, Exercise 1: Who Am I? Identity Mind Map Activity Sheet, Exercise 2: Lifeline Activity Sheet, Exercise 3: Defining Values Activity Sheet, Exercise 4: Reimagining Future Career Story Activity Sheet.

Preparation Needed: Copies of activity sheets.

Activity Directions:

1. Ask clients how they would describe themselves to someone who did not know them. In preparation for this activity, give them Exercise 1, the Who Am I? Identity Mind Map. During this co-construction phase, you are helping clients to uncover and explore their life/career narrative.
2. Next, give clients Exercise 2, the Lifeline Activity Sheet, along with some newsprint and colored pencils or markers, and ask them to chart a lifeline of defining and memorable episodes in their life/career story, including the high points and times of distress and hardship. After allowing sufficient time to complete the lifeline, ask clients to describe the impact, both positive and negative, of these events on their lives. Your role, as counselor, is to listen without criticism in order to develop an understanding of the experiences, events, and people that clients thought were important. During this storytelling time, ask both facilitating and clarifying questions, such as: *What does that experience say about what's important to you?* or *What is the significance of that time in your life?* or *What have you learned from that experience?* (Brott, 2011).
3. Moving into the deconstruction or unpacking phase of the session, help clients to identify patterns or themes in their narratives and unproductive rules or strategies they chose to live by that may have been influenced by the events or people in their lives. In addition, explore with clients missed opportunities, the road not taken, that may have occurred due to life events, such as the sudden death of a parent during childhood or adolescence, divorce, an unexpected move, or severe illness. Point out to clients developmental demands on decision making, and help them to understand that decisions and events in the past do not dictate decisions and choices in the future. Encourage clients that they are active agents in their own life/career stories and can author new and enriched narratives to follow that road not taken.
4. Continuing with the deconstruction phase, provide clients with the Defining Values Activity, Exercise 3, to help determine the best direction toward their life/career goals. Ask clients to identify the top 10 values they hold most dear in living and working. To facilitate this activity, invite clients to identify times when they were happiest, most proud, and most fulfilled and satisfied. When they are ready, have them talk through their chosen values in rank order.
5. To help them reauthor their life/career story in more powerful and positive directions, work together with clients to consider different perspectives on life strategies that incorporate their personal life/work values and strengths.
6. Then team with clients to create a goal map together, Reimagining Future Career Story, Exercise 4, to explore options as a way of reauthoring the future. This activity helps clients to clarify their choices, generate alternatives, and extend the story into the future. Have an obstacles category and then identify resources, bridges, and solutions to overcome these obstacles (construction process).
7. To conclude the session, guide clients to create three steps toward reaching their career goal.

EXERCISE 1: WHO AM I? IDENTITY MIND MAP ACTIVITY SHEET

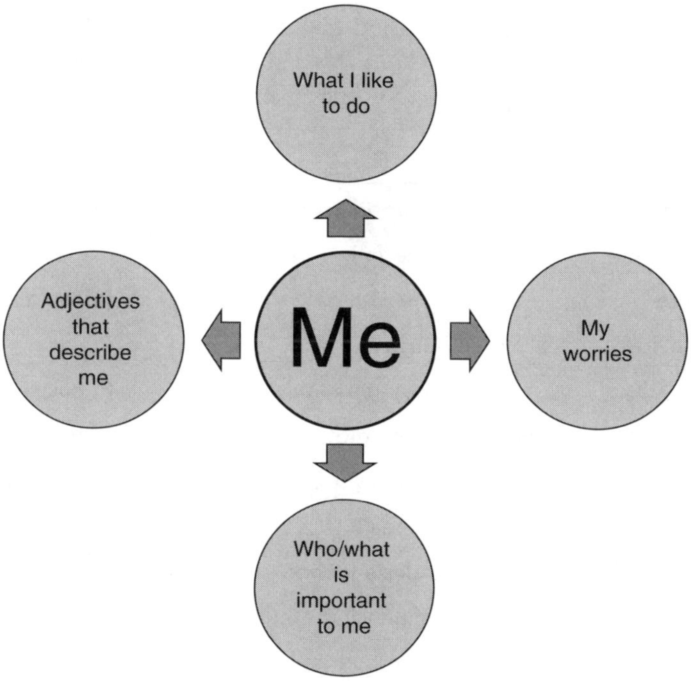

Directions: Create a Mind Map using the paper provided that depicts characteristics and qualities that you feel are important in defining who you are. You can use the previous example to get you started, and then add more circles as you complete your self-description.

EXERCISE 2: LIFELINE ACTIVITY SHEET

Directions: Chart the memorable events in your life, both positive and negative. Use the newsprint and colored pencils/markers provided.

EXERCISE 3: DEFINING VALUES ACTIVITY SHEET

Directions: This exercise is designed to help you reach a better understanding of your most significant values. From this list of values (both career and life), circle the 10 that are most important to you as guides for how to behave and/or as components of a valued way of life. Feel free to add any values of your own to this list.

Achievement	Financial gain	Physical challenge
Advancement	Freedom	Pleasure
Adventure	Friendships	Power and authority
Affection (love and caring)	Growth	Privacy
Arts	Having a family	Public service
Being around people who are open and honest	Helping other people	Purity
Challenging problems	Helping society	Quality of what I take part in
Change and variety	Honesty	Quality relationships
Close relationships	Independence	Recognition
Community	Influencing others	Religion
Competence	Inner harmony	Reputation
Competition	Integrity	Responsibility
Cooperation	Intellectual status	Security
Country	Involvement	Self-respect
Creativity	Job tranquility	Serenity
Decisiveness	Knowledge	Sophistication
Democracy	Leadership	Stability
Ecological awareness	Location	Status
Economic security	Loyalty	Supervising others
Effectiveness	Market position	Time freedom
Efficiency	Meaningful work	Truth
Ethical practice	Merit	Wealth
Excellence	Money	Work under pressure
Excitement	Nature	Work with others
Fame	Order (tranquility and conformity)	Working alone
Fast living	Personal development	

EXERCISE 4: REIMAGINING FUTURE CAREER STORY ACTIVITY SHEET

Career Goal: ______________________________

Obstacles:	Resources:
______________	______________
______________	______________
______________	______________
______________	______________

Three Steps to Take Toward Reaching Goal:

1. ______________________________

2. ______________________________

3. ______________________________

UNVEILING INSTITUTIONAL BARRIERS WHILE EMPOWERING INDIVIDUALS FOR SUCCESS

Erin N. Friedman and Katherine M. Wix

Currently, minorities, including formerly incarcerated individuals, are facing a number of barriers in the workplace, including institutional bias, differential workplace treatment, and microaggressions. By combining the principles of cognitive behavioral therapy and the creative underpinnings of narrative therapy, clients can explore negative patterns of thinking and processing embedded stereotype threats impacting their career identities. Clients work to story edit based on new cognitive perceptions. Story-editing approaches can reduce stigma, improve personal strengths, regulate emotions, and create goals by teaching clients how to revise negative stories or tweak personal stories in beneficial ways (Cook, 2011). This intervention helps clients identify stereotypes of differential treatment they are experiencing in the workplace, discuss the effects this treatment or different expectations can have on their identity, and recognize workplace discrimination and change their own thought processes to reduce its harmful effects and empowering themselves. The objectives of this intervention include the following: empower clients in their career setting and reimagine career identity, replace harmful internalized messages with positive messages, and recognize and acknowledge the existence and impact of discrimination and stereotypes.

Materials Required: Paper, highlighter, and writing utensils.

Preparation Needed: None.

Activity Directions:

1. This activity uses story editing to address discrimination and stereotypes in addition to increasing career self-concept through reflective writing exercises. Begin the session by describing institutional bias and discrimination in the workplace. You can also discuss how these negative stereotypes or differential treatment based on an individual's identity can be internalized and lead to harmful beliefs about oneself as well as impede performance. Direct clients to write out their personal career stories, including as much detail as possible (their narrative). Clients will need to include all barriers they have encountered in the workplace or during their career endeavors. Once clients have written out their story, you and the clients work together to identify (and highlight) all negative stereotypes woven throughout the story. Provide a questionnaire on workplace discrimination to help clients identify areas of discrimination they have personally experienced, because clients may not be able to readily generate experiences of institutional or personal discrimination. Given the nature of how deep-seated many of these beliefs are, it is important that you allow clients a space to process feelings and beliefs about inadequacies that relate to career experiences. Describe the role story editing can play in both the clients' career experiences and personal life. With the clients, you will process possible solutions, identify strengths, and create new goals to reach career aspirations.

Process Questions:

1. *What did you learn about yourself through the story-editing process?*
2. *What barriers will you need to confront?*
3. *What are some possible new strategies you can implement?*
4. *How can you use your story edits to address moments of discrimination in your work setting?*
5. *In the face of discrimination, what will your role be?*

Follow-Up:

1. Counselors will have clients write a letter (or series of letters) to themselves before they terminate work with one another. Counselors will then send clients this letter (or series of letters) that specifies the client strengths, accomplishments, alternative stories (generated by the clients), and any other key reminders they would like to remind themselves of the work they did with counselors.

APPENDIX N

INTERVENTIONS FOR DIVERSE INDIVIDUALS

Please note that each of the following interventions can be easily modified to work with individuals who represent any of a variety of diversities.

CAREER CROSSROADS: SUPPORTING TRANSGENDER CLIENTS IN TRANSITION

Melissa Luke, Kristopher M. Goodrich, and Shalom Bond

Research has indicated the relevance of a number of career development factors when working with lesbian, gay, bisexual, and transgender (LGBT) clients (Schmidt, Miles, & Welsh, 2011; Tomlinson & Fassinger, 2003). The following activity can be used with transgender clients who are anticipating or involved in transitioning from living and working as one gender to living and working as another gender. As transition can involve major behavioral, emotional, and systemic challenges, this intervention is designed to support clients in all three areas by:

a. identifying some of the career-related tasks that are inherent in transitioning (e.g., changing gender marker, name on driver's license or other identity documents used within employment, and obtaining references in changed name).

b. exploring the varied and sometimes conflicting cognitive and emotional experiences related to the process of transitioning (e.g., relief, excitement, and resonance associated with living and working gender congruently; fear, grief, and loss associated with safety concerns; vulnerability within some relationships; and uncertainty about potential repercussions).

c. consideration of cost–benefit of remaining in the same career and/or securing employment in a more gender-typical field, as well as reflection on what might be required to succeed in a chosen career and living and working in the new gender role.

Following this intervention, clients will be able to name at least two behaviors, two thoughts–emotions, and two systemic considerations for employment associated with their transitioning.

Materials Required: This intervention requires a piece of legal-sized paper or large poster board that can be divided into three columns. Writing and drawing implements are also needed. Counselors may also wish to have magazines or other visual material, scissors, and glue.

Preparation Needed: Prior to implementing the intervention, the counselor can label each of the three columns as shown in Figure N.1. The counselor, prior to creating the paper, can ask his or her clients if any future categories or topics need exploration as part of this activity. If clients affirm that they wish to explore other elements, the counselor can expand the paper grid to include them.

Activity Directions:

Counselor's Pre-Activities

1. Before working with trans* clients, you should seek out professional development and training related to ethical and effective work with trans* clients. Review the Competencies for Counseling Transgender Clients (ALGBTIC, 2009), drafted by the Association for Lesbian, Gay, Bisexual, and Transgender Issues in Counseling and endorsed by the American Counseling Association.
2. You should also create a safe and encouraging environment for clients. Display affirmative symbols or texts within your office and understand clients' pronoun usage in the counselor-client relationship. Foster a safe environment by ensuring clients' identities are visible during the intake process (i.e., asking for preferred name) and by using each client's preferred terminology when discussing identity and transition.
3. As part of all ethical counselor development, career counselors new to working with trans* clients should also seek regular supervision of their work.

Activity Facilitation

1. Begin introducing the concept of career and employment as part of transitioning and discuss some of what this might raise within the client. For some clients, this might entail seeking employment in a career that better matches the identity they wish to transition to; for others, it might involve remaining in their current profession and reflect a gender syntonic or dystonic match with their current career. Some clients may wish to remain employed in the same company or setting, whereas others may wish to find new employment to match the new life changes that they are pursuing. Each of the decisions comes with a variety of complexities that can be reviewed in counseling.
2. Next, frame the complexities for the client by utilizing the three-column paper addressed previously. Within the columns, there are spaces for the client (with your help, if needed) to complete: behaviors, thoughts–emotions, and systemic considerations. Although behaviors are listed to the left, with other columns to the right, it should not be suggested that the client necessarily completes the column in a left to right fashion; instead, the client can complete the activity in whichever column or direction that might be

guiding his or her thoughts or reactions at the time. Within the "behaviors" column, the client will be asked what behaviors he or she might consider or utilize to obtain career or occupational goals. Under the "thoughts–emotions" column, the client is asked to address the thoughts and feelings that he or she might have about these career/occupational goals and the potential career/occupational transitions. Finally, within the "systemic considerations" column, the client is asked to list the considerations outside of himself or herself that might influence success in occupations or careers. As a counselor, you may be reviewing with clients some jobs or careers that may not be accepting of persons from different backgrounds. Do not lead clients to decisions to enter or leave professions; instead, highlight to the client different factors that influence or relate to certain decisions. *Note*: Some clients might identify additional topics that they wish to explore that fall outside of the three-column grid. The grid can be expanded to address these clients' needs.

3. The client will complete the columned paper in a way that best reflects his or her understanding or needs. For some, it might involve beginning with behavioral actions that the client is considering taking, and then exploring the thoughts/feelings that might follow those behaviors and the systemic considerations that might occur following those actions. Other clients may wish to start with systemic considerations, thinking about the contexts they are considering working in, or exploring the struggles or successes they may be currently facing. This might follow with behavioral actions clients could take to respond to these considerations, or thoughts or emotions that clients might experience. A different alternative could have clients start with their thoughts or emotions. It would end with systemic considerations needed for them to be successful or how to address systemic barriers. In whichever way the client explores this experience, support the client in processing personal experiences through each lens. If additional topics were developed in the previous step, you are asked to assist the clients in exploring these topics as well.
4. Following the completion of the three- (or more) column grid, ask your client to review the work and express his or her reactions to the experience of putting these different issues and concerns on paper. Together with the client, review the client's impressions of what he or she learned about the occupational/career choice as a result of doing this activity and any follow-up activities/behaviors that the client will need to engage in to achieve his or her career goal. For some clients, this might involve revising or editing the occupational/career goal, whereas for others it might be creating a new goal all-together. Finally, for some clients, it will involve the solidification of goals they already created and setting up a structured plan so the goals can be made tangible.

Post-Activity

Following the client's processing of the activity, you can create follow-up appointments with the client to track his or her progress and measure the outcomes. With the client, you can negotiate concrete goals and specific time periods to complete goals. Develop a check-up plan as well.

Specific Considerations for Clients Seeking New Work

1. Clients may have difficulty obtaining work references following transition. Previous positions are likely associated with a former name. Help clients review their work history to identify references who are most likely to be supportive. Clients may need to contact these individuals about name and gender changes to ensure an appropriate reference.
2. Clients may experience stress and fear of discrimination around disclosing their trans status. Disclosing trans status may be necessary during career transitions, such as to inform references of a name change, explain mismatched documents to new employers, and so on. You can assist clients with this process by helping them to consider the costs and benefits of disclosures and role-playing with clients.
3. The trans community can be an invaluable resource during transition. Individuals benefit from forming relationships with other trans people and receiving advice from those who have transitioned. Become familiar with LGBT organizations in the community. Informed counselors can provide clients referrals to community resources.

Specific Considerations for Clients Remaining in the Same Position

Clients who will remain in the same position during and after transition face unique challenges. It may be necessary to disclose transition plans to supervisors and coworkers. Help clients to consider their priorities and options. The client can form a plan to navigate transition at the workplace. Encourage the client to review nondiscrimination workplace policies and identify any supervisors or coworkers who are likely to be supportive. When possible, the client may wish to inform a supervisor, human resources representative, or supportive coworker first and enlist that person's assistance in informing the rest of the organization.

Behaviors	Thoughts-Emotions	Systemic Considerations

FIGURE N.1 Client's Complexities Table.

CAREER EXPLORATION OF TRANSGENDER YOUTH THROUGH SANDTRAY

Varunee Faii Sangganjanavanich

The purpose of this intervention is to facilitate career exploration of transgender youth through the use of sandtrays and miniatures. It facilitates the exploration of career choices in the context of clients' gender identity and expression in a safe and supportive environment.

Materials Required:

Sandtrays. Two blue plastic trays with 12- to 16-inch diameters are preferred; each tray should be two thirds filled with sand.

Miniatures. Diverse presentation (e.g., race, age, gender, accessibility, cultural, career items) of miniatures is important. The counselor may also consider having more quantities for common items that the client may be likely to use (e.g., people, trees, gender symbols).

Table or Shelf. For visibility and accessibility, a table or shelf is used to display all miniatures. The decision whether to use a table or shelf depends on the counselor's preference and convenience.

Water (optional). Water can be provided for the client to work with the sand.

Preparation Needed:

All miniatures should be displayed and visible to the client. There is no restriction on how to place each miniature; however, miniatures that appear to be in the same category (e.g., people, household, animal, nature, creative, mystical categories) should be grouped and displayed in the same location. Sandtrays could be placed on the table or floor depending on room arrangement and should be set up next to each other, leaving at least one foot in between trays. The table or shelf and the tray placement should be in a close proximity for the client to easily access the miniatures during the activity.

Activity Directions:

1. To begin building the trays, ask the client to select one occupation of his or her interest.
2. Ask the client to use the miniatures to narrate how he or she sees himself or herself in that occupation in the first tray and how he or she believes his or her transgender identity affects him or her in that occupation in the second tray. You may say: *There are two trays. For the first tray, please use the miniatures, as many as you like, to tell me how you see yourself in the occupation you have in mind. The second tray is a place for you to talk about the perceived impacts of trans identity on the occupation you choose. I will sit here quietly while you are making your trays. Please spend around 15–20 minutes completing your trays. After you are done, we can begin our discussion.*
3. Once the client completes both trays, invite the client to share them by saying: *I am curious to learn about your trays. Tell me about them. Start with the first tray—you in that occupation*. While describing trays, it is not uncommon if the

client goes back and forth between two trays as they are often interconnected. When the client describes the trays, consistently show and maintain curiosity through verbal and nonverbal language. You should refrain from giving your judgment and/or opinion on the client's trays.

4. In addition to the factual information about the occupation and the client's perception, process insight that the client gains during the activity by asking: *Tell me what it was like building and talking about your trays?*
5. If the client has more than one interested occupation, repeat this activity.

COMING OUT AT WORK

Varunee Faii Sangganjanavanich

Gender transition refers to a process of adopting a new gender role by living full time as the desired gender and is a period in which transgender individuals come out to others, including at work. Coming out at work presents unique career benefits as well as challenges. Therefore, it is important that individuals manage challenges with a thoughtfully constructed plan and careful preparation. This intervention helps transgender clients address concerns about coming out at work, identify challenges, and discuss resources that facilitate the process. This intervention allows verbalization and visual representation of career concerns about coming out at work.

Materials Required: Poster-size paper, round-shape papers (several pieces of paper in multiple colors), person-shape papers (several pieces of paper in multiple colors), glue, and markers.

Preparation Needed: Divide the poster size paper into four rows using a marker.

Activity Directions:

1. Ask the client to write down each of his or her concerns about coming out at work on a blank round-shape paper. Glue them on the first row of the poster-size paper. Allow the client to fully describe each concern.
2. Ask the client to generate a list of people whom he or she needs to inform about coming out and to identify each person on a person-shape paper. Glue them on the second row of the poster size paper. Allow the client to fully discuss his or her thoughts and feelings associated with each person's reaction to his or her coming out.
3. Ask the client to identify potential career challenges on his or her decision to come out at work and to write down each of the career challenges on a blank round-shape paper. Glue them on the third row of the poster size paper.
4. Using a marker(s), ask the client to generate ways and resources that he or she could utilize to deal with potential career challenges associated with coming out at work on the last row of the poster-size paper.
5. Process the intervention using the following questions: *What was it like talking about your coming out at work? What is your newfound awareness from this activity? If you were to come out at work tomorrow, how confident are you in dealing with those challenges?*

CO-CONSTRUCTING THE CAREER STORY: WORKING WITH DIVERSE CLIENTS

Ricardo Phipps and Lucy Parker

Narrative approaches to career counseling allow individuals to construct their own selves and career paths according to changing values and changing sense of self that arise through changing relationships (Brott, 2005). In narrative career counseling, individuals write their own life stories, integrating aspects of life from outside of work and taking into account their roles as family member, worker, and member of their community. This activity is a conceptualization of process questions that can facilitate co-construction of the client's career story.

Materials Required: Co-construction Questionnaire, journal, pencil.

Preparation Needed: An understanding of narrative theory.

Activity Directions:

Narrative career counseling typically involves the counselor engaging the client in a very collaborative fashion in which the counselor relinquishes the role of expert. Three basic phases characterize the helping process (Locke & Gibbons, 2008).

1. *Co-construction phase*—This involves the counselor and client uncovering the life story of the client and the overarching themes that create personal meaning for the client.
2. *Deconstruction phase*—This involves exploring different viewpoints and different possibilities in the search for the preferred way of being of the client.
3. *Future story construction*— This is based on the identified values and meanings individual clients would like to have guiding their future. Narrative counseling uses techniques that empower clients as authors in their own story. The Co-construction Questionnaire worksheet is one technique used to consider a client's career story.

Co-construction Questionnaire

Questions of construction of story themes and chapters include:

1. Story plot (i.e., client motivations):
   a. *What careers are you considering currently?*
   b. *What careers did you consider in the past?*
2. Story setting (i.e., cultural residence):
   a. *Who are you?*
   b. *What is your cultural identity?*
   c. *What are your cultural values?*
   d. *How do your cultural identity and values influence the careers that you are or are not considering?*

3. Story characters (i.e., one's multifaceted cultural identity):
   a. *How have your family experiences influenced your career dreams?*
   b. *How has your cultural identity influenced your career dreams?*
4. Cumulative chapters (i.e., past work experiences and anticipations for future work):
   a. *How have past and current experiences influenced your career goals?*
   b. *Were there past experiences where you faced microinvalidations and/or microaggressions?*
   c. *How have these experiences influenced your choices about career opportunities?*
   d. *What do you value?*
   e. *What is your dream career?*

The counselor and client may process this story construction using various questions and dialogue, including:

a. What is the most powerful theme for you that emerges from your dialogue?
b. What feelings did you experience when considering these questions?
c. What did you enjoy about considering these questions?
d. What are some uncertainties and/or struggles you experienced regarding career choice?
e. What else did you learn about yourself in the process of collaborating about your career story?
f. Were there any new insights about you after creating this activity?
g. Were there any new insights about your career options after creating this activity?
h. From this experience, what will you take with you as you continue and/or enter into the workforce?
i. Is there any other important message or discussion point you can think of after collaborating about your career story?
j. How can I make this activity more meaningful for you in your career considerations?

Narrative career counseling may resonate highly with clients who have cultural backgrounds that hold storytelling very precious (Stebleton, 2007). Narrative career counseling is most effective when counselors are not limited by strict time constraints. The goal is to facilitate empowerment in clients so that they feel free to travel career paths beyond those imposed by the expectations of others.

APPENDIX O

INTERVENTIONS USING SANDTRAY

SANDTRAY CAREER GENOGRAM VARIATIONS

Please note that these are variations in the use of sandtray techniques for career counseling. These interventions should be used only if you have training and experience in sandtray. In addition, it is helpful to have sandtray figures that represent individuals in as wide a variety of diverse careers as possible.

SANDTRAY GENOGRAM VARIATION 1

Imelda N. Bratton

Preparation Needed:

In addition to the collection of miniatures, also have available a variety of colors and lengths of pipe cleaners and a variety of colored rocks; these should be placed beside the sandtray. Develop a symbol key using the colors of pipe cleaners and rocks. The symbol key should identify pipe cleaner symbols such as: enjoyed career, did not enjoy career, did not work, began working at an early age, began working later in life, higher education, limited education, and so on. The symbol key can also use rocks to identify similar career choices between family members or other career choices the counselor would like to emphasize when looking at the career genogram *sandworld*. A career genogram *sandworld* is a visual representation of the client's career world as the client perceives it. It is made using sand and figures.

Activity Directions:

1. Introduce the activity to the client by noting: *In a moment you will create a career genogram* sandworld. *A genogram is like a family tree, but with more information than just names. The genogram you will create today will show the different jobs or careers your family members have held. We will have a chance to talk about your career genogram* sandworld *and you may reflect on your family's history and dynamics. I would like for you to take a moment and think about your family members and types of jobs or careers they have held.*
2. Provide a few moments of silence. Continue by saying: *Figurines are selected to represent the career or job of each family member. If a family member has held many positions, then you may select a figurine that best represents that persons' overall career choice. Family members should be placed in clusters similar to what would be found in a diagram of a family tree in the sandtray.* Let the client know he or she may begin creating the career genogram *sandworld* when ready.
3. Many times, it is helpful to observe the client as the *sandworld* is created. Observe how the client selects figurines and places them in the sandtray. Also, watch for times when the client seems to have difficulty in creating the *sandworld*. Examples can include when a client focuses on a particular figurine or family member or if a family member is left out of the *sandworld*.
4. Discuss the careers or jobs each family member has held when the client has completed the *sandworld*. Review the symbol key with the client. Let the client know that the pipe cleaners and rock symbols will be placed in the *sandworld* throughout the discussion. Either you or the client may place the symbols in the *sandworld*, depending on therapeutic goals.
5. Process the career genogram *sandworld* using the following questions (as appropriate): *Who are you most like in your family? How are you similar to that person? Who are you most different than in your family? How are you different than that person? What stands out to you as you look at your career genogram* sandworld*? How do you feel when you reflect on your career genogram* sandworld*? Describe*

your personal career journey up to this point in time; which member in your family is it most like? Which member is it most different than? As you think about your future, whom do you want to be more like? Whom do you want to be different than?

6. Allow the client to reflect on the discussion. It can be helpful to take a digital picture of the career genogram *sandworld* and e-mail it to the client to view as needed. The visual image can be a way to further reflect and process information discussed in session. Additionally, the photograph may be used in case notes for reference.

SANDTRAY GENOGRAM VARIATION 2

Edward F. Hudspeth

Activity Directions:

1. Ask the client to select the miniatures to represent the members of his or her family. Begin with spouse/partner, parents, siblings, and children (i.e., if the client has children who have careers). Make sure that the client does not forget to include himself or herself. Use the following prompts: *Select a miniature to represent each family member. Remember to consider your family member's career while selecting. When choosing the miniature for each family member, consider the family member's thoughts and feelings about, and satisfaction with, his or her career. When choosing the miniature to represent you, consider your thoughts and feelings about, and satisfaction with, your career.*
2. Instruct the client to place the miniatures in the tray and arrange them in the order that fits his or her family structure.
3. Ask the client to place, with each miniature, any other miniature that represents that individual's thoughts and feelings about, or satisfaction with, his or her career.
4. Ask the client to select and place miniatures that represent the bonds between family members.
5. Process the sandtray using any or all of the following statements: *Tell me about (how does) the miniature(s) you chose to represent _______ (family member) and their career. Tell me about (how does) the miniature(s) you chose to represent ______ (family member's) thoughts and feelings about, and satisfaction with, his or her career. Describe that person's thoughts and feelings about his or her career. Tell me about the miniature(s) you selected to represent family bonds. Tell me about the miniature(s) you selected to represent yourself. Are there any similarities between the miniature that represents you and any family member? What have you learned from doing this career sandtray genogram about family career roles and expectations?*
6. When processing the sandtray creation, the client has the opportunity to view his or her career world more objectively. The client also has opportunities to imagine himself or herself in the sandtray career world, moving about day to day.
7. When processing the sandtray, focus on the here and now and thoughts and feelings the client may have had while doing the sandtray. Focus more on the process than the content.
8. Finally, take a photograph of the career sandtray genogram to facilitate further processing in future sessions.

SANDTRAY GENOGRAM VARIATION 3

Marta M. Garrett

Activity Directions:

1. Ask the client to create a family tree in the sandtray using miniature people to represent the family members. Depending on the age of the client, you may want the client to create two generations back (if he or she has this information) and also include information about the client's children if he or she has adult children. Individual family members can be placed in the traditional family tree format or layout or they may be placed in relational groups (based on how they get along or how close they are or were).
2. Process this tray with the client by asking questions about each family member that the client has included (this will help the client to think in more depth about each family member and strengthen the client's ability to respond to future prompts). For complex family trees, it might be helpful for you to list names of family members or take simple notes to help guide your memory during the discussion of the sandtray. You may want to ask questions such as: *What do you remember most about this person?* (For a person who may be distantly related, living far away, or deceased.) *What do you like most about this person? (For a relative who is still living, or more closely connected to the client.) Where did this person live? Who are the important people (or family members) in this person's life? How close was this person to his or her siblings or parents or children? How close were/are you to this person? How would you describe your relationship with this person? If you had to describe this person with one or two words, what would they be? If I asked other family members to describe this person, what might they say?*
3. Next, ask the client to go back and select items that help to describe what kind of work each person represented in the family tree did in his or her life and place these items next to each person in the tray. This may include multiple miniatures for people who did various jobs.
4. Process this tray by asking questions to clarify the kinds of work that individuals may have done and how this work influenced other life choices, if known. For example: *What kind of work did this person do? What do you know about this person's career or work life? Based on what you know about this person's work, what do you find appealing about this career choice? What are the negative aspects to this kind of work? How long has this person been doing this work? How long did he/ she work before retiring or dying? Do you know if he/she went to school or special training for this job/career? As far as you know, was this person happy in his/her job? How do you know this? Would you consider this person successful? Why or why not?*
5. When the processing comes to a lull or is completed, take a photo of the tray. You may choose to send this picture home with the client or use the photo for further processing in a follow-up session. Suggested journaling questions (to

send home with the client) or follow-up processing questions (in future sessions) or if time permits include: *What kinds of patterns do you see in the various career choices in your family?* (Career choices, lifestyle choices, levels of happiness, etc.—this follow up can be specifically designed to meet the client's goals and/or to complement his or her cultural background.) *Is there anything that you didn't see in the tray that you might have expected to see? Did anything in the tray/family career tree surprise you? Which of these career choices would you like to learn more about? How might you learn more about this career? Which people in this tray seemed to have a good fit with their personality and their career choice; why? Were there any that you noticed did not have a good fit; why not? What would have made this person or these individuals more successful; happier?*

UNCOVERING SOLUTIONS TO CAREER CHALLENGES

Charles E. Myers and Margo D. Sutorius-Milano

This activity is helpful for clients struggling to identify a career direction. Through symbolic representation and metaphor development, career counselors can facilitate clients in identifying and communicating unrealized and nonverbalized goals, barriers, and obstacles in reaching those goals and strategies for success.

Activity Directions:

Part 1—Identifying Career Aspirations

1. Invite the client to: *Think about your past jobs and activities. Consider the aspects of those careers and activities that you enjoyed. Please select as few or as many miniatures as you like that represent those positive elements and place them in the sandtray in any way you like. In other words, use the miniatures to create your world of the positive activities you enjoyed from your past jobs or hobbies.*
2. Process and discuss the client's sandtray when completed with questions such as: *Take a few moments and take in what you have created. Look at it from different angles.... What stands out for you?* Using reflection of content and feelings, expand the meaning of the scene with the client. Respond to what the client says and what you see in the sandtray scene, invite the client to expand on what the imagery represents, and develop therapeutic metaphors for future sessions. Listen for opportunities to connect the client's narrative with other assessments and dialogue with the client.
3. Next, ask the client: *What other characteristics would you like in a career? What do you feel was missing from your previous jobs? Place some miniatures to represent those missing elements. In other words, use the miniatures to create your world of missing job activities you would like to involve in your future.*
4. Process the sandtray when the client is done. Ask the client: *Please tell me about what you added. How important is it for you to have those elements?* Invite the client to prioritize the positive elements of past careers and wants for future careers. Ask the client: *Which elements in the sandtray are needs and which ones are wants? Which elements are most possible and which are least possible? Where do those thoughts come from?*

Part 2—Identifying Barriers and Obstacles

1. Invite the client to: *Think about any barriers or obstacles experienced in past positions. Consider what barriers and obstacles you anticipate in pursuing a future career. Please select as few or as many miniatures as you like that represent those barriers and obstacles and place them in the sandtray in any way you like. In other words, use the miniatures to create a world of the obstacles you once experienced.*
2. Process and discuss the client's sandtray when completed: *Take a few moments and take in what you have created. Look at it from different angles.... What stands out for you?* Using reflection of content and feelings, expand the meaning of the scene with the client. Respond to what the client says and what you

see in the sandtray scene, invite the client to expand on what the imagery represents, and develop therapeutic metaphors for future sessions. Ask the client: *Which of these barriers and obstacles represent severe challenges and which ones represent minor challenges?* Listen for opportunities to connect the client's narrative with other assessments and dialogue with the client.

3. Invite the client to: *Think about what strategies you implemented to deal with challenges in the past. Consider the effectiveness of strategies, then select some miniatures that represent those effective strategies and add them to the sandtray.*
4. Process the sandtray when the client is done. Ask the client: *Please tell me about what you added. What are those strategies and how effective were they in overcoming barriers and obstacles?* Facilitate discussion with the client on how to use past effective strategies in overcoming future challenges and how to adapt those strategies to be more effective.

Part 3—Bringing It All Together

1. Invite the client to: *Think about the career you want. Reflect on what elements you want in your career. Consider the barriers and obstacles you will face in pursuing that career and the strategies you will employ to overcome those challenges. Now please select as few or as many miniatures as you like and create a scene in the sandtray that represents the journey you are embarking on. In other words, use the miniatures to create your future career that involves the tasks and activities you enjoy in addition to the strategies you will use to obtain this career and overcome obstacles and challenges.*
2. Process and discuss the client's sandtray when completed. Invite the client to: *Take a few moments and take in what you have created. Look at it from different angles.... What stands out for you?* Using reflection of content and feelings, expand the meaning of the scene with the client. Respond to what the client says and what you see in the sandtray scene, invite the client to expand on what the imagery represents, and develop therapeutic metaphors for future sessions using the following prompts: *Please share with me the journey that you have created. What challenges will you face and how will you overcome them?*
3. Facilitate career exploration using the sandtrays as material to help the client identify career goals and to map out strategies for achieving those goals.

APPENDIX P

APPENDICES REFERENCES

ALGBTIC Competencies Taskforce. (2009). Association for lesbian, gay, bisexual, and transgender issues in counseling competencies for counseling with transgender clients. *Journal of LGBT Issues in Counseling, 4*(3), 135–159.

Alonso-Almeida, M. (2014). Women (and mothers) in the workforce: Worldwide factors. *Women's Studies International Forum, 44*, 164–171.

Amundson, N. E., Borgen, W. A., Iaquinta, M., Butterfield, L. D., & Koert, E. (2010). Career decisions from the decider's perspective. *The Career Development Quarterly, 58*(4), 336–351.

Bridges, W. (2009). *Transitions: Making Sense of Life's Changes*, Boston, MA: Da Capo Press.

Brott, P. E. (2005). A constructivist look at life roles. *The Career Development Quarterly, 54*, 138–149.

Brott, P. E. (2011). The storied approach: A postmodern perspective for career counseling. *The Career Development Quarterly, 49*, 304–313.

Brown, D., & Associates. (2002). *Career choice and development* (4th ed.). San Francisco, CA: Jossey-Bass.

Chae, M. H. (2002). Counseling reentry women: An overview. *Journal of Employment Counseling, 39*(4), 146–152.

Cochrane, S. V. (2001). Psychotherapy with men navigating midlife terrain. In G. R. Brooks & G. E. Good (Eds.), *The new handbook of psychotherapy and counseling with men: A comprehensive guide to settings, problems, and treatment approaches* (pp. 444–463). San Francisco, CA: Jossey-Bass.

Cook, G. (2011). How to improve your life with "story editing." *Scientific American.* Retrieved from http://www.scientificamerican.com/article/how-to-improve-your-life-with-story-editing/

Erford, B. T. (2014). *Forty techniques every counselor should know.* Upper Saddle River, NJ: Pearson Merrill Prentice Hall.

Ericksen, K. S., Jurgens, J. C., Garrett, M. T., & Swedburg, R. B. (2008). Should I stay at home or should I go back to work? Workforce reentry influences on a mother's decision-making process. *Journal of Employment Counseling, 45*(4), 156–167.

Ettinger, J. M. (1991). *Improved career decision making in a changing world: Integrating occupational information and guidance.* Washington, DC: National Occupational Information Coordinating Committee.

Greenberg, L. S. (2004). Emotion–focused therapy. *Clinical Psychology & Psychotherapy, 11*(1), 3–16.

Hall, D. T., & Murvis, P. H. (1995). The new career contract: Developing the whole person at midlife and beyond. *Journal of Vocational Behavior, 47*, 269–289.

Holland, J. L. (1992). *Making vocational choice: A theory of vocational personalities and work environments* (2nd ed.). Odessa, FL: Psychological Assessment Resources.

Holland, J. L. (1994). *Self-directed search, form r: You and your career* (4th ed.). Odessa, FL: Psychological Assessment Resources.

http://blog.dwwtc.com/veterans-workforce-transition/for-returning-veterans-7-myths-and-realities-of-organizations

Krumboltz, J. D. (2009). The happenstance learning theory. *Journal of Career Assessment, 17*(2), 135–154.

Landreth, G. L. (1991). *Play therapy: The art of the relationship*. Bristol, PA: Accelerated Development.

Leahy, R. L. (1996). *Cognitive therapy: Basic principles and applications*. Northvale, NJ: Jason Aronson Publishing.

Locke, W. S., & Gibbons, M. M. (2008). On her own again: The use of narrative therapy in career counseling with displaced new traditionalists. *The Family Journal, 16*(2), 132–138.

Merriam-Webster. (2005). *Merriam-Webster's collegiate dictionary* (11th ed.). Springfield, MA: Author.

Minor, C. W., & Celotta, B. (2000). Career services I needed. In M. Pope & C. Minor (Eds.), *Experiential activities for teaching career classes of facilitating career groups* (p. 5). Broken Arrow, OK: National Career Development Association.

Mitchell, K. E., Levin, S., & Krumboltz, J. D. (1999). Planned happenstance: Constructing unexpected career opportunities. *Journal of Counseling & Development, 77*, 115–124.

Motulsky, S. L. (2010). Relational processes in career transition: Extending theory, research, and practice. *Counseling Psychologist, 38*, 1078–1114.

Murphy, R. A., & Fairbank, J. A. (2013). Implementation and dissemination of military informed and evidence-based interventions for community dwelling military families. *Clinical Child and Family Psychology Review, 16*(4), 348–364.

Nafziger, J., & DeKruyf, L. (2013). Narrative counseling for professional school counselors. *Professional School Counseling, 16*(5), 290–302.

National Military Family Association. (2015). *Children's education*. Retrieved from http://www.militaryfamily.org/kids-operation-purple/education.html

Niles, S. G., & Harris-Bowlsbey, J. E. (2013). *Career development interventions in the 21st century* (4th ed.). Upper Saddle River, NJ: Pearson.

Rehfuss, M. C. (2009). The future career autobiography: A narrative measure of career intervention effectiveness. *The Career Development Quarterly, 58*(1), 82–90.

Saka, N., Gati, I., & Kelly, K. R. (2008). Emotional and personality-related aspects of career decision-making difficulties. *Journal of Career Assessment, 16*(4), 403–424.

Saltzman, W. R., Lester, P., Beardslee, W. R., Layne, C. M., Woodward, K., & Nash, W. P. (2011). Mechanisms of risk and resilience in military families: Theoretical and empirical basis of a family-focused resilience enhancement program. *Clinical Child and Family Psychology Review, 14*(3), 213–230.

Savickas, M. L., & Porfeli, E. J. (2012). Career Adapt-Abilities Scale: Construction, reliability, and measurement equivalence across 13 countries. *Journal of Vocational Behavior, 80*, 661–673. doi:10.1016/j.jvb.2012.01.011

Schmidt, C. K., Miles, J. R., & Welsh, A. C. (2011). Perceived discrimination and social support: The influences on career development and college adjustment of LGBT college clients. *Journal of Career Development, 38*(4), 293–309.

Schultheiss, D. E. P. (2007). The emergence of relational cultural paradigm for vocational psychology. *International Journal of Educational and Vocational Guidance, 7*, 191–201.

Schultheiss, D. E. P., Kress, H. M., & Manzi, J. A. J. (2001). Relational influences in career development: A qualitative inquiry. *The Counseling Psychologist, 29*(2), 216–241.

Slaten, C. D., & Baskin T. W. (2014). Examining the impact of peer and family belongingness on the career decision-making difficulties of young adults: A path analytic approach. *Journal of Career Assessment, 22*(1), 59–74.

Stebleton, M. J. (2007). Career counseling with African immigrant college clients: Theoretical approaches and implications for practice. *The Career Development Quarterly, 55*(4), 290–312.

Super, D. E. (1957). *The psychology of careers: An introduction to vocational development*. Oxford, England: Harper & Brothers.

Super, D. E. (1990). A life-span, life-space approach to career development. In D. Brown & L. Brooks (Eds.), *Career choice and development: Applying contemporary theories to practice* (2nd ed., pp. 197–269). San Francisco, CA: Jossey Bass.

Super, D. E., Savickas, M. L., & Super, C. M. (1996). The life-span, life-space approach to careers. In D. Brown & L. Brooks (Eds.), *Career choice and development* (3rd ed., pp. 121–178). San Francisco, CA: Jossey Bass.

Thomas, D. A., & Gibbons, M. M. (2009). Narrative theory: A career counseling approach for adolescents of divorce. *Professional School Counseling, 12*(3), 223–229.

Tomlinson, M. J., & Fassinger, R. E. (2003). Career development, lesbian identity development, and campus climate among lesbian college clients. *Journal of College Client Development, 44*(6), 845–860. doi:10.1353/csd.2003.0078

U.S. Department of Labor. (2014). *O*NET OnLine.* Retrieved from http://www.onetonline.org/

White, M. (2007). *Maps of narrative practice* (1st ed.). New York, NY: W. W. Norton.

White, M., & Epston, D. (1990). *Narrative means to therapeutic ends.* New York, NY: Norton.

Wonder, S. (2011). *Songs in the key of life–Remastered.* [Originally Recorded by Wonder, S. 1976]. Santa Monica, CA : Universal Music Group.

Yalom, I. (2002). *The gift of therapy: An open letter to a new generation of therapists and their patients.* New York, NY: HarperCollins.

INDEX